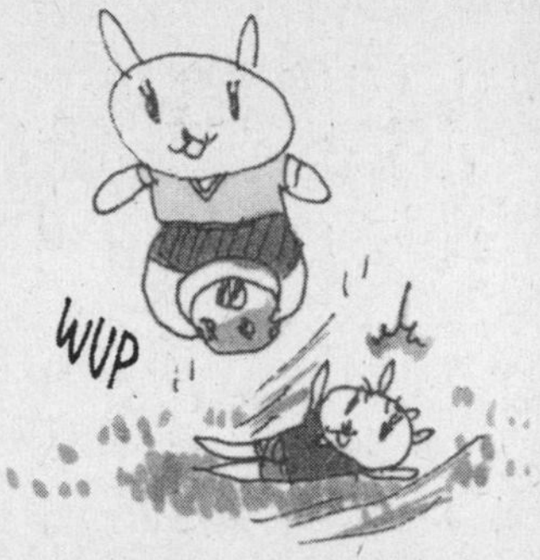
WUP

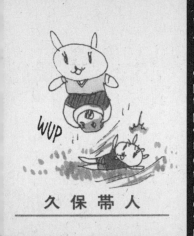

久保帯人

Writer and friend busy moving.
The writer is in the air.

I moved. My phone number changed. It's a very good phone number. It's super easy to remember. It's the best phone number. But for some strange reason, I get wrong numbers a lot. One I was especially surprised by was: "Is this the XX (I cannot reveal the name of the country) embassy?" and a phone call from a foreigner going off on me speaking really fast in Russian (I think). Well, it's funny so I don't really mind.
Tite Kubo

BLEACH is author Tite Kubo's second title. Kubo made his debut with ***ZOMBIE POWDER***, a four-volume series for ***WEEKLY SHONEN JUMP***. To date, ***BLEACH*** has sold nearly 7 million volumes and has been translated into seven different languages. Beginning its serialization in 2001, ***BLEACH*** is still a mainstay in the pages of ***WEEKLY SHONEN JUMP***.

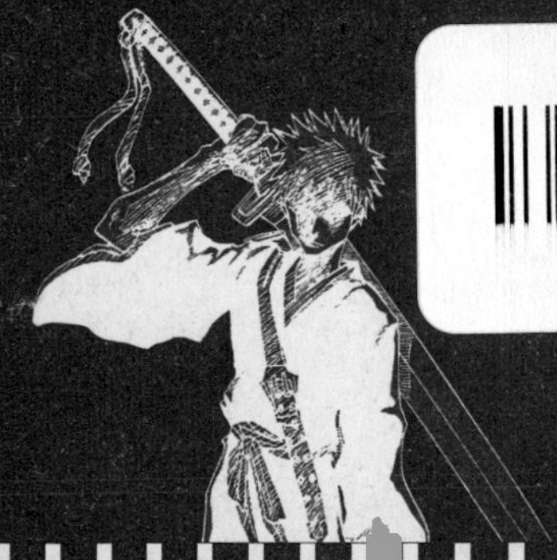

BLEACH
Vol. 4: QUINCY ARCHER HATES YOU
The SHONEN JUMP Graphic Novel Edition

STORY AND ART BY TITE KUBO

English Adaptation/Lance Caselman
Translation/Joe Yamazaki
Touch-Up Art & Lettering/Dave Lanphear
Design/Sean Lee
Editor/Kit Fox

Managing Editor/Elizabeth Kawasaki
Director of Production/Noboru Watanabe
Editorial Director/Alvin Lu
Executive Vice President & Editor in Chief/Hyoe Narita
Sr. Director of Licensing & Acquisitions/Rika Inouye
Vice President of Sales & Marketing/Liza Coppola
Vice President of Strategic Development/Yumi Hoashi
Publisher/Seiji Horibuchi

Printed in the U.S.A.

Published by VIZ, LLC
P.O. Box 77010
San Francisco, CA 94107

SHONEN JUMP Graphic Novel Edition
10 9 8 7 6 5 4 3 2 1
First printing, November 2004

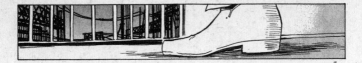

We are drawn to each other
Like drops of water, like the planets
We repulse each other
Like magnets, like the colors of our skin

BLEACH 4

QUINCY ARCHER HATES YOU

Shonen Jump Graphic Novel

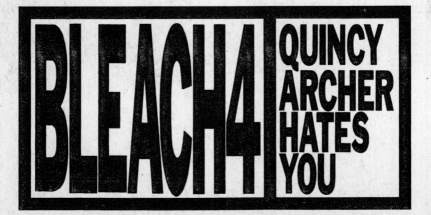

STARS AND

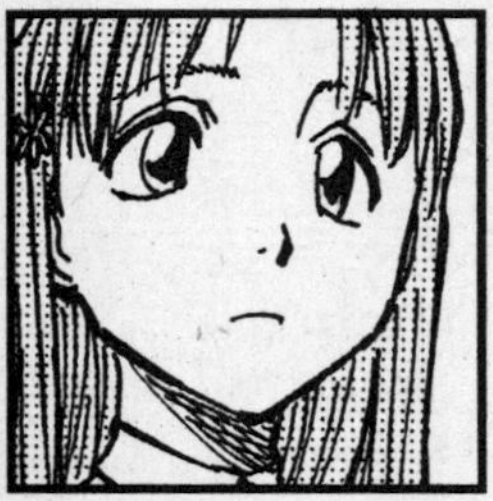

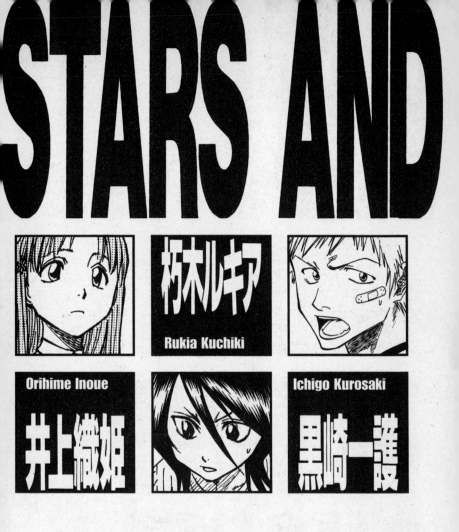

朽木ルキア

Rukia Kuchiki

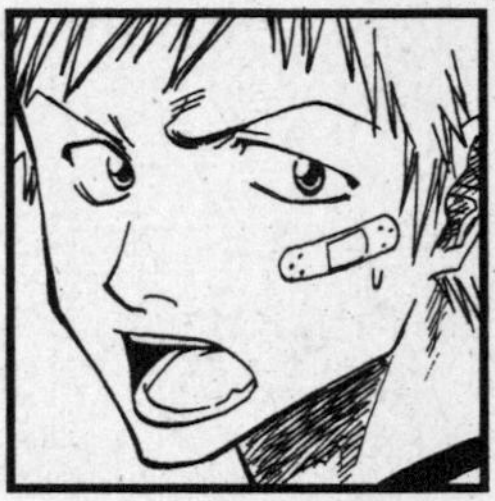

Orihime Inoue

井上織姫

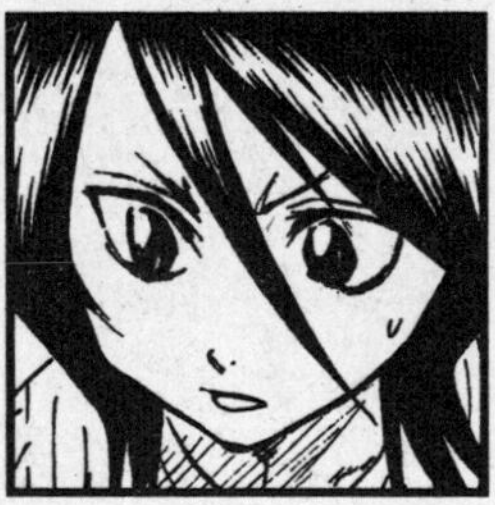

Ichigo Kurosaki

黒崎一護

plot

Ichigo Kurosaki, 15 years old. Except for being able to see ghosts, he is an ordinary (?) high school student. But when he encounters Soul Reaper Rukia Kuchiki, his life takes a dramatic turn. Because of his strong spiritual powers and good heart, Ichigo decides to help Rukia with her job as a Soul Reaper.

A Soul Reaper cleanses lost souls called "Hollows" and guides them to the Soul Society. Ichigo gets used to his bizarre new job, and eventually encounters the Hollow that killed his mother. Despite Ichigo's best efforts, the wicked Hollow gets away, leaving Ichigo painfully aware of his short-comings and determined to get stronger, but...

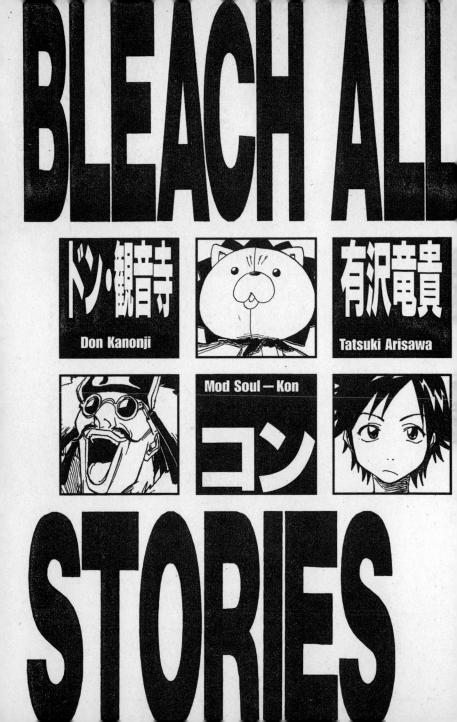

BLEACH ALL

ドン・観音寺

Don Kanonji

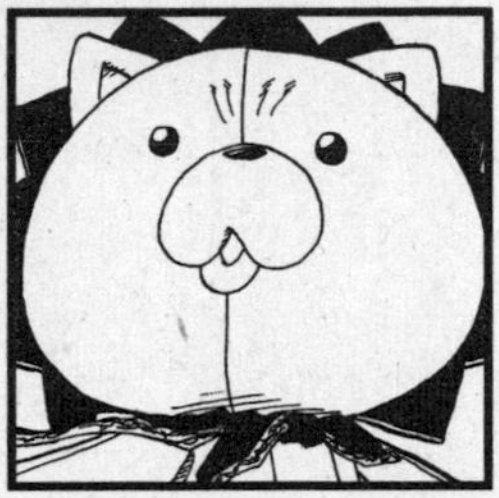

有沢竜貴

Tatsuki Arisawa

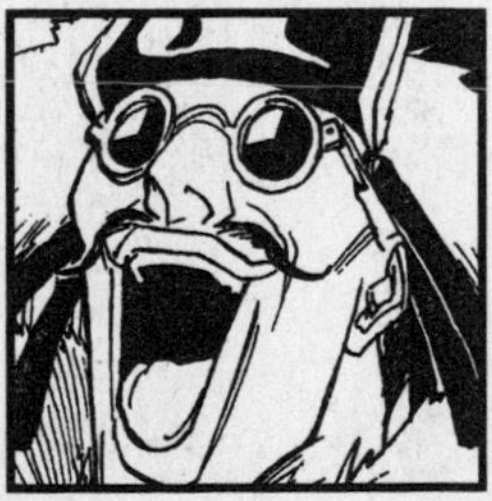

Mod Soul — Kon

コン

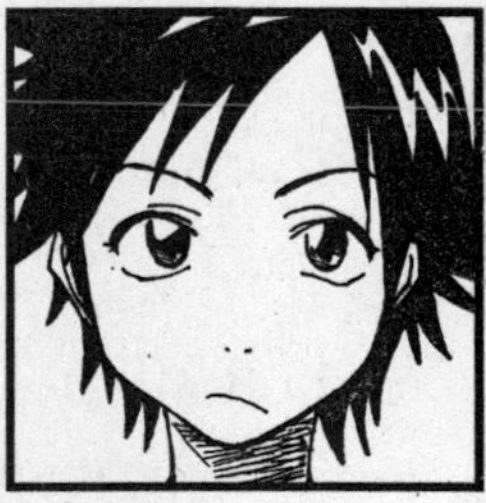

STORIES

BLEACH4

QUINCY ARCHER HATES YOU

Contents

26. Paradise Is Nowhere

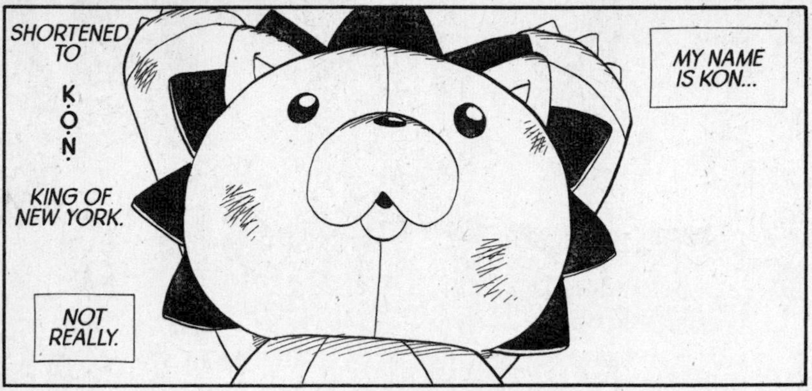
MY NAME IS KON...
SHORTENED TO K·O·N·
KING OF NEW YORK.
NOT REALLY.

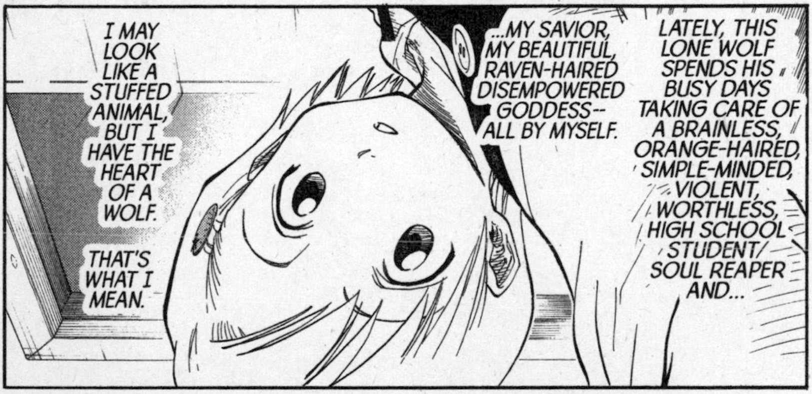
LATELY, THIS LONE WOLF SPENDS HIS BUSY DAYS TAKING CARE OF A BRAINLESS, ORANGE-HAIRED, SIMPLE-MINDED, VIOLENT, WORTHLESS, HIGH SCHOOL STUDENT/ SOUL REAPER AND...
...MY SAVIOR, MY BEAUTIFUL, RAVEN-HAIRED DISEMPOWERED GODDESS-- ALL BY MYSELF.
I MAY LOOK LIKE A STUFFED ANIMAL, BUT I HAVE THE HEART OF A WOLF.
THAT'S WHAT I MEAN.

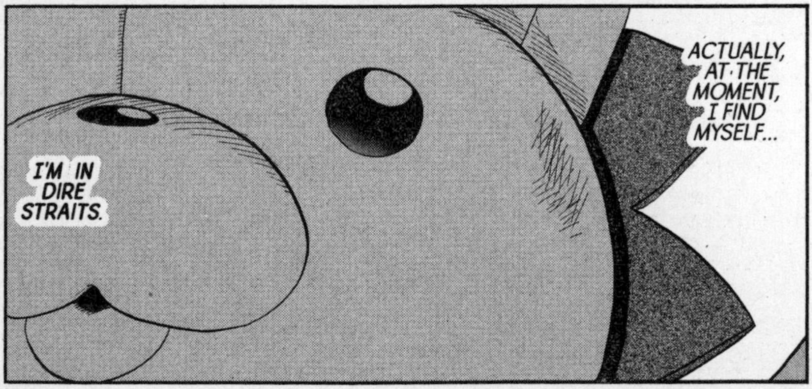
ACTUALLY, AT THE MOMENT, I FIND MYSELF...
I'M IN DIRE STRAITS.

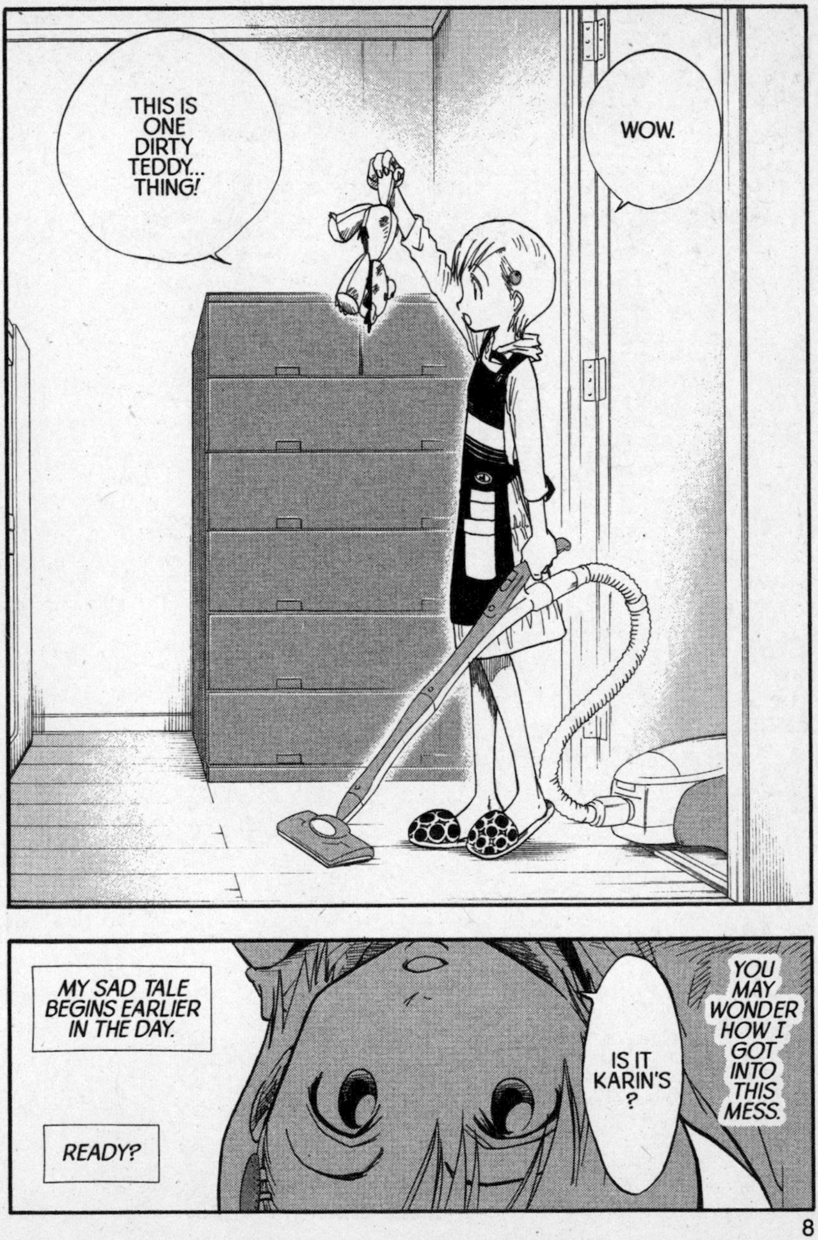
WOW.
THIS IS ONE DIRTY TEDDY... THING!
YOU MAY WONDER HOW I GOT INTO THIS MESS.
IS IT KARIN'S?
MY SAD TALE BEGINS EARLIER IN THE DAY.
READY?

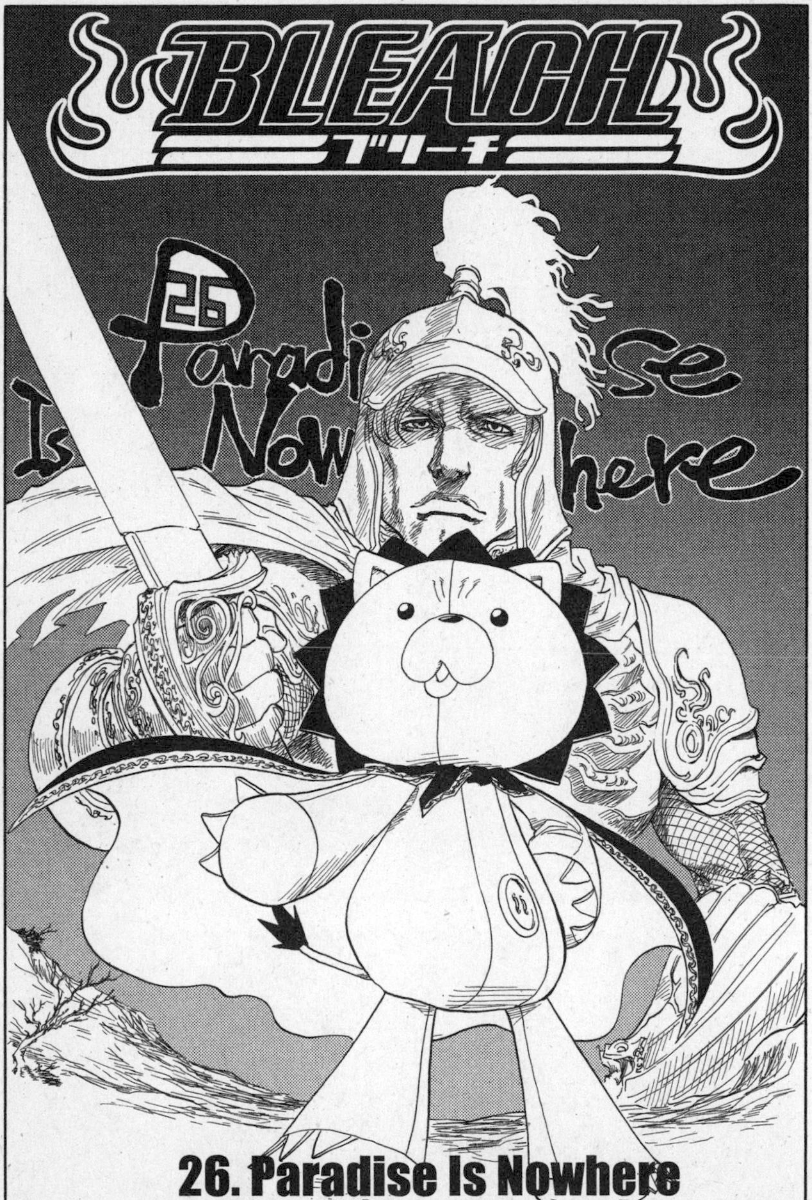
BLEACH
ブリーチ
26 Paradise Is Nowhere

26. Paradise Is Nowhere

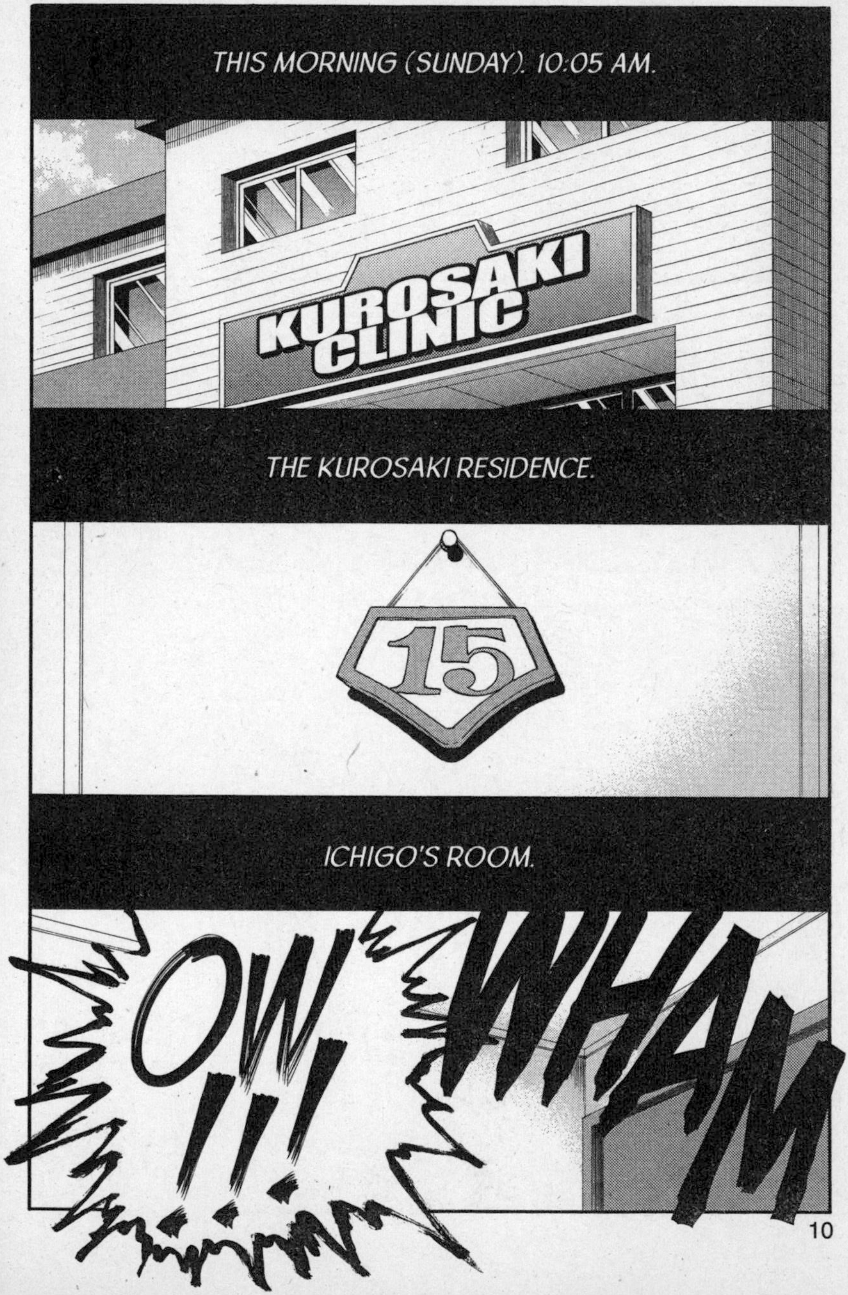
THIS MORNING (SUNDAY). 10:05 AM.
KUROSAKI CLINIC
THE KUROSAKI RESIDENCE.
15
ICHIGO'S ROOM.
WHAM
OW!!

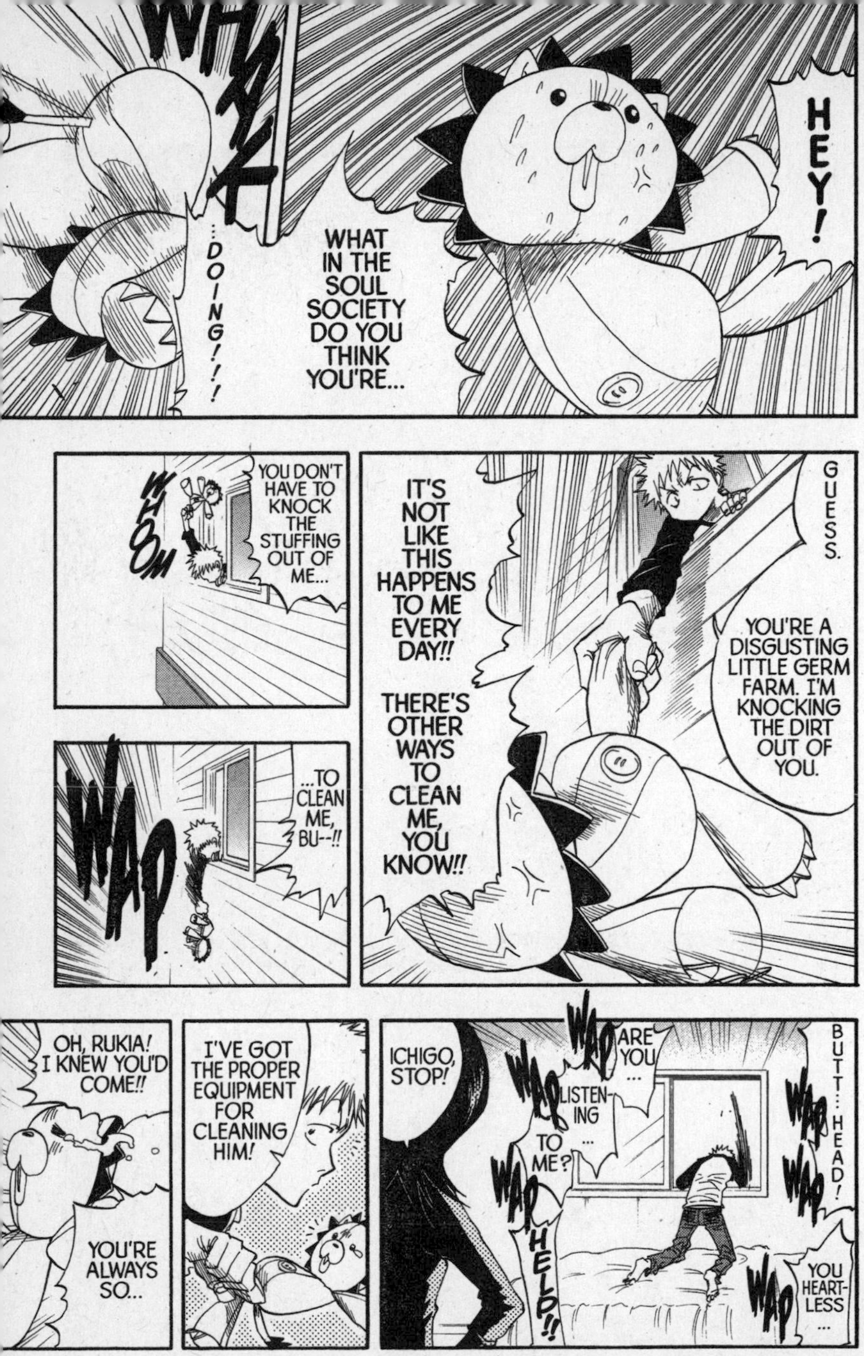
HEY!
WHAT IN THE SOUL SOCIETY DO YOU THINK YOU'RE...
...DOING!!!
WHAAK
GUESS.
YOU'RE A DISGUSTING LITTLE GERM FARM. I'M KNOCKING THE DIRT OUT OF YOU.
IT'S NOT LIKE THIS HAPPENS TO ME EVERY DAY!!
THERE'S OTHER WAYS TO CLEAN ME, YOU KNOW!!
YOU DON'T HAVE TO KNOCK THE STUFFING OUT OF ME...
WHOOM
...TO CLEAN ME, BU--!!
WAP
BUTT... HEAD!
WAP
WAP
YOU HEARTLESS...
WAP
ARE YOU...
LISTENING...
TO ME?
WAP
WAP
WAP
HELP!!
ICHIGO, STOP!
I'VE GOT THE PROPER EQUIPMENT FOR CLEANING HIM!
OH, RUKIA! I KNEW YOU'D COME!!
YOU'RE ALWAYS SO...

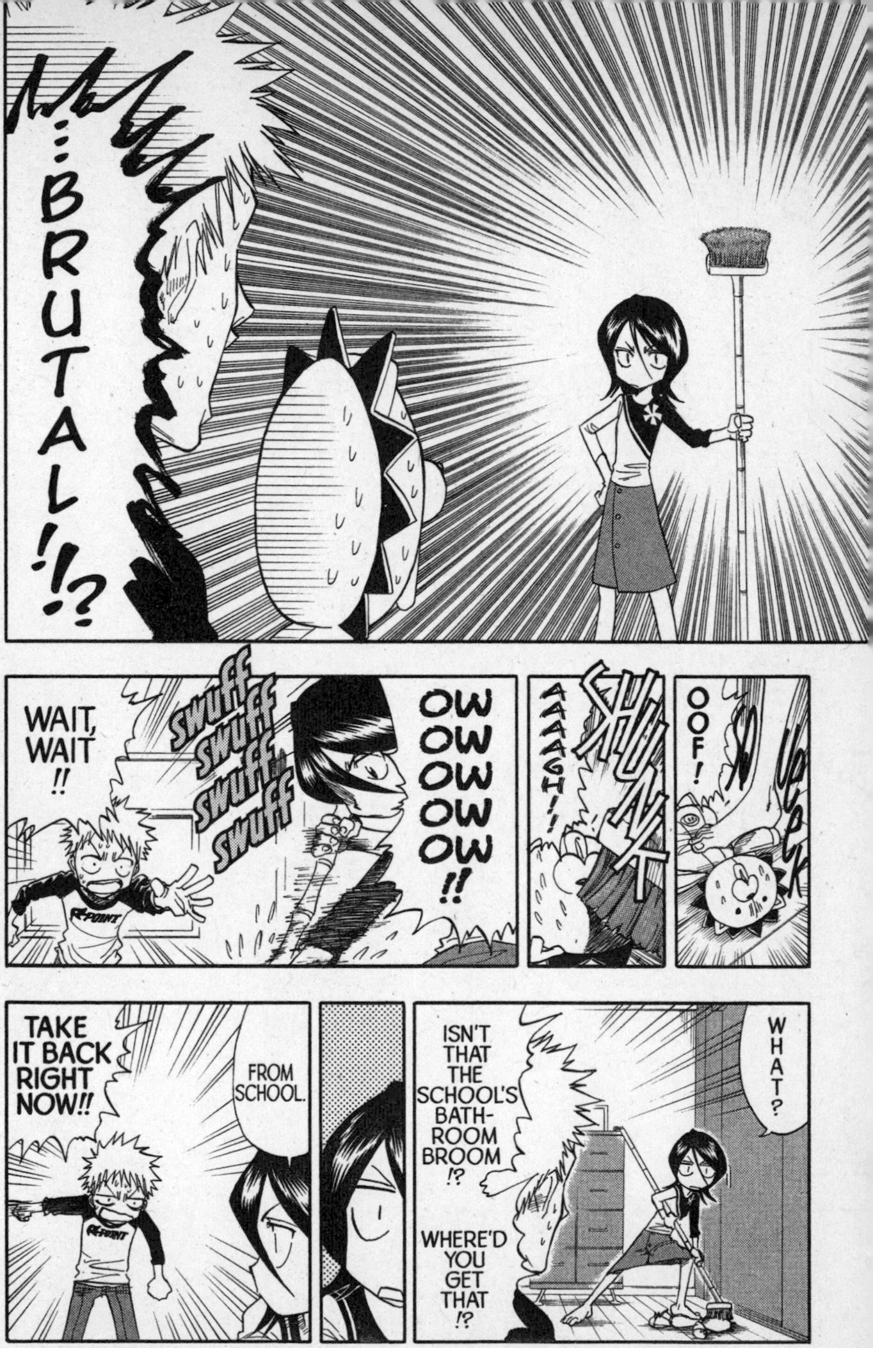
...BRUTAL!!?
OOF!
AAAAAAGH!!
OWOWOWOWOWOW!!
SWUFF SWUFF SWUFF SWUFF
WAIT, WAIT!!
WHAT?
ISN'T THAT THE SCHOOL'S BATH-ROOM BROOM!?
WHERE'D YOU GET THAT!?
FROM SCHOOL.
TAKE IT BACK RIGHT NOW!!

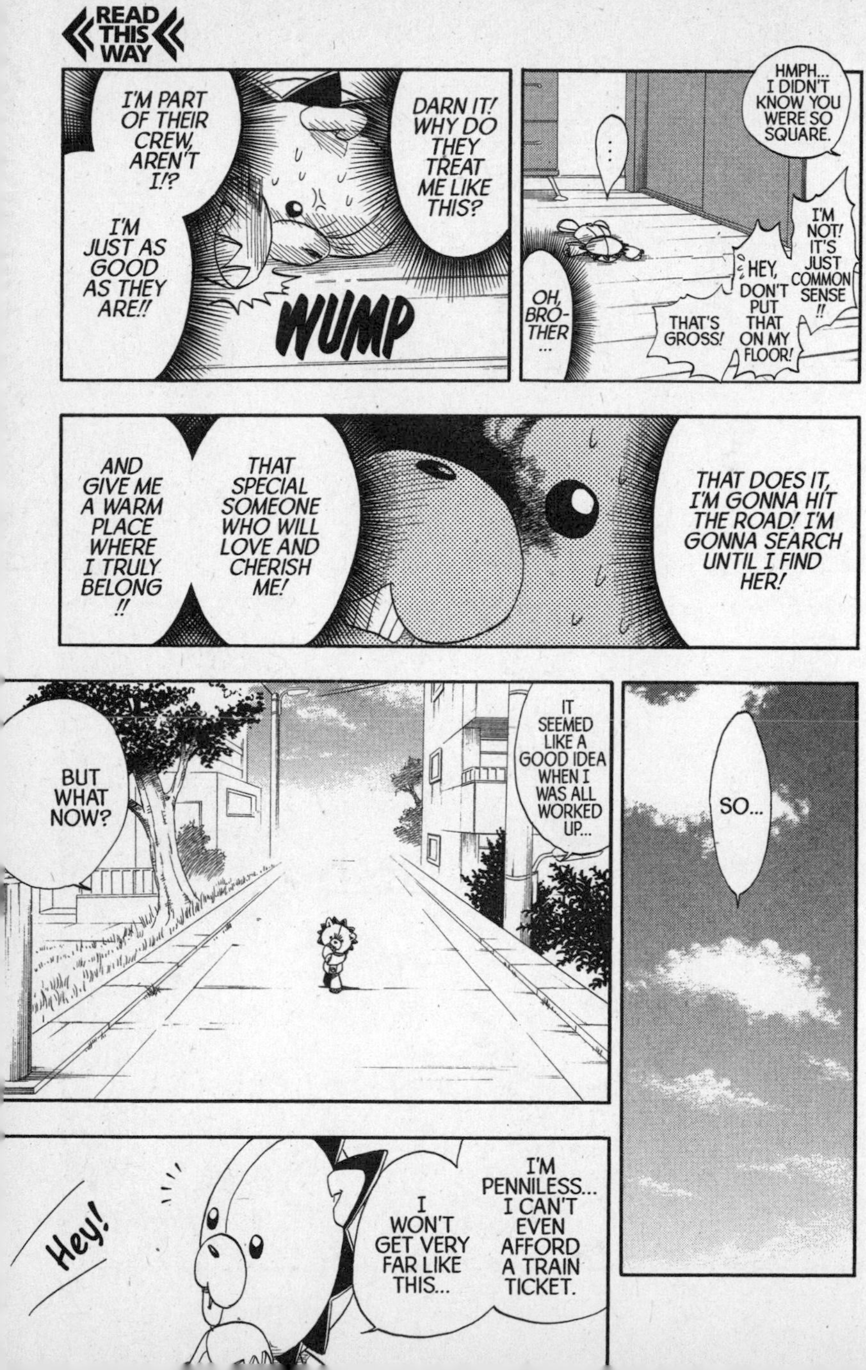
READ THIS WAY
…
HMPH… I DIDN'T KNOW YOU WERE SO SQUARE.
I'M NOT! IT'S JUST COMMON SENSE!!
HEY, DON'T PUT THAT ON MY FLOOR!
THAT'S GROSS!
OH, BROTHER…
DARN IT! WHY DO THEY TREAT ME LIKE THIS?
I'M PART OF THEIR CREW, AREN'T I!?
I'M JUST AS GOOD AS THEY ARE!!
WUMP
THAT DOES IT, I'M GONNA HIT THE ROAD! I'M GONNA SEARCH UNTIL I FIND HER!
THAT SPECIAL SOMEONE WHO WILL LOVE AND CHERISH ME!
AND GIVE ME A WARM PLACE WHERE I TRULY BELONG!!
SO…
IT SEEMED LIKE A GOOD IDEA WHEN I WAS ALL WORKED UP…
BUT WHAT NOW?
I'M PENNILESS… I CAN'T EVEN AFFORD A TRAIN TICKET.
I WON'T GET VERY FAR LIKE THIS…
Hey!

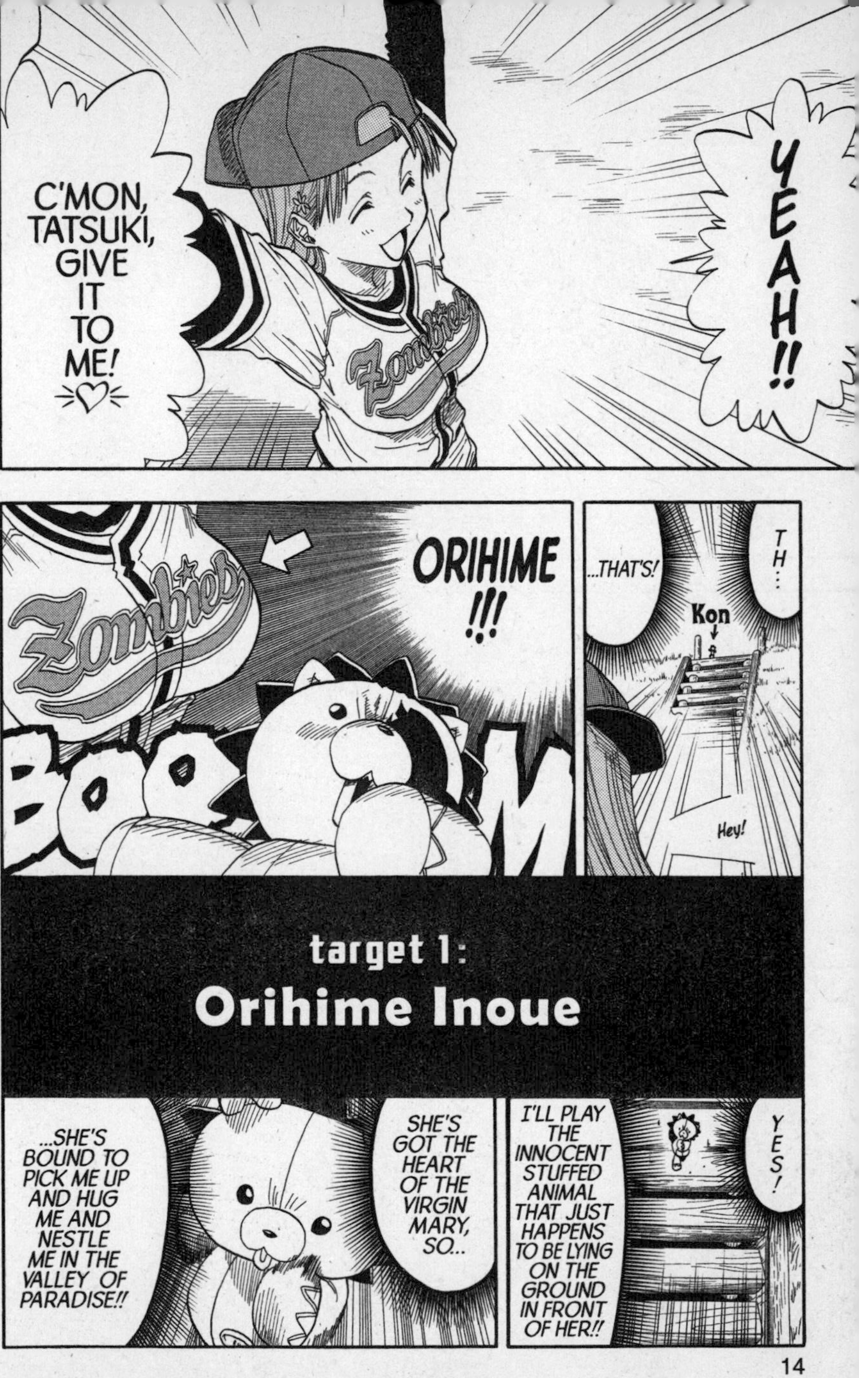
YEAH!!
C'MON, TATSUKI, GIVE IT TO ME! ♡
TH...
...THAT'S!
Kon
Hey!
ORIHIME!!!
BOOM
target 1:
Orihime Inoue
YES!
I'LL PLAY THE INNOCENT STUFFED ANIMAL THAT JUST HAPPENS TO BE LYING ON THE GROUND IN FRONT OF HER!!
SHE'S GOT THE HEART OF THE VIRGIN MARY, SO...
...SHE'S BOUND TO PICK ME UP AND HUG ME AND NESTLE ME IN THE VALLEY OF PARADISE!!

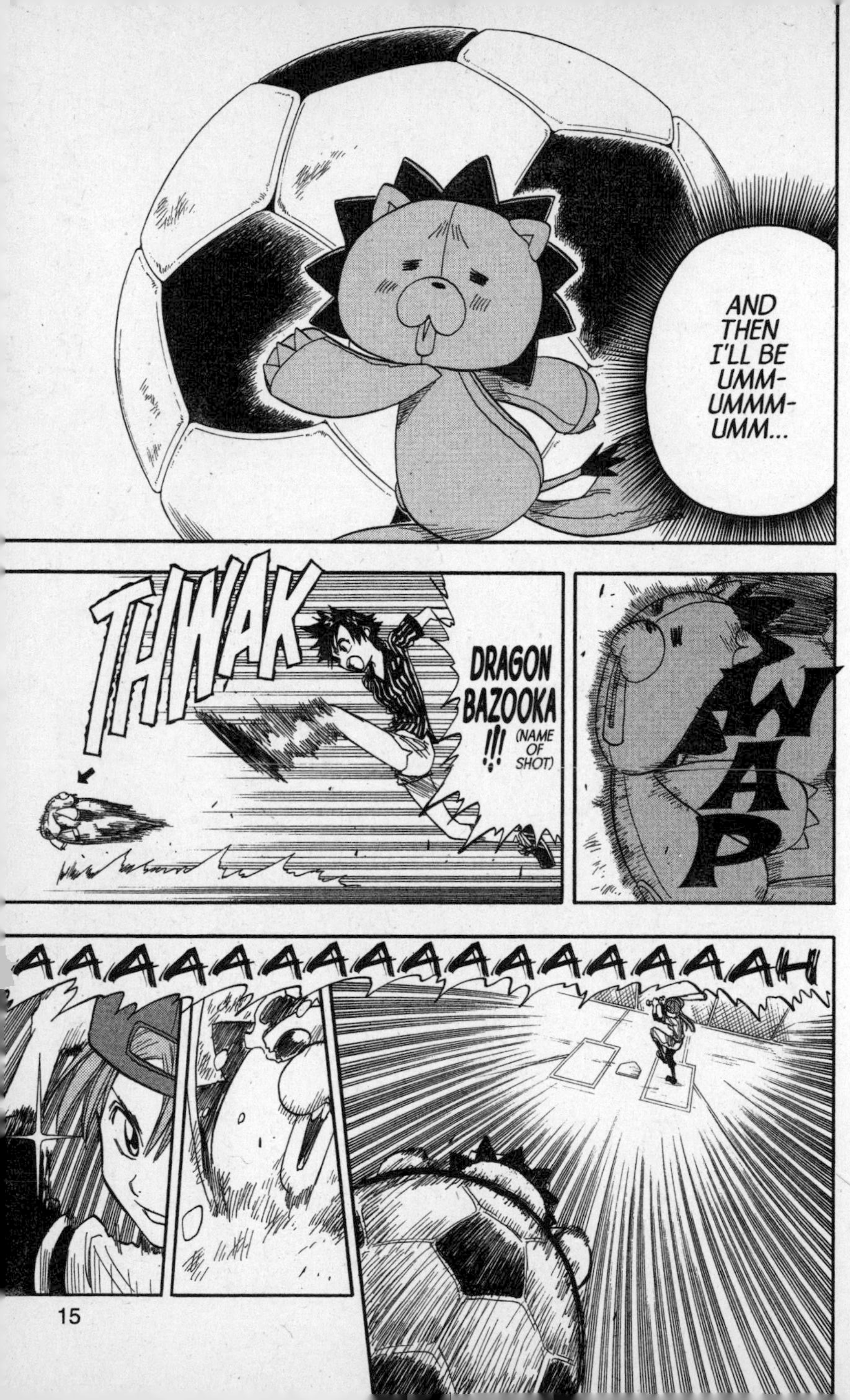
AND THEN I'LL BE UMM-UMMM-UMM...
SWAP
THWAK
DRAGON BAZOOKA!!!
(NAME OF SHOT)
AAAAAAAAAAAAAAAAH

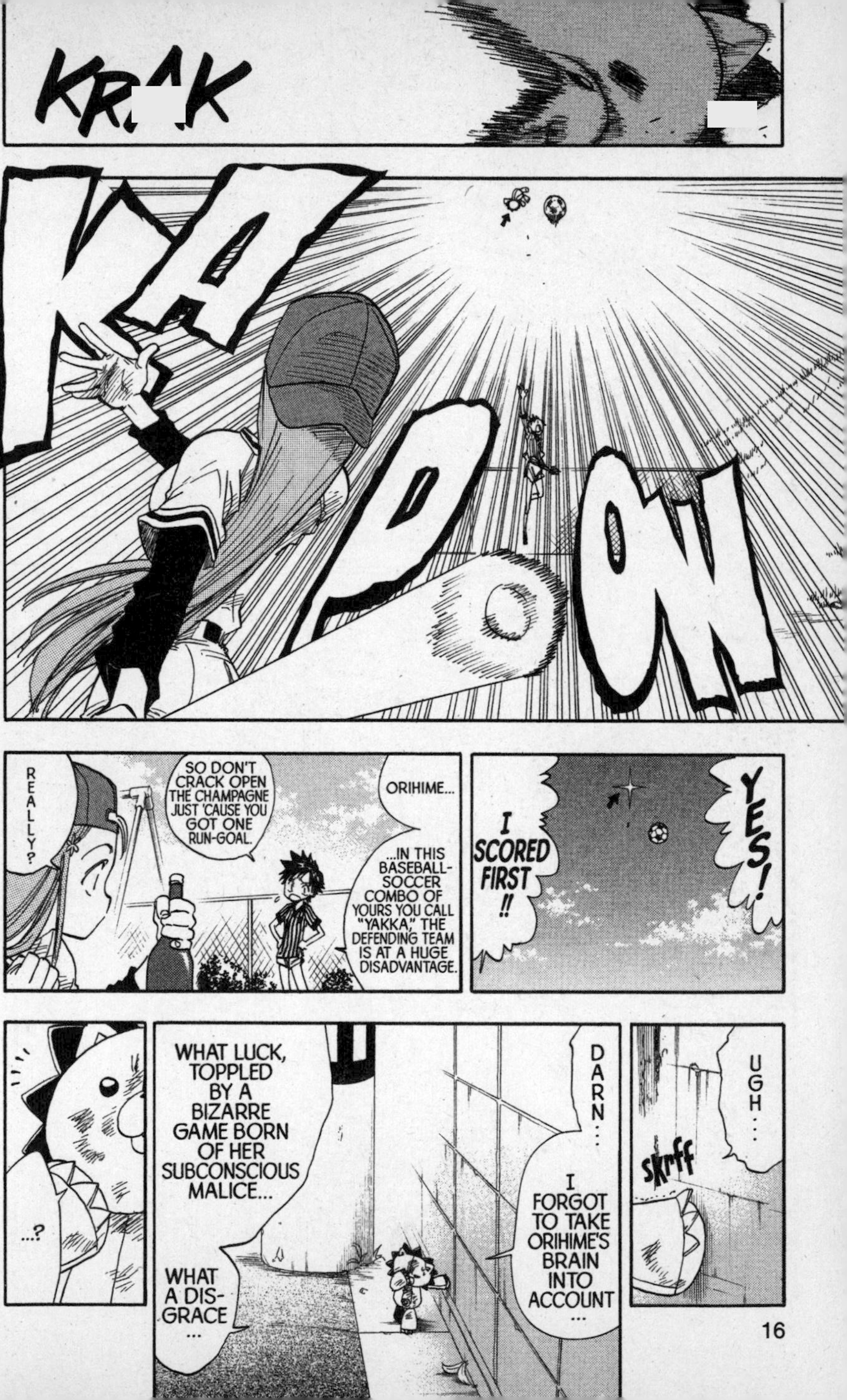
KRAK
KAPOW
YES!
I SCORED FIRST!!
ORIHIME...
...IN THIS BASEBALL-SOCCER COMBO OF YOURS YOU CALL "YAKKA," THE DEFENDING TEAM IS AT A HUGE DISADVANTAGE.
SO DON'T CRACK OPEN THE CHAMPAGNE JUST 'CAUSE YOU GOT ONE RUN-GOAL.
REALLY?
UGH...
SKRFF
DARN...
I FORGOT TO TAKE ORIHIME'S BRAIN INTO ACCOUNT...
WHAT LUCK, TOPPLED BY A BIZARRE GAME BORN OF HER SUBCONSCIOUS MALICE...
WHAT A DISGRACE...
...?

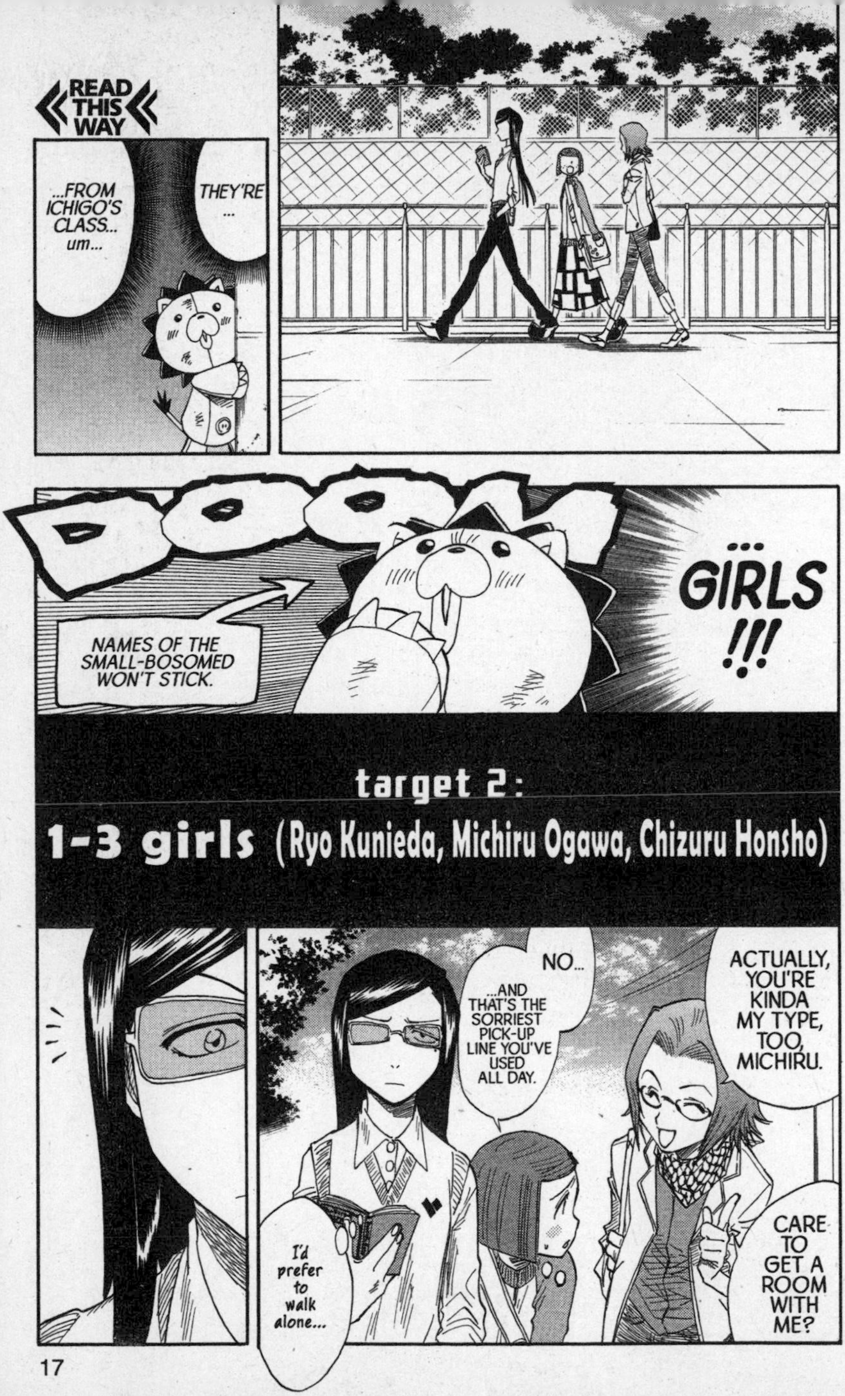
READ THIS WAY
THEY'RE ...
...FROM ICHIGO'S CLASS... um...
...GIRLS !!!
NAMES OF THE SMALL-BOSOMED WON'T STICK.
target 2:
1-3 girls (Ryo Kunieda, Michiru Ogawa, Chizuru Honsho)
ACTUALLY, YOU'RE KINDA MY TYPE, TOO, MICHIRU.
CARE TO GET A ROOM WITH ME?
NO...
...AND THAT'S THE SORRIEST PICK-UP LINE YOU'VE USED ALL DAY.
I'd prefer to walk alone...

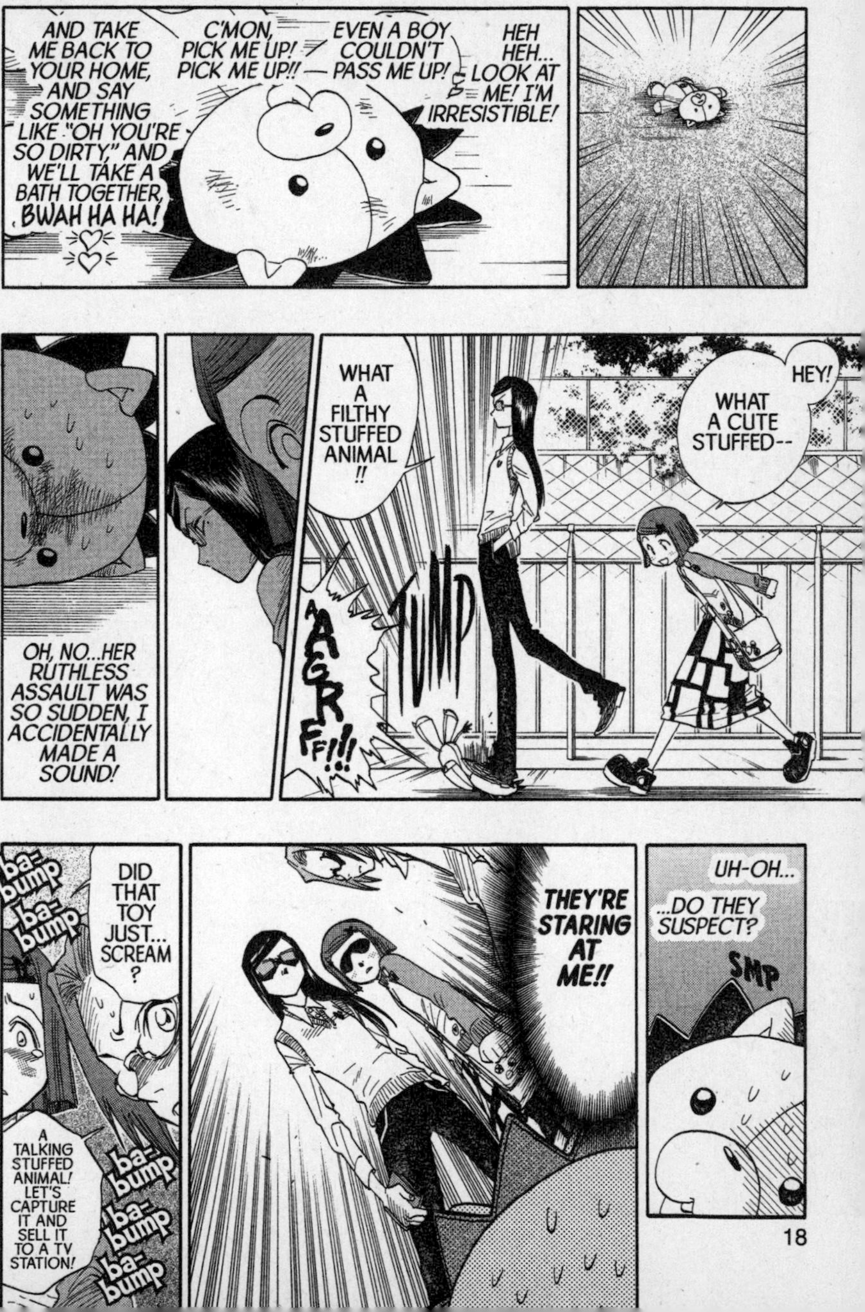
HEH HEH... LOOK AT ME! I'M IRRESISTIBLE!
EVEN A BOY COULDN'T PASS ME UP!
C'MON, PICK ME UP! PICK ME UP!!
AND TAKE ME BACK TO YOUR HOME, AND SAY SOMETHING LIKE "OH YOU'RE SO DIRTY," AND WE'LL TAKE A BATH TOGETHER, BWAH HA HA!
HEY!
WHAT A CUTE STUFFED--
WHAT A FILTHY STUFFED ANIMAL!!
TUMP
AGRFF!!!
OH, NO...HER RUTHLESS ASSAULT WAS SO SUDDEN, I ACCIDENTALLY MADE A SOUND!
UH-OH...
...DO THEY SUSPECT?
SMP
THEY'RE STARING AT ME!!
ba-bump ba-bump
DID THAT TOY JUST... SCREAM?
A TALKING STUFFED ANIMAL! LET'S CAPTURE IT AND SELL IT TO A TV STATION!
ba-bump ba-bump ba-bump

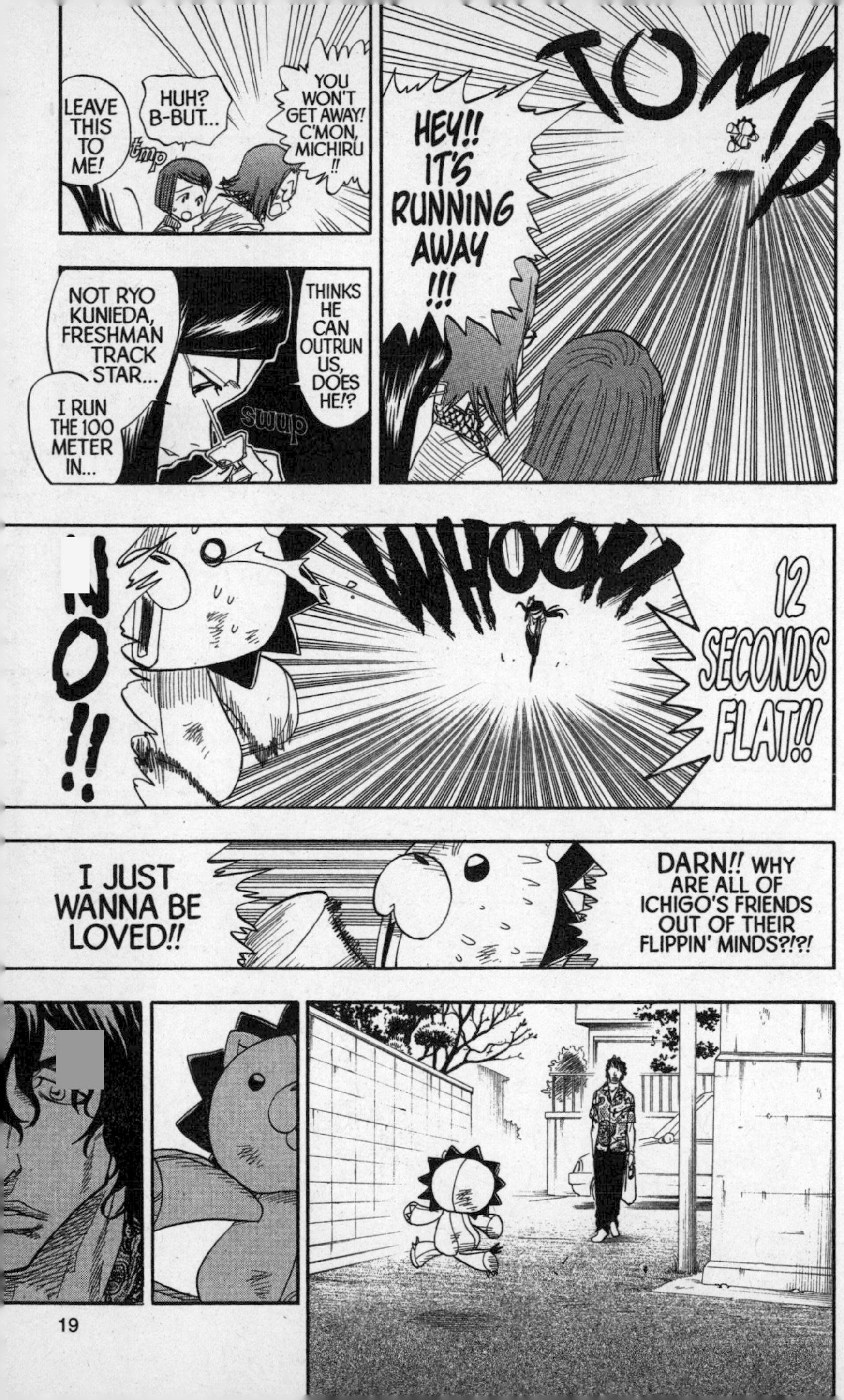
TOMP
HEY!! IT'S RUNNING AWAY!!!
YOU WON'T GET AWAY! C'MON, MICHIRU!!
HUH? B-BUT...
tmp
LEAVE THIS TO ME!
THINKS HE CAN OUTRUN US, DOES HE!?
NOT RYO KUNIEDA, FRESHMAN TRACK STAR...
swup
I RUN THE 100 METER IN...
12 SECONDS FLAT!!
WHOOM
NO!!
DARN!! WHY ARE ALL OF ICHIGO'S FRIENDS OUT OF THEIR FLIPPIN' MINDS?!?!
I JUST WANNA BE LOVED!!

target 3:
Chad (unintentional)

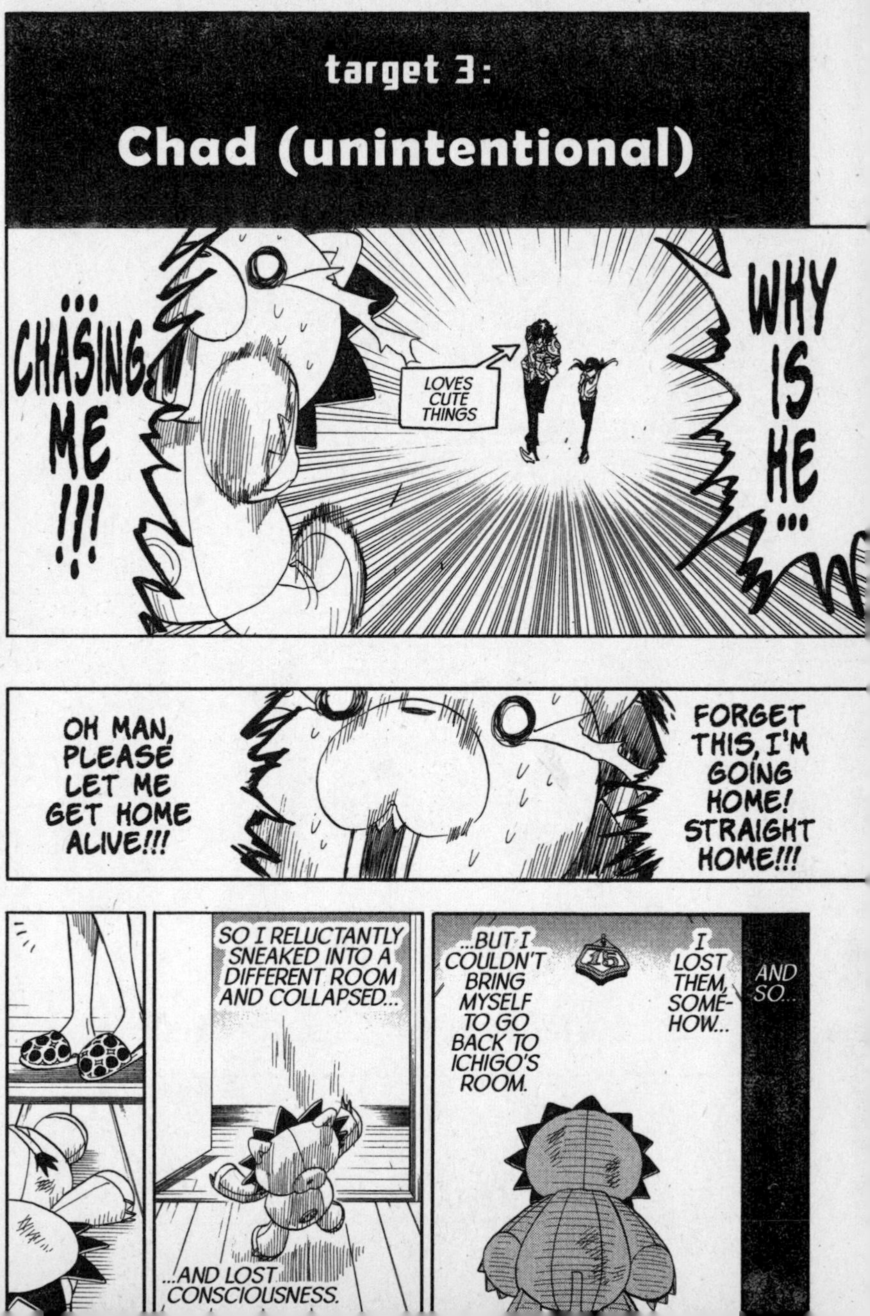
WHY IS HE...
LOVES CUTE THINGS
...CHASING ME!!!
FORGET THIS, I'M GOING HOME! STRAIGHT HOME!!!
OH MAN, PLEASE LET ME GET HOME ALIVE!!!
AND SO...
I LOST THEM, SOMEHOW...
...BUT I COULDN'T BRING MYSELF TO GO BACK TO ICHIGO'S ROOM.
SO I RELUCTANTLY SNEAKED INTO A DIFFERENT ROOM AND COLLAPSED...
...AND LOST CONSCIOUSNESS.

READ THIS WAY

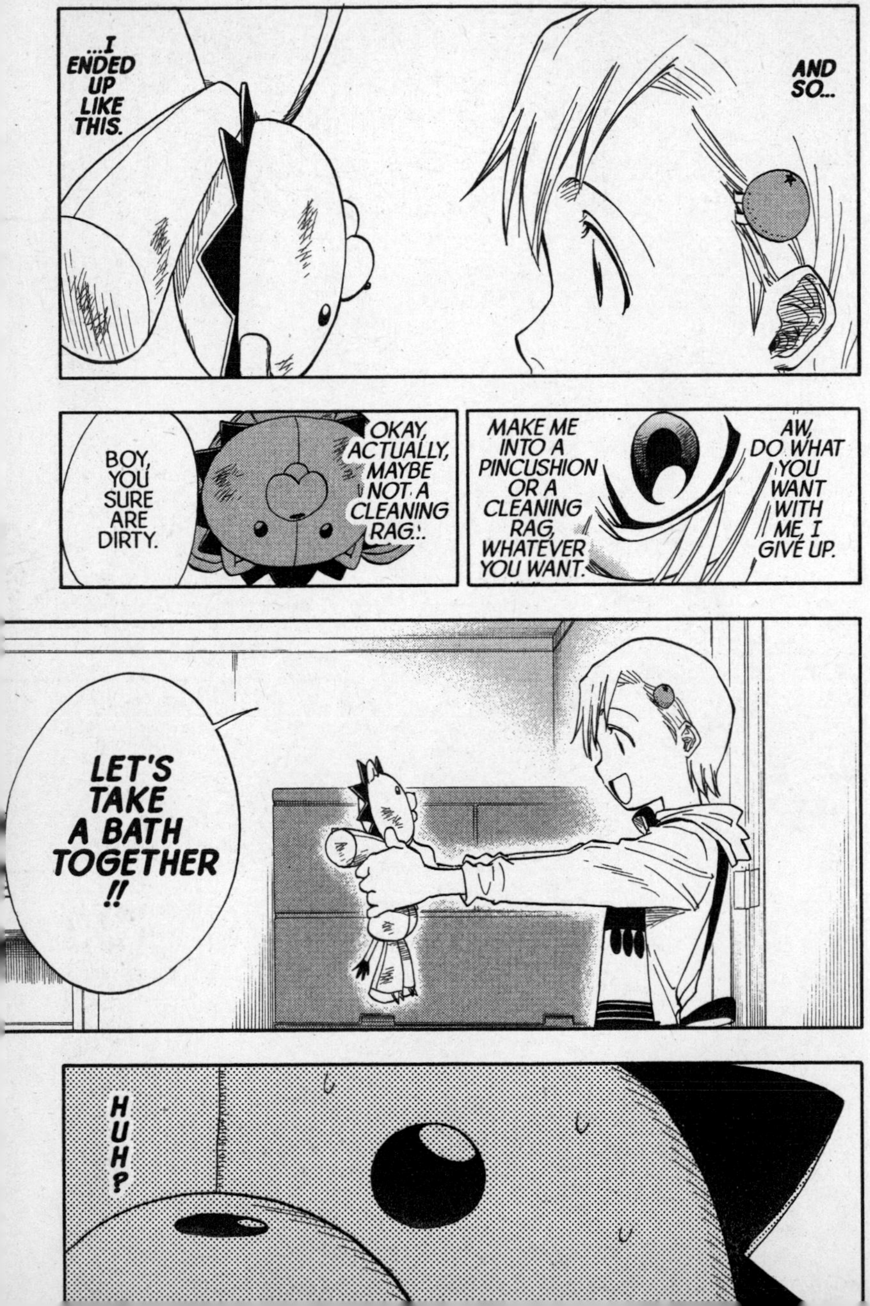
AND SO...
...I ENDED UP LIKE THIS.
AW, DO WHAT YOU WANT WITH ME, I GIVE UP.
MAKE ME INTO A PINCUSHION OR A CLEANING RAG, WHATEVER YOU WANT.
OKAY, ACTUALLY, MAYBE NOT A CLEANING RAG...
BOY, YOU SURE ARE DIRTY.
LET'S TAKE A BATH TOGETHER!!
HUH?

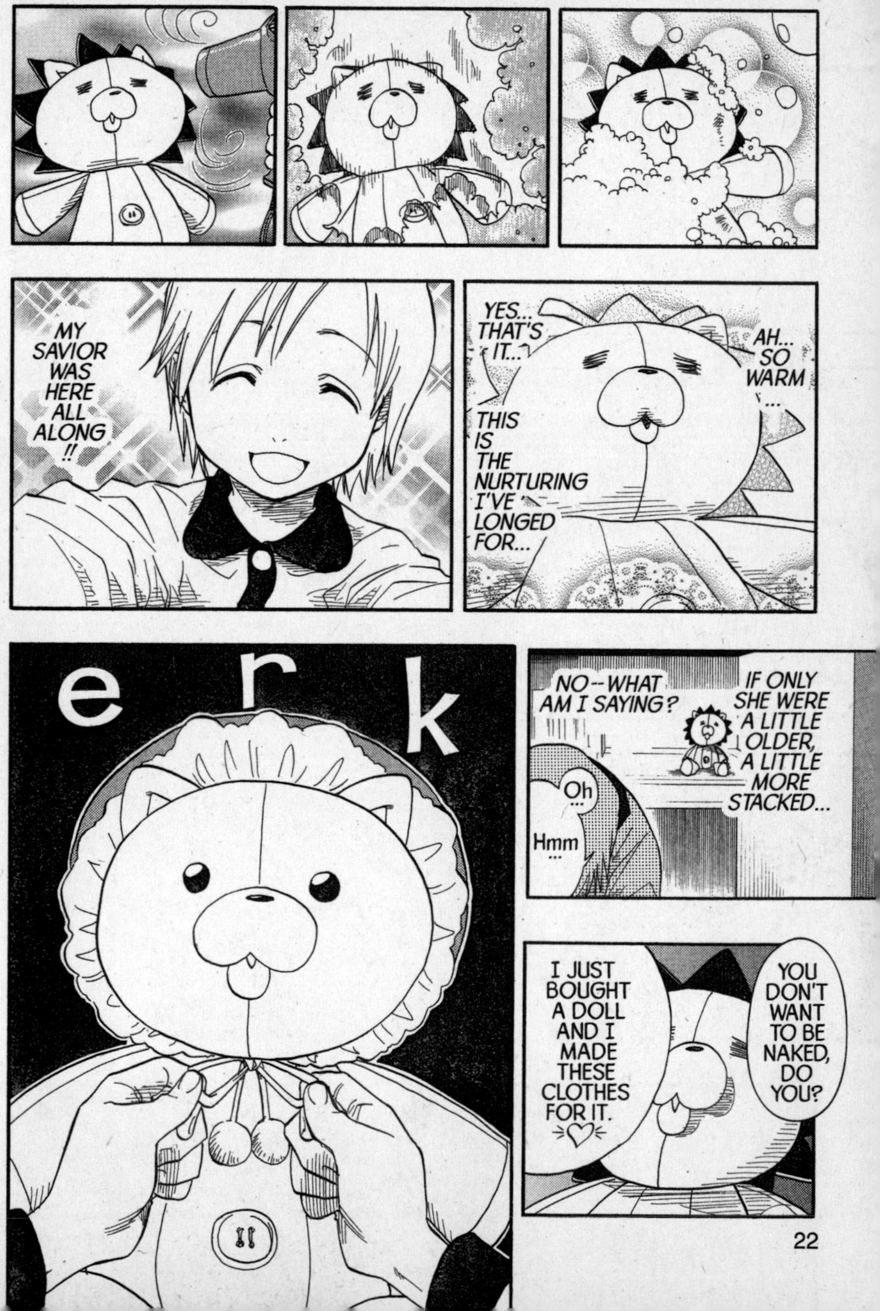
AH... SO WARM...
YES... THAT'S IT...
THIS IS THE NURTURING I'VE LONGED FOR...
MY SAVIOR WAS HERE ALL ALONG!!
IF ONLY SHE WERE A LITTLE OLDER, A LITTLE MORE STACKED...
NO--WHAT AM I SAYING?
Oh...
Hmm...
YOU DON'T WANT TO BE NAKED, DO YOU?
I JUST BOUGHT A DOLL AND I MADE THESE CLOTHES FOR IT. ♡
e r k

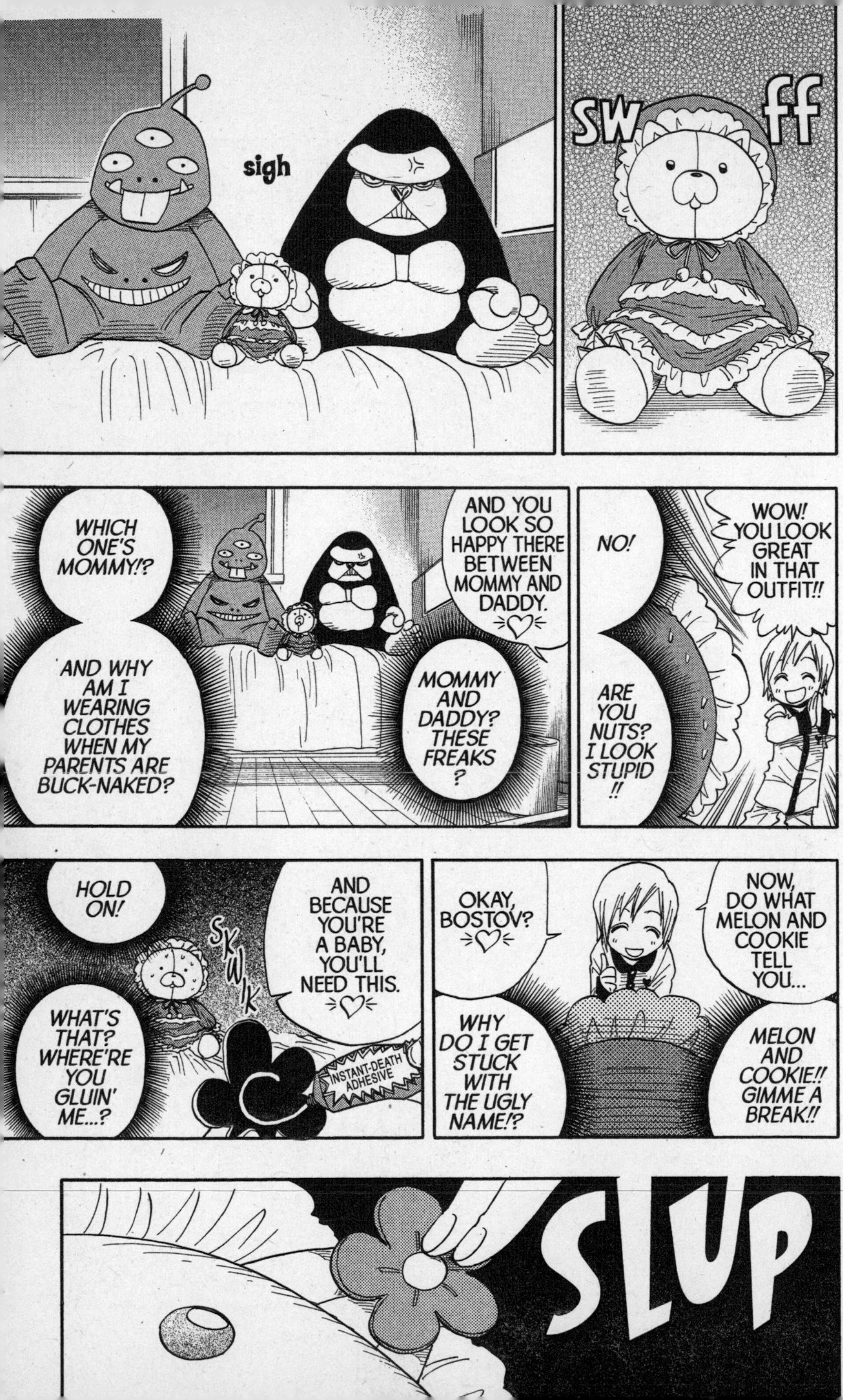
sw ff
sigh
WOW! YOU LOOK GREAT IN THAT OUTFIT!!
NO!
ARE YOU NUTS? I LOOK STUPID!!
AND YOU LOOK SO HAPPY THERE BETWEEN MOMMY AND DADDY. ♡
MOMMY AND DADDY? THESE FREAKS?
WHICH ONE'S MOMMY!?
AND WHY AM I WEARING CLOTHES WHEN MY PARENTS ARE BUCK-NAKED?
NOW, DO WHAT MELON AND COOKIE TELL YOU...
OKAY, BOSTOV? ♡
MELON AND COOKIE!! GIMME A BREAK!!
WHY DO I GET STUCK WITH THE UGLY NAME!?
AND BECAUSE YOU'RE A BABY, YOU'LL NEED THIS. ♡
HOLD ON!
SKWIK
INSTANT-DEATH ADHESIVE
WHAT'S THAT? WHERE'RE YOU GLUIN' ME...?
SLUP

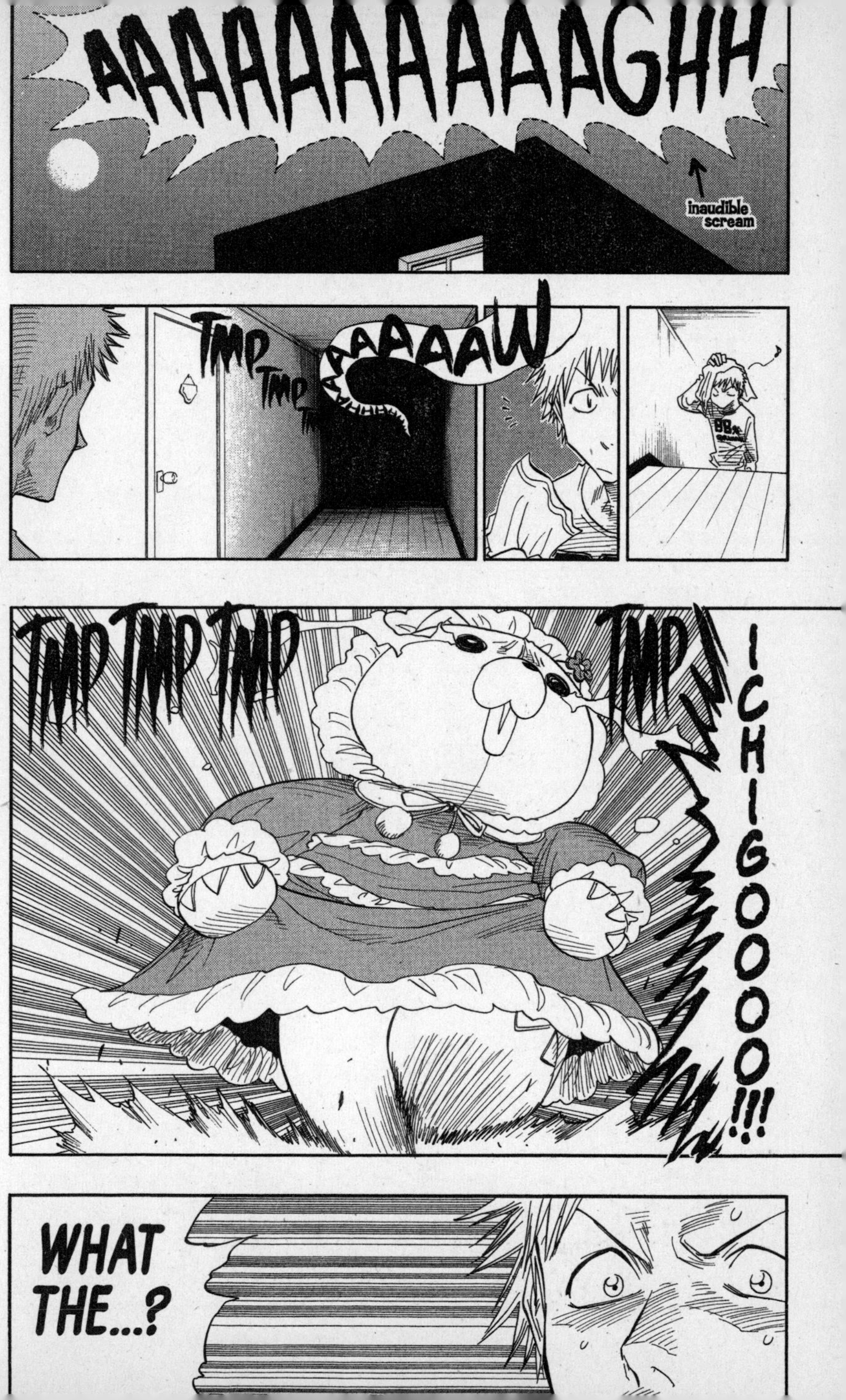
AAAAAAAAAAAGHH
inaudible scream
AAAAAAAW
TMP TMP TMP
TMP TMP TMP TMP!
ICHIGOOOOOO!!!
WHAT THE...?

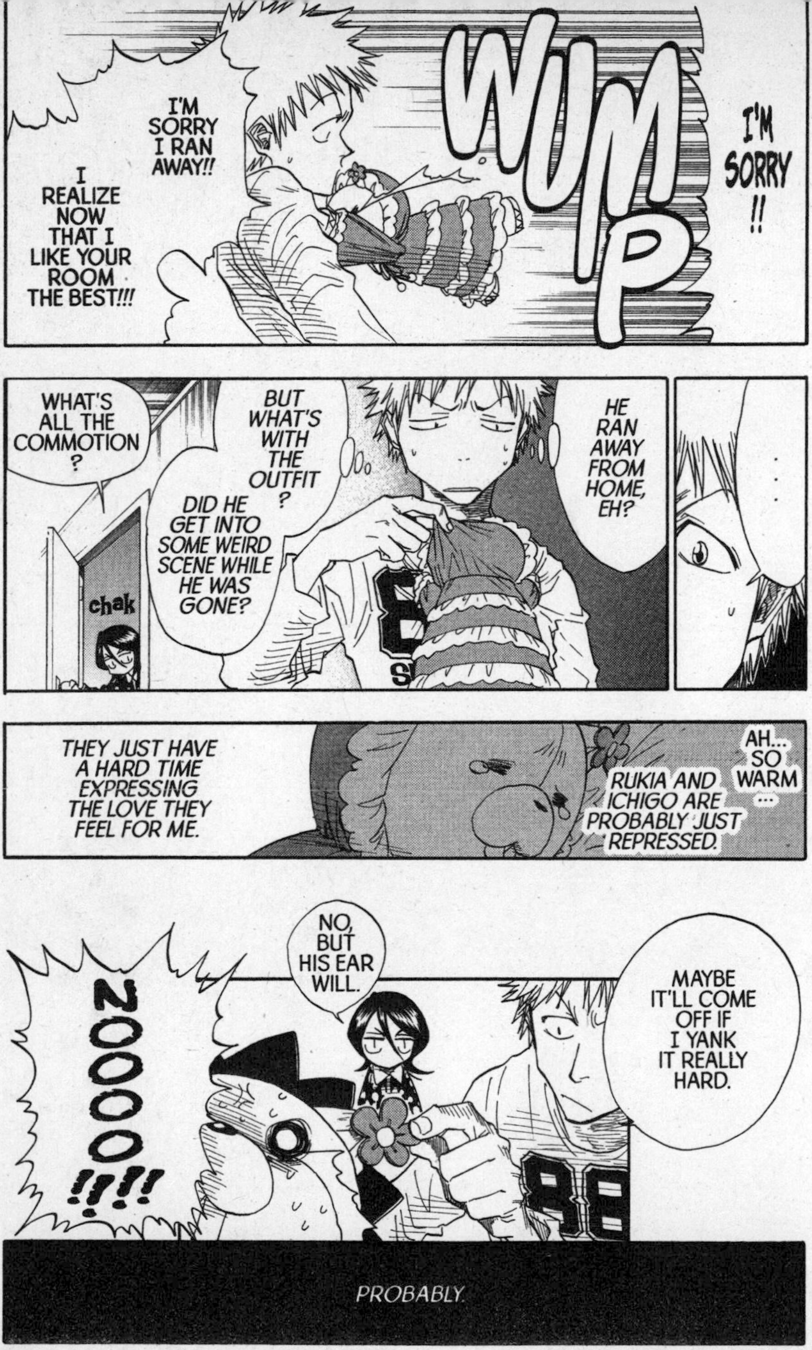
I'M SORRY !!
WUMP
I'M SORRY I RAN AWAY!!
I REALIZE NOW THAT I LIKE YOUR ROOM THE BEST!!!
...
HE RAN AWAY FROM HOME, EH?
BUT WHAT'S WITH THE OUTFIT?
DID HE GET INTO SOME WEIRD SCENE WHILE HE WAS GONE?
WHAT'S ALL THE COMMOTION?
chak
AH... SO WARM...
RUKIA AND ICHIGO ARE PROBABLY JUST REPRESSED.
THEY JUST HAVE A HARD TIME EXPRESSING THE LOVE THEY FEEL FOR ME.
MAYBE IT'LL COME OFF IF I YANK IT REALLY HARD.
NO, BUT HIS EAR WILL.
NOOOO!!?!!
PROBABLY.

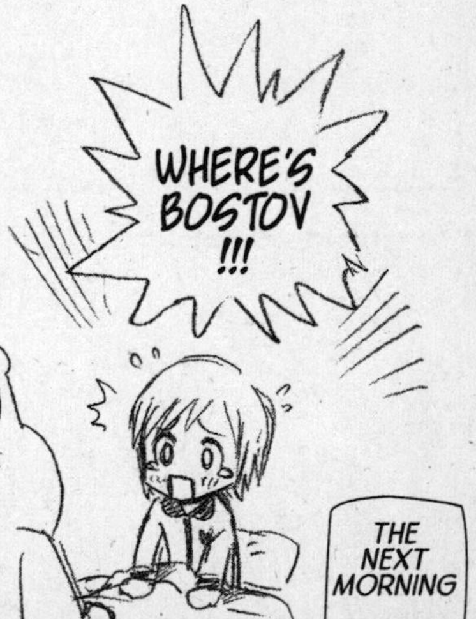
THE NEXT MORNING
WHERE'S BOSTOV !!!

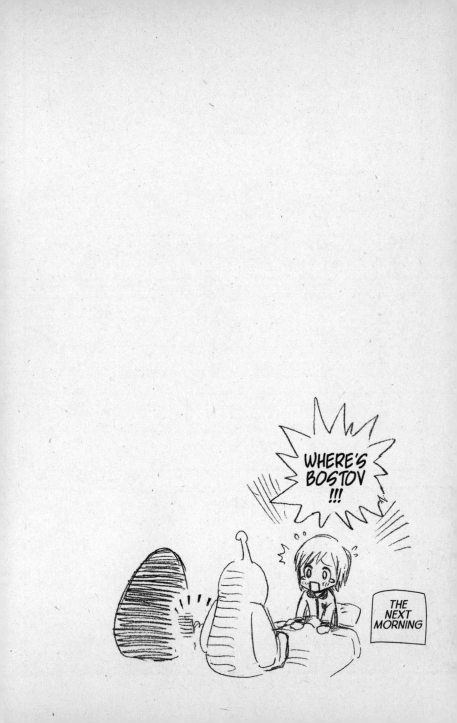

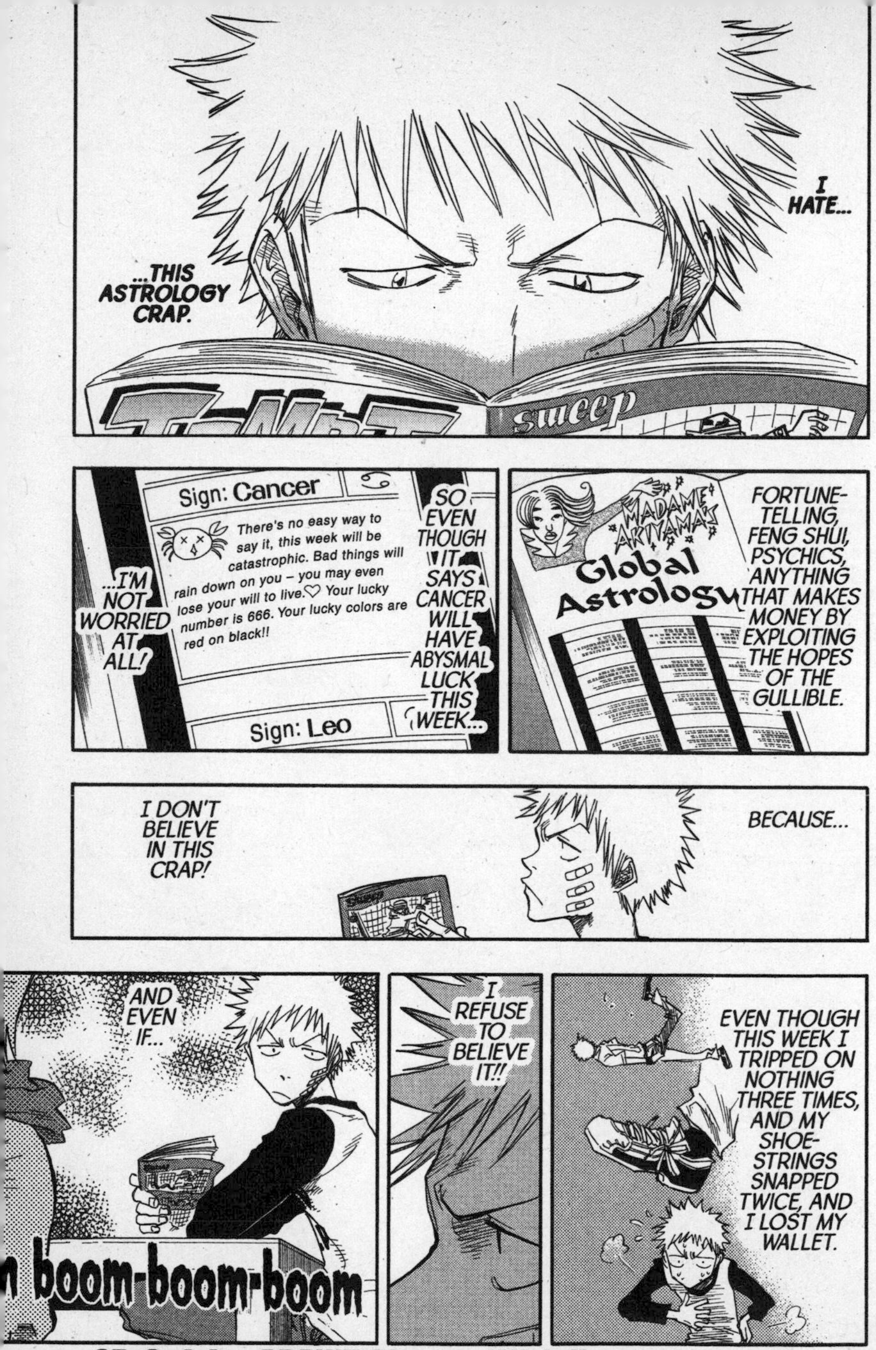
I HATE...
...THIS ASTROLOGY CRAP.
sweep
MADAME AKIYAMA'S
Global Astrology
FORTUNE-TELLING, FENG SHUI, PSYCHICS, ANYTHING THAT MAKES MONEY BY EXPLOITING THE HOPES OF THE GULLIBLE.
Sign: Cancer
There's no easy way to say it, this week will be catastrophic. Bad things will rain down on you – you may even lose your will to live.♡ Your lucky number is 666. Your lucky colors are red on black!!
Sign: Leo
SO EVEN THOUGH IT SAYS CANCER WILL HAVE ABYSMAL LUCK THIS WEEK...
...I'M NOT WORRIED AT ALL!
BECAUSE...
I DON'T BELIEVE IN THIS CRAP!
EVEN THOUGH THIS WEEK I TRIPPED ON NOTHING THREE TIMES, AND MY SHOE-STRINGS SNAPPED TWICE, AND I LOST MY WALLET.
I REFUSE TO BELIEVE IT!!
AND EVEN IF...
boom-boom-boom

27. Spirits AREN'T Always With Us

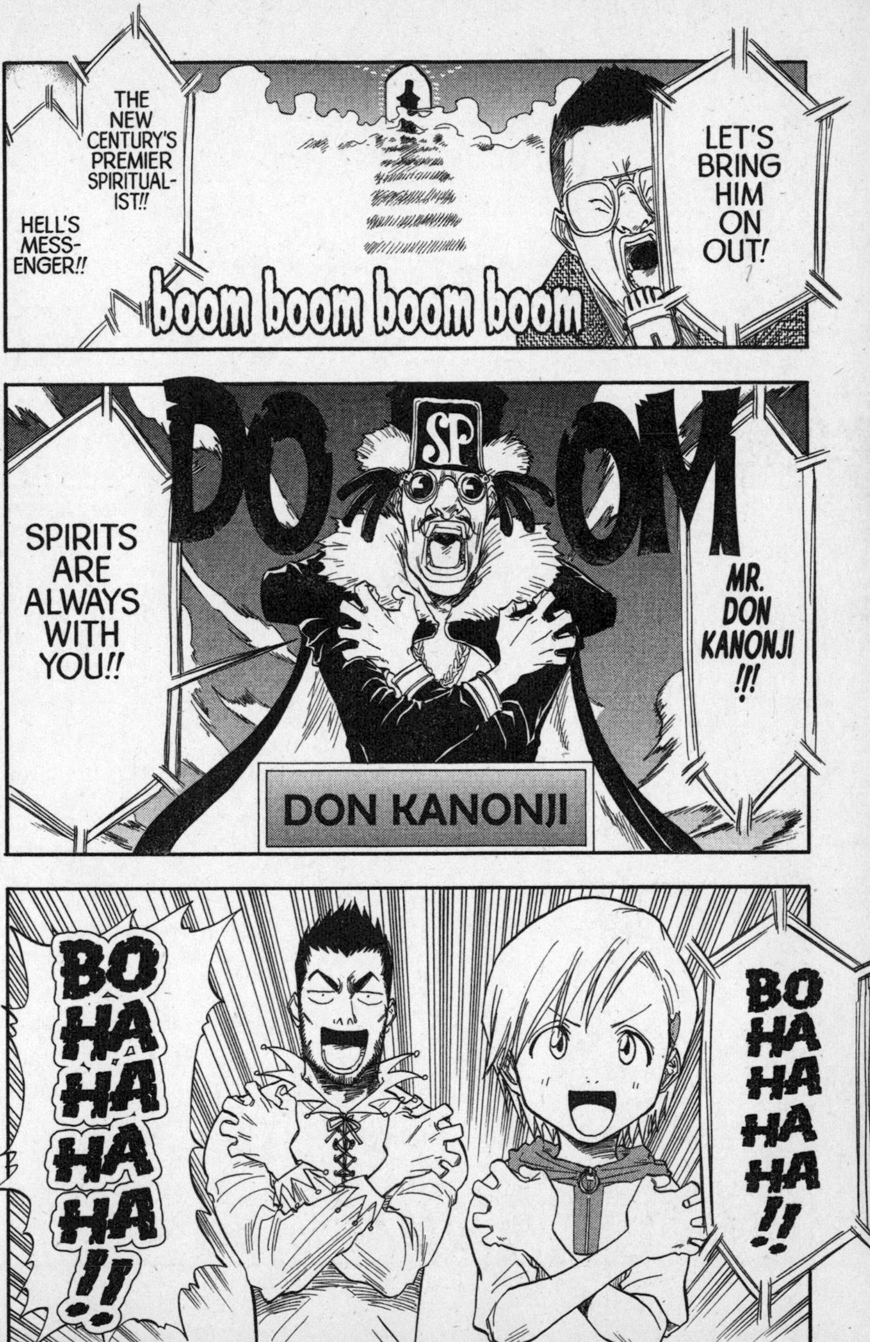
LET'S BRING HIM ON OUT!
THE NEW CENTURY'S PREMIER SPIRITUAL-IST!!
HELL'S MESS-ENGER!!
boom boom boom boom
MR. DON KANONJI!!!
SPIRITS ARE ALWAYS WITH YOU!!
DO OM
DON KANONJI
BO HA HA HA HA HA HA!!
BO HA HA HA HA HA HA!!

READ THIS WAY

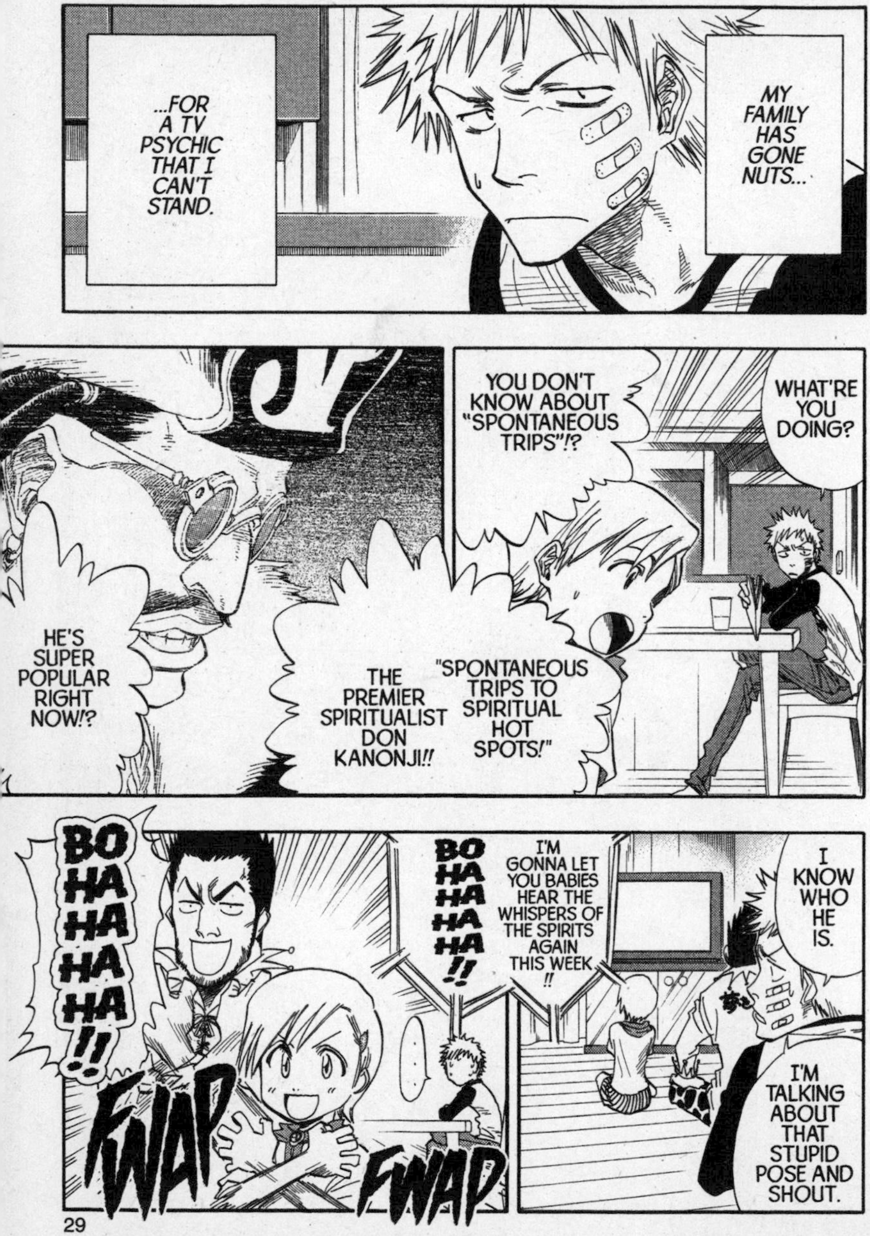

MY FAMILY HAS GONE NUTS...
...FOR A TV PSYCHIC THAT I CAN'T STAND.
WHAT'RE YOU DOING?
YOU DON'T KNOW ABOUT "SPONTANEOUS TRIPS"!?
"SPONTANEOUS TRIPS TO SPIRITUAL HOT SPOTS!"
THE PREMIER SPIRITUALIST DON KANONJI!!
HE'S SUPER POPULAR RIGHT NOW!?
I KNOW WHO HE IS.
I'M TALKING ABOUT THAT STUPID POSE AND SHOUT.
I'M GONNA LET YOU BABIES HEAR THE WHISPERS OF THE SPIRITS AGAIN THIS WEEK !!
BO HA HA HA HA!!
BO HA HA HA HA HA!!
...
FWAP
FWAP

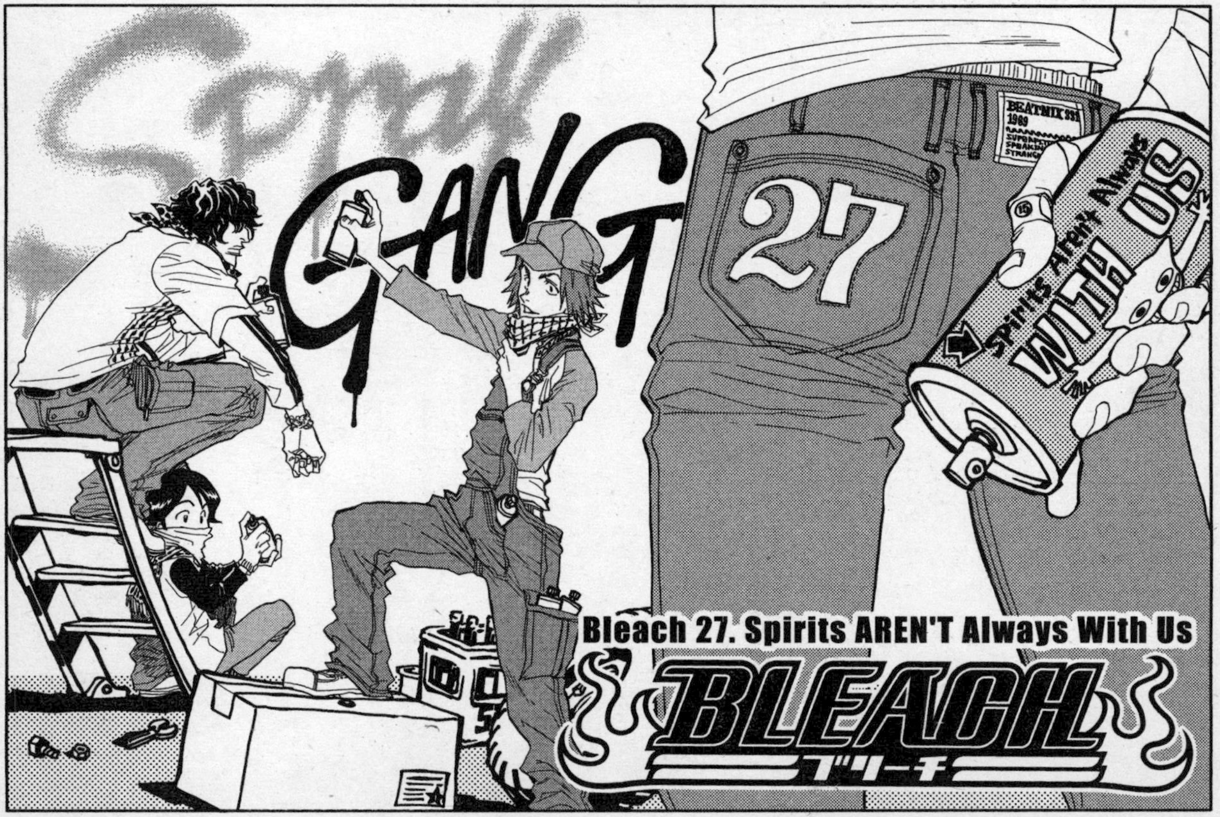
GANG
27
BEATMIX 999
1969
Spirits Aren't Always
WITH US
Bleach 27. Spirits AREN'T Always With Us
BLEACH
ブリーチ

READ THIS WAY

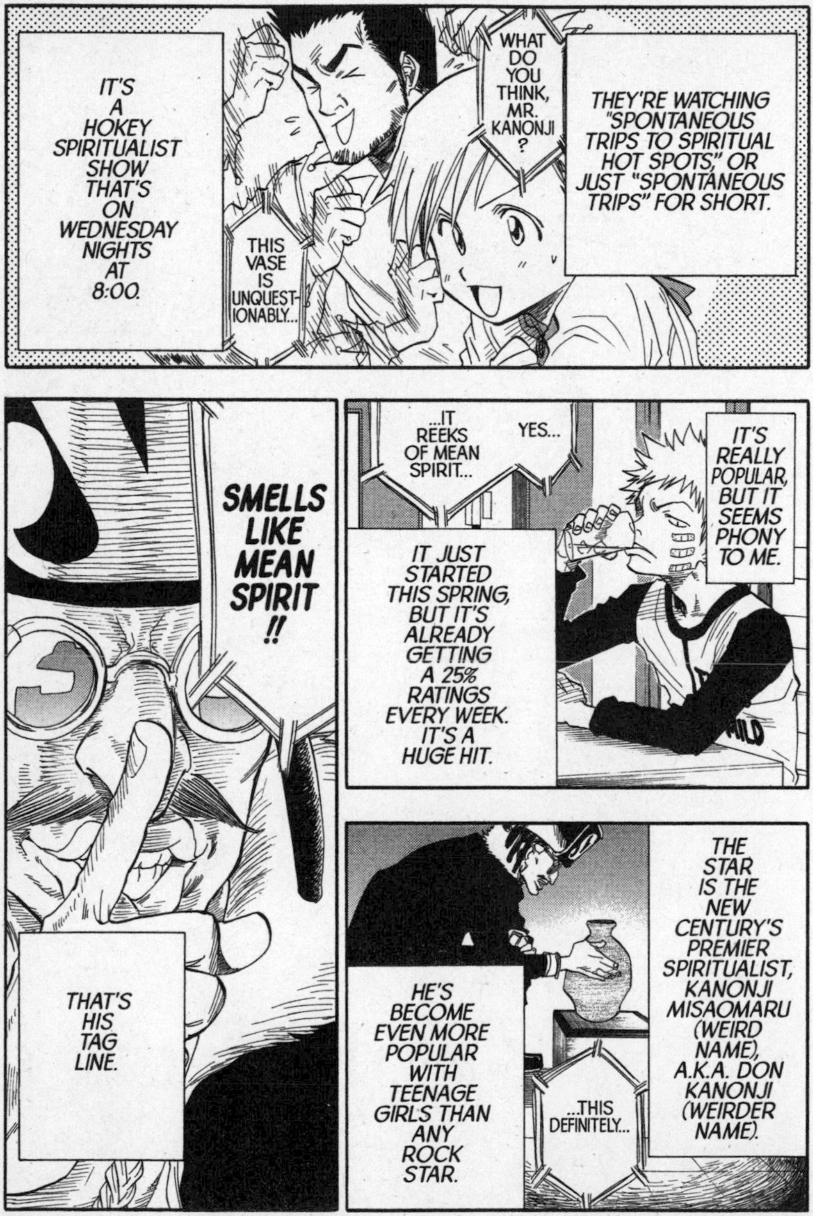
THEY'RE WATCHING "SPONTANEOUS TRIPS TO SPIRITUAL HOT SPOTS," OR JUST "SPONTANEOUS TRIPS" FOR SHORT.
WHAT DO YOU THINK, MR. KANONJI?
THIS VASE IS UNQUESTIONABLY...
IT'S A HOKEY SPIRITUALIST SHOW THAT'S ON WEDNESDAY NIGHTS AT 8:00.
IT'S REALLY POPULAR, BUT IT SEEMS PHONY TO ME.
YES...
...IT REEKS OF MEAN SPIRIT...
IT JUST STARTED THIS SPRING, BUT IT'S ALREADY GETTING A 25% RATINGS EVERY WEEK. IT'S A HUGE HIT.
THE STAR IS THE NEW CENTURY'S PREMIER SPIRITUALIST, KANONJI MISAOMARU (WEIRD NAME), A.K.A. DON KANONJI (WEIRDER NAME).
...THIS DEFINITELY...
HE'S BECOME EVEN MORE POPULAR WITH TEENAGE GIRLS THAN ANY ROCK STAR.
SMELLS LIKE MEAN SPIRIT!!
THAT'S HIS TAG LINE.

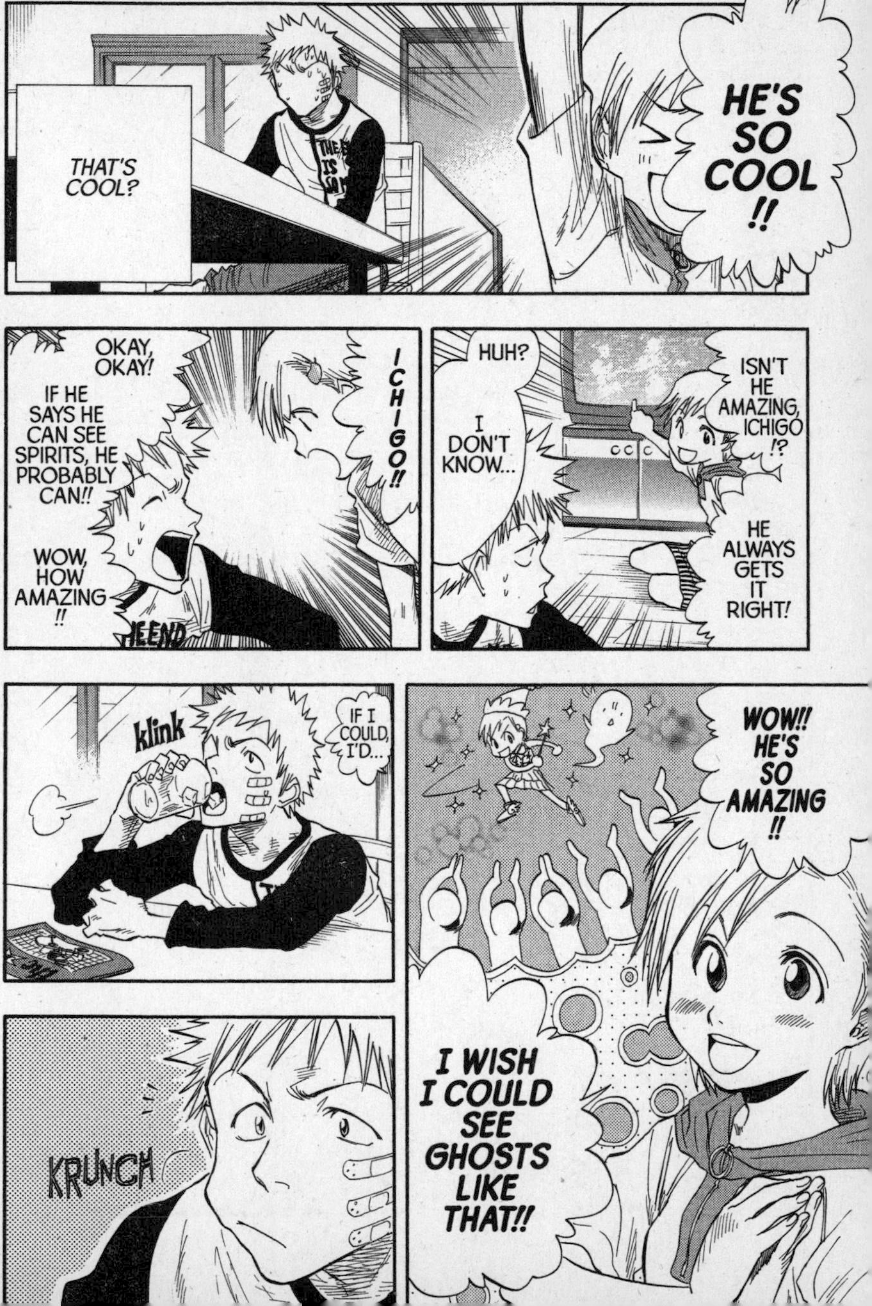
HE'S SO COOL!!
THAT'S COOL?
ISN'T HE AMAZING, ICHIGO!?
HUH?
HE ALWAYS GETS IT RIGHT!
I DON'T KNOW...
ICHIGO!!
OKAY, OKAY!
IF HE SAYS HE CAN SEE SPIRITS, HE PROBABLY CAN!!
WOW, HOW AMAZING!!
WOW!! HE'S SO AMAZING!!
I WISH I COULD SEE GHOSTS LIKE THAT!!
IF I COULD, I'D...
klink
KRUNCH

READ THIS WAY

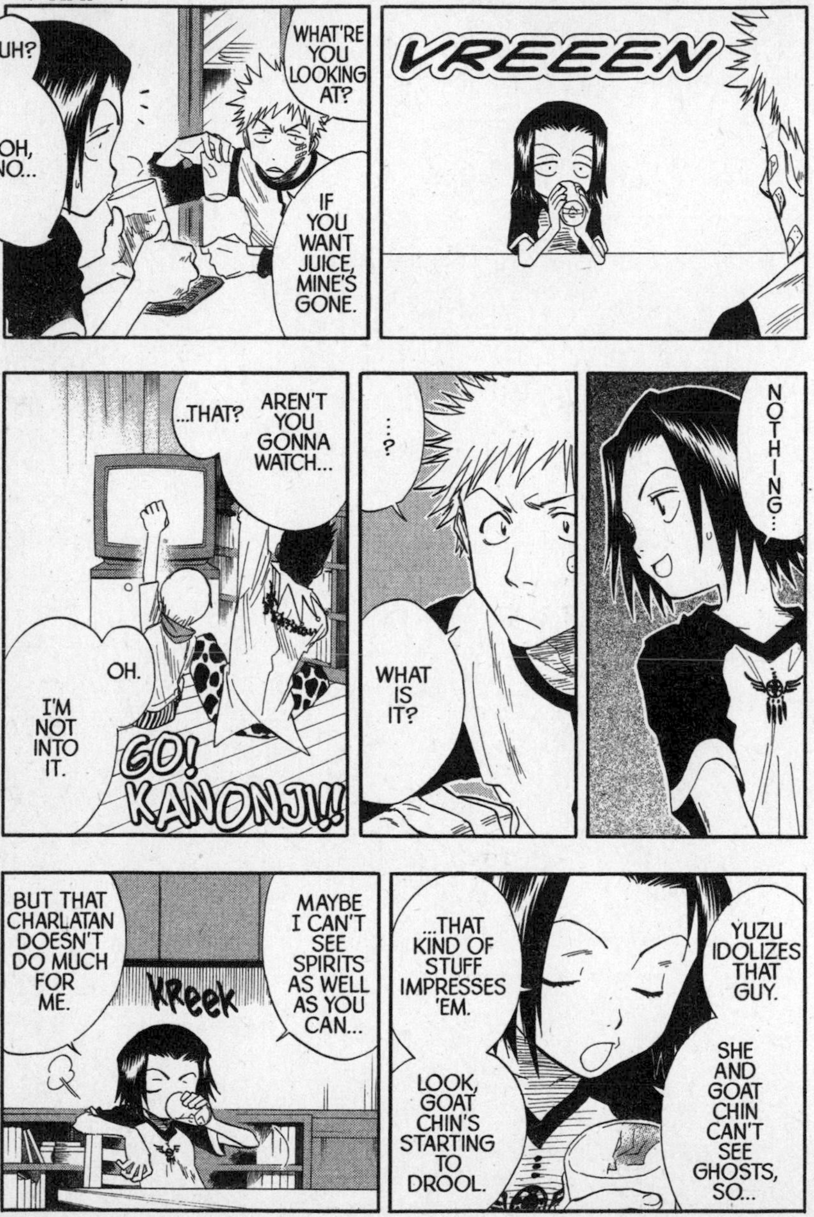
VREEEN
WHAT'RE YOU LOOKING AT?
HUH?
IF YOU WANT JUICE, MINE'S GONE.
OH, NO...
NOTHING...
...?
WHAT IS IT?
AREN'T YOU GONNA WATCH...
...THAT?
OH.
I'M NOT INTO IT.
GO! KANONJI!!
YUZU IDOLIZES THAT GUY.
SHE AND GOAT CHIN CAN'T SEE GHOSTS, SO...
...THAT KIND OF STUFF IMPRESSES 'EM.
LOOK, GOAT CHIN'S STARTING TO DROOL.
MAYBE I CAN'T SEE SPIRITS AS WELL AS YOU CAN...
BUT THAT CHARLATAN DOESN'T DO MUCH FOR ME.
KREEK

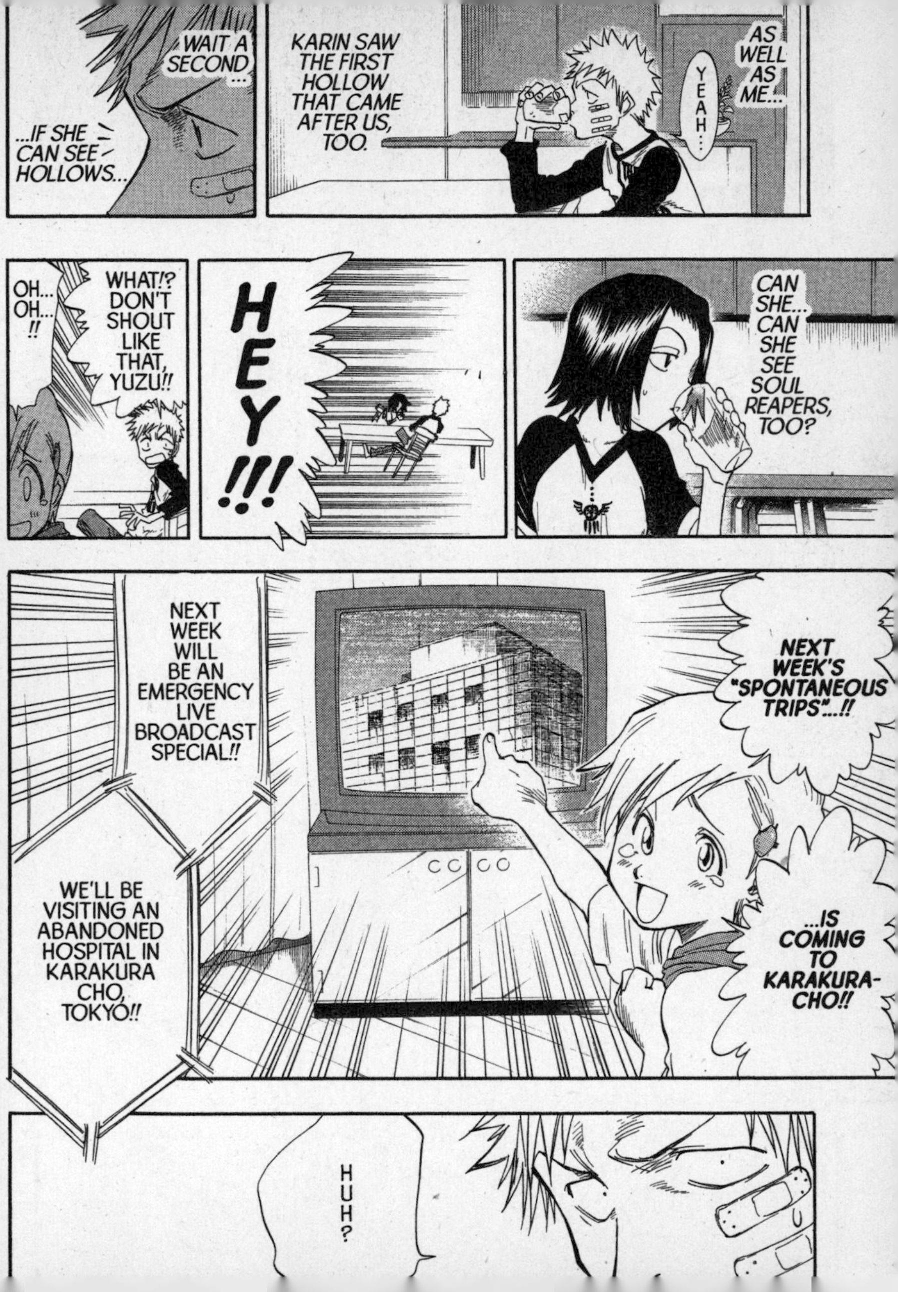
AS WELL AS ME...
YEAH...
KARIN SAW THE FIRST HOLLOW THAT CAME AFTER US, TOO.
WAIT A SECOND ...
...IF SHE CAN SEE HOLLOWS...
CAN SHE... CAN SHE SEE SOUL REAPERS, TOO?
HEY!!!
WHAT!? DON'T SHOUT LIKE THAT, YUZU!!
OH... OH... !!
NEXT WEEK'S "SPONTANEOUS TRIPS"...!!
...IS COMING TO KARAKURA-CHO!!
NEXT WEEK WILL BE AN EMERGENCY LIVE BROADCAST SPECIAL!!
WE'LL BE VISITING AN ABANDONED HOSPITAL IN KARAKURA CHO, TOKYO!!
HUH?

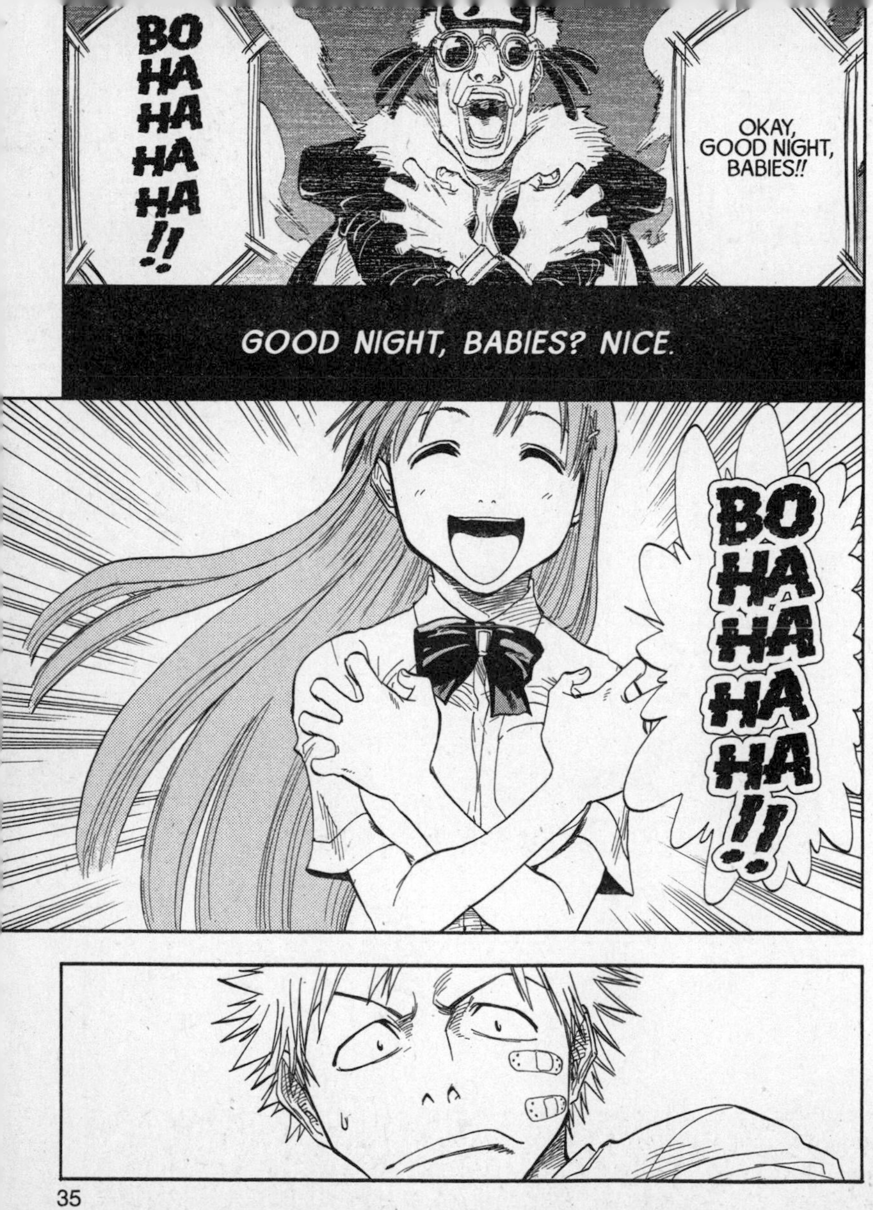
OKAY, GOOD NIGHT, BABIES!!
BO HA HA HA HA!!
GOOD NIGHT, BABIES? NICE.
BO HA HA HA HA!!

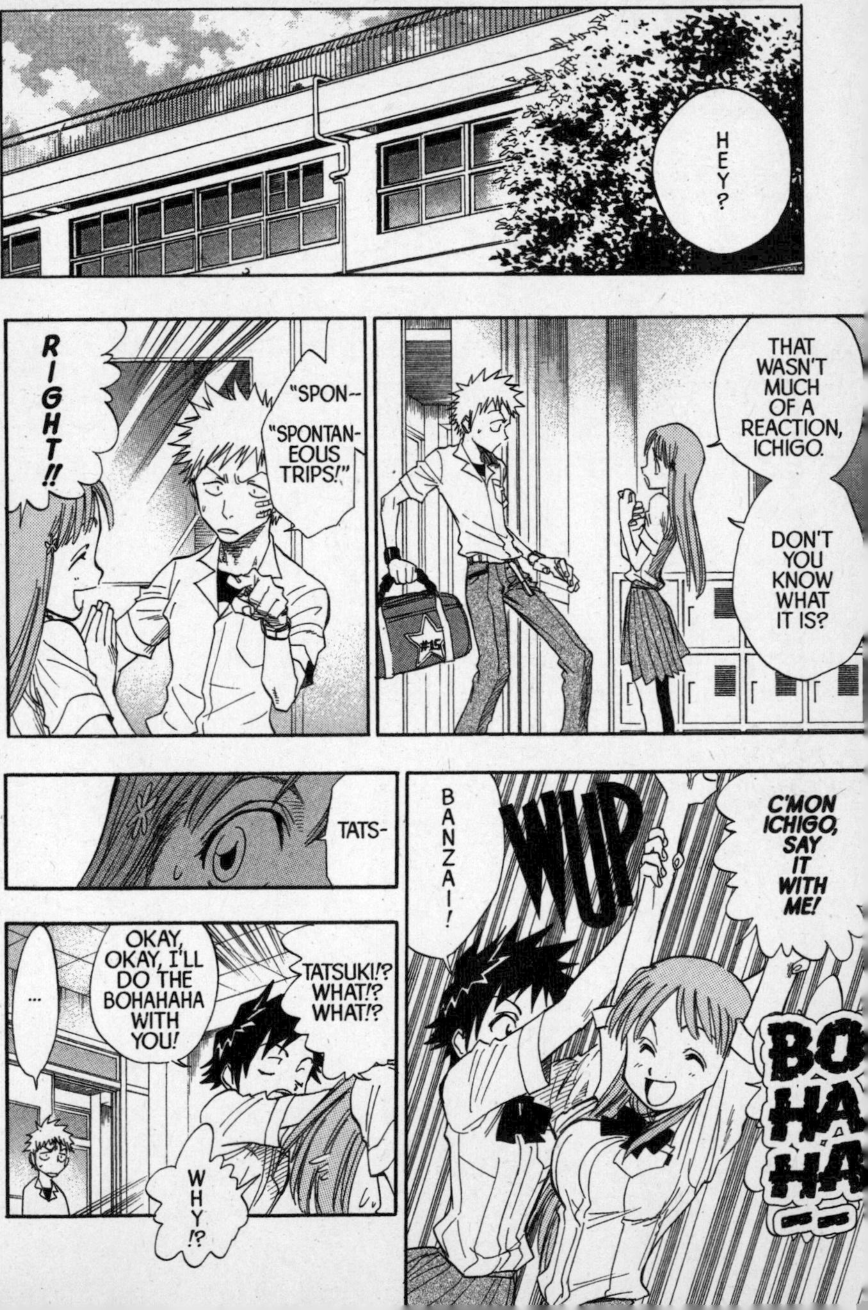
HEY?
THAT WASN'T MUCH OF A REACTION, ICHIGO.
DON'T YOU KNOW WHAT IT IS?
"SPON--
"SPONTANEOUS TRIPS!"
RIGHT!!
C'MON ICHIGO, SAY IT WITH ME!
WUP
BANZAI!
BOHAHAHA--
TATS-
TATSUKI!? WHAT!? WHAT!?
OKAY, OKAY, I'LL DO THE BOHAHAHA WITH YOU!
...
WHY!?

READ THIS WAY

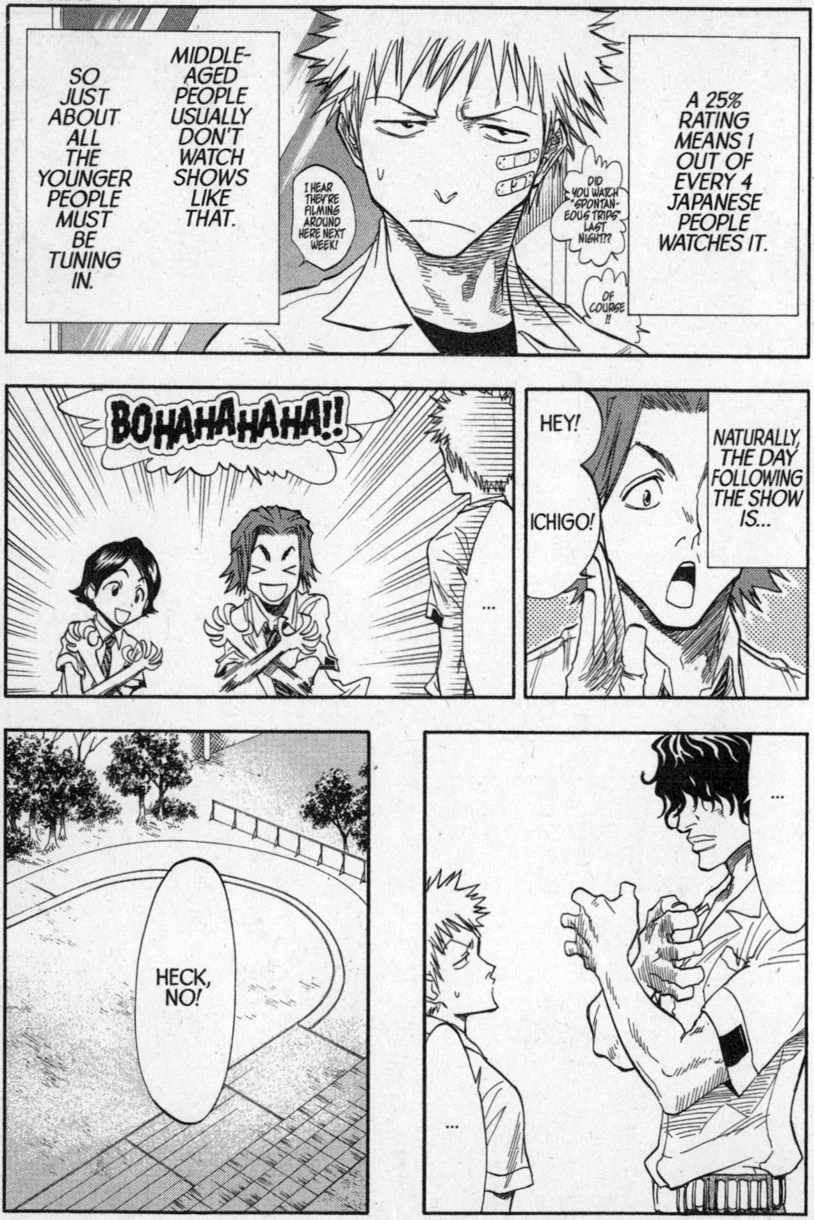

A 25% RATING MEANS 1 OUT OF EVERY 4 JAPANESE PEOPLE WATCHES IT.
DID YOU WATCH "SPONTANEOUS TRIPS" LAST NIGHT!?
OF COURSE!!
I HEAR THEY'RE FILMING AROUND HERE NEXT WEEK!
MIDDLE-AGED PEOPLE USUALLY DON'T WATCH SHOWS LIKE THAT.
SO JUST ABOUT ALL THE YOUNGER PEOPLE MUST BE TUNING IN.
NATURALLY, THE DAY FOLLOWING THE SHOW IS...
HEY!
ICHIGO!
BOHAHAHAHA!!
...
...
...
HECK, NO!

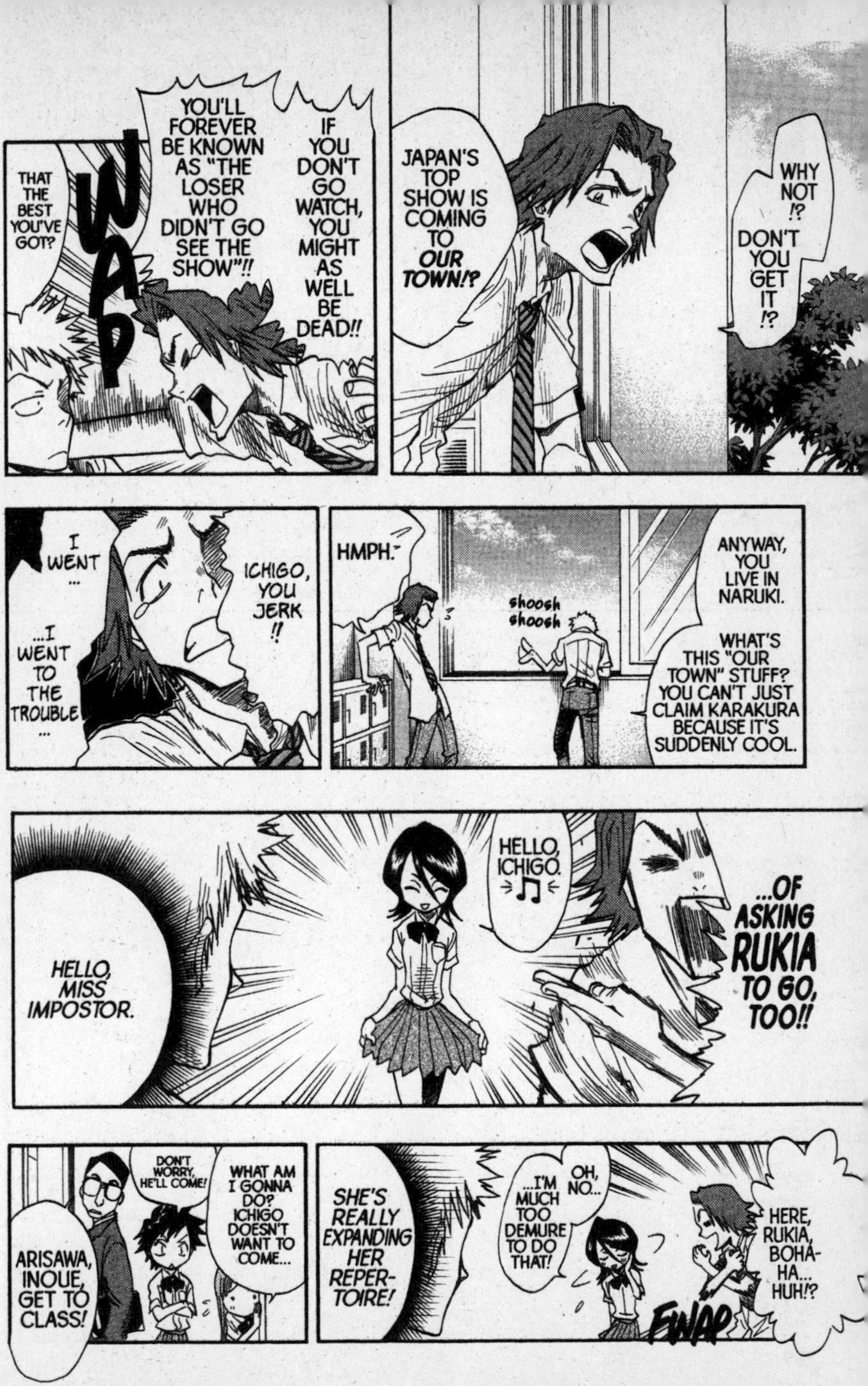
WHY NOT!? DON'T YOU GET IT!?
JAPAN'S TOP SHOW IS COMING TO OUR TOWN!?
IF YOU DON'T GO WATCH, YOU MIGHT AS WELL BE DEAD!!
YOU'LL FOREVER BE KNOWN AS "THE LOSER WHO DIDN'T GO SEE THE SHOW"!!
WAP
THAT THE BEST YOU'VE GOT?
ANYWAY, YOU LIVE IN NARUKI.
WHAT'S THIS "OUR TOWN" STUFF? YOU CAN'T JUST CLAIM KARAKURA BECAUSE IT'S SUDDENLY COOL.
shoosh shoosh
HMPH.
ICHIGO, YOU JERK!!
I WENT...
...I WENT TO THE TROUBLE...
...OF ASKING RUKIA TO GO, TOO!!
HELLO, ICHIGO. ♫
HELLO, MISS IMPOSTOR.
HERE, RUKIA, BOHAHA... HUH!?
FWAP
OH, NO...
...I'M MUCH TOO DEMURE TO DO THAT!
SHE'S REALLY EXPANDING HER REPERTOIRE!
WHAT AM I GONNA DO? ICHIGO DOESN'T WANT TO COME...
DON'T WORRY, HE'LL COME!
ARISAWA, INOUE, GET TO CLASS!

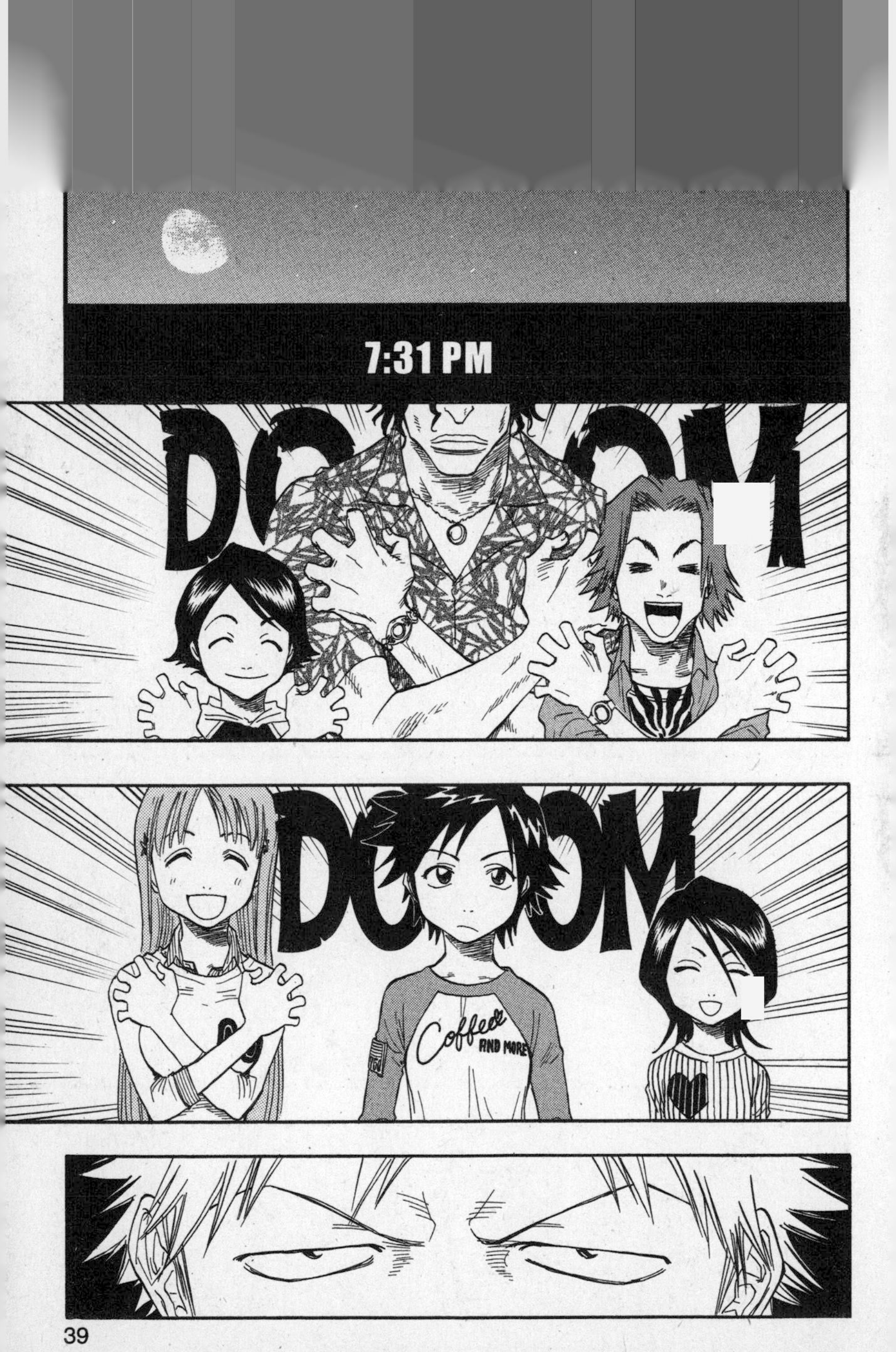
7:31 PM
Coffee
AND MORE

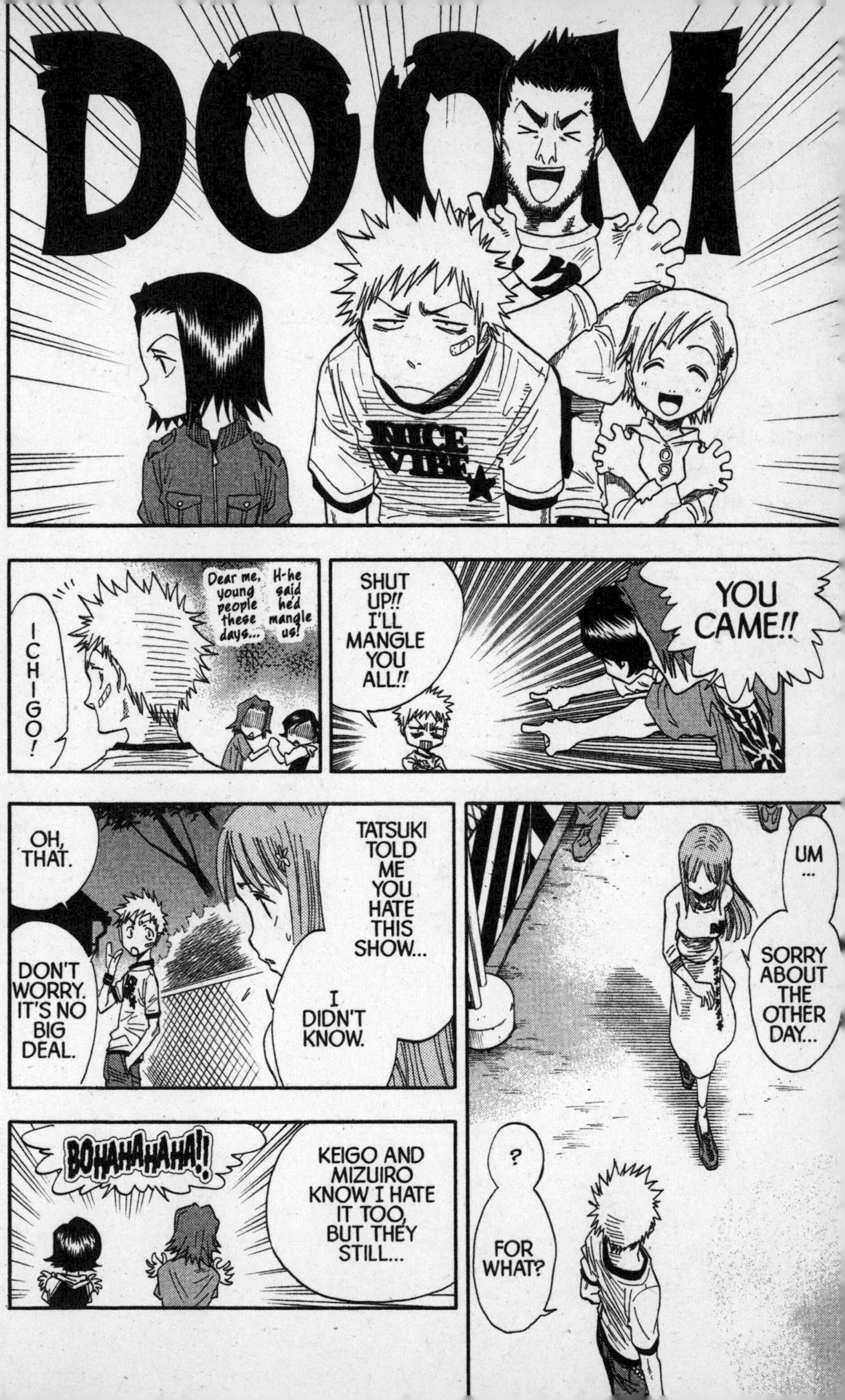
DOOM
YOU CAME!!
SHUT UP!! I'LL MANGLE YOU ALL!!
H-he said he'd mangle us!
Dear me, young people these days...
ICHIGO!
UM...
SORRY ABOUT THE OTHER DAY...
?
FOR WHAT?
TATSUKI TOLD ME YOU HATE THIS SHOW...
I DIDN'T KNOW.
OH, THAT.
DON'T WORRY. IT'S NO BIG DEAL.
KEIGO AND MIZUIRO KNOW I HATE IT TOO, BUT THEY STILL...
BOHAHAHAHA!!

READ THIS WAY

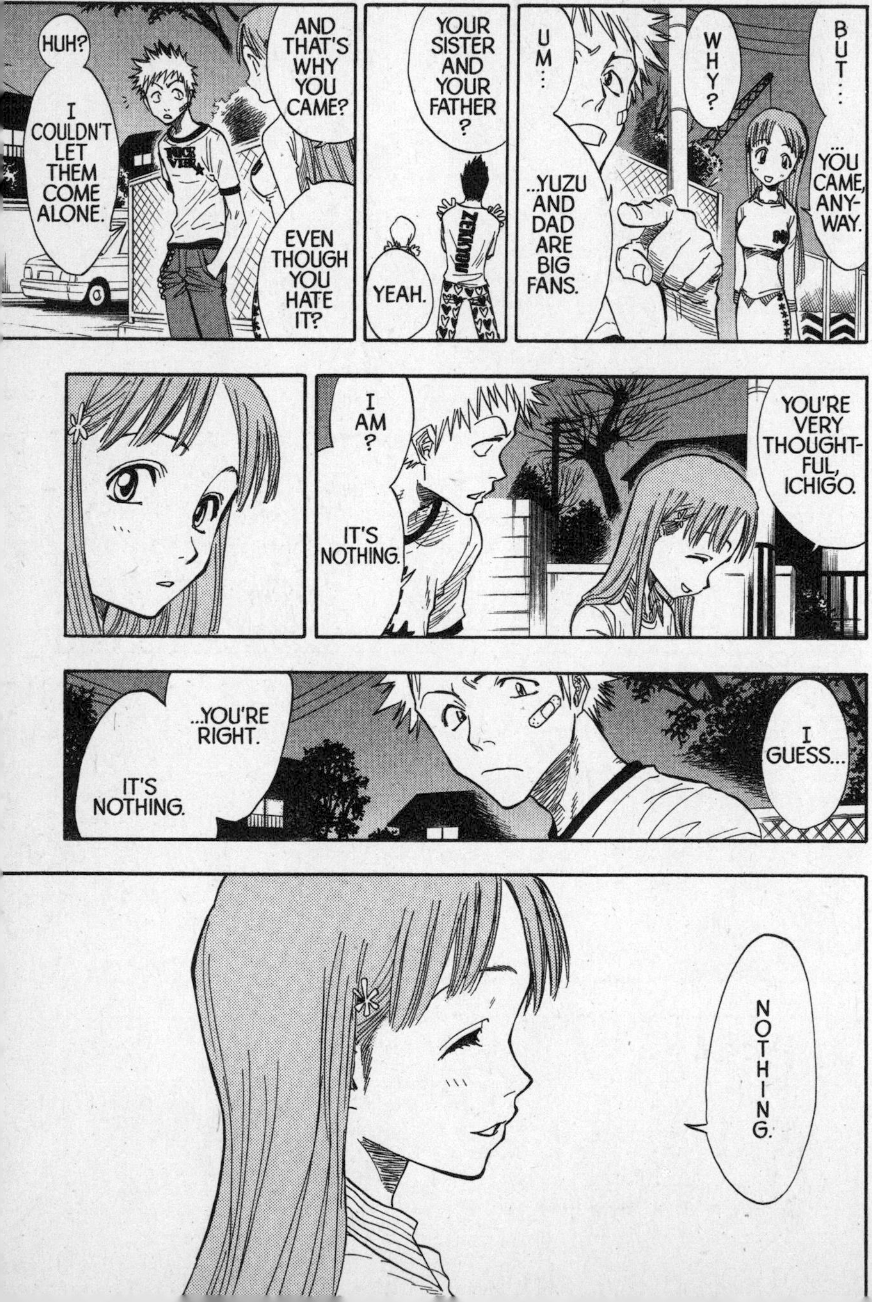
BUT...
...YOU CAME, ANYWAY.
WHY?
UM...
...YUZU AND DAD ARE BIG FANS.
YOUR SISTER AND YOUR FATHER?
YEAH.
AND THAT'S WHY YOU CAME?
EVEN THOUGH YOU HATE IT?
HUH?
I COULDN'T LET THEM COME ALONE.
YOU'RE VERY THOUGHTFUL, ICHIGO.
I AM?
IT'S NOTHING.
I GUESS...
...YOU'RE RIGHT.
IT'S NOTHING.
NOTHING.

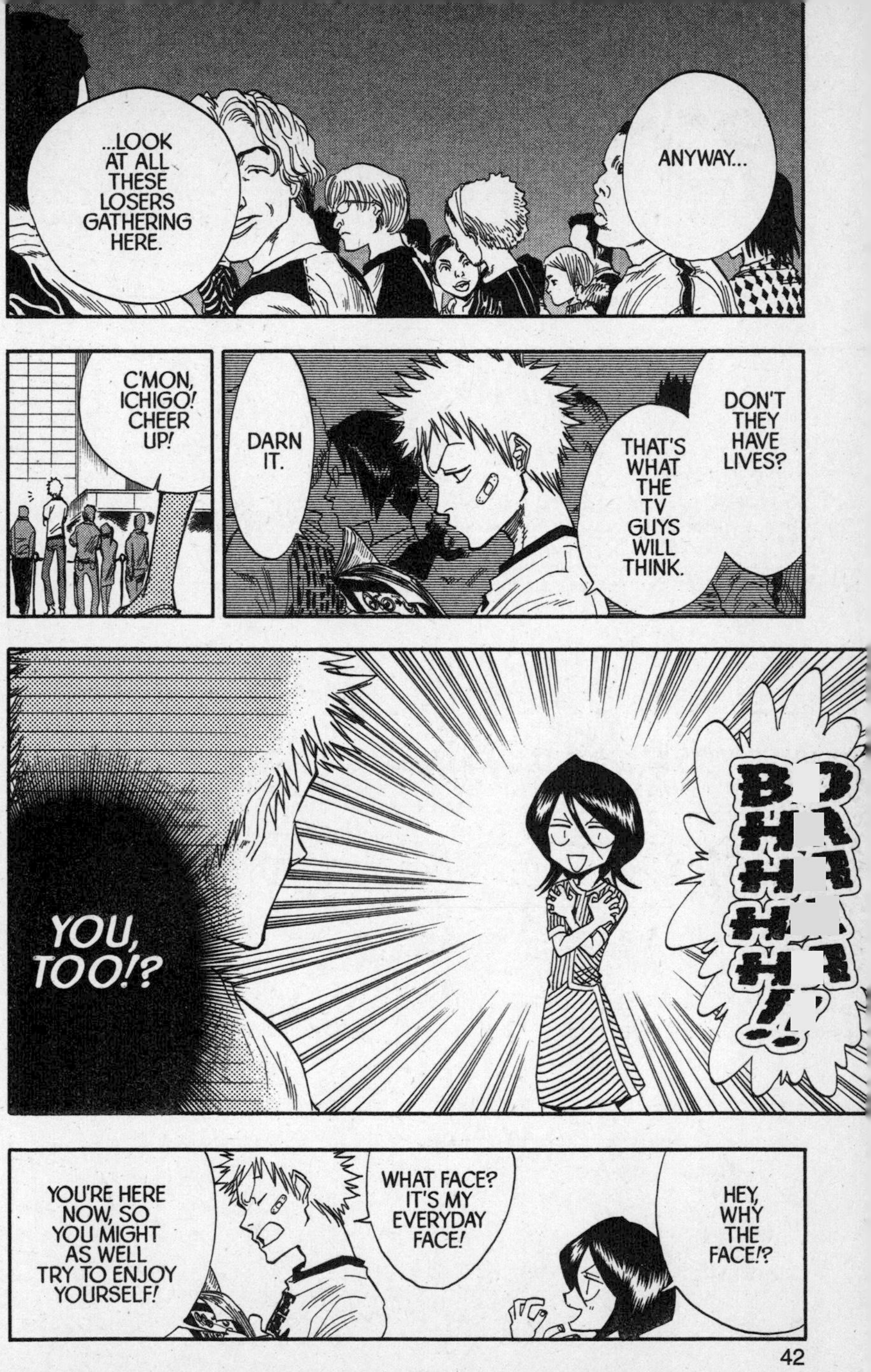
ANYWAY...
...LOOK AT ALL THESE LOSERS GATHERING HERE.
DON'T THEY HAVE LIVES?
THAT'S WHAT THE TV GUYS WILL THINK.
DARN IT.
C'MON, ICHIGO! CHEER UP!
YOU, TOO!?
HEY, WHY THE FACE!?
WHAT FACE? IT'S MY EVERYDAY FACE!
YOU'RE HERE NOW, SO YOU MIGHT AS WELL TRY TO ENJOY YOURSELF!

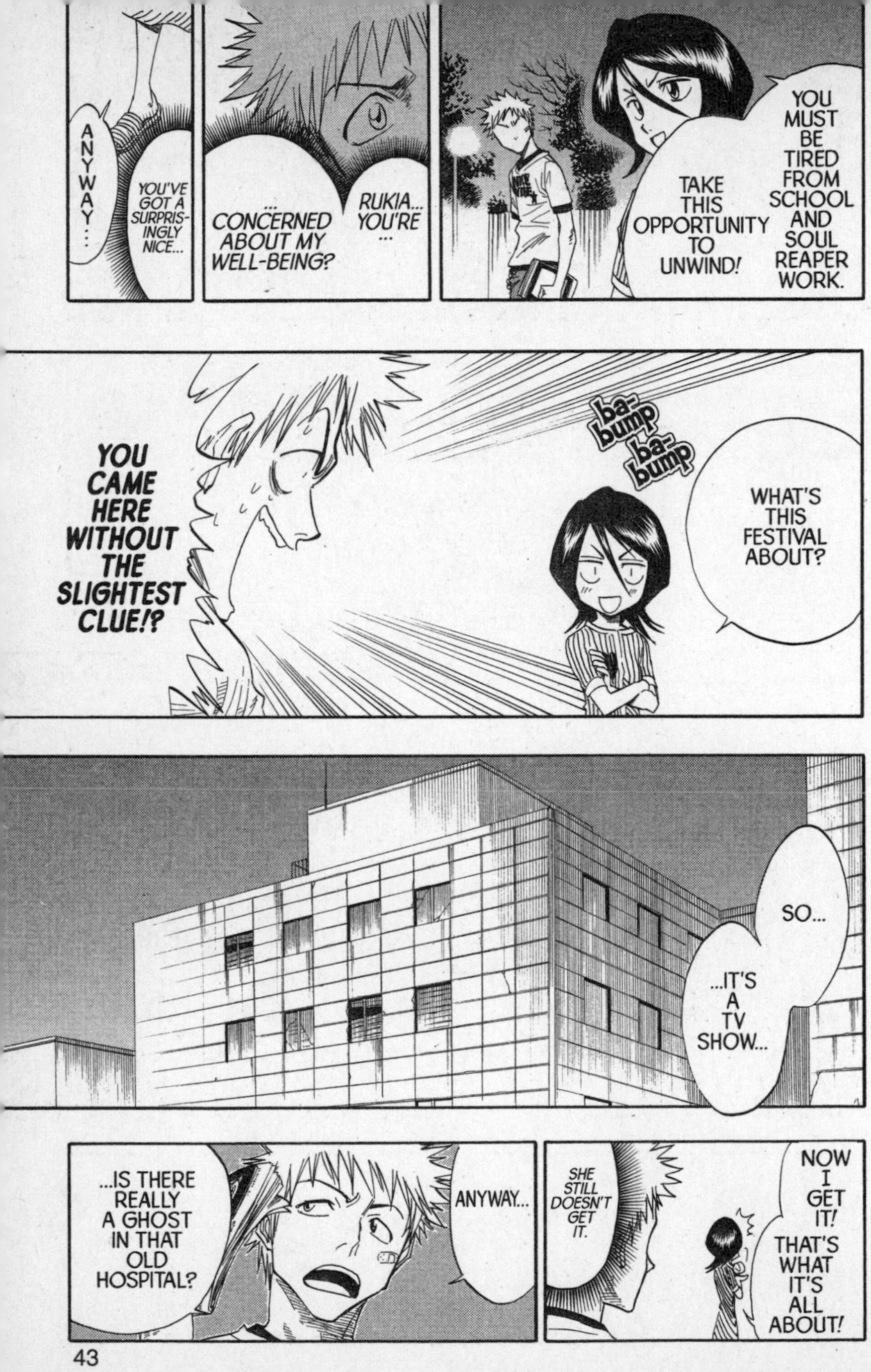
YOU MUST BE TIRED FROM SCHOOL AND SOUL REAPER WORK.
TAKE THIS OPPORTUNITY TO UNWIND!
RUKIA... YOU'RE ...
... CONCERNED ABOUT MY WELL-BEING?
YOU'VE GOT A SURPRISINGLY NICE...
ANYWAY...
WHAT'S THIS FESTIVAL ABOUT?
ba-bump ba-bump
YOU CAME HERE WITHOUT THE SLIGHTEST CLUE!?
SO...
...IT'S A TV SHOW...
NOW I GET IT! THAT'S WHAT IT'S ALL ABOUT!
SHE STILL DOESN'T GET IT.
ANYWAY...
...IS THERE REALLY A GHOST IN THAT OLD HOSPITAL?

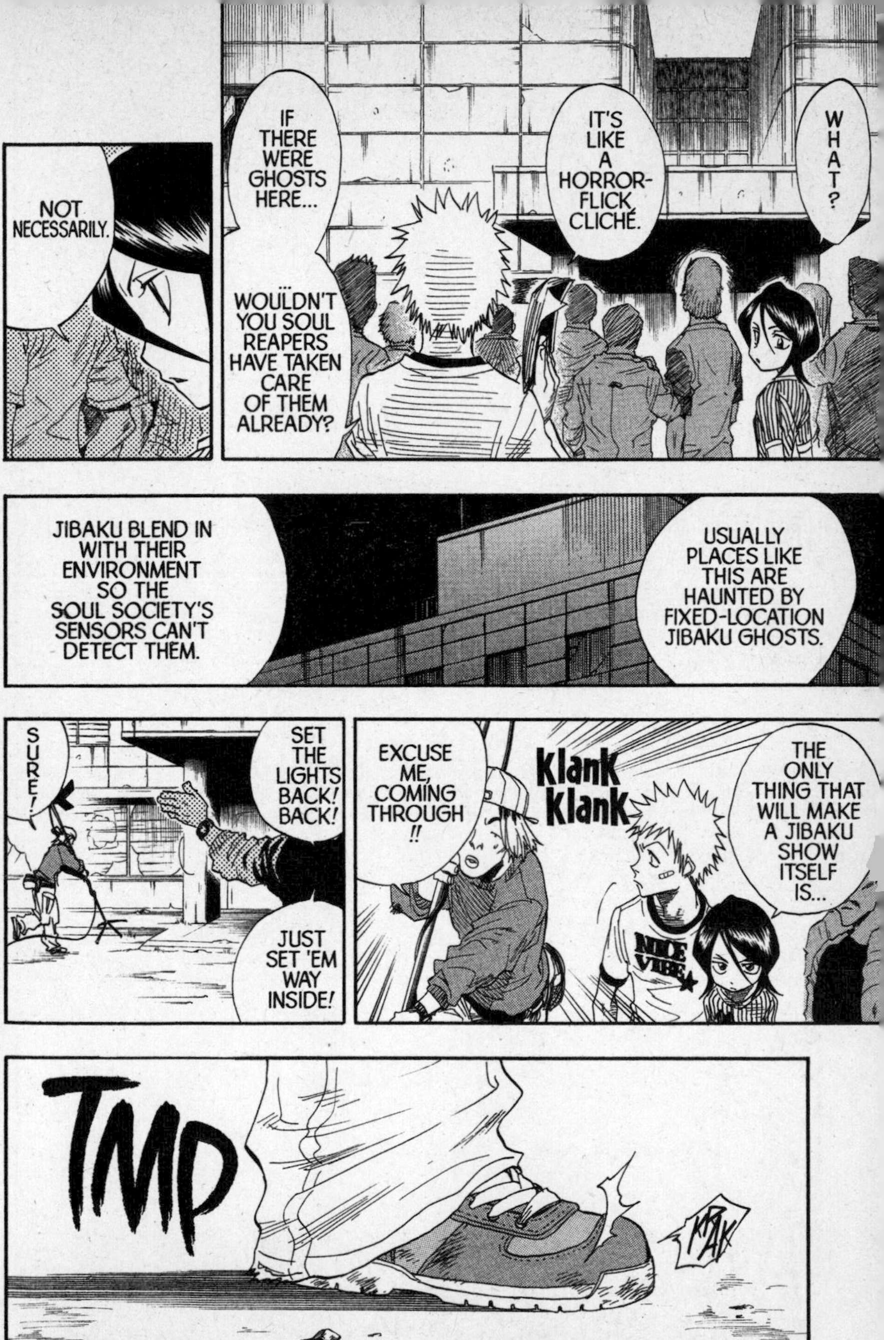
WHAT?
IT'S LIKE A HORROR-FLICK CLICHÉ.
IF THERE WERE GHOSTS HERE...
...WOULDN'T YOU SOUL REAPERS HAVE TAKEN CARE OF THEM ALREADY?
NOT NECESSARILY.
USUALLY PLACES LIKE THIS ARE HAUNTED BY FIXED-LOCATION JIBAKU GHOSTS.
JIBAKU BLEND IN WITH THEIR ENVIRONMENT SO THE SOUL SOCIETY'S SENSORS CAN'T DETECT THEM.
THE ONLY THING THAT WILL MAKE A JIBAKU SHOW ITSELF IS...
Klank Klank
EXCUSE ME, COMING THROUGH!!
SET THE LIGHTS BACK! BACK!
JUST SET 'EM WAY INSIDE!
SURE!
TMP
KRAK

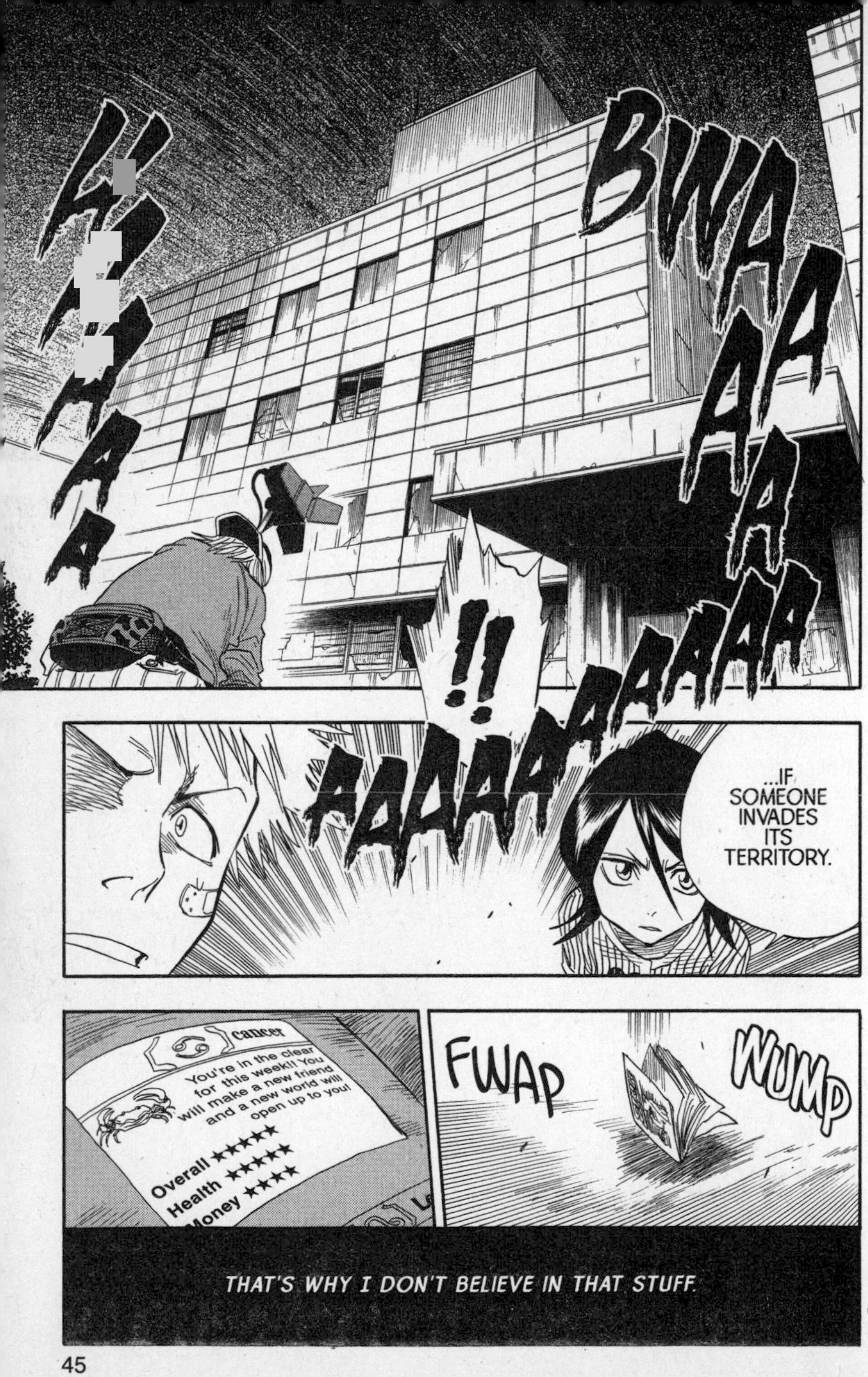
BWAAAAAAAAAAAAAAAA
!!
...IF SOMEONE INVADES ITS TERRITORY.
WUMP
FWAP
cancer
You're in the clear for this week!! You will make a new friend and a new world will open up to you!
Overall ★★★★★
Health ★★★★★
Money ★★★★
THAT'S WHY I DON'T BELIEVE IN THAT STUFF.

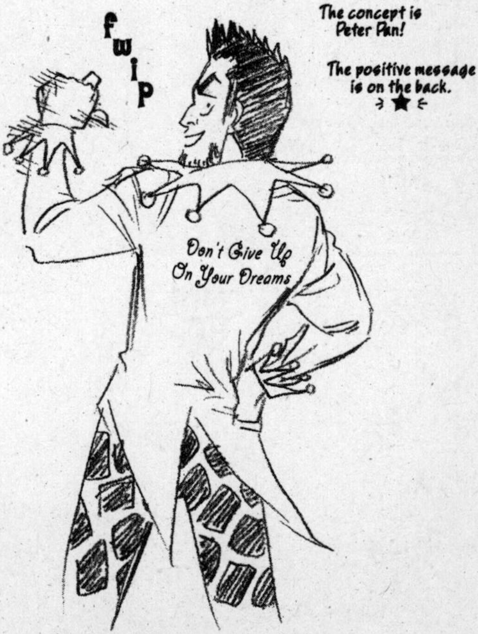
The concept is Peter Pan!
The positive message is on the back.
fwip
Don't Give Up On Your Dreams

28. Symptom of Synesthesia

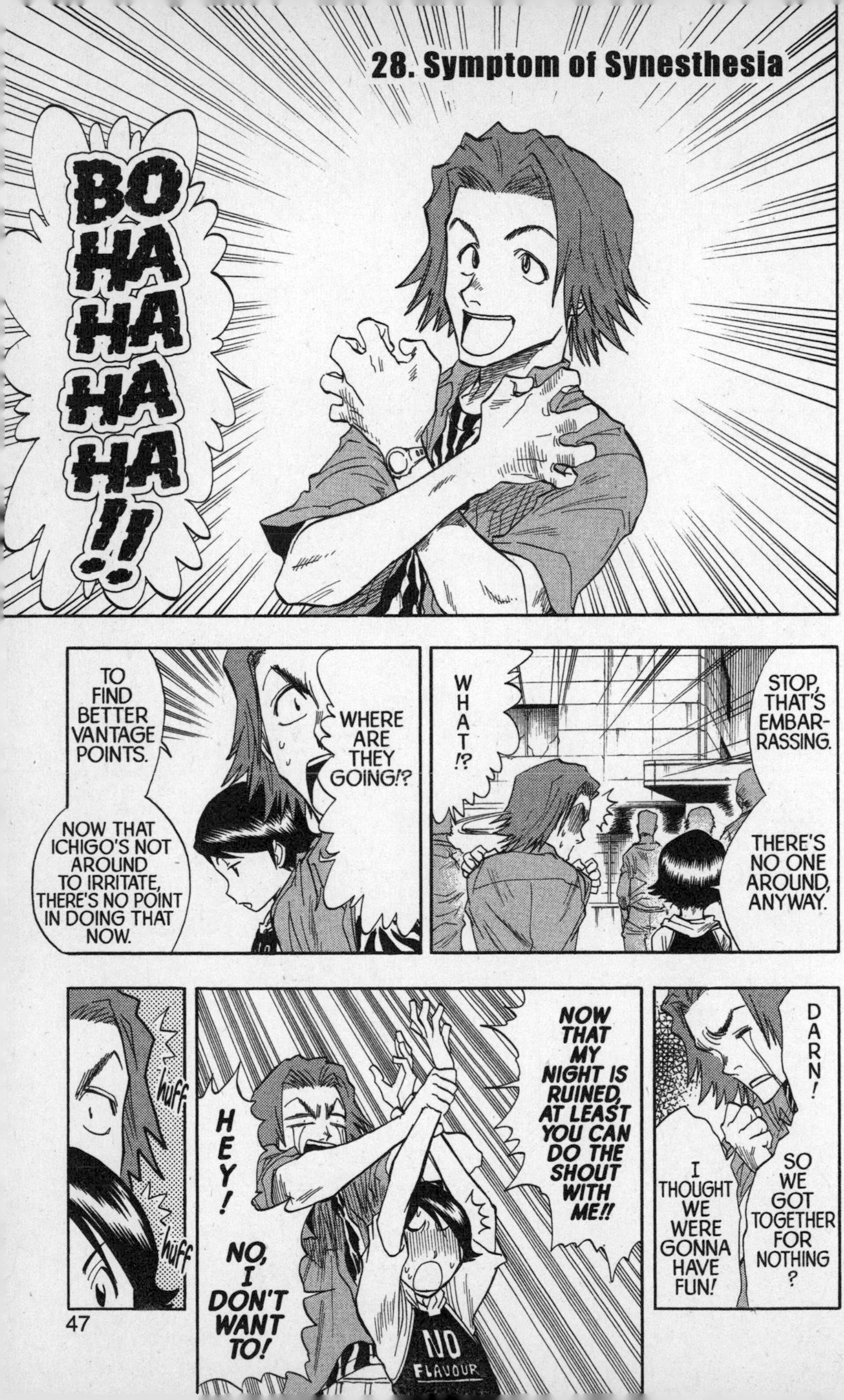
BOHAHAHAHAHA!!
STOP, THAT'S EMBARRASSING.
THERE'S NO ONE AROUND, ANYWAY.
WHAT!?
WHERE ARE THEY GOING!?
TO FIND BETTER VANTAGE POINTS.
NOW THAT ICHIGO'S NOT AROUND TO IRRITATE, THERE'S NO POINT IN DOING THAT NOW.
DARN!
SO WE GOT TOGETHER FOR NOTHING?
I THOUGHT WE WERE GONNA HAVE FUN!
NOW THAT MY NIGHT IS RUINED, AT LEAST YOU CAN DO THE SHOUT WITH ME!!
HEY!
NO, I DON'T WANT TO!
NO FLAVOUR
huff
huff

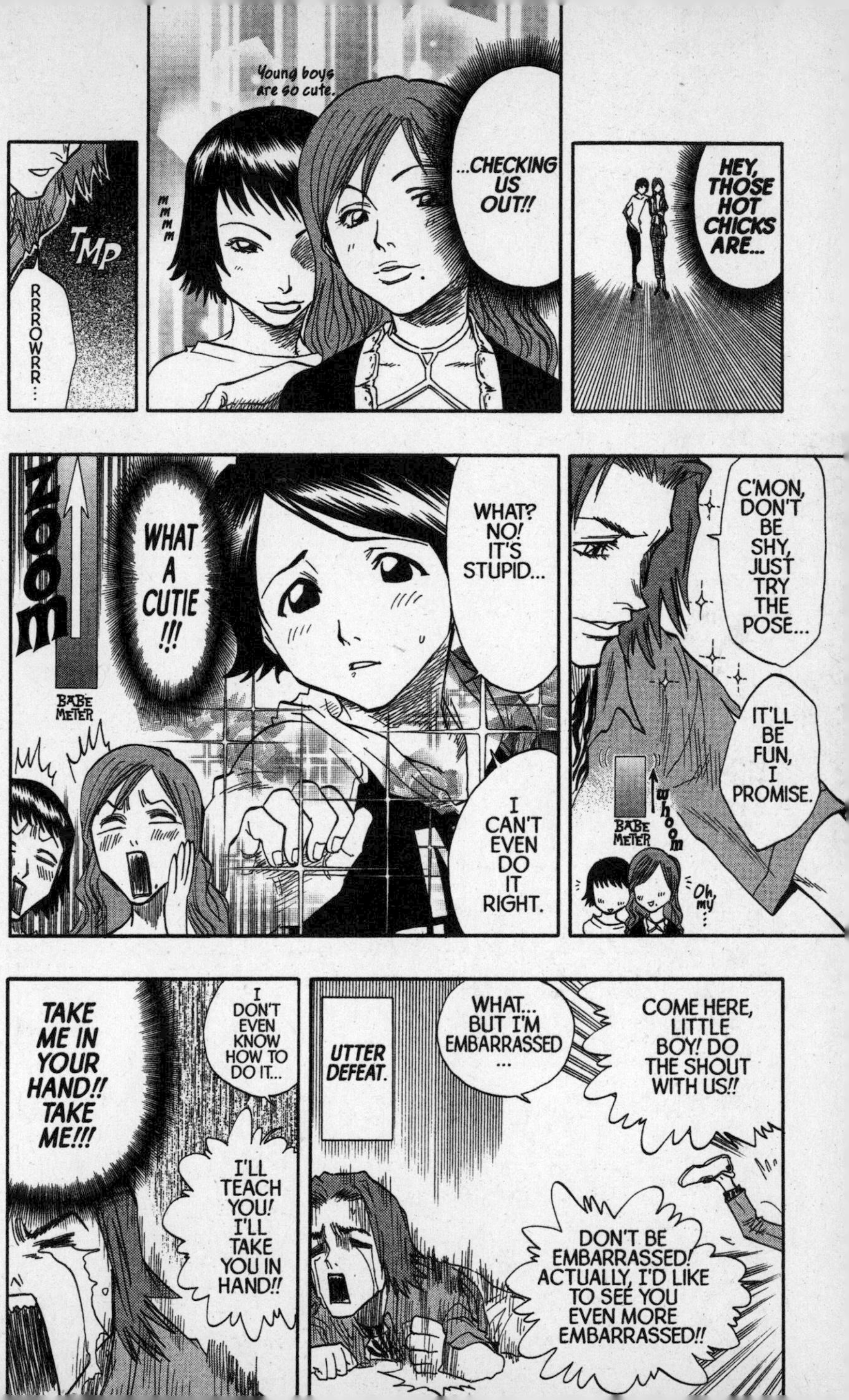
HEY, THOSE HOT CHICKS ARE...
...CHECKING US OUT!!
Young boys are so cute.
mmmm
TMP
RRROWRR...
C'MON, DON'T BE SHY, JUST TRY THE POSE...
IT'LL BE FUN, I PROMISE.
BABE METER
whoom
Oh, my...
WHAT? NO! IT'S STUPID...
I CAN'T EVEN DO IT RIGHT.
WHAT A CUTIE!!!
ZOOM
BABE METER
COME HERE, LITTLE BOY! DO THE SHOUT WITH US!!
WHAT... BUT I'M EMBARRASSED...
UTTER DEFEAT.
DON'T BE EMBARRASSED! ACTUALLY, I'D LIKE TO SEE YOU EVEN MORE EMBARRASSED!!
I DON'T EVEN KNOW HOW TO DO IT...
TAKE ME IN YOUR HAND!! TAKE ME!!!
I'LL TEACH YOU! I'LL TAKE YOU IN HAND!!

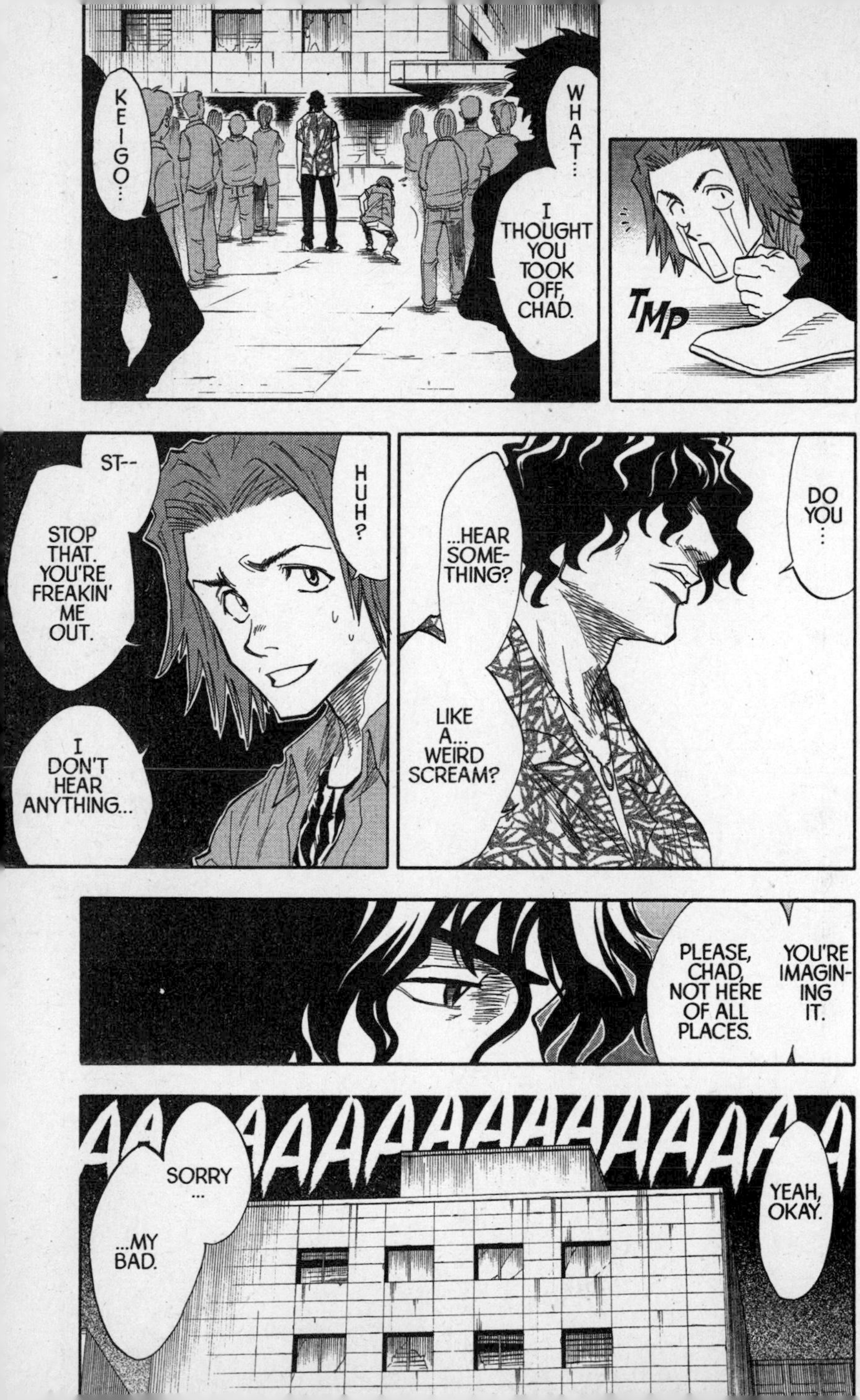
TMP
WHAT... I THOUGHT YOU TOOK OFF, CHAD.
KEIGO...
DO YOU...
...HEAR SOMETHING?
LIKE A... WEIRD SCREAM?
HUH?
ST--
STOP THAT. YOU'RE FREAKIN' ME OUT.
I DON'T HEAR ANYTHING...
YOU'RE IMAGINING IT.
PLEASE, CHAD, NOT HERE OF ALL PLACES.
AAAAAAAAAAAAAAAAAA
YEAH, OKAY.
SORRY...
...MY BAD.

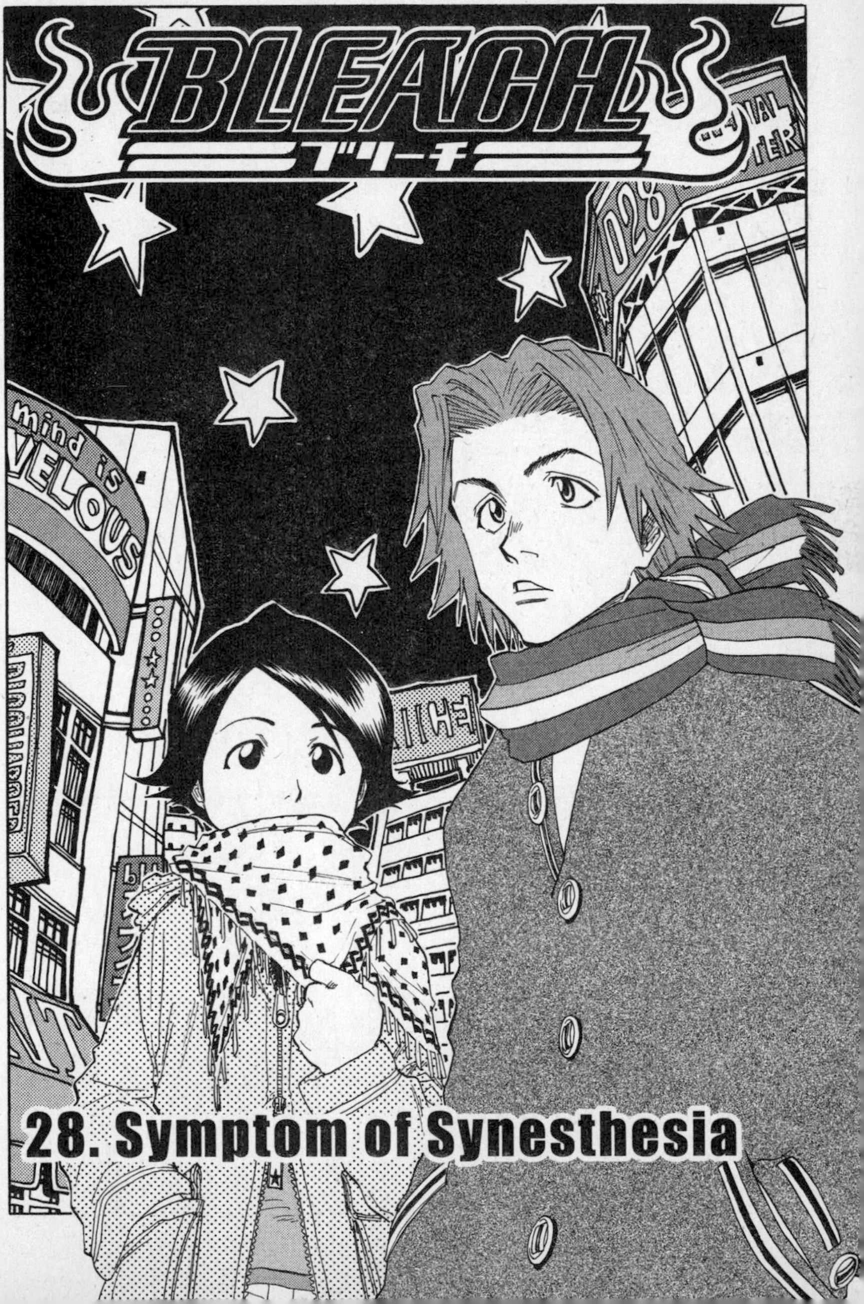
BLEACH
ブリーチ
mind is
VELOUS
028

28. Symptom of Synesthesia

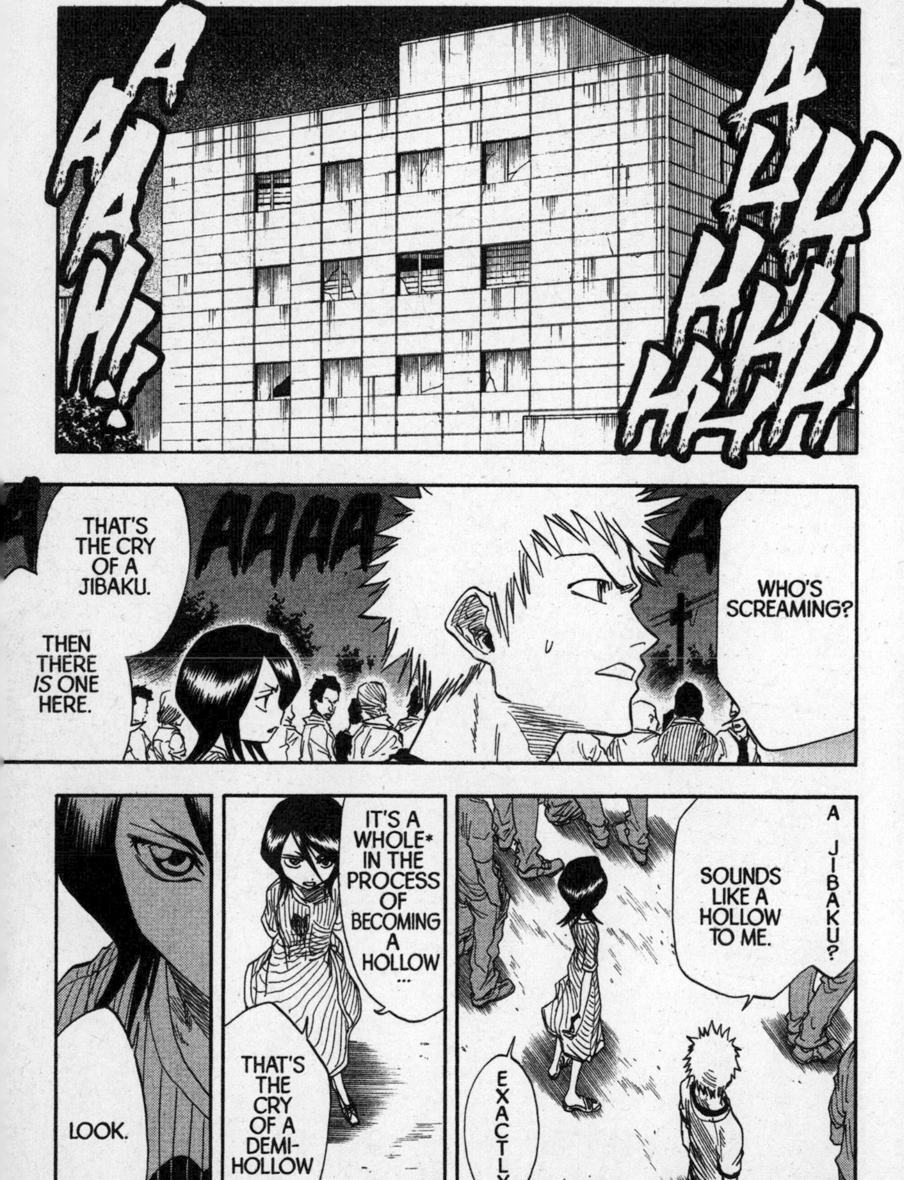
AAAAHHHHHHH
AAAAH!
WHO'S SCREAMING?
AAAAA
THAT'S THE CRY OF A JIBAKU.
THEN THERE *IS* ONE HERE.
A JIBAKU?
SOUNDS LIKE A HOLLOW TO ME.
EXACTLY.
IT'S A WHOLE* IN THE PROCESS OF BECOMING A HOLLOW...
THAT'S THE CRY OF A DEMI-HOLLOW...
LOOK.

*Whole: a good spirit.

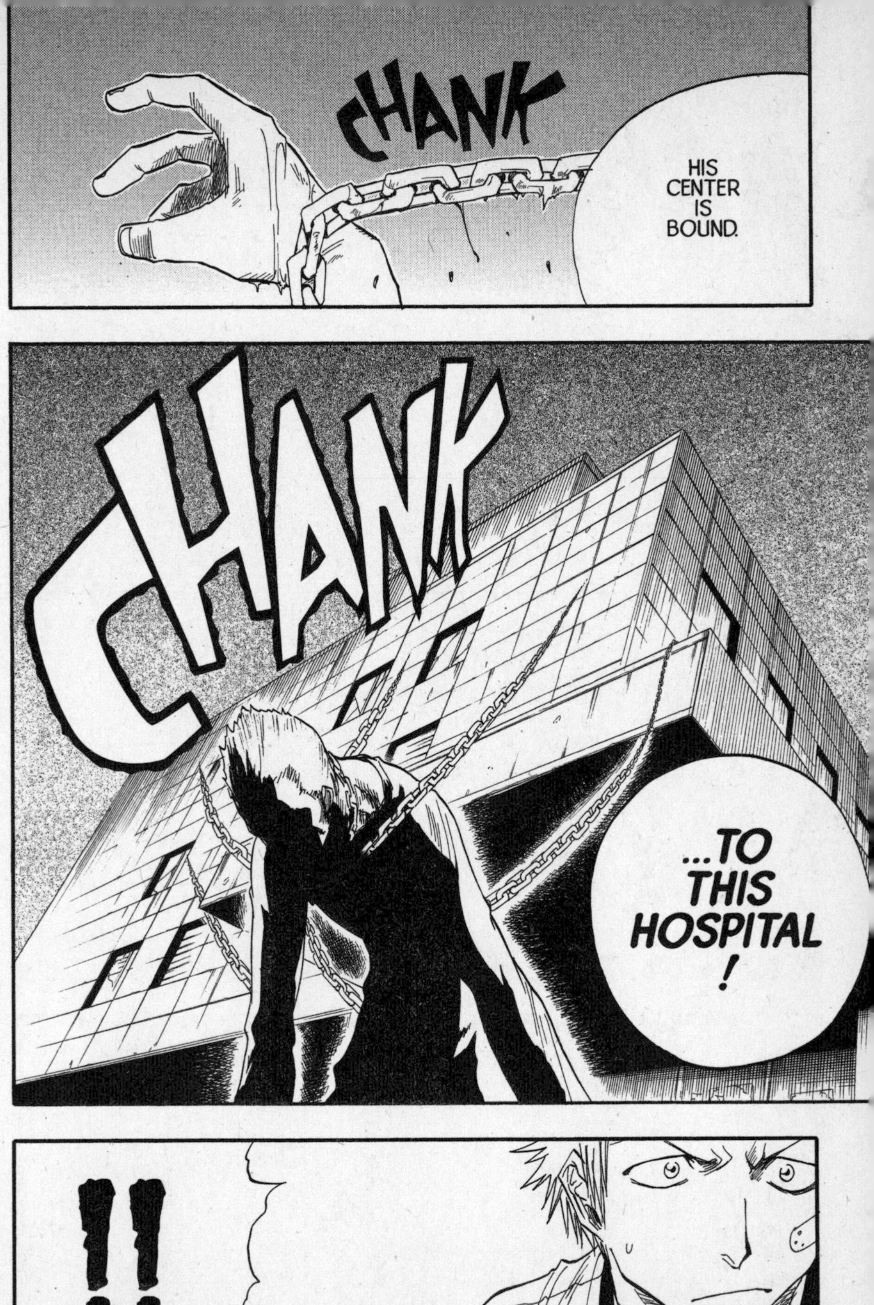
HIS CENTER IS BOUND.
CHANK
CHANK
...TO THIS HOSPITAL!
!!

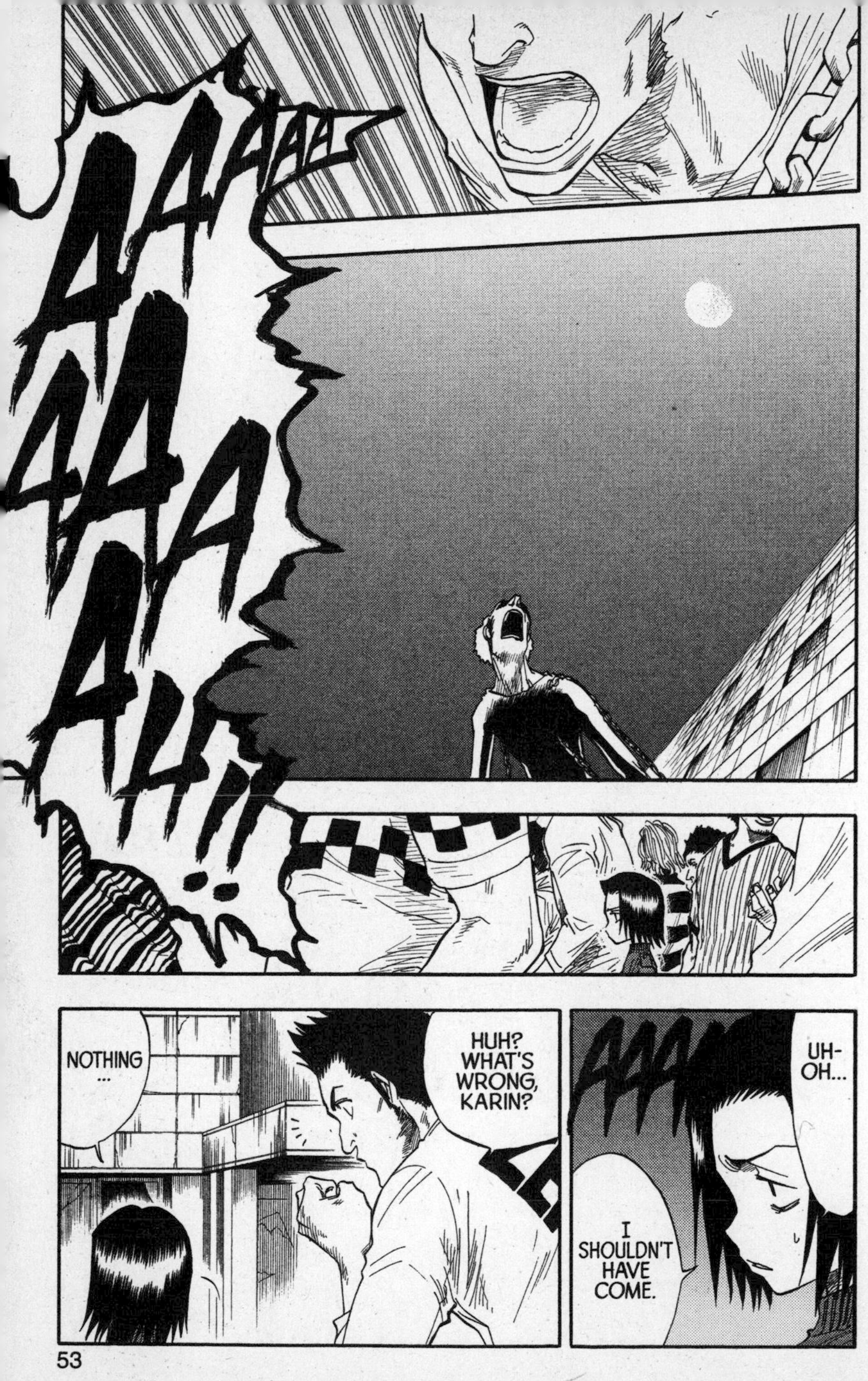

AAAAAAAAAAAAAH!!
AAAA
UH-OH...
I SHOULDN'T HAVE COME.
HUH? WHAT'S WRONG, KARIN?
NOTHING ...

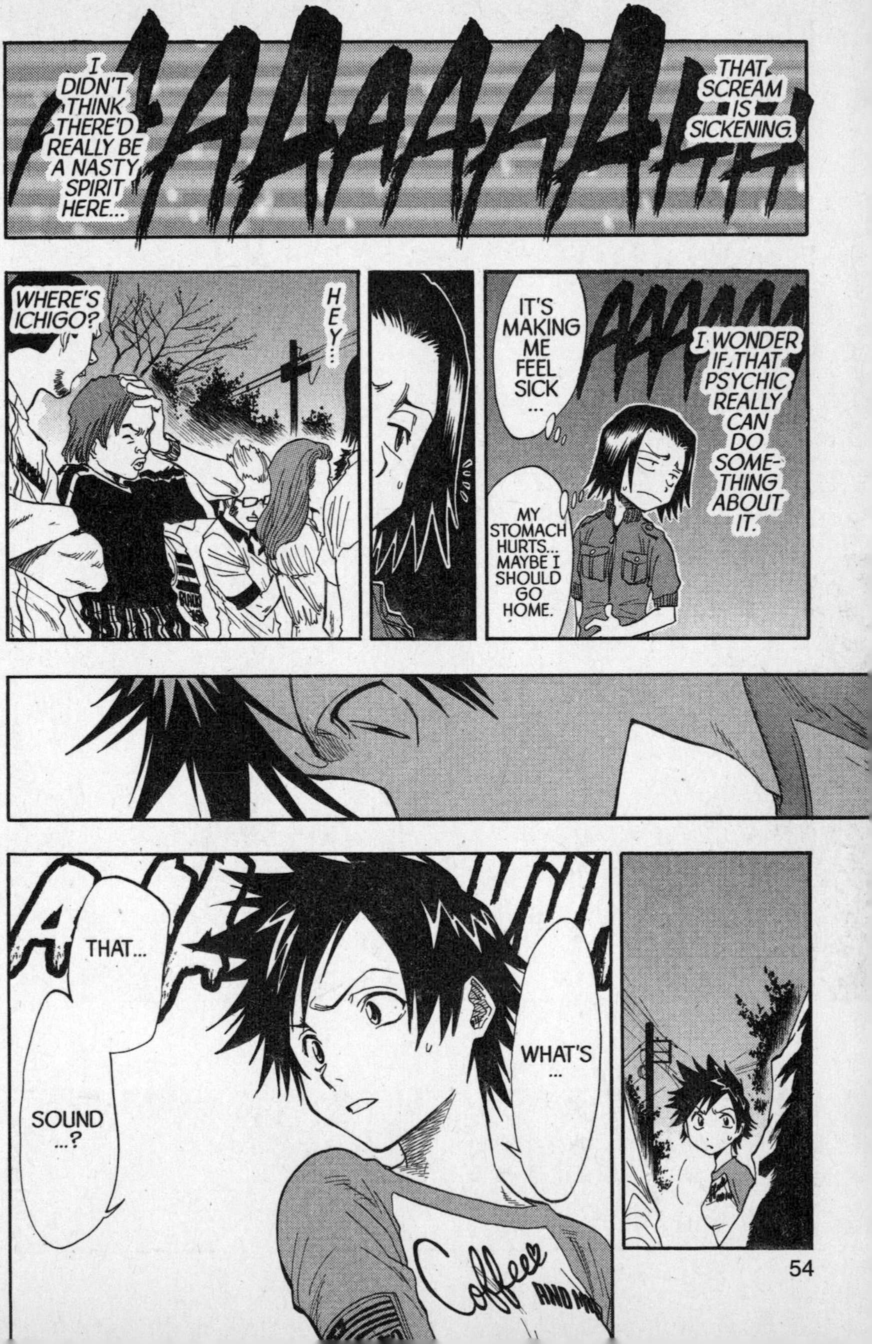
THAT SCREAM IS SICKENING.
AAAAAAHH
I DIDN'T THINK THERE'D REALLY BE A NASTY SPIRIT HERE...
I WONDER IF THAT PSYCHIC REALLY CAN DO SOMETHING ABOUT IT.
IT'S MAKING ME FEEL SICK...
MY STOMACH HURTS... MAYBE I SHOULD GO HOME.
HEY...
WHERE'S ICHIGO?
WHAT'S...
THAT...
SOUND...?

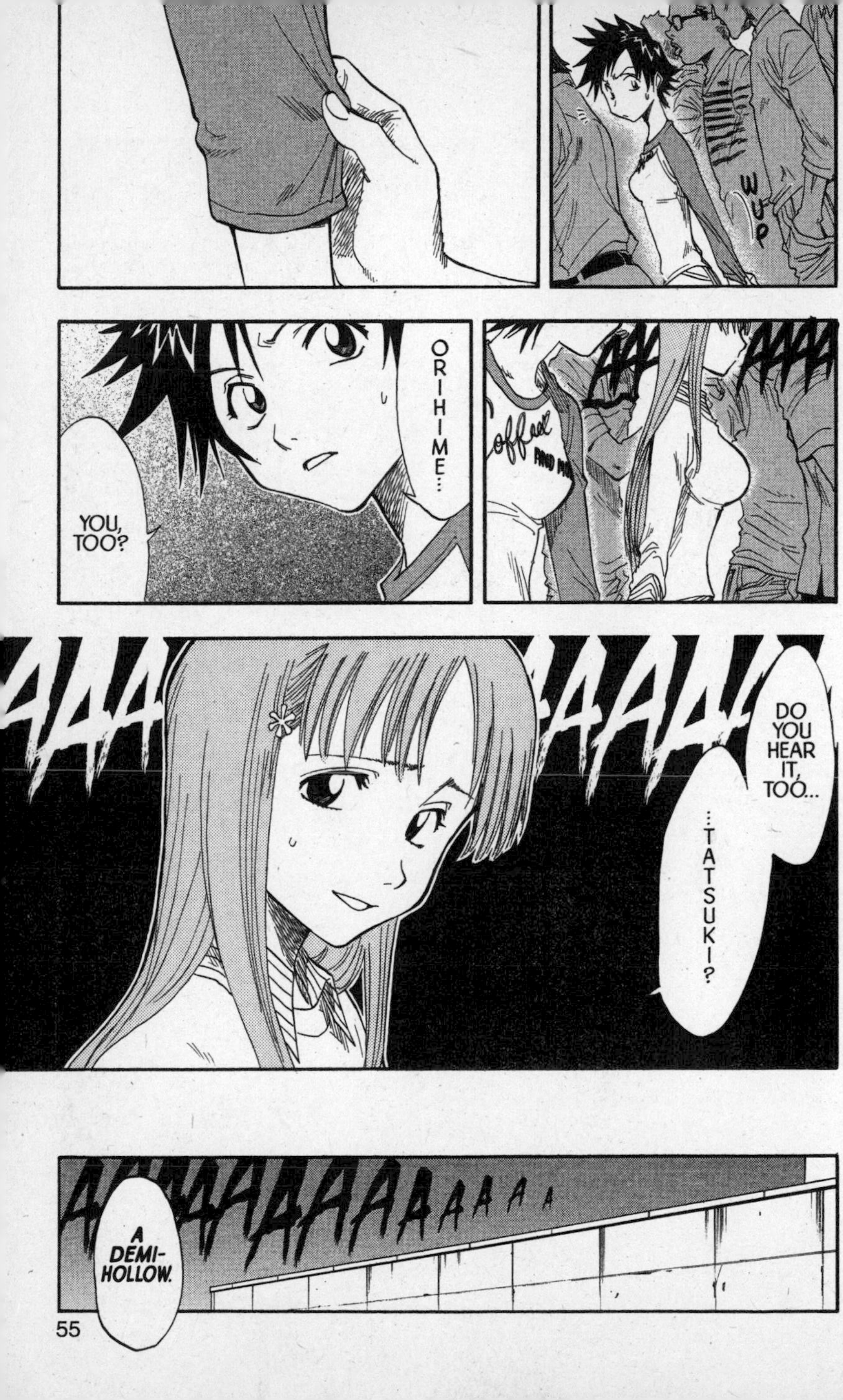
WUP
AAAA
AAAA
ORIHIME...
YOU, TOO?
AAAAAAAAA
DO YOU HEAR IT, TOO...
...TATSUKI?
AAAAAAAAAAAAA
A DEMI-HOLLOW.

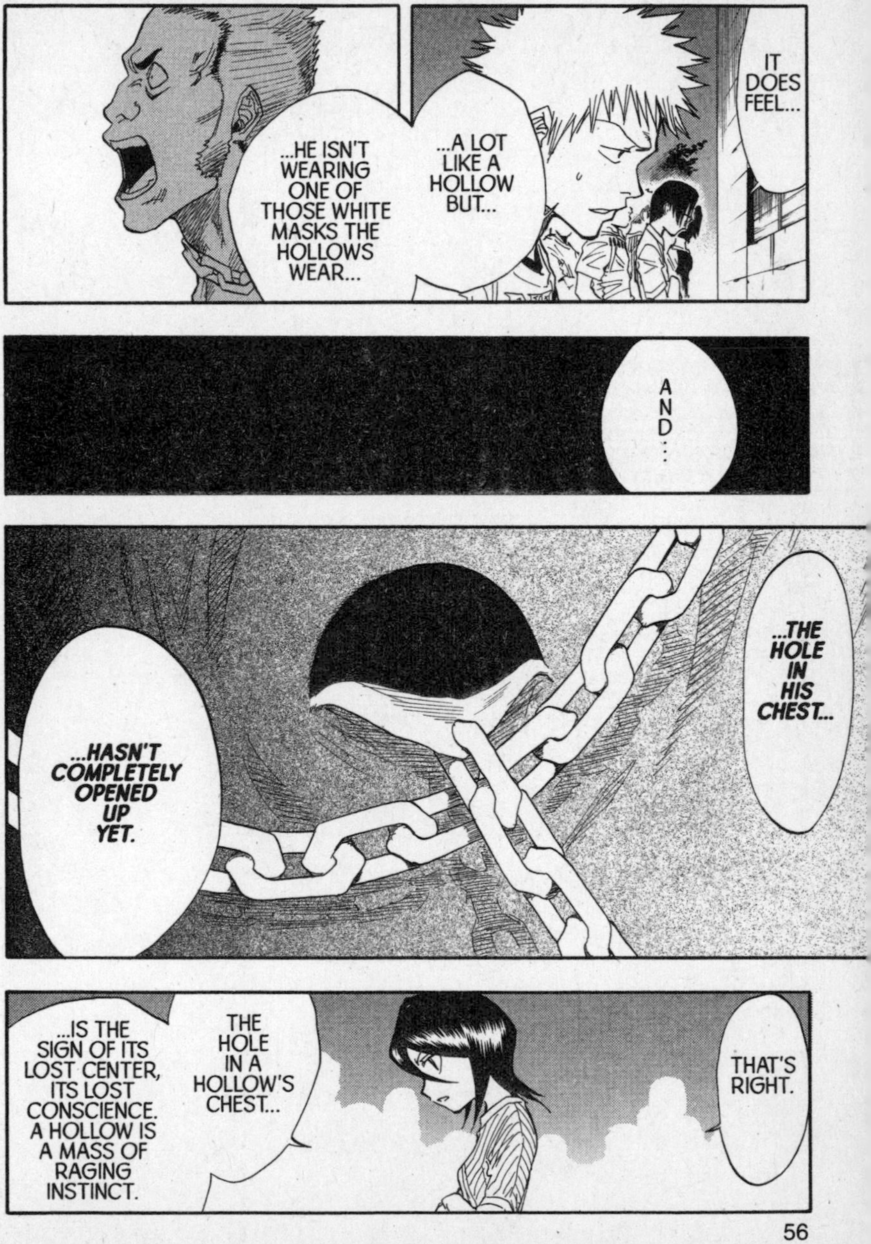
IT DOES FEEL...
...A LOT LIKE A HOLLOW BUT...
...HE ISN'T WEARING ONE OF THOSE WHITE MASKS THE HOLLOWS WEAR...
AND...
...THE HOLE IN HIS CHEST...
...HASN'T COMPLETELY OPENED UP YET.
THAT'S RIGHT.
THE HOLE IN A HOLLOW'S CHEST...
...IS THE SIGN OF ITS LOST CENTER, ITS LOST CONSCIENCE. A HOLLOW IS A MASS OF RAGING INSTINCT.

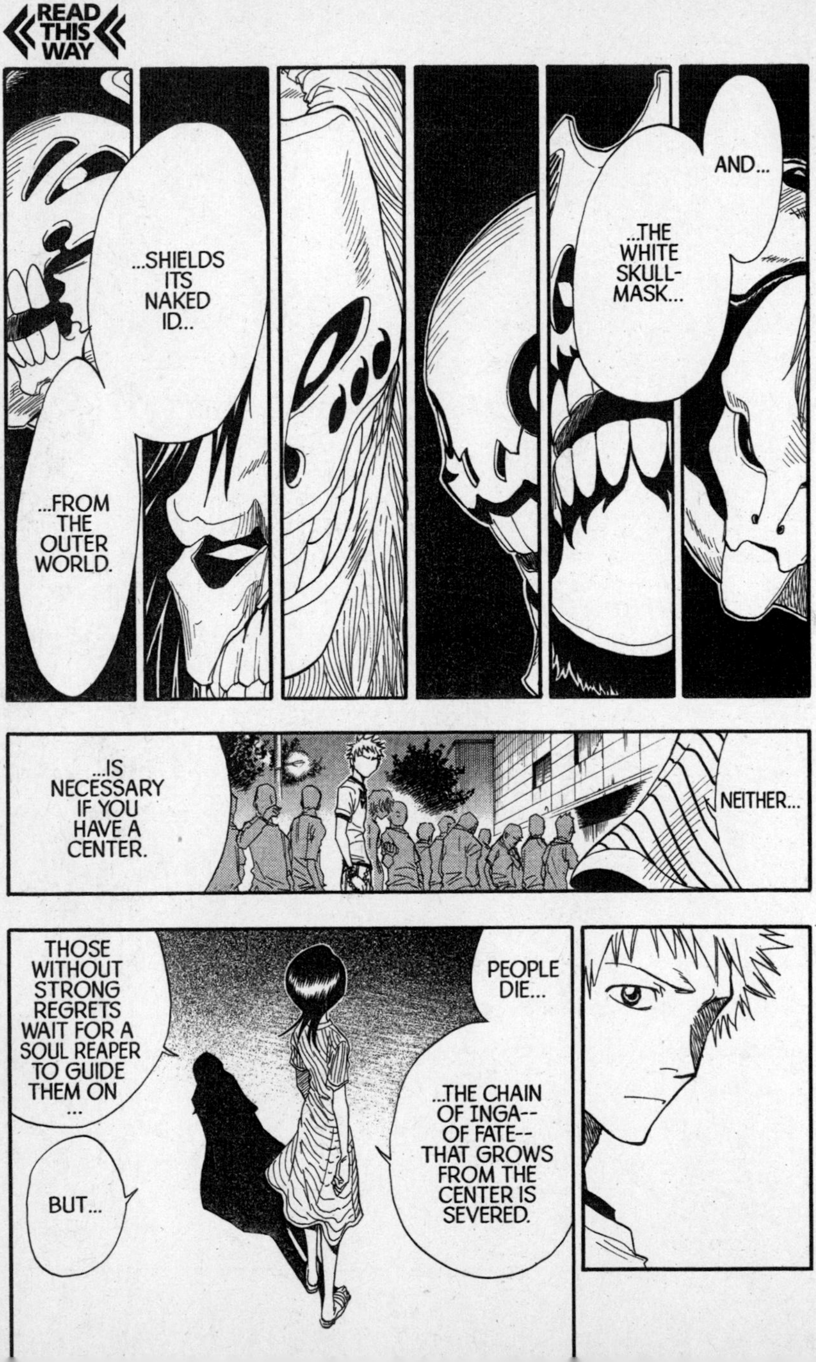
READ THIS WAY
AND...
...THE WHITE SKULL-MASK...
...SHIELDS ITS NAKED ID...
...FROM THE OUTER WORLD.
NEITHER...
...IS NECESSARY IF YOU HAVE A CENTER.
PEOPLE DIE...
...THE CHAIN OF INGA-- OF FATE-- THAT GROWS FROM THE CENTER IS SEVERED.
THOSE WITHOUT STRONG REGRETS WAIT FOR A SOUL REAPER TO GUIDE THEM ON ...
BUT...

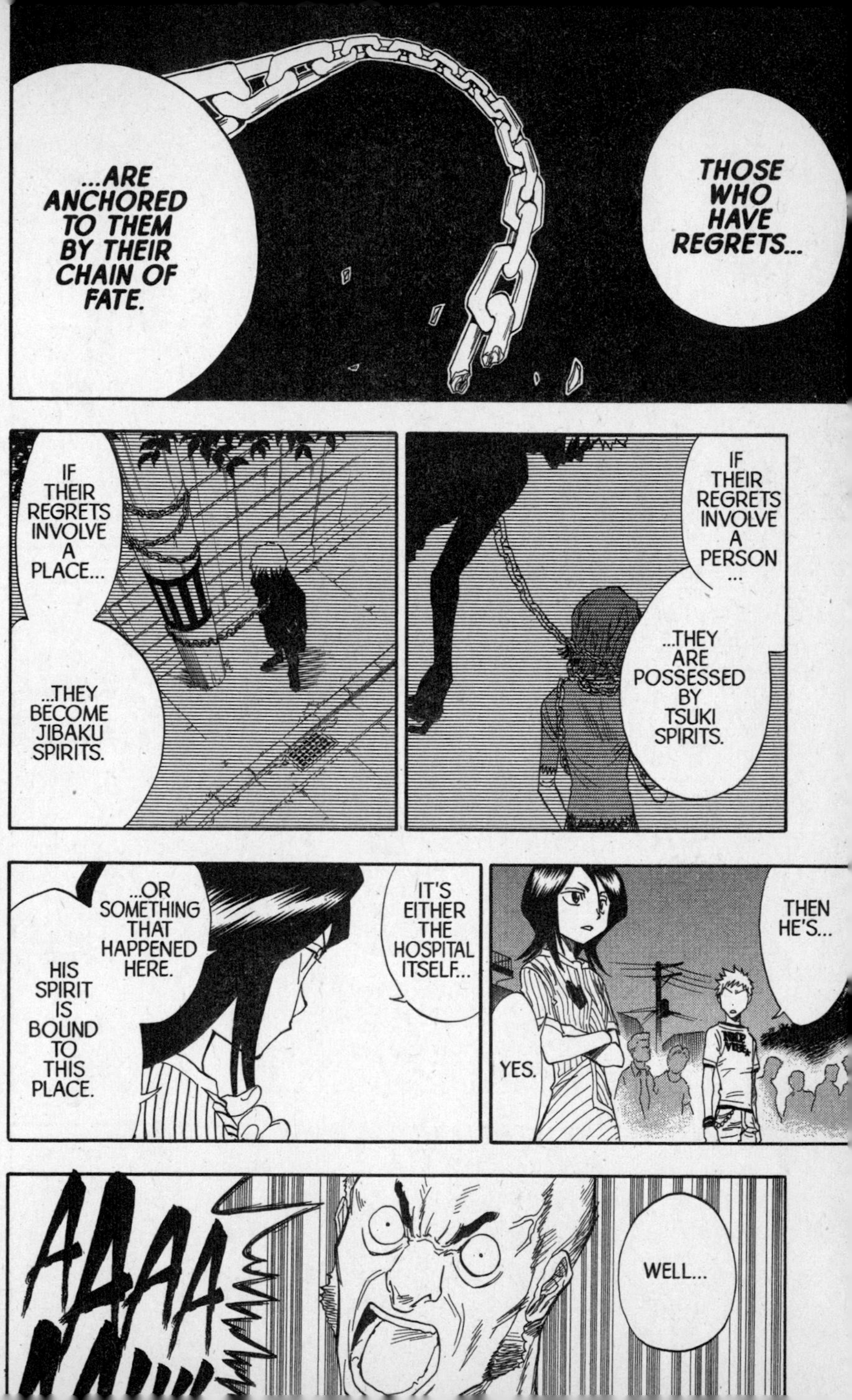
THOSE WHO HAVE REGRETS...
...ARE ANCHORED TO THEM BY THEIR CHAIN OF FATE.
IF THEIR REGRETS INVOLVE A PERSON...
...THEY ARE POSSESSED BY TSUKI SPIRITS.
IF THEIR REGRETS INVOLVE A PLACE...
...THEY BECOME JIBAKU SPIRITS.
THEN HE'S...
YES.
IT'S EITHER THE HOSPITAL ITSELF...
...OR SOMETHING THAT HAPPENED HERE.
HIS SPIRIT IS BOUND TO THIS PLACE.
WELL...
AAAA

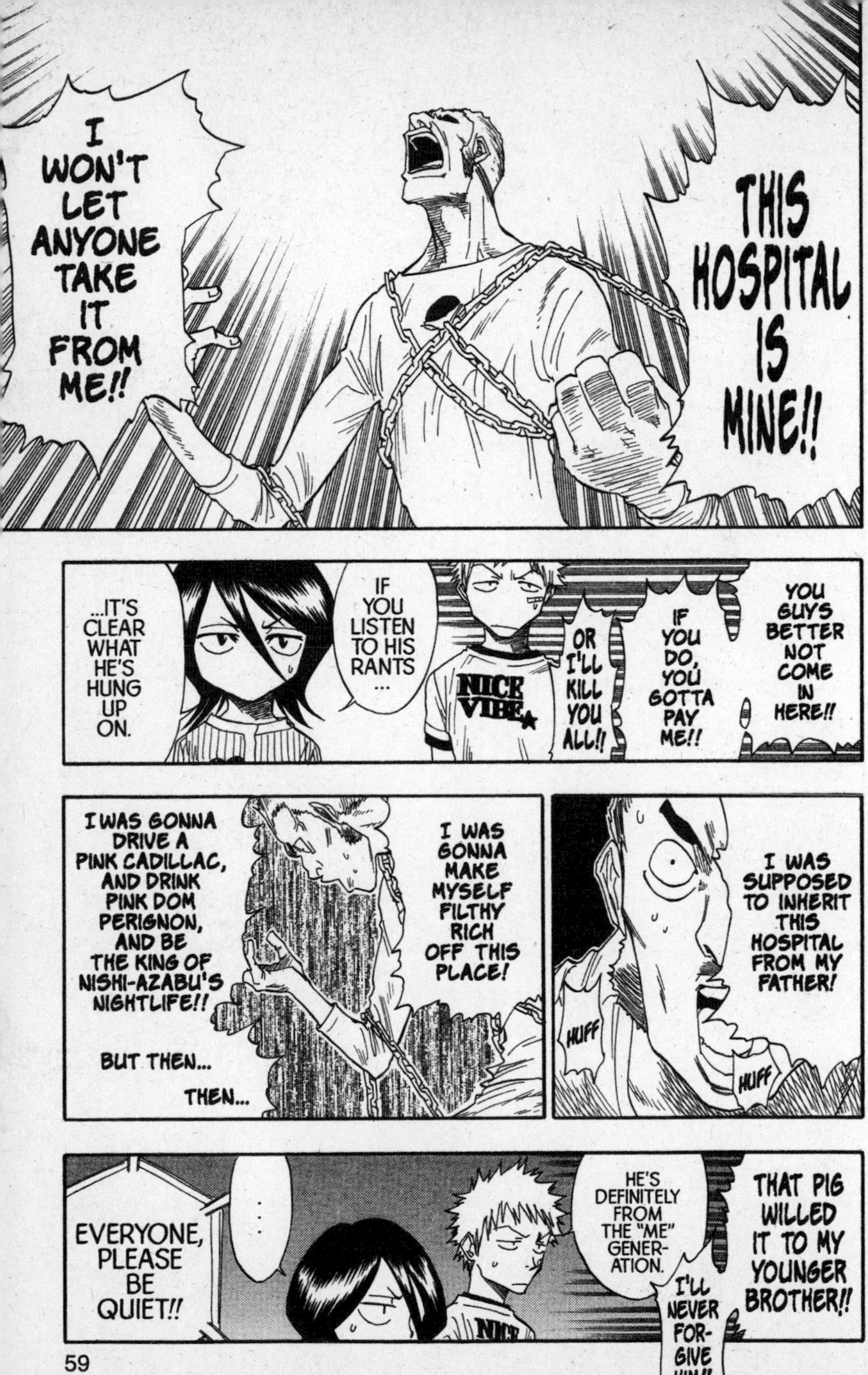
THIS HOSPITAL IS MINE!!
I WON'T LET ANYONE TAKE IT FROM ME!!
YOU GUYS BETTER NOT COME IN HERE!!
IF YOU DO, YOU GOTTA PAY ME!!
OR I'LL KILL YOU ALL!!
IF YOU LISTEN TO HIS RANTS ...
...IT'S CLEAR WHAT HE'S HUNG UP ON.
I WAS SUPPOSED TO INHERIT THIS HOSPITAL FROM MY FATHER!
HUFF
HUFF
I WAS GONNA MAKE MYSELF FILTHY RICH OFF THIS PLACE!
I WAS GONNA DRIVE A PINK CADILLAC, AND DRINK PINK DOM PERIGNON, AND BE THE KING OF NISHI-AZABU'S NIGHTLIFE!!
BUT THEN...
THEN...
THAT PIG WILLED IT TO MY YOUNGER BROTHER!!
I'LL NEVER FOR-GIVE HIM!!
HE'S DEFINITELY FROM THE "ME" GENER-ATION.
...
EVERYONE, PLEASE BE QUIET!!

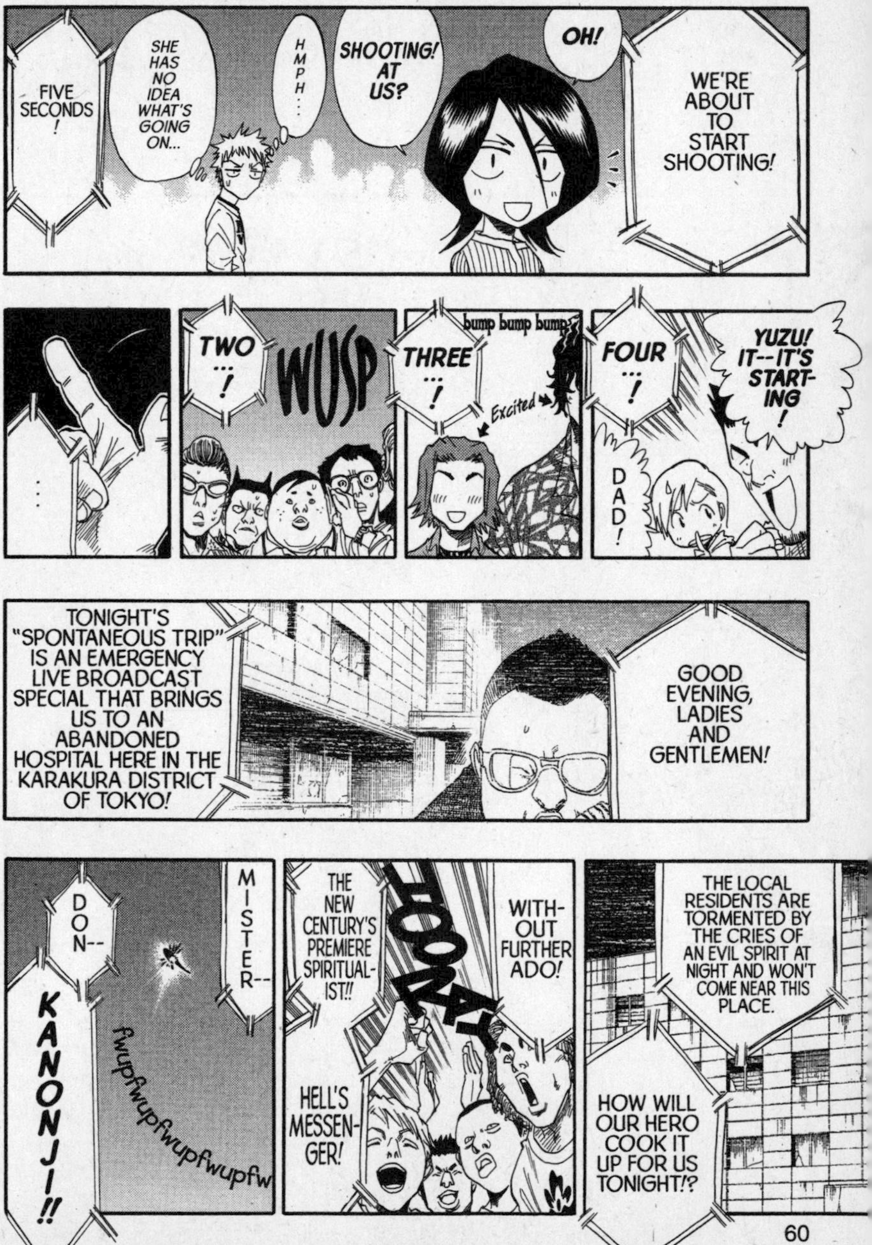
WE'RE ABOUT TO START SHOOTING!
OH!
SHOOTING! AT US?
HMPH...
SHE HAS NO IDEA WHAT'S GOING ON...
FIVE SECONDS!
FOUR...!
YUZU! IT--IT'S STARTING!
DAD!
bump bump bump
THREE...!
Excited
TWO...!
WUSP
...
GOOD EVENING, LADIES AND GENTLEMEN!
TONIGHT'S "SPONTANEOUS TRIP" IS AN EMERGENCY LIVE BROADCAST SPECIAL THAT BRINGS US TO AN ABANDONED HOSPITAL HERE IN THE KARAKURA DISTRICT OF TOKYO!
THE LOCAL RESIDENTS ARE TORMENTED BY THE CRIES OF AN EVIL SPIRIT AT NIGHT AND WON'T COME NEAR THIS PLACE.
HOW WILL OUR HERO COOK IT UP FOR US TONIGHT!?
WITHOUT FURTHER ADO!
THE NEW CENTURY'S PREMIERE SPIRITUALIST!!
HOORAY
HELL'S MESSENGER!
MISTER--
DON--
KANONJI!!
fwupfwupfwupfwupfw

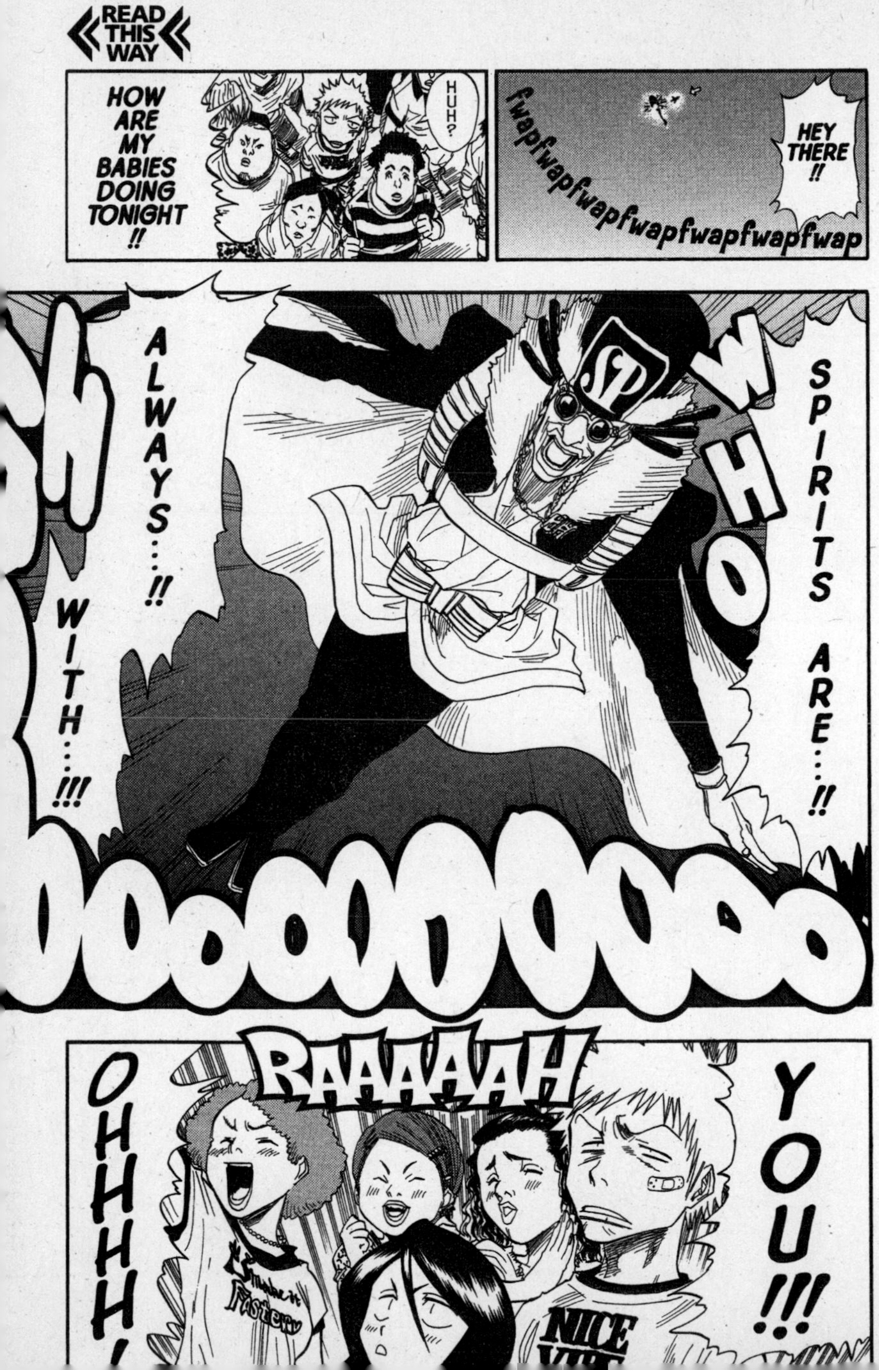
READ THIS WAY
HEY THERE!!
fwapfwapfwapfwapfwapfwapfwap
HUH?
HOW ARE MY BABIES DOING TONIGHT!!
SPIRITS ARE...!!
WHOOOOOOOOOOOh
ALWAYS...!!
WITH...!!!
YOU!!!
RAAAAAH
OHHHHH!
NICE

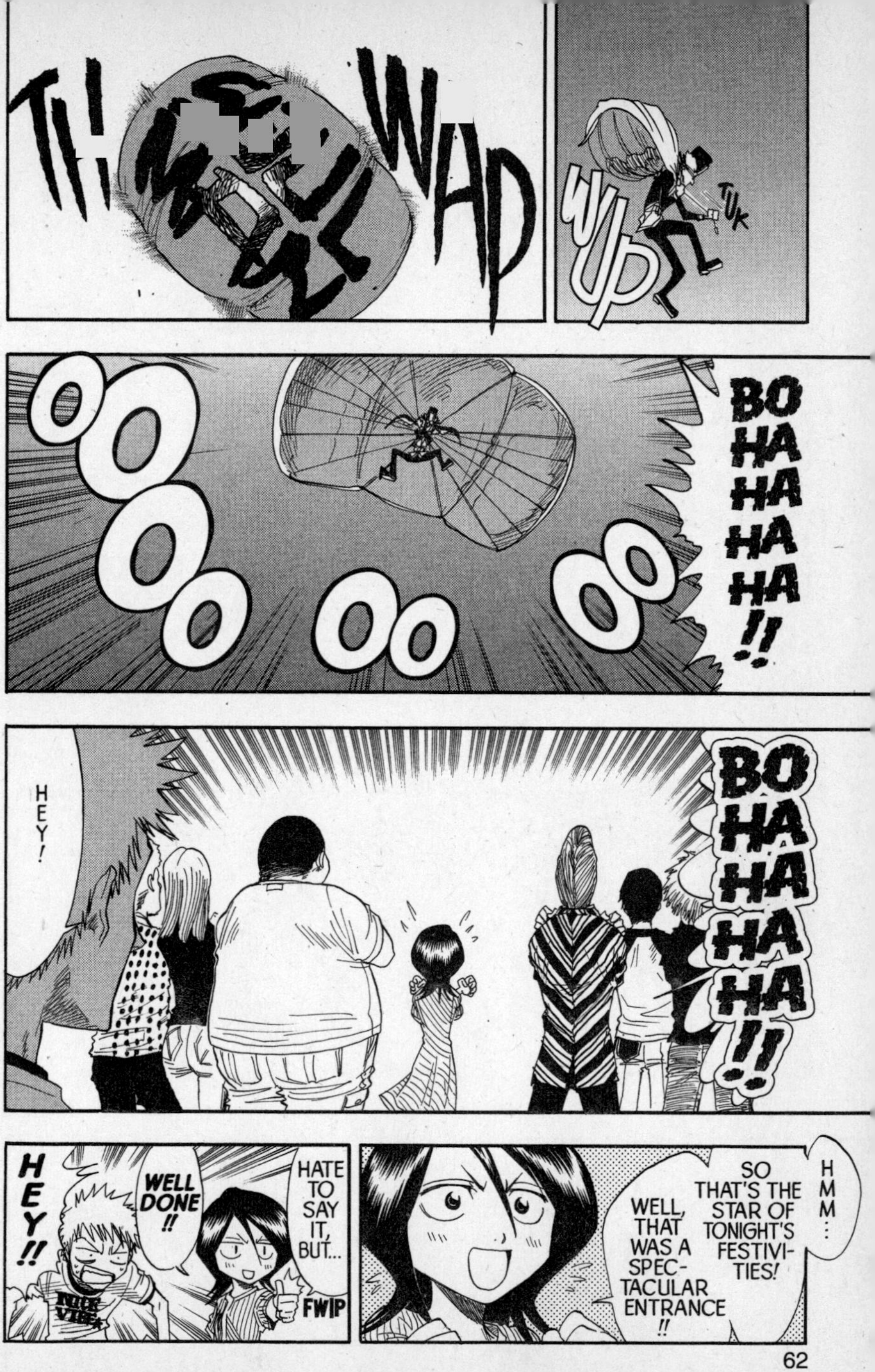
WUP
TUK
WAP
BOHAHAHAHAHA!!
OOOOOOOOO
BOHAHAHAHAHAHA!!
HEY!
HMM...
SO THAT'S THE STAR OF TONIGHT'S FESTIVITIES!
WELL, THAT WAS A SPECTACULAR ENTRANCE!!
HATE TO SAY IT, BUT...
FWIP
WELL DONE!!
HEY!!
NICE VIBES

READ THIS WAY

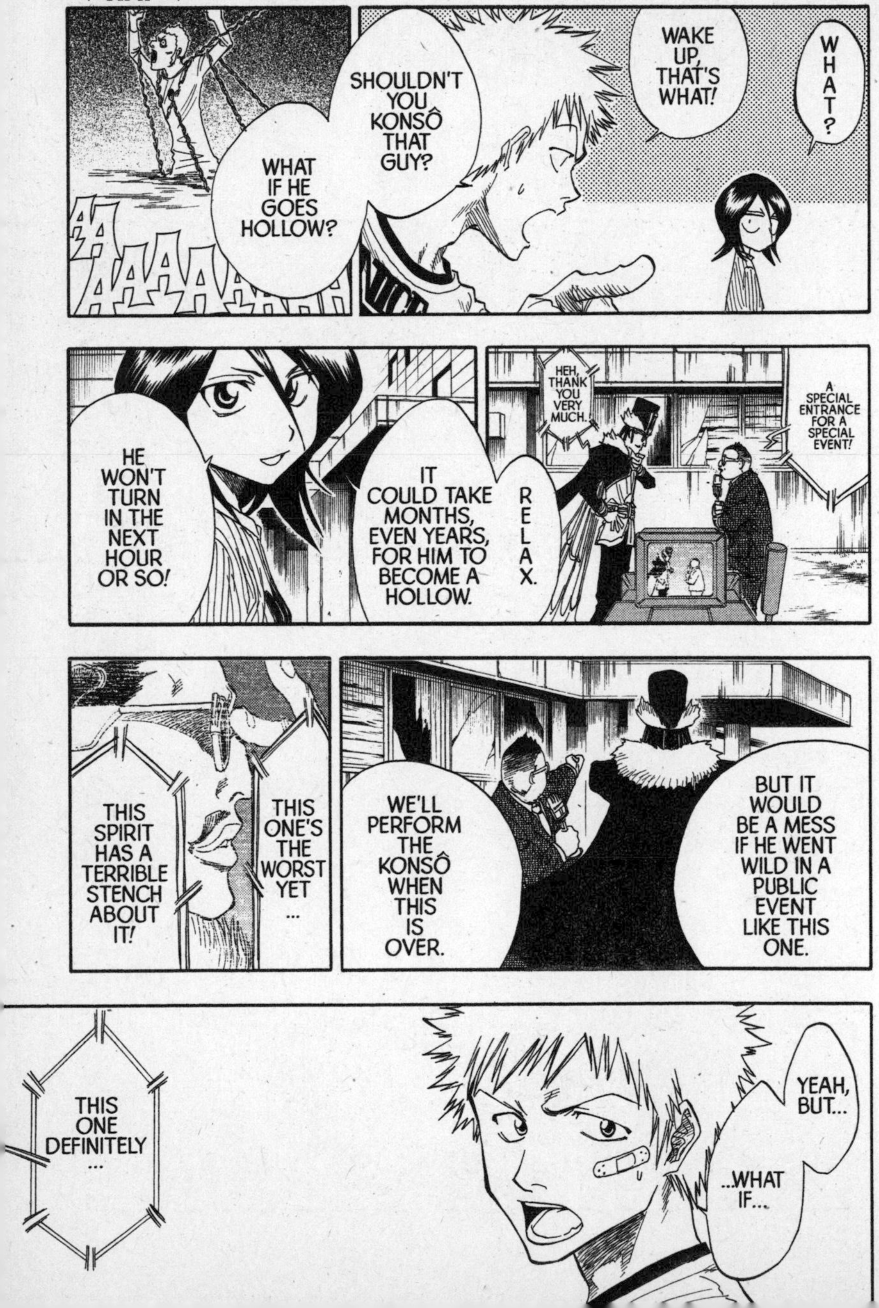
WHAT?
WAKE UP, THAT'S WHAT!
SHOULDN'T YOU KONSÔ THAT GUY?
WHAT IF HE GOES HOLLOW?
AAAAAAA
A SPECIAL ENTRANCE FOR A SPECIAL EVENT!
HEH, THANK YOU VERY MUCH.
RELAX.
IT COULD TAKE MONTHS, EVEN YEARS, FOR HIM TO BECOME A HOLLOW.
HE WON'T TURN IN THE NEXT HOUR OR SO!
BUT IT WOULD BE A MESS IF HE WENT WILD IN A PUBLIC EVENT LIKE THIS ONE.
WE'LL PERFORM THE KONSÔ WHEN THIS IS OVER.
THIS ONE'S THE WORST YET...
THIS SPIRIT HAS A TERRIBLE STENCH ABOUT IT!
YEAH, BUT...
...WHAT IF...
THIS ONE DEFINITELY...

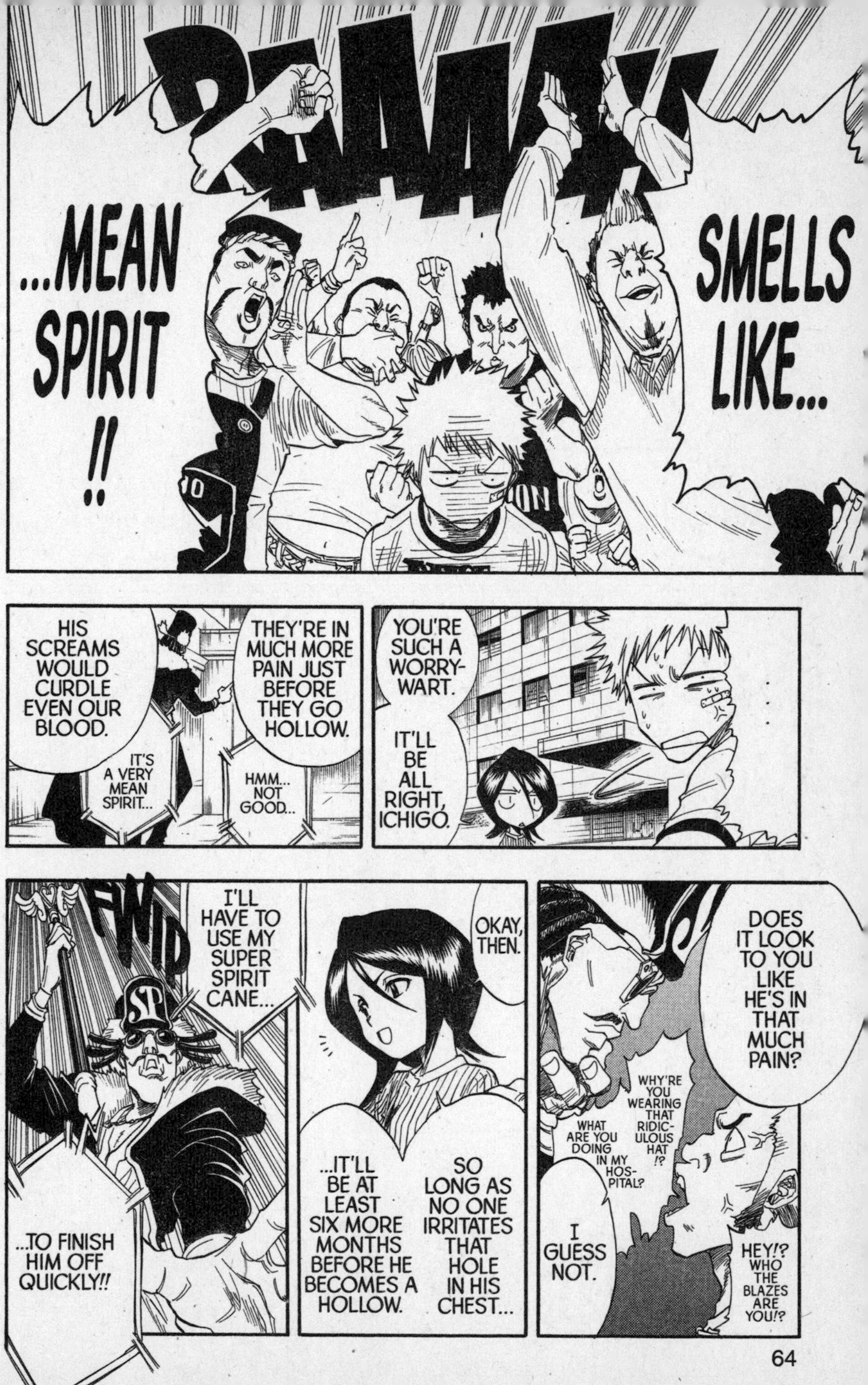
SMELLS LIKE...
...MEAN SPIRIT!!
YOU'RE SUCH A WORRY-WART.
IT'LL BE ALL RIGHT, ICHIGO.
THEY'RE IN MUCH MORE PAIN JUST BEFORE THEY GO HOLLOW.
HMM... NOT GOOD...
HIS SCREAMS WOULD CURDLE EVEN OUR BLOOD.
IT'S A VERY MEAN SPIRIT...
DOES IT LOOK TO YOU LIKE HE'S IN THAT MUCH PAIN?
WHY'RE YOU WEARING THAT RIDICULOUS HAT!?
WHAT ARE YOU DOING IN MY HOSPITAL?
HEY!? WHO THE BLAZES ARE YOU!?
I GUESS NOT.
OKAY, THEN.
SO LONG AS NO ONE IRRITATES THAT HOLE IN HIS CHEST...
...IT'LL BE AT LEAST SIX MORE MONTHS BEFORE HE BECOMES A HOLLOW.
I'LL HAVE TO USE MY SUPER SPIRIT CANE...
...TO FINISH HIM OFF QUICKLY!!

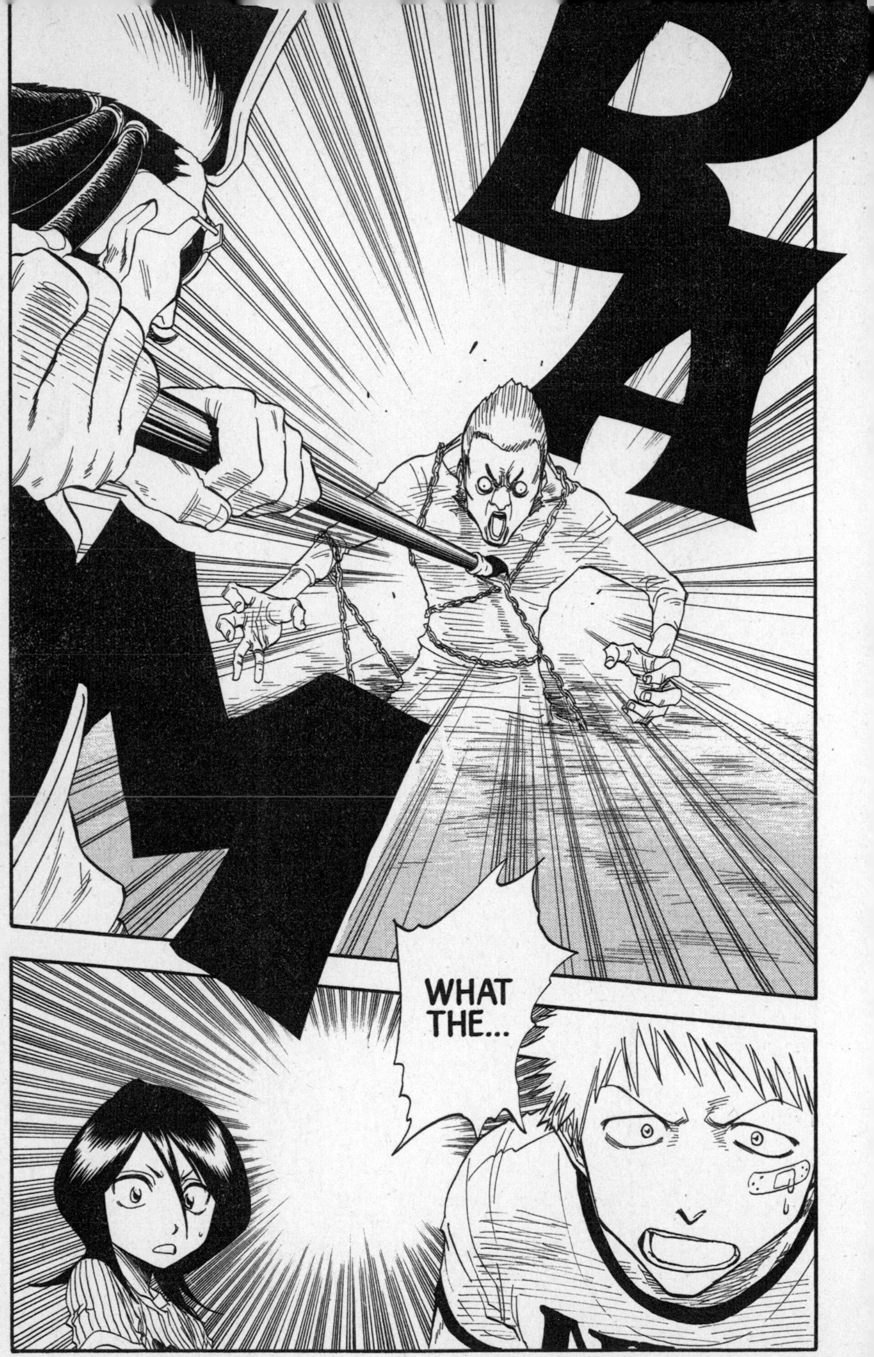
BA
WHAT THE...

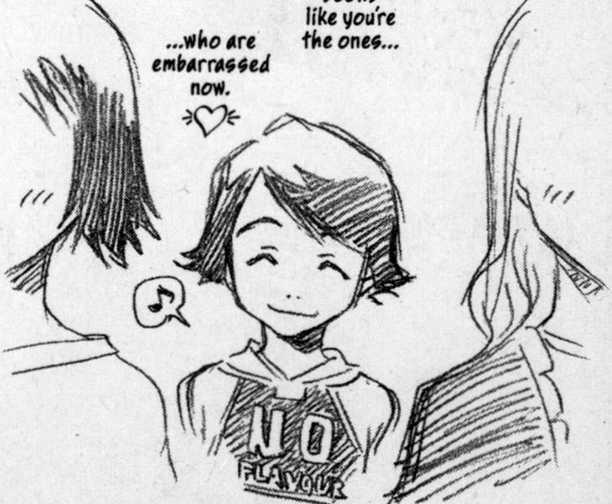
Sorry.
Looks like you're the ones...
...who are embarrassed now.
NO FLAVOUR

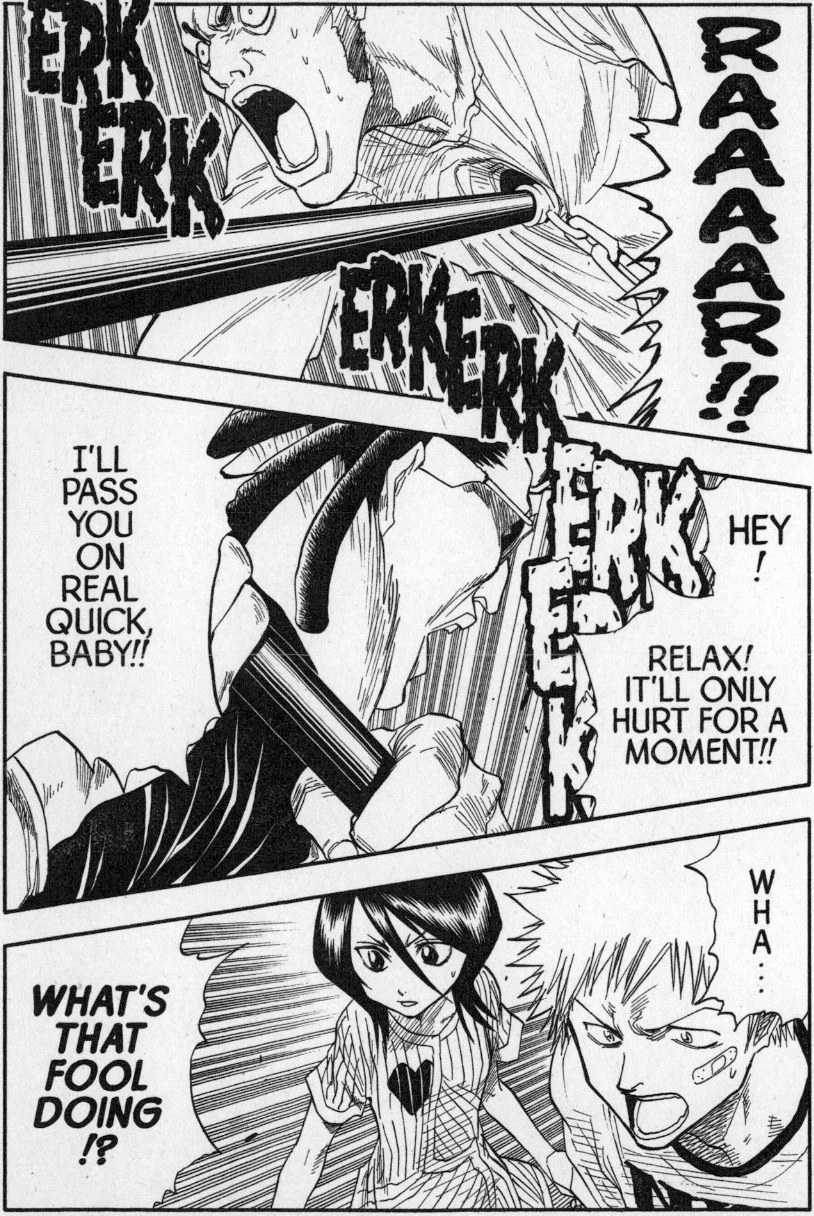
RAAAAR!!
ERK ERK
ERK ERK
HEY!
RELAX! IT'LL ONLY HURT FOR A MOMENT!!
ERK ERK
I'LL PASS YOU ON REAL QUICK, BABY!!
WHA...
WHAT'S THAT FOOL DOING!?

29. Stop That, Stupid!!

29. Stop That, Stupid!!

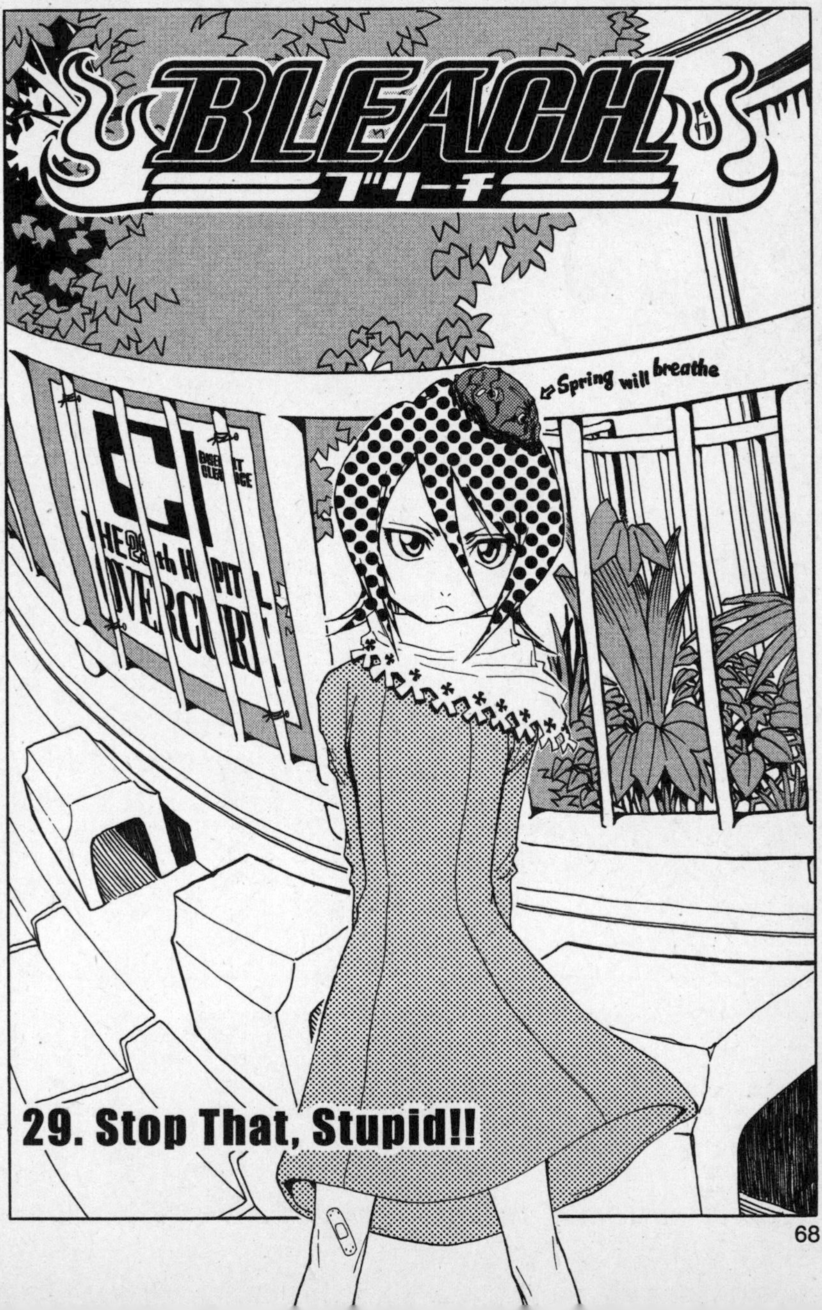
BLEACH
ブリーチ
Spring will breathe

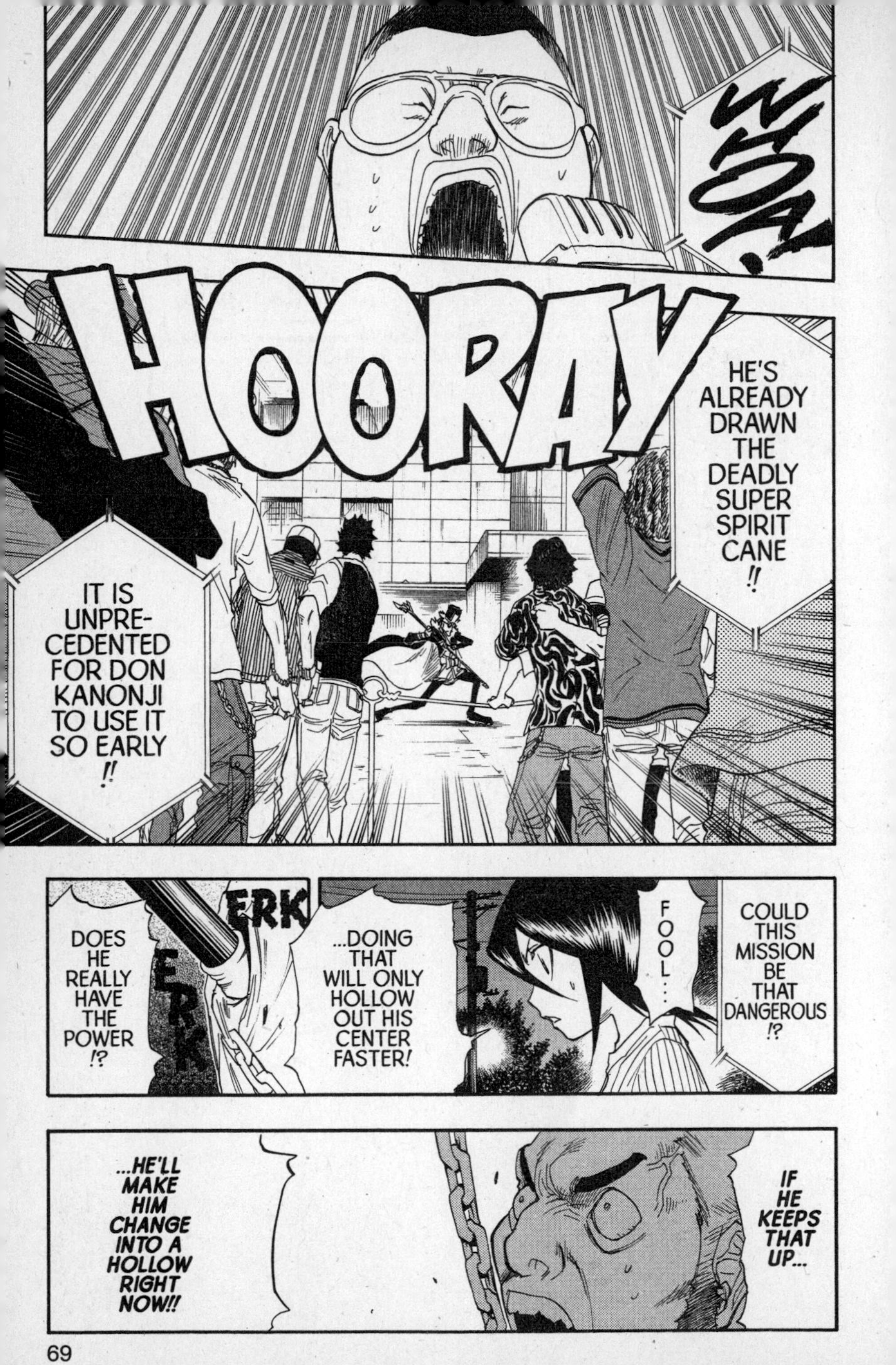
WHOA!
HOORAY
HE'S ALREADY DRAWN THE DEADLY SUPER SPIRIT CANE!!
IT IS UNPRECEDENTED FOR DON KANONJI TO USE IT SO EARLY!!
COULD THIS MISSION BE THAT DANGEROUS!?
FOOL...
...DOING THAT WILL ONLY HOLLOW OUT HIS CENTER FASTER!
ERK
ERK
DOES HE REALLY HAVE THE POWER!?
IF HE KEEPS THAT UP...
...HE'LL MAKE HIM CHANGE INTO A HOLLOW RIGHT NOW!!

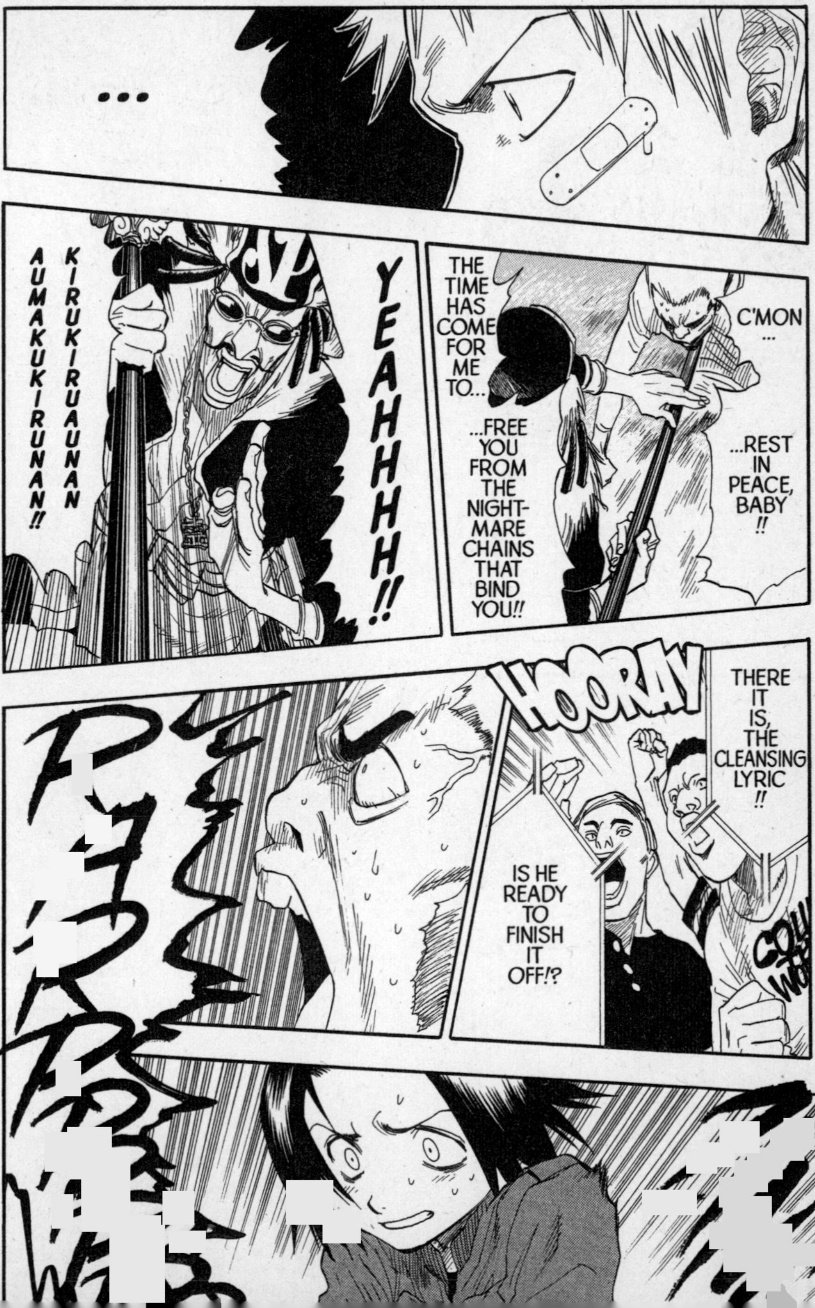
...
C'MON ...
...REST IN PEACE, BABY!!
THE TIME HAS COME FOR ME TO...
...FREE YOU FROM THE NIGHT-MARE CHAINS THAT BIND YOU!!
YEAHHHHHH!!
KIRUKIRUAUNAN
AUMAKUKIRUNAN!!
THERE IT IS, THE CLEANSING LYRIC!!
HOORAY
IS HE READY TO FINISH IT OFF!?

READ THIS WAY

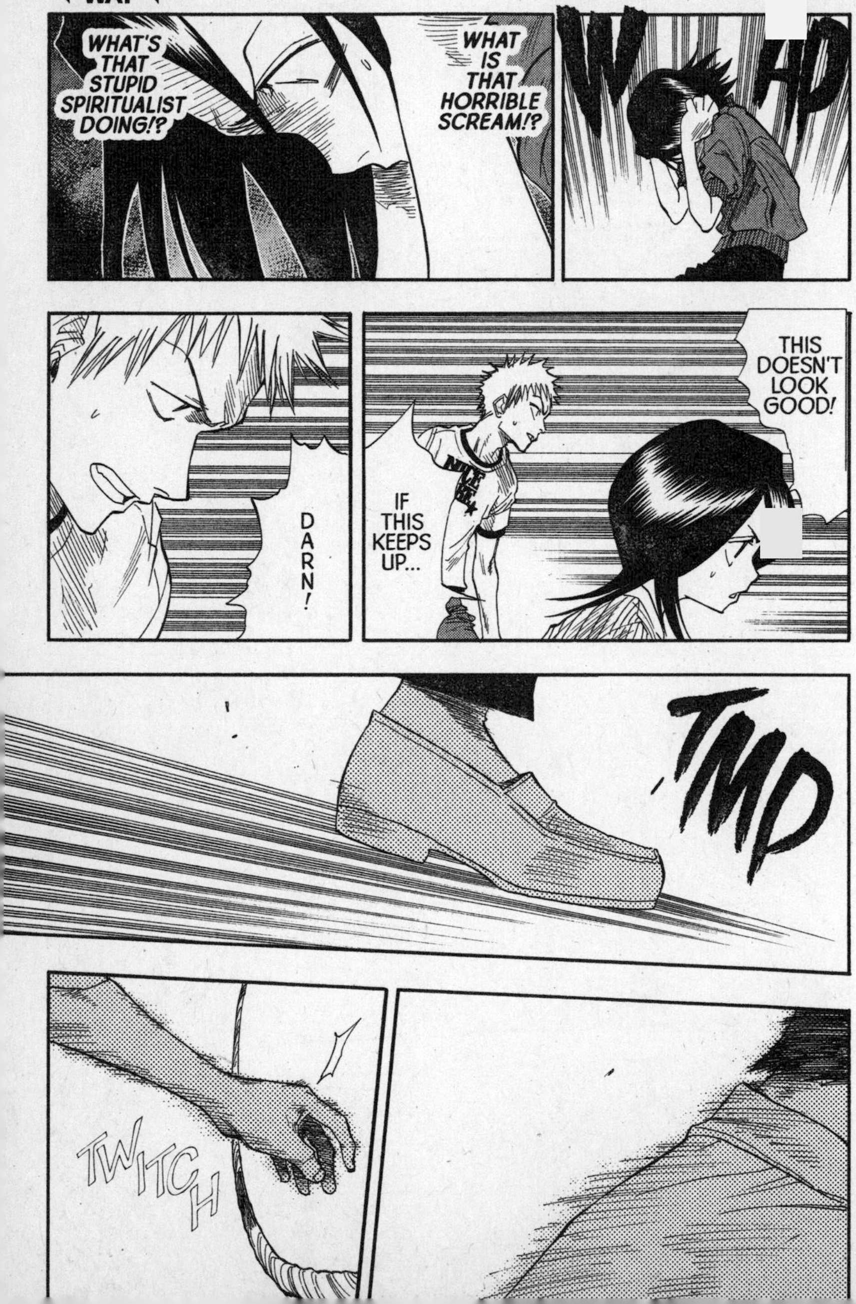
WHAT IS THAT HORRIBLE SCREAM!?
WHAT'S THAT STUPID SPIRITUALIST DOING!?
THIS DOESN'T LOOK GOOD!
IF THIS KEEPS UP...
DARN!
TMP
TWITCH

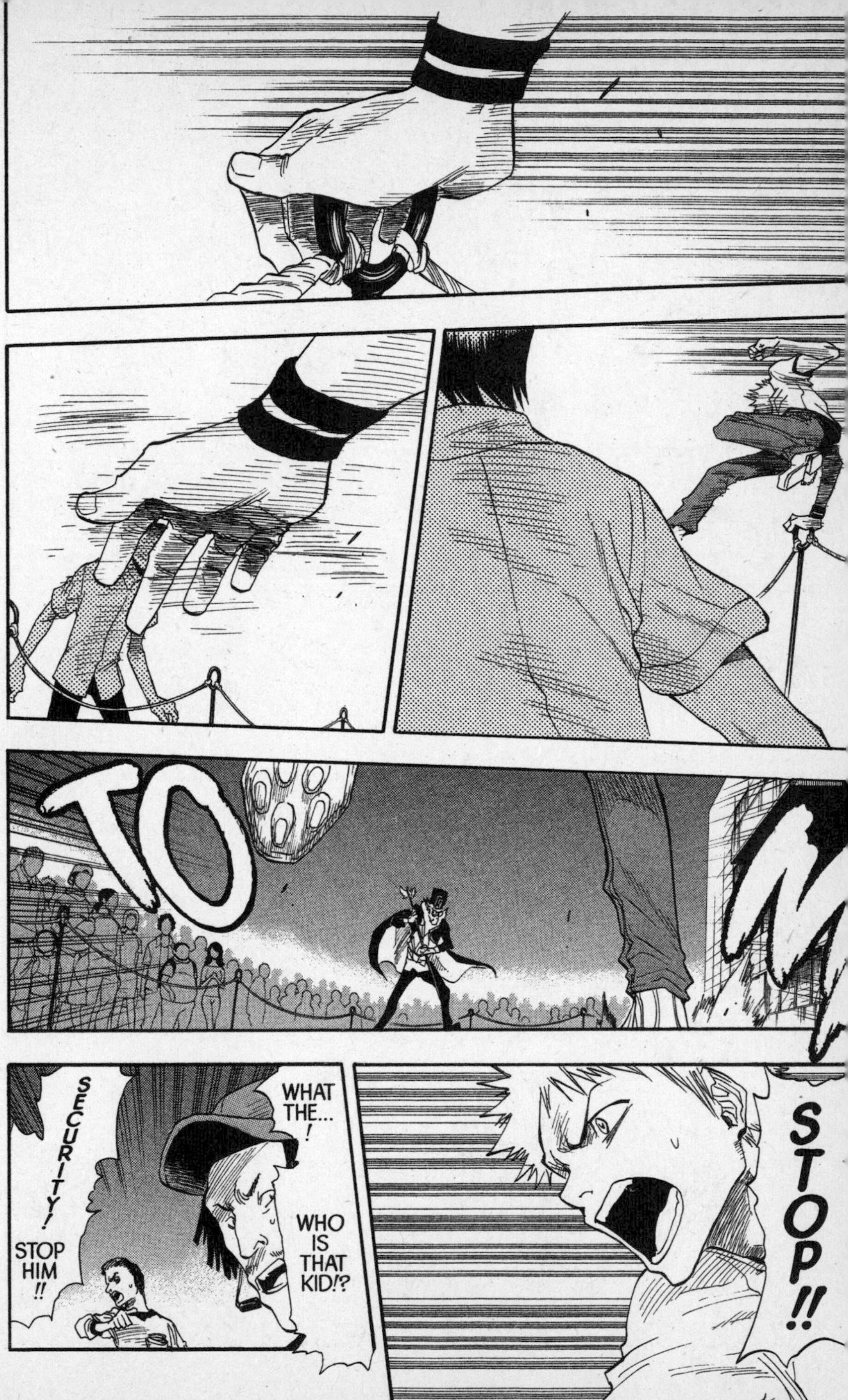
TO
STOP!!
WHAT THE...!
WHO IS THAT KID!?
SECURITY!
STOP HIM!!

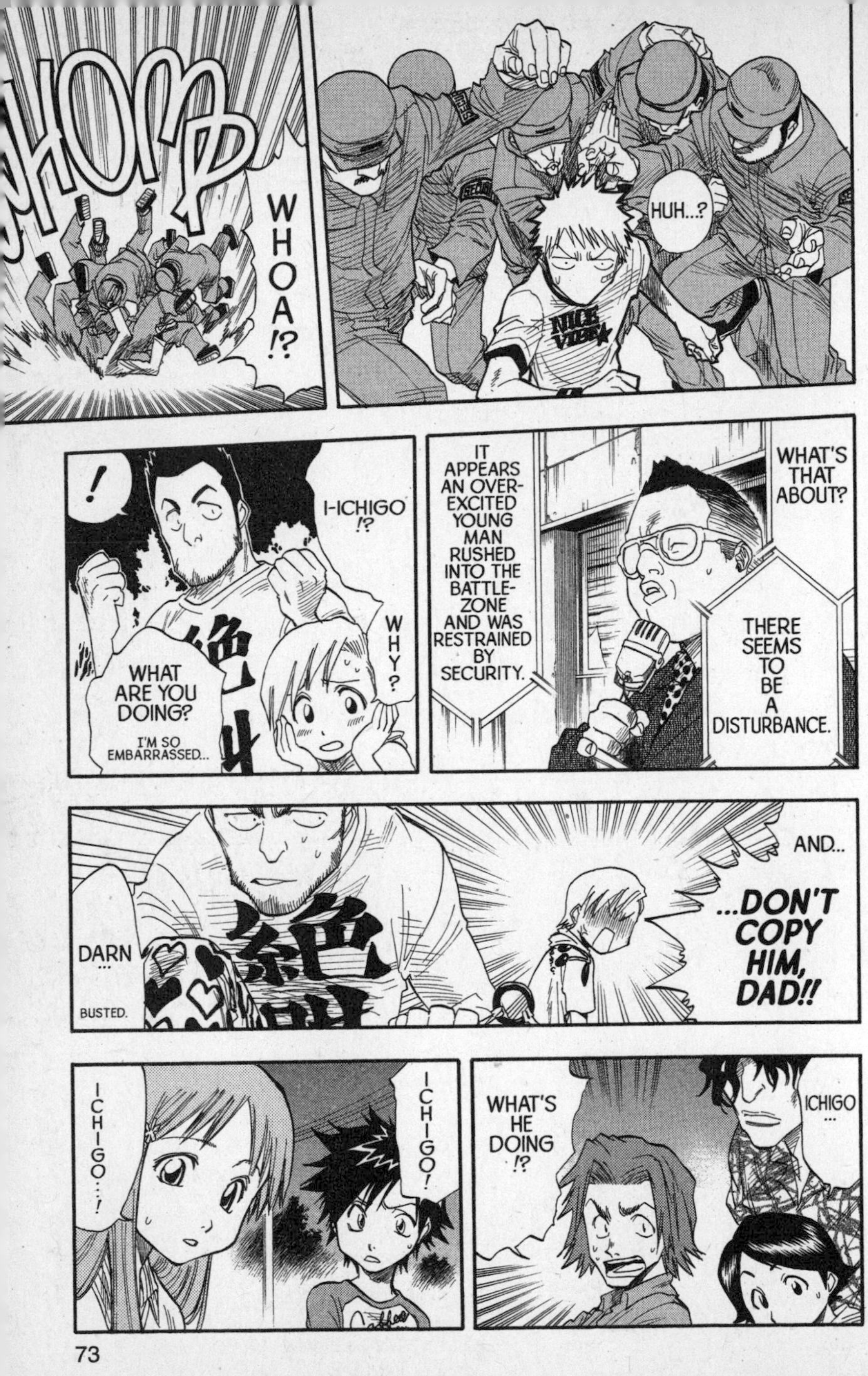
HUH...?
WHOMP
WHOA!?
WHAT'S THAT ABOUT?
THERE SEEMS TO BE A DISTURBANCE.
IT APPEARS AN OVER-EXCITED YOUNG MAN RUSHED INTO THE BATTLE-ZONE AND WAS RESTRAINED BY SECURITY.
!
I-ICHIGO!?
WHY?
WHAT ARE YOU DOING?
I'M SO EMBARRASSED...
AND...
...DON'T COPY HIM, DAD!!
DARN...
BUSTED.
ICHIGO...
WHAT'S HE DOING!?
ICHIGO!
ICHIGO...!

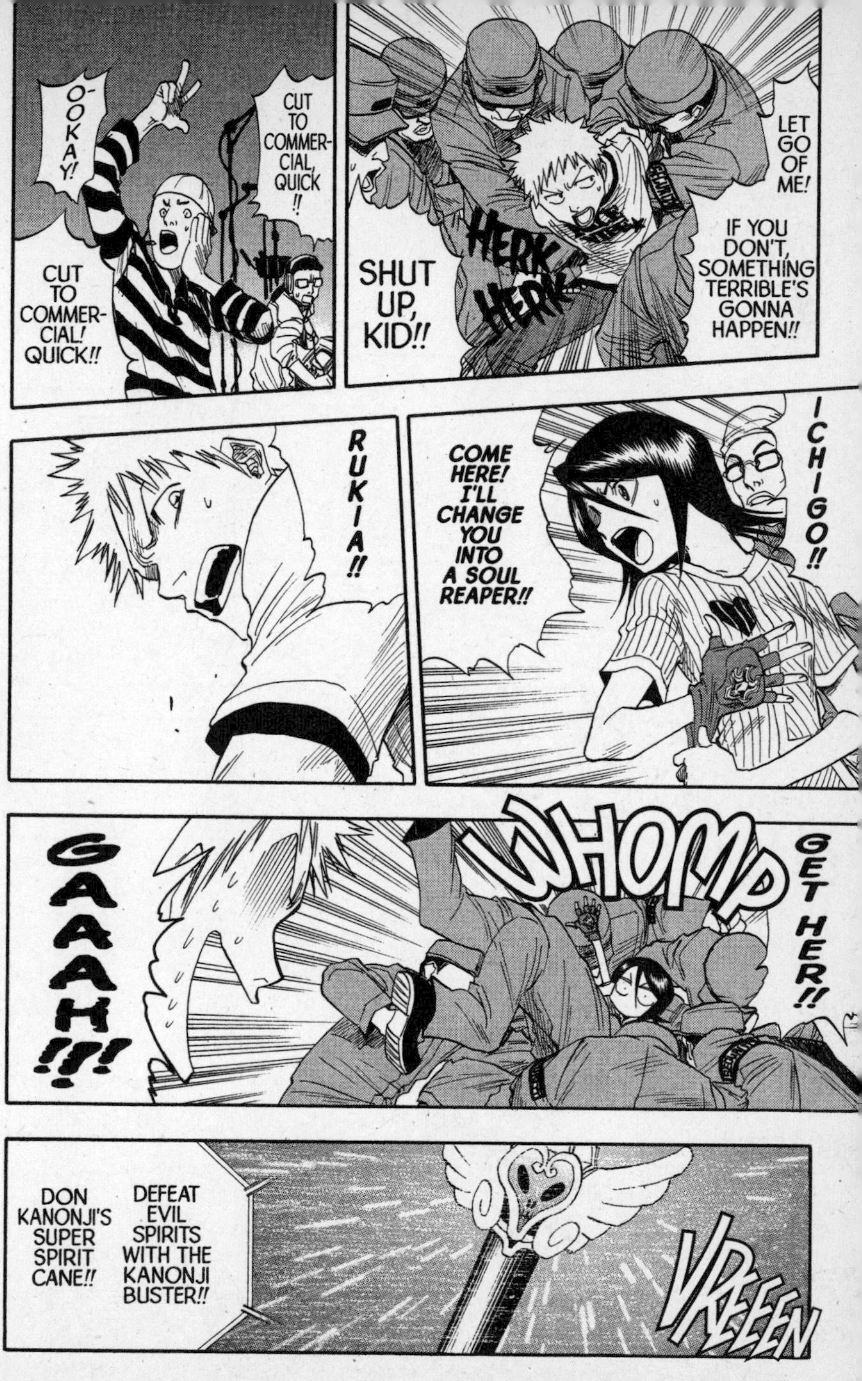

LET GO OF ME!
IF YOU DON'T, SOMETHING TERRIBLE'S GONNA HAPPEN!!
HERK HERK
SHUT UP, KID!!
CUT TO COMMERCIAL, QUICK!!
O-OOKAY!
CUT TO COMMERCIAL! QUICK!!
ICHIGO!!
COME HERE! I'LL CHANGE YOU INTO A SOUL REAPER!!
RUKIA!!
GET HER!!
WHOMP
GAAAAH!!!
VREEEN
DEFEAT EVIL SPIRITS WITH THE KANONJI BUSTER!!
DON KANONJI'S SUPER SPIRIT CANE!!

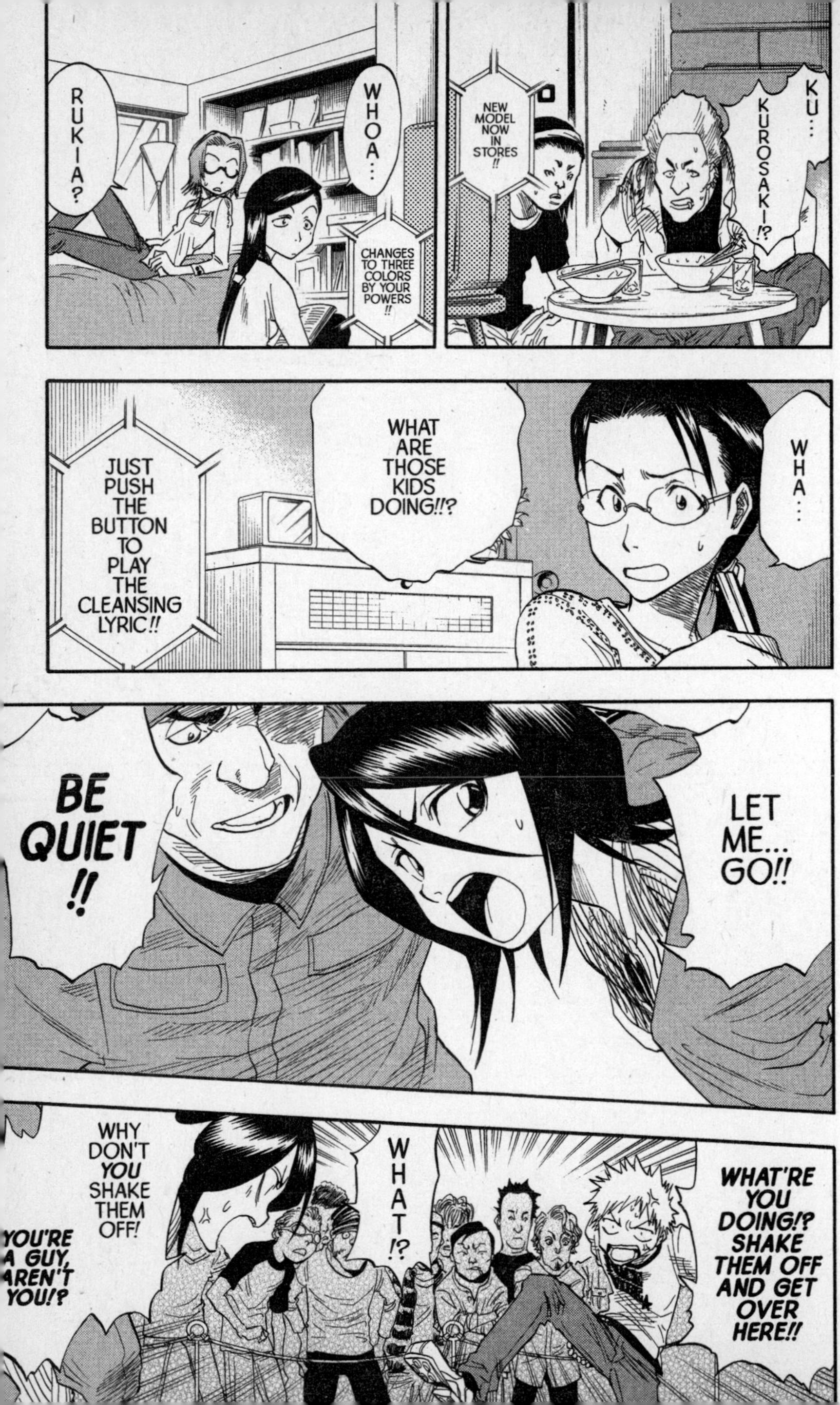

KU... KUROSAKI!?
NEW MODEL NOW IN STORES!!
WHOA...
CHANGES TO THREE COLORS BY YOUR POWERS!!
RUKIA?
WHA...
WHAT ARE THOSE KIDS DOING!!?
JUST PUSH THE BUTTON TO PLAY THE CLEANSING LYRIC!!
LET ME... GO!!
BE QUIET!!
WHAT'RE YOU DOING!? SHAKE THEM OFF AND GET OVER HERE!!
WHAT!?
WHY DON'T YOU SHAKE THEM OFF!
YOU'RE A GUY, AREN'T YOU!?

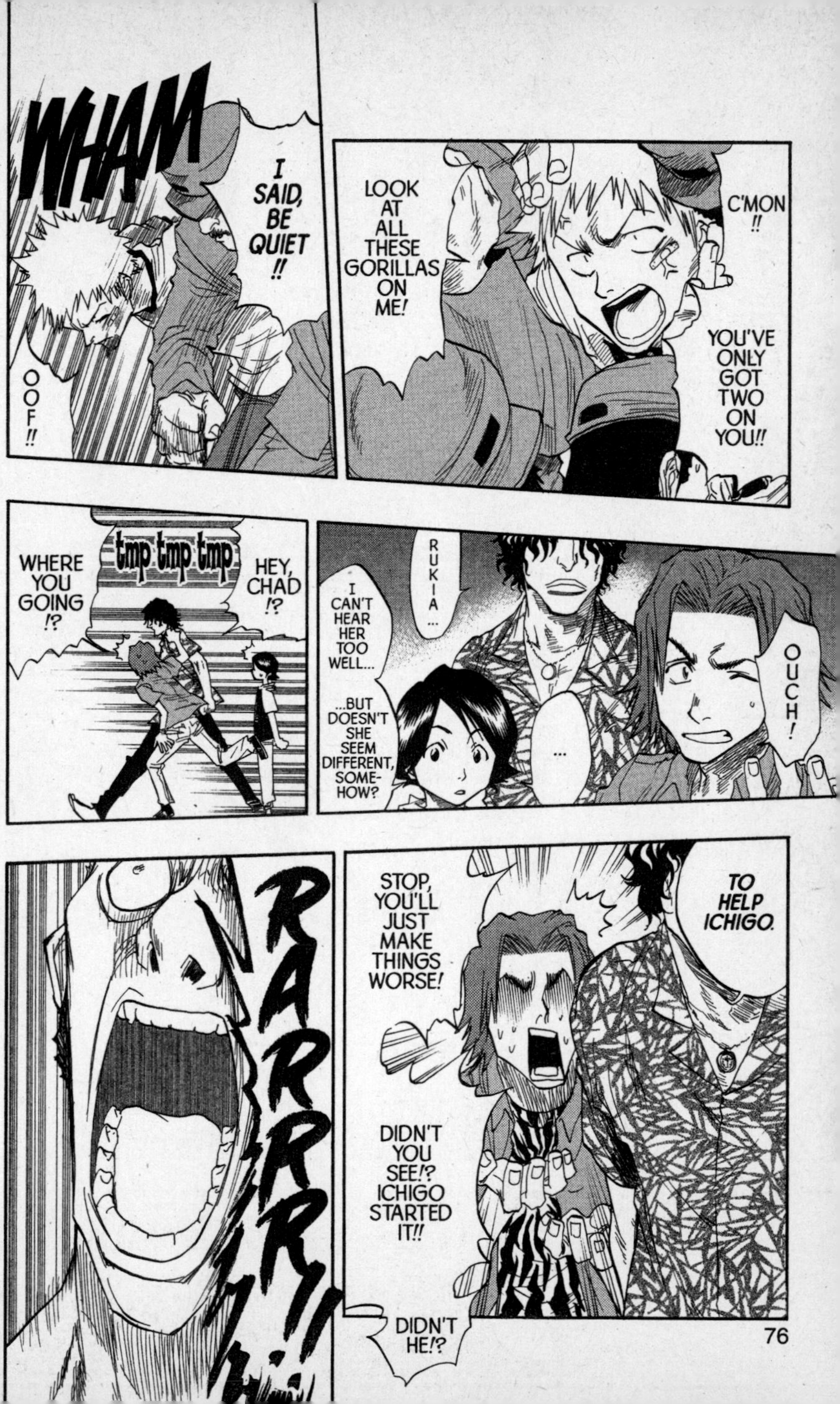
C'MON!!
LOOK AT ALL THESE GORILLAS ON ME!
YOU'VE ONLY GOT TWO ON YOU!!
I SAID, BE QUIET!!
WHAM
OOF!!
OUCH!
RUKIA...
I CAN'T HEAR HER TOO WELL...
...BUT DOESN'T SHE SEEM DIFFERENT, SOME-HOW?
...
HEY, CHAD!?
tmp tmp tmp
WHERE YOU GOING!?
TO HELP ICHIGO.
STOP, YOU'LL JUST MAKE THINGS WORSE!
DIDN'T YOU SEE!? ICHIGO STARTED IT!!
DIDN'T HE!?
RARRR!!

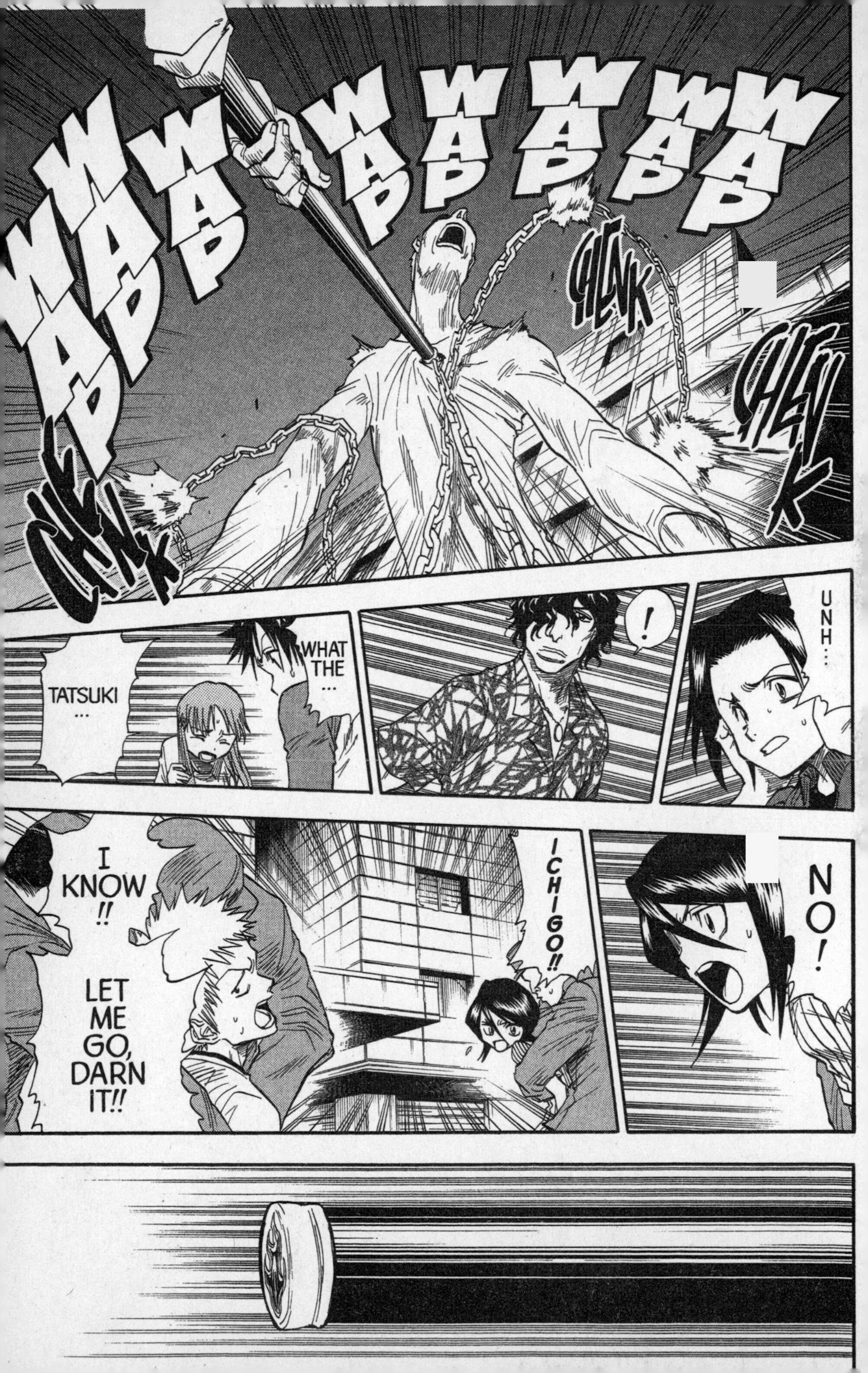
WAP WAP WAP WAP WAP WAP WAP
CHINK
CHINK
CHINK
UNH...
!
WHAT THE ...
TATSUKI ...
NO!
ICHIGO!!
I KNOW!!
LET ME GO, DARN IT!!

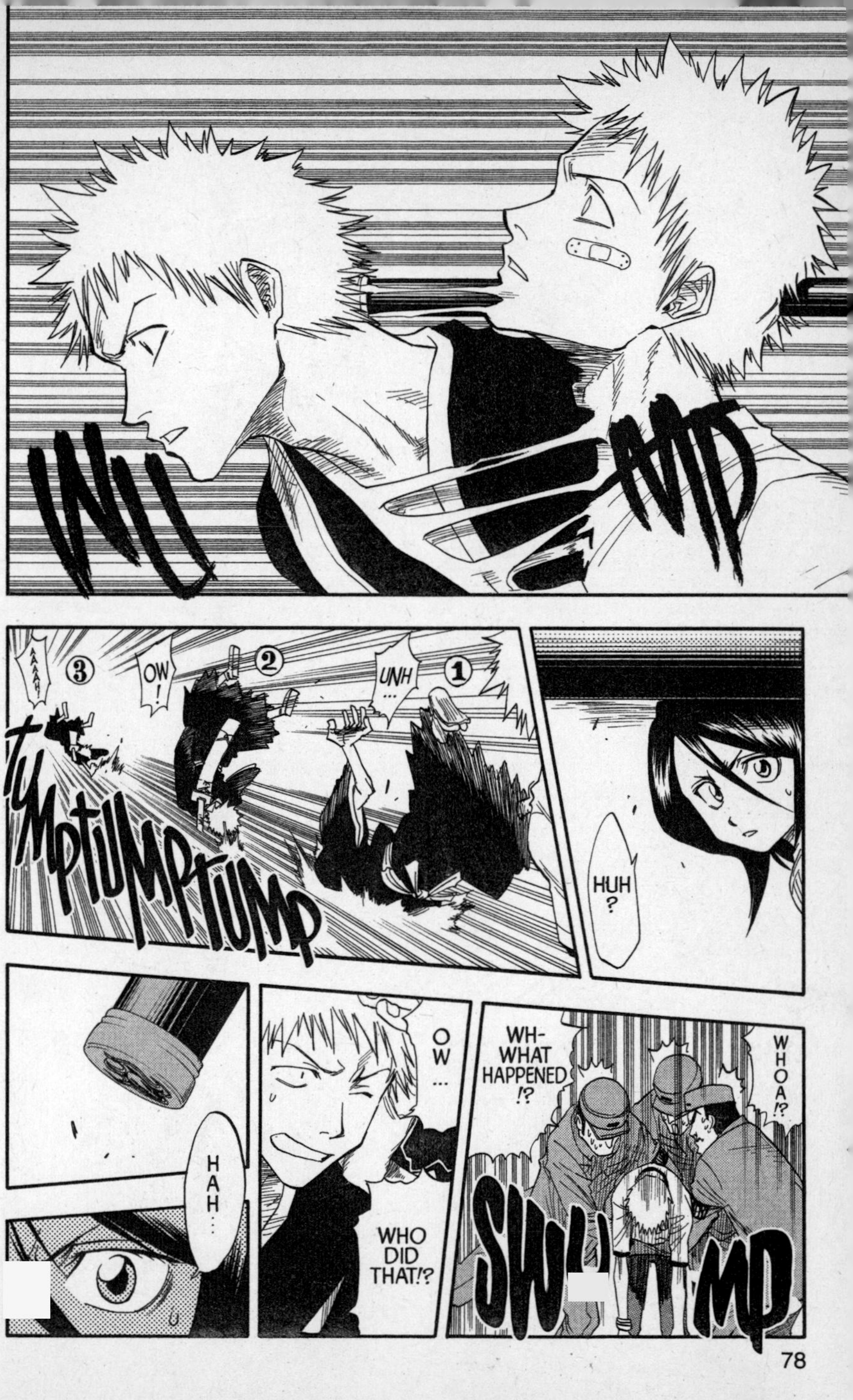
WHUMP
HUH?
UNH...
OW!
AAAH!
TUMPTUMPTUMPTUMP
WHOA!?
WH-WHAT HAPPENED!?
SWUMP
OW...
WHO DID THAT!?
HAH...

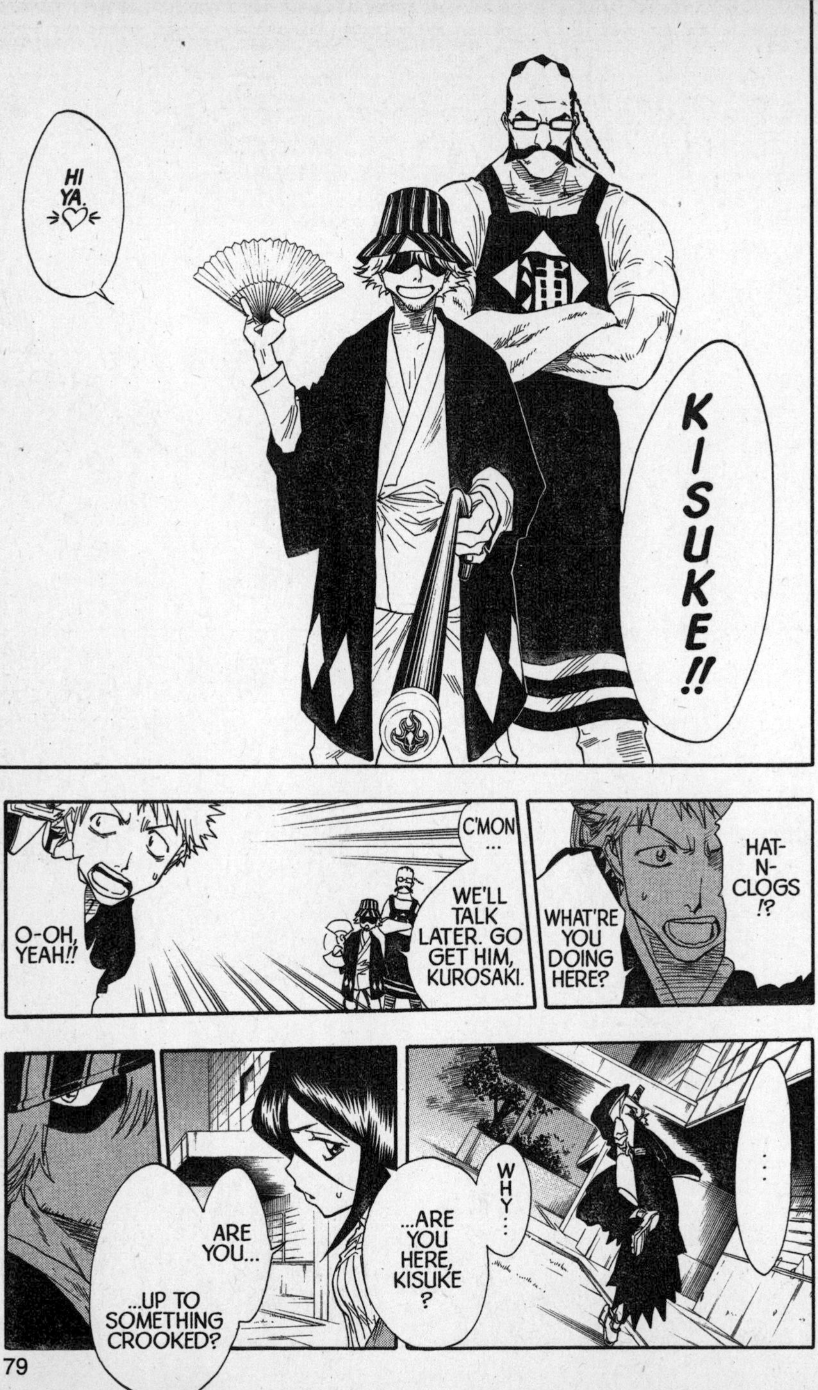
KISUKE!!
HI YA. ♡
HAT-N-CLOGS!?
WHAT'RE YOU DOING HERE?
C'MON...
WE'LL TALK LATER. GO GET HIM, KUROSAKI.
O-OH, YEAH!!
...
WHY...
...ARE YOU HERE, KISUKE?
ARE YOU...
...UP TO SOMETHING CROOKED?

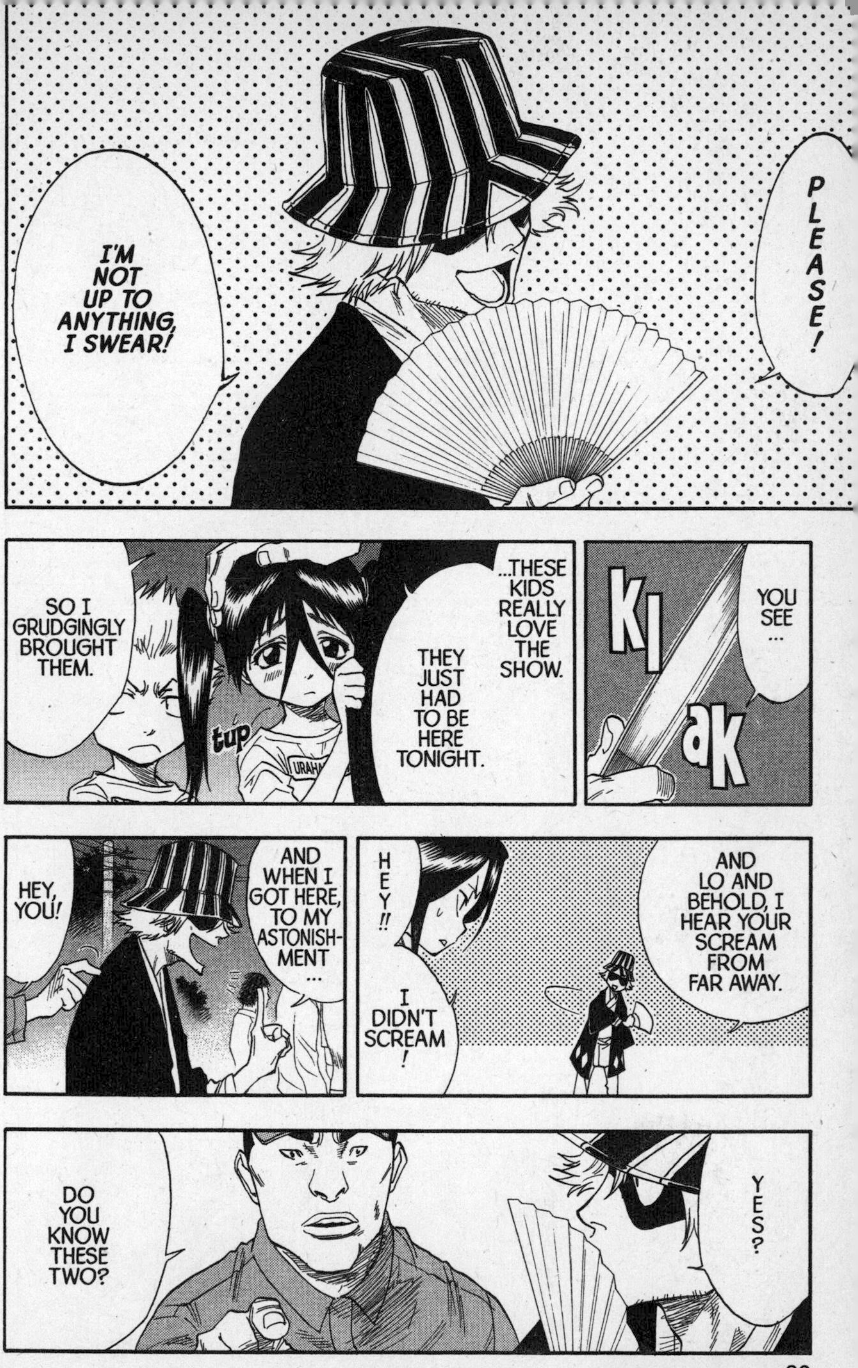
PLEASE!
I'M NOT UP TO ANYTHING, I SWEAR!
YOU SEE ...
KLAK
...THESE KIDS REALLY LOVE THE SHOW.
THEY JUST HAD TO BE HERE TONIGHT.
tup
SO I GRUDGINGLY BROUGHT THEM.
AND LO AND BEHOLD, I HEAR YOUR SCREAM FROM FAR AWAY.
HEY!!
I DIDN'T SCREAM!
AND WHEN I GOT HERE, TO MY ASTONISHMENT ...
HEY, YOU!
YES?
DO YOU KNOW THESE TWO?

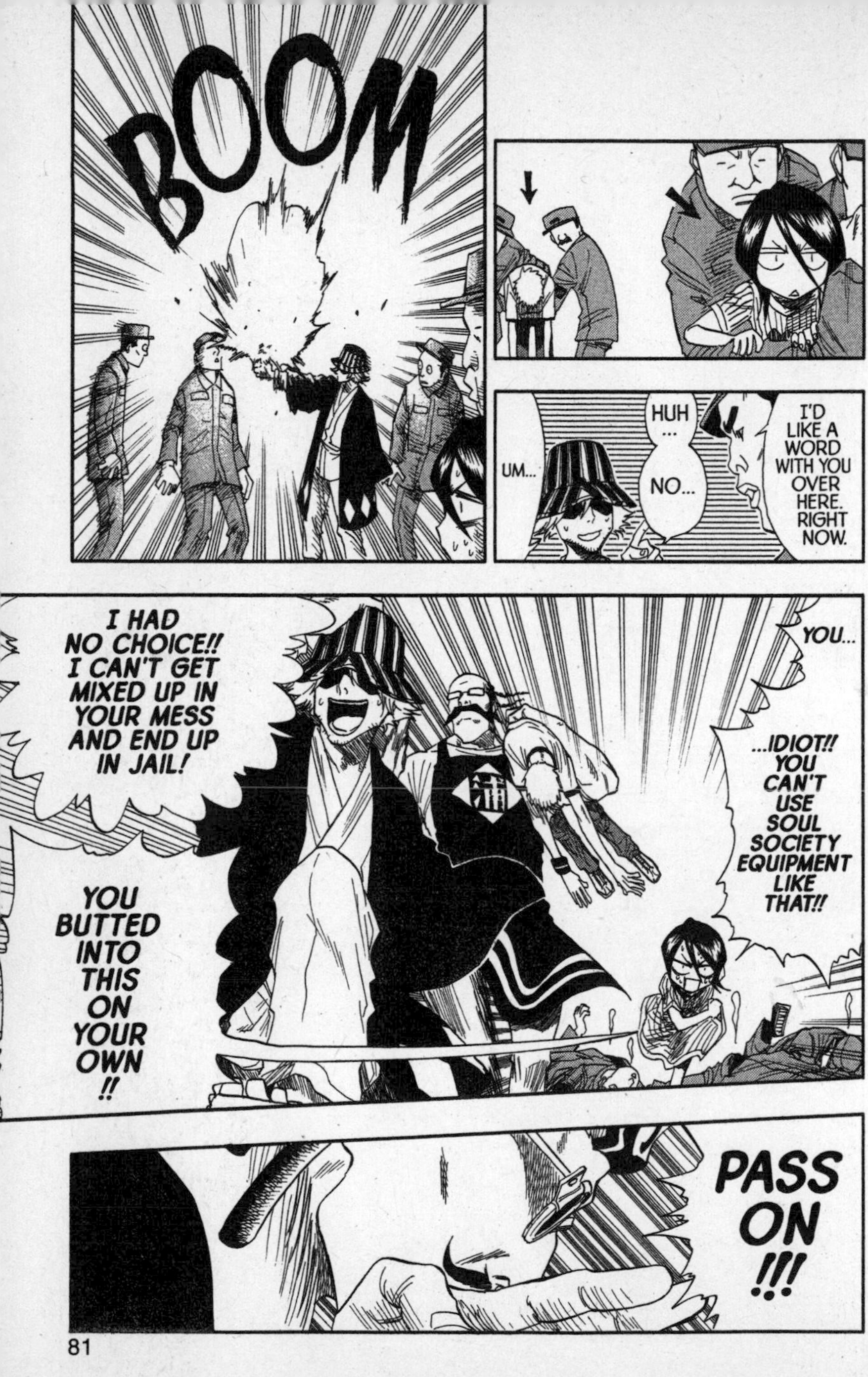
I'D LIKE A WORD WITH YOU OVER HERE. RIGHT NOW.
HUH... NO...
UM...
BOOM
YOU...
...IDIOT!! YOU CAN'T USE SOUL SOCIETY EQUIPMENT LIKE THAT!!
I HAD NO CHOICE!! I CAN'T GET MIXED UP IN YOUR MESS AND END UP IN JAIL!
YOU BUTTED INTO THIS ON YOUR OWN!!
PASS ON!!!

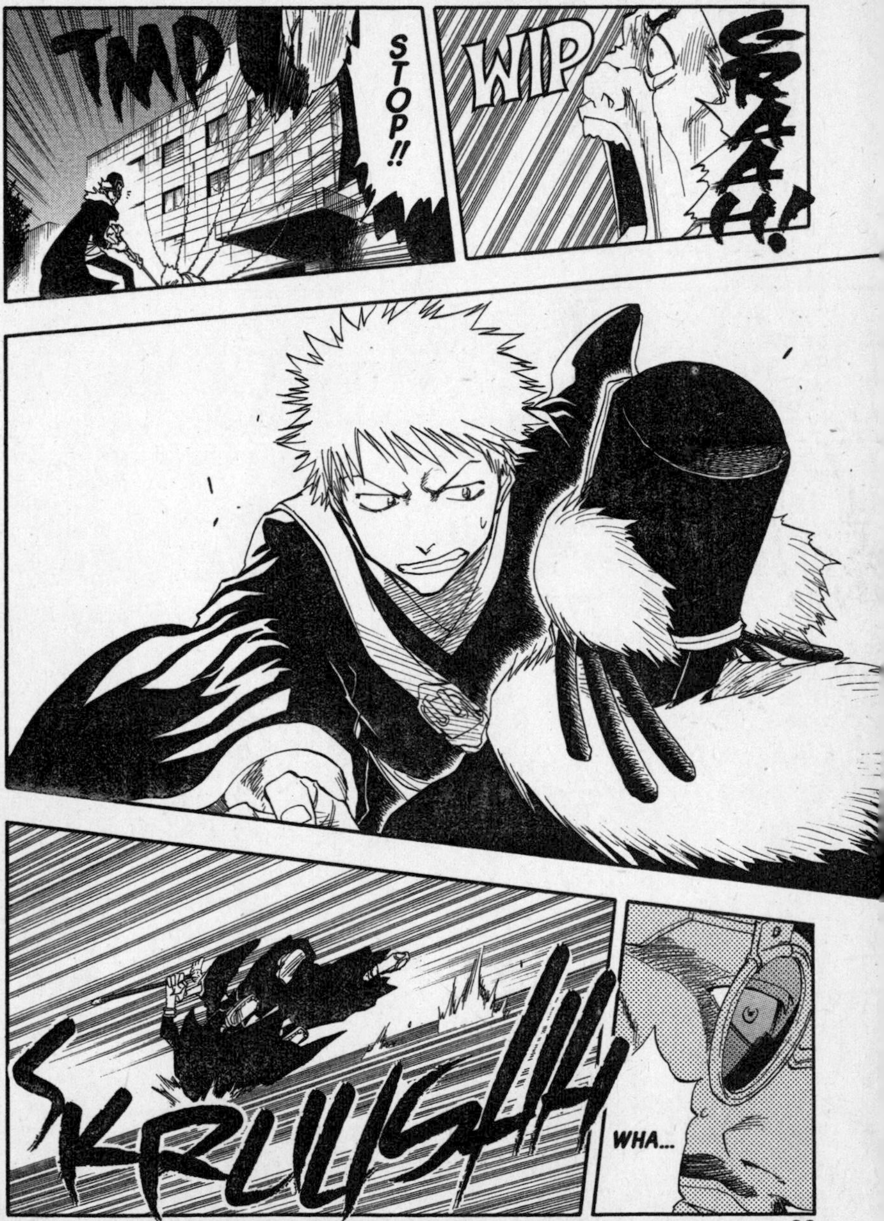
WIP
GRAAH!
TMD
STOP!!
WHA...
SKRUSH

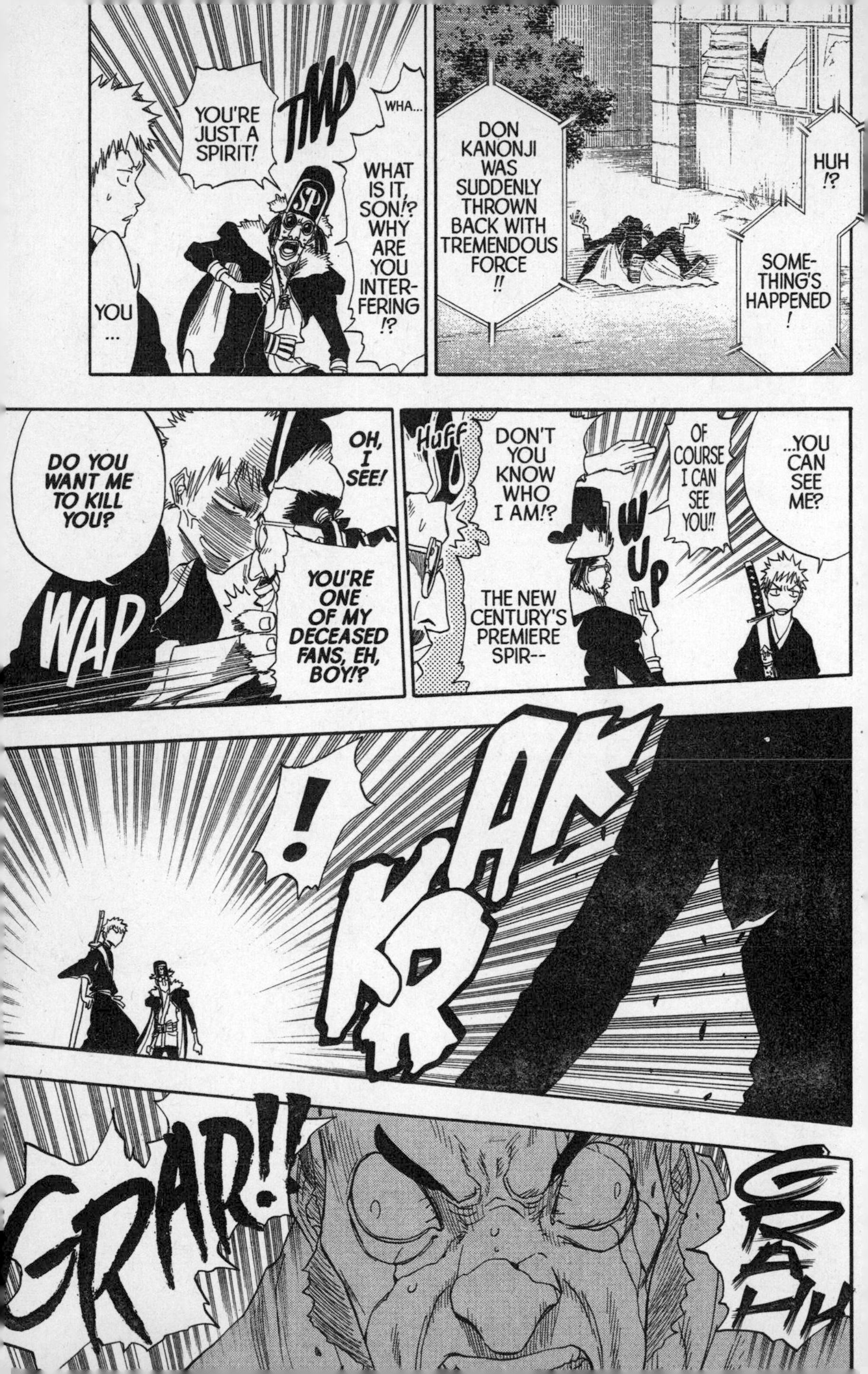
HUH !?
SOME-THING'S HAPPENED!
DON KANONJI WAS SUDDENLY THROWN BACK WITH TREMENDOUS FORCE!!
WHA...
TMP
WHAT IS IT, SON!? WHY ARE YOU INTERFERING!?
YOU'RE JUST A SPIRIT!
YOU...
...YOU CAN SEE ME?
OF COURSE I CAN SEE YOU!!
WUP
DON'T YOU KNOW WHO I AM!?
Huff
THE NEW CENTURY'S PREMIERE SPIR--
OH, I SEE!
YOU'RE ONE OF MY DECEASED FANS, EH, BOY!?
DO YOU WANT ME TO KILL YOU?
WAP
KRAK
!
GRAAH
GRAR!!

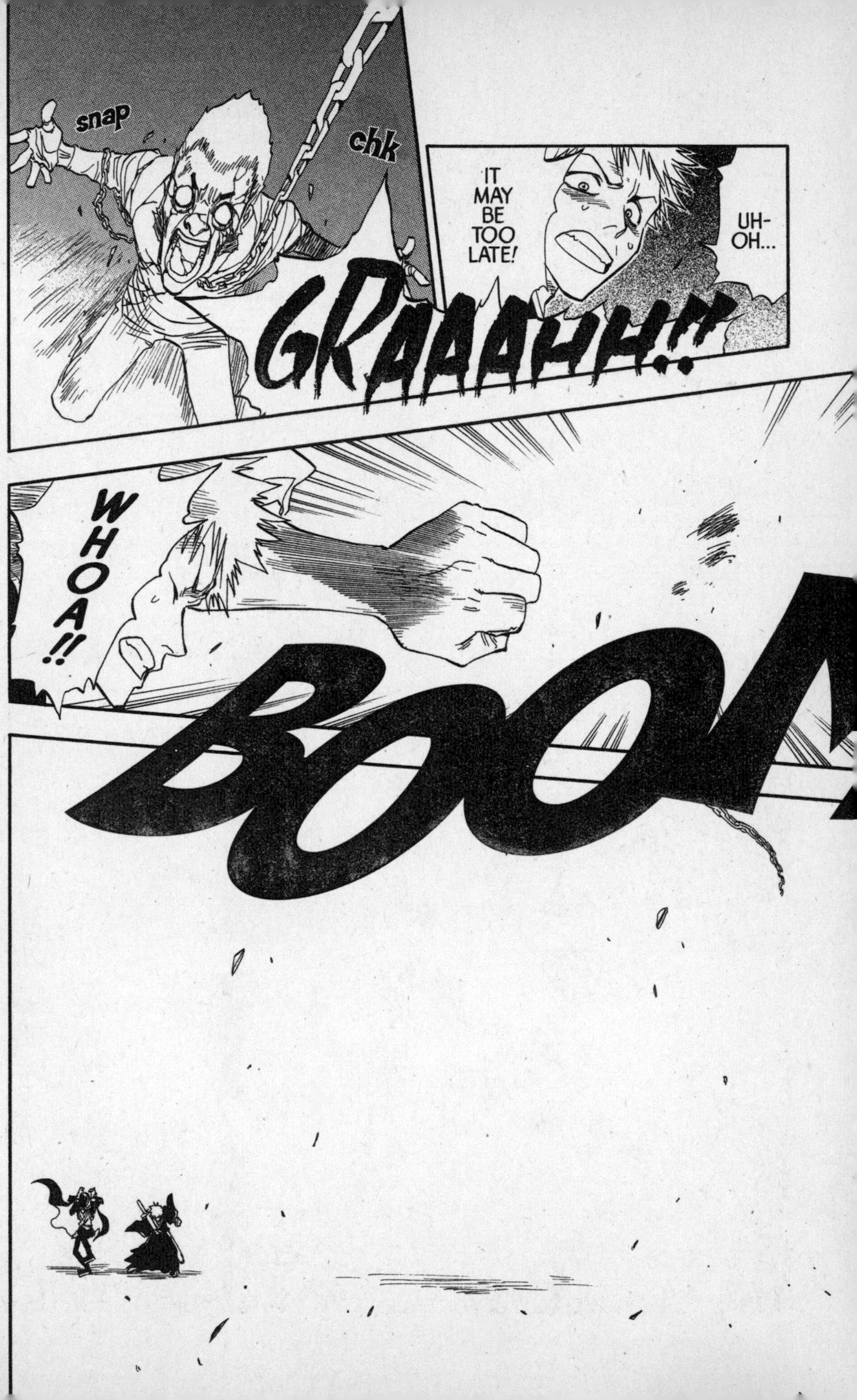
UH-OH...
IT MAY BE TOO LATE!
snap
chk
GRAAAHH!!
WHOA!!
BOO

READ THIS WAY

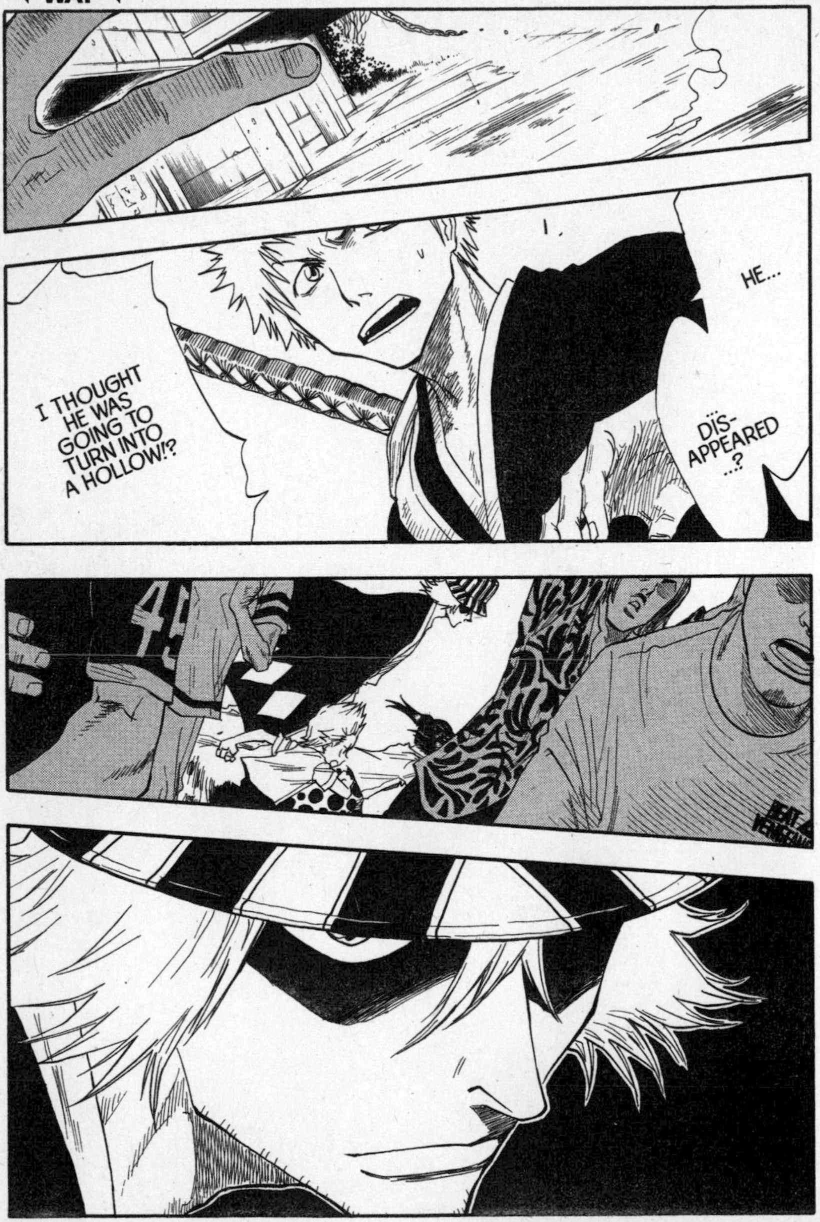
HE...
...DIS-APPEARED...?
I THOUGHT HE WAS GOING TO TURN INTO A HOLLOW!?

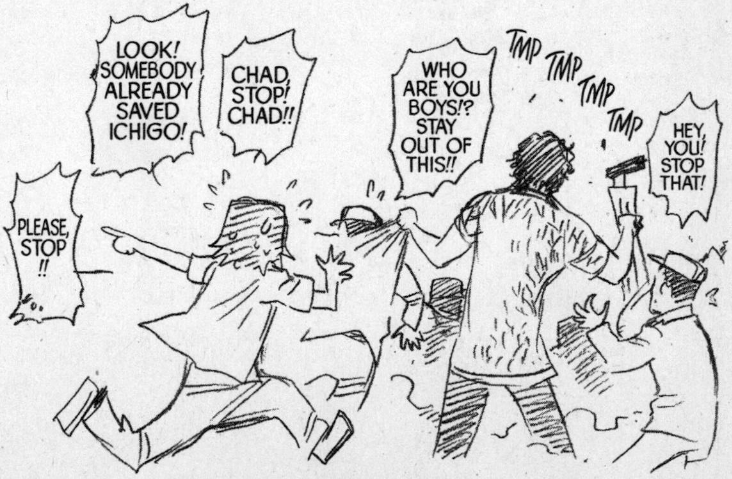
HEY, YOU! STOP THAT!
TMP TMP TMP TMP
WHO ARE YOU BOYS!? STAY OUT OF THIS!!
CHAD, STOP! CHAD!!
LOOK! SOMEBODY ALREADY SAVED ICHIGO!
PLEASE, STOP!!

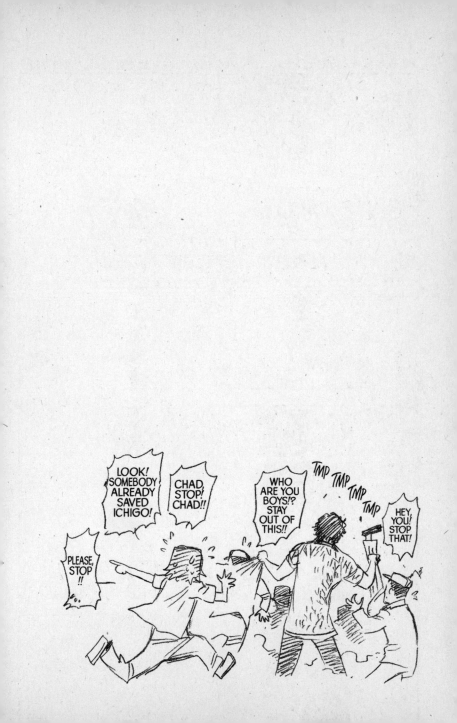

30. Second Contact (it was beyond the scope of our understanding)

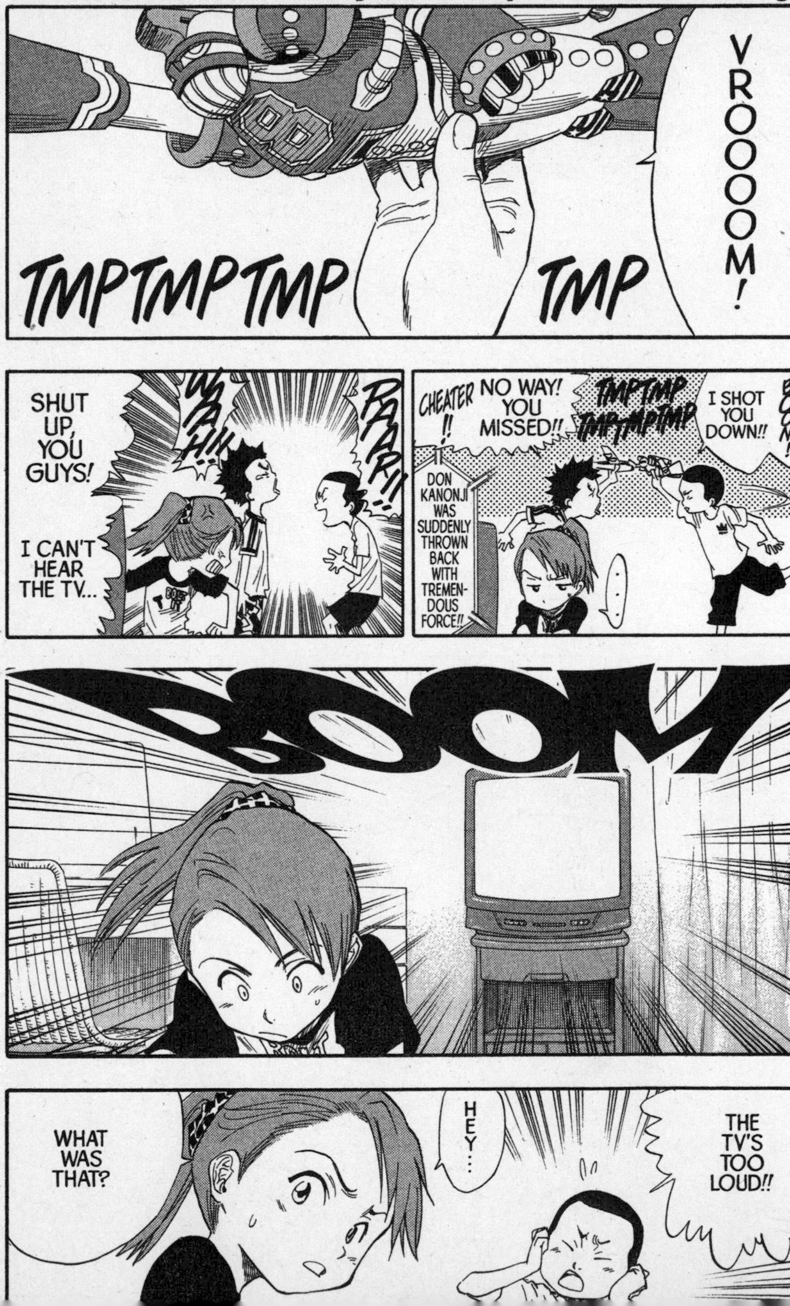

VROOOOOM!
TMP
TMPTMPTMP
BOOM!
I SHOT YOU DOWN!!
TMPTMP TMPTMPTMP
NO WAY! YOU MISSED!!
CHEATER!!
DON KANONJI WAS SUDDENLY THROWN BACK WITH TREMENDOUS FORCE!!
...
SHUT UP, YOU GUYS!
I CAN'T HEAR THE TV...
BOOM
THE TV'S TOO LOUD!!
HEY...
WHAT WAS THAT?

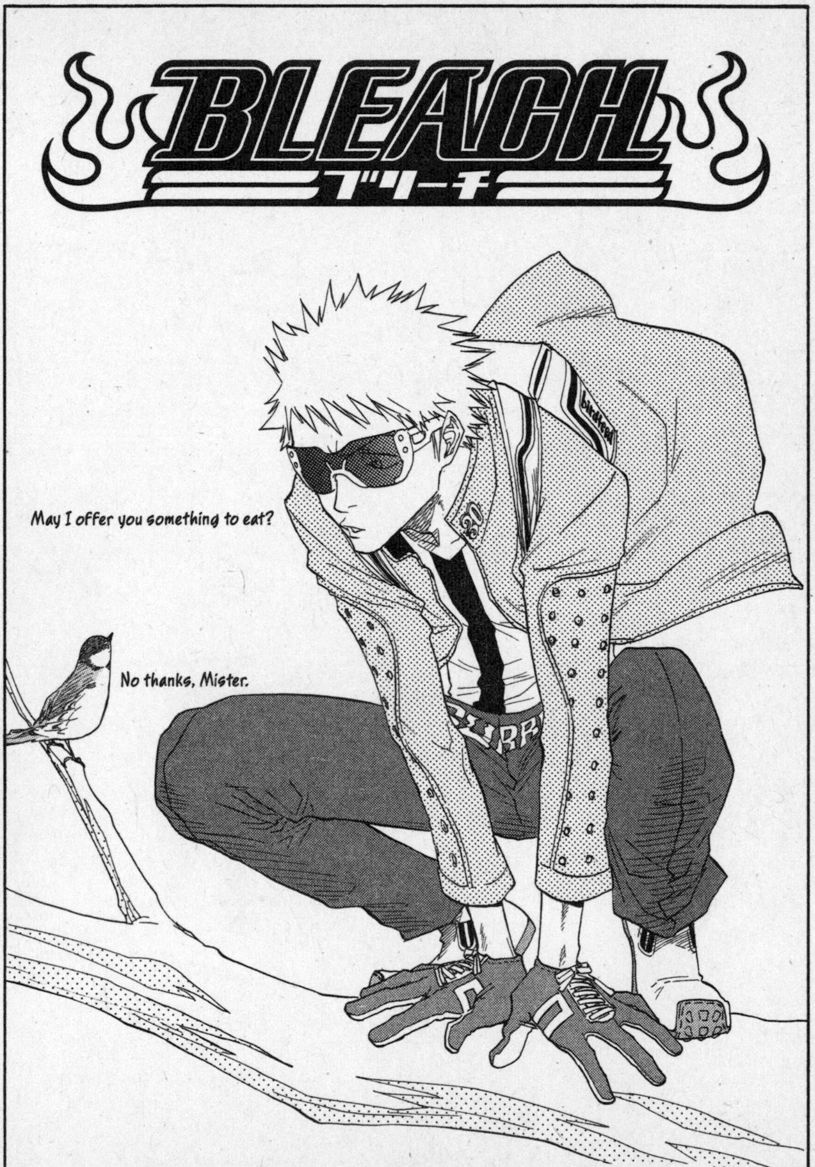
BLEACH
ブリーチ
May I offer you something to eat?
No thanks, Mister.

30. Second Contact (it was beyond the scope of our understanding)

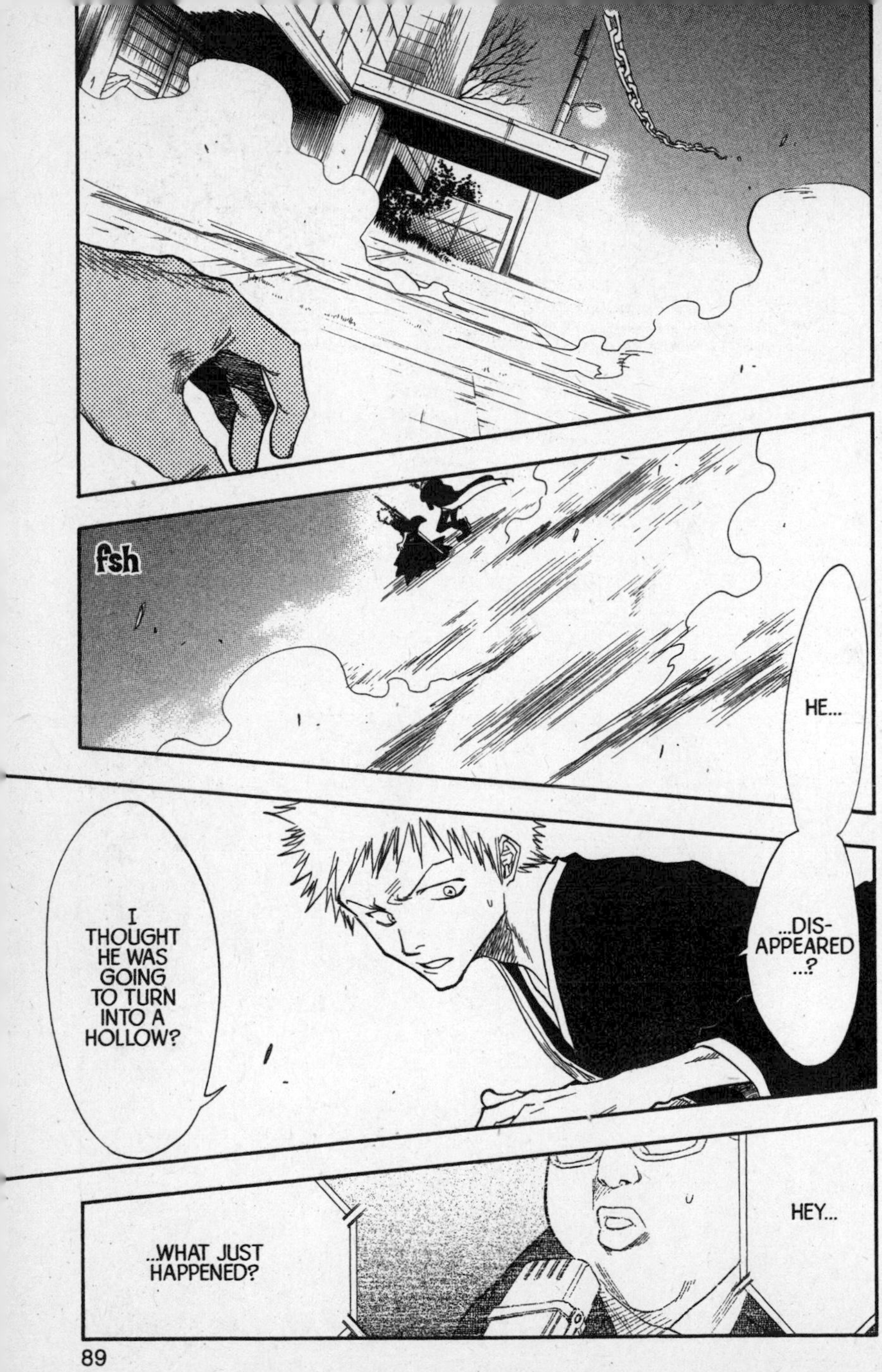
fsh
HE...
...DIS-APPEARED ...?
I THOUGHT HE WAS GOING TO TURN INTO A HOLLOW?
HEY...
...WHAT JUST HAPPENED?

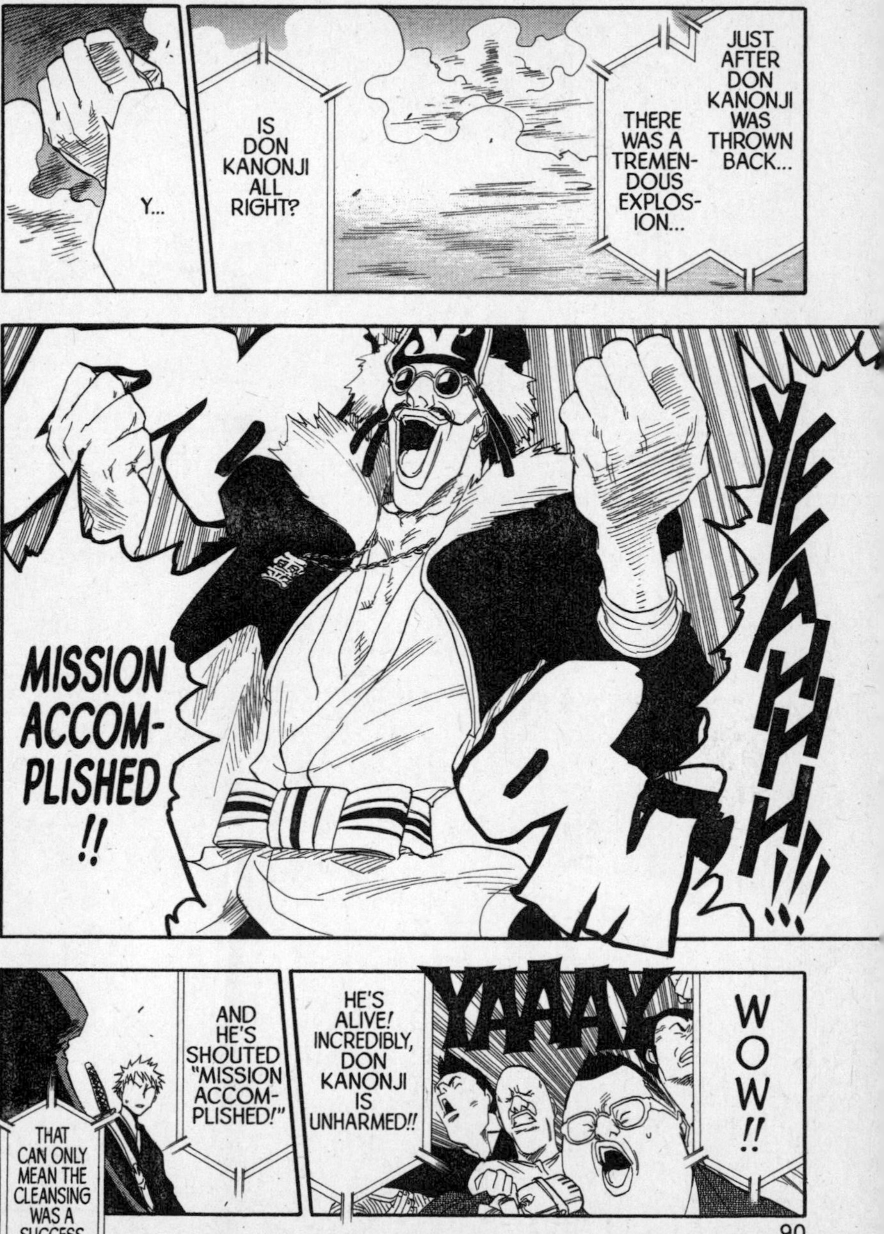
JUST AFTER DON KANONJI WAS THROWN BACK...
THERE WAS A TREMENDOUS EXPLOSION...
IS DON KANONJI ALL RIGHT?
Y...
YEAAHHH!!!
MISSION ACCOMPLISHED!!
WOW!!
YAAAY
HE'S ALIVE! INCREDIBLY, DON KANONJI IS UNHARMED!!
AND HE'S SHOUTED "MISSION ACCOMPLISHED!"
THAT CAN ONLY MEAN THE CLEANSING WAS A SUCCESS!!

READ THIS WAY

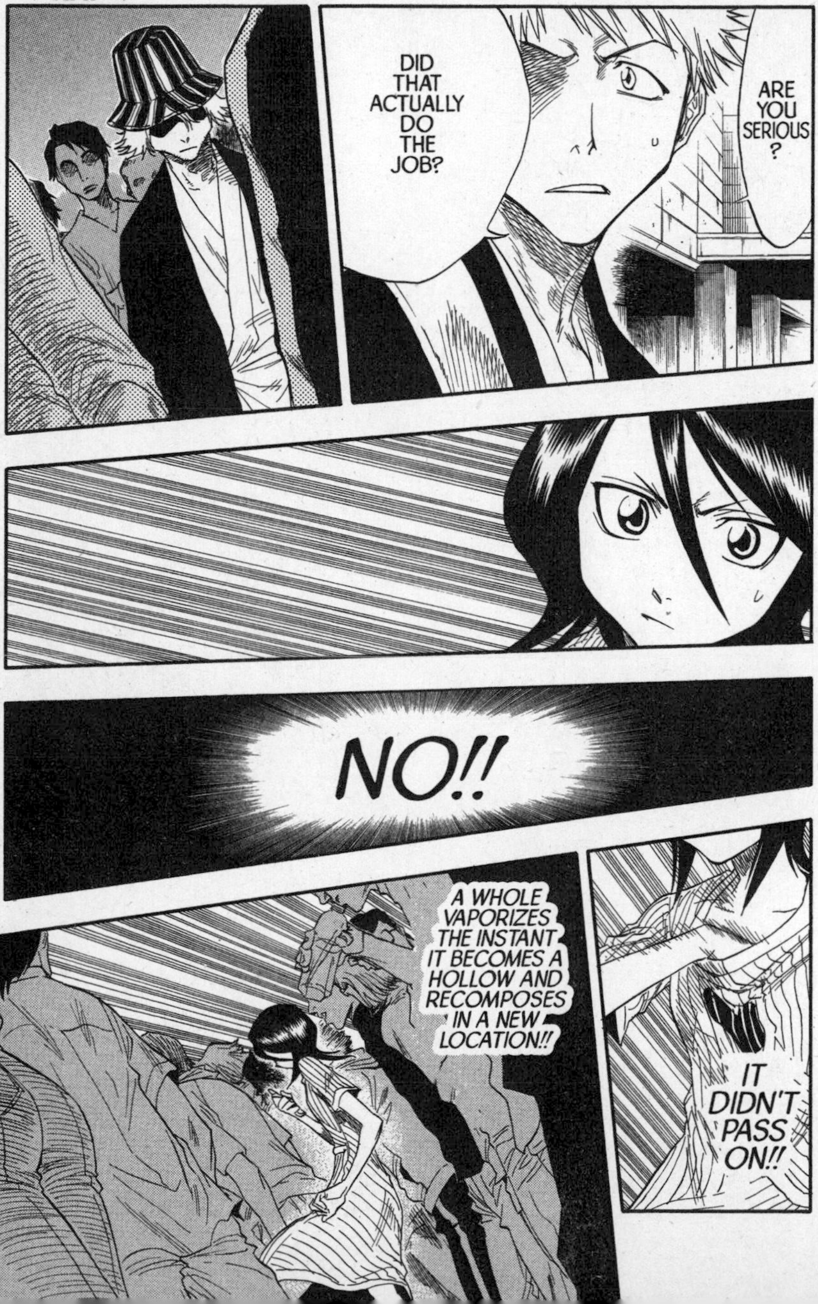
ARE YOU SERIOUS?
DID THAT ACTUALLY DO THE JOB?
NO!!
IT DIDN'T PASS ON!!
A WHOLE VAPORIZES THE INSTANT IT BECOMES A HOLLOW AND RECOMPOSES IN A NEW LOCATION!!

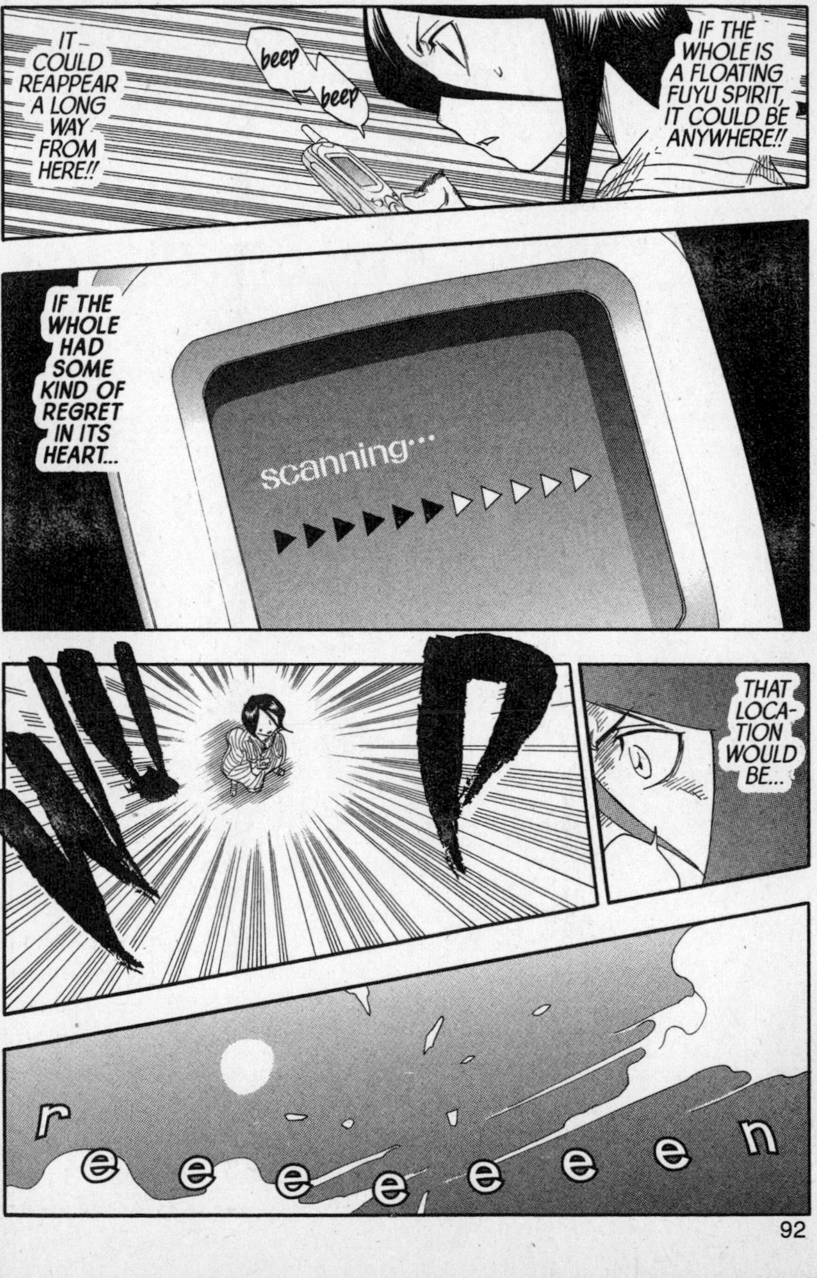
IF THE WHOLE IS A FLOATING FUYU SPIRIT, IT COULD BE ANYWHERE!!
beep
beep
IT COULD REAPPEAR A LONG WAY FROM HERE!!
IF THE WHOLE HAD SOME KIND OF REGRET IN ITS HEART...
scanning···
THAT LOCATION WOULD BE...
r e e e e e e e n

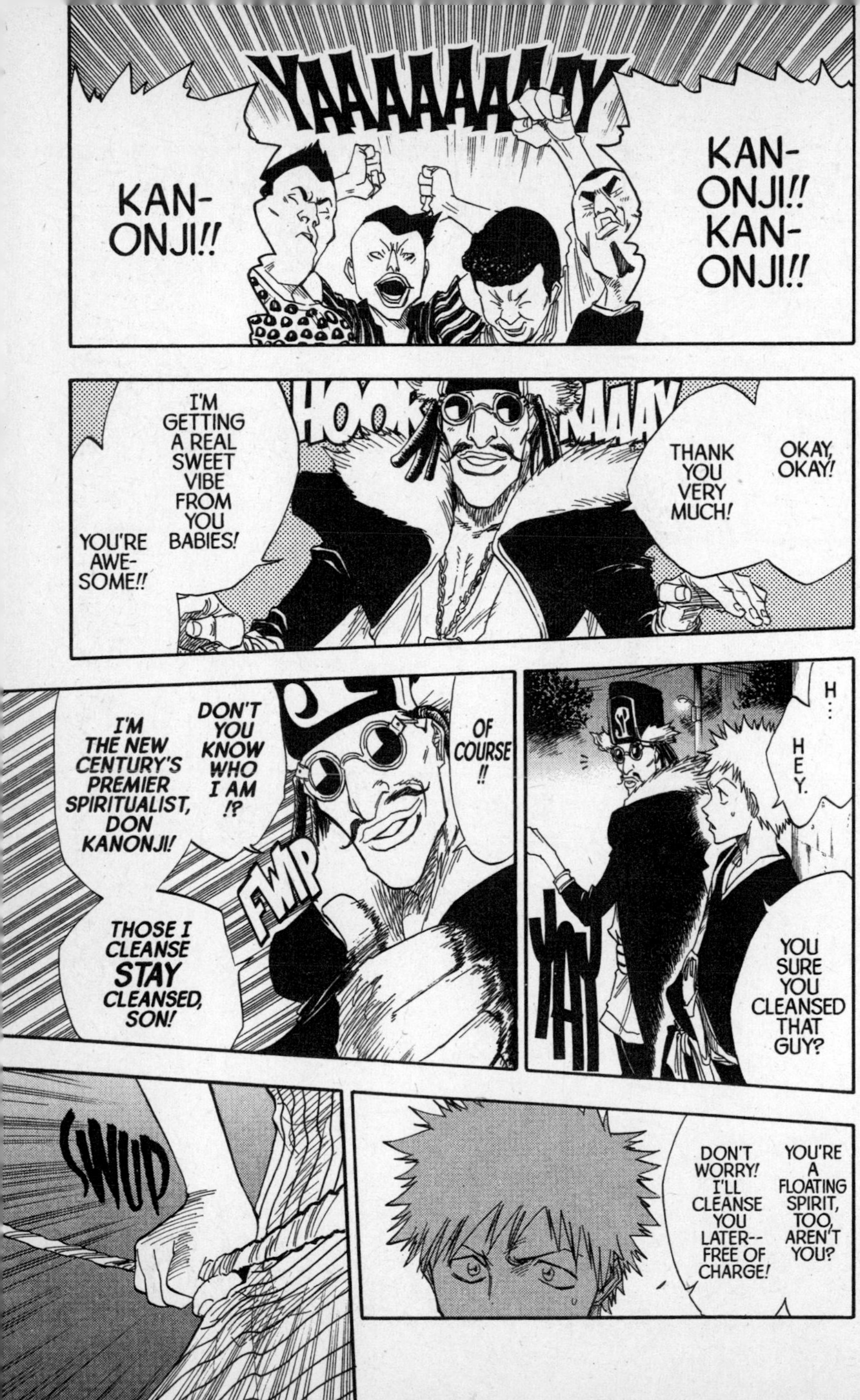
YAAAAAAAY
KAN-ONJI!! KAN-ONJI!!
KAN-ONJI!!
OKAY, OKAY!
THANK YOU VERY MUCH!
I'M GETTING A REAL SWEET VIBE FROM YOU BABIES!
YOU'RE AWE-SOME!!
H... HEY.
YOU SURE YOU CLEANSED THAT GUY?
YAY
OF COURSE!!
DON'T YOU KNOW WHO I AM!?
I'M THE NEW CENTURY'S PREMIER SPIRITUALIST, DON KANONJI!
FWIP
THOSE I CLEANSE STAY CLEANSED, SON!
YOU'RE A FLOATING SPIRIT, TOO, AREN'T YOU?
DON'T WORRY! I'LL CLEANSE YOU LATER-- FREE OF CHARGE!
SWUP

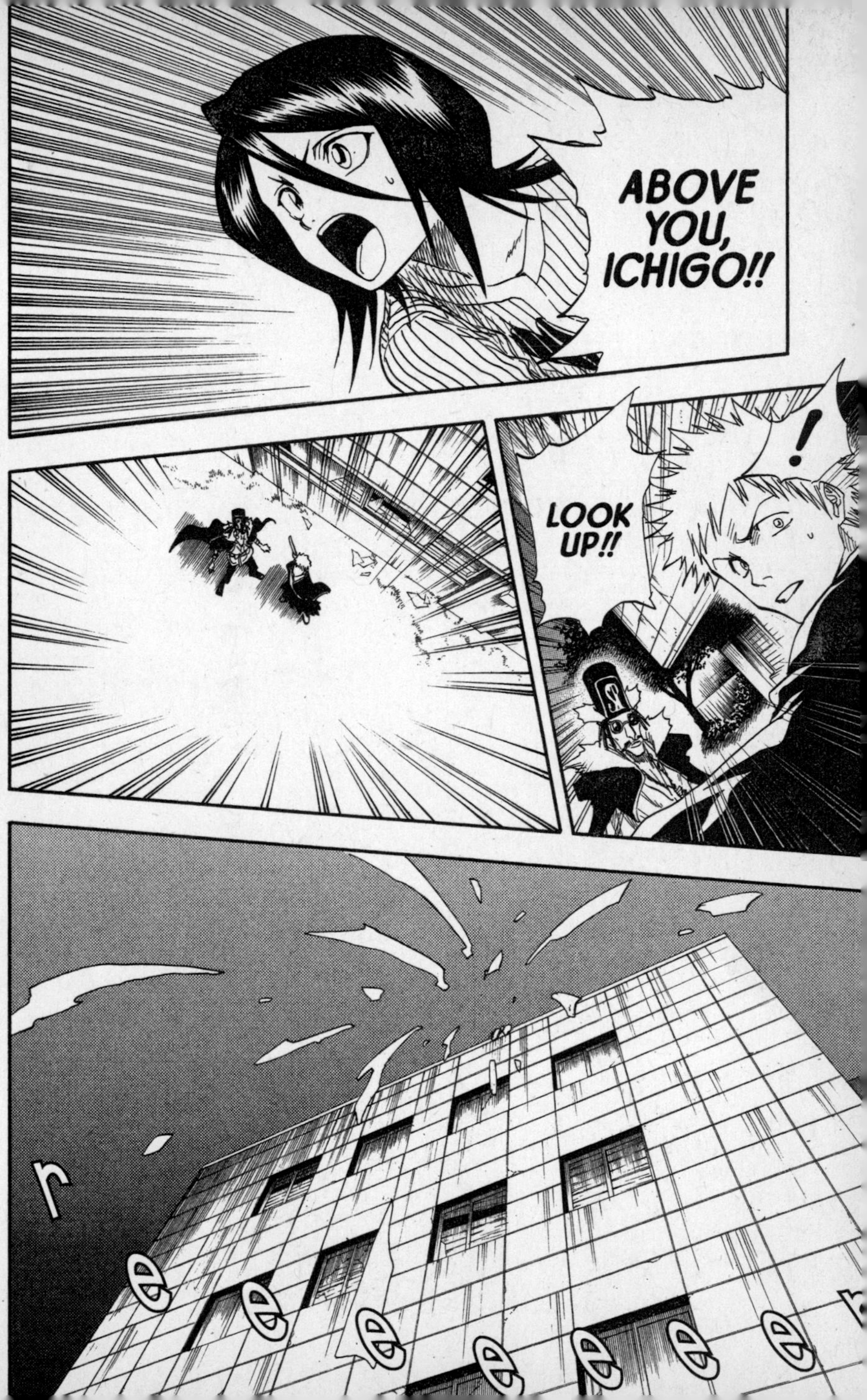
ABOVE YOU, ICHIGO!!
!
LOOK UP!!

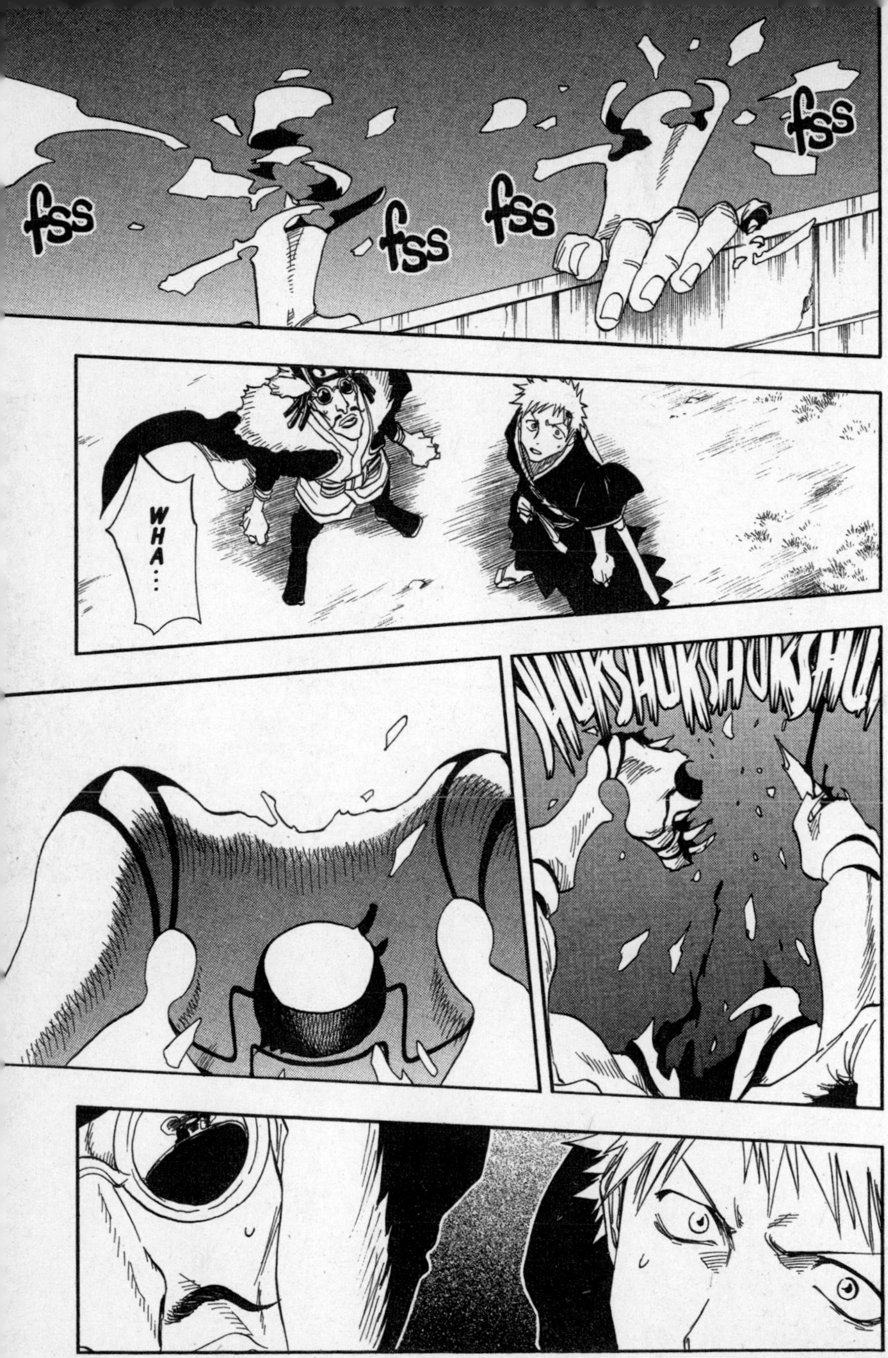
fss
fss
fss
fss
WHA...
SHUKSHUKSHUKSHU

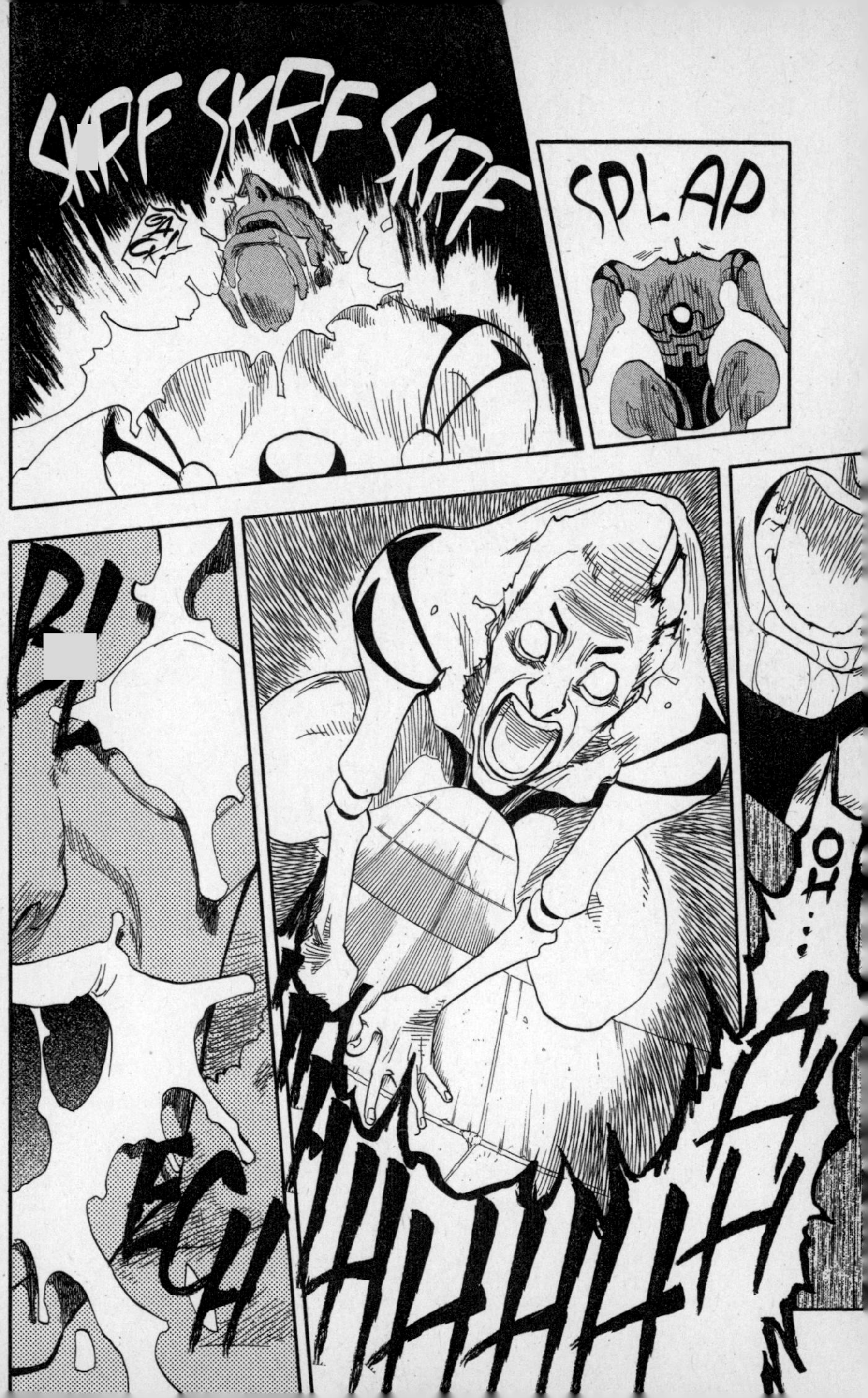
SPLAP
SKRF SKRF SKRF
GACK
OH...
AAAHHHHH
AAAHHHHH
BLECH

READ THIS WAY

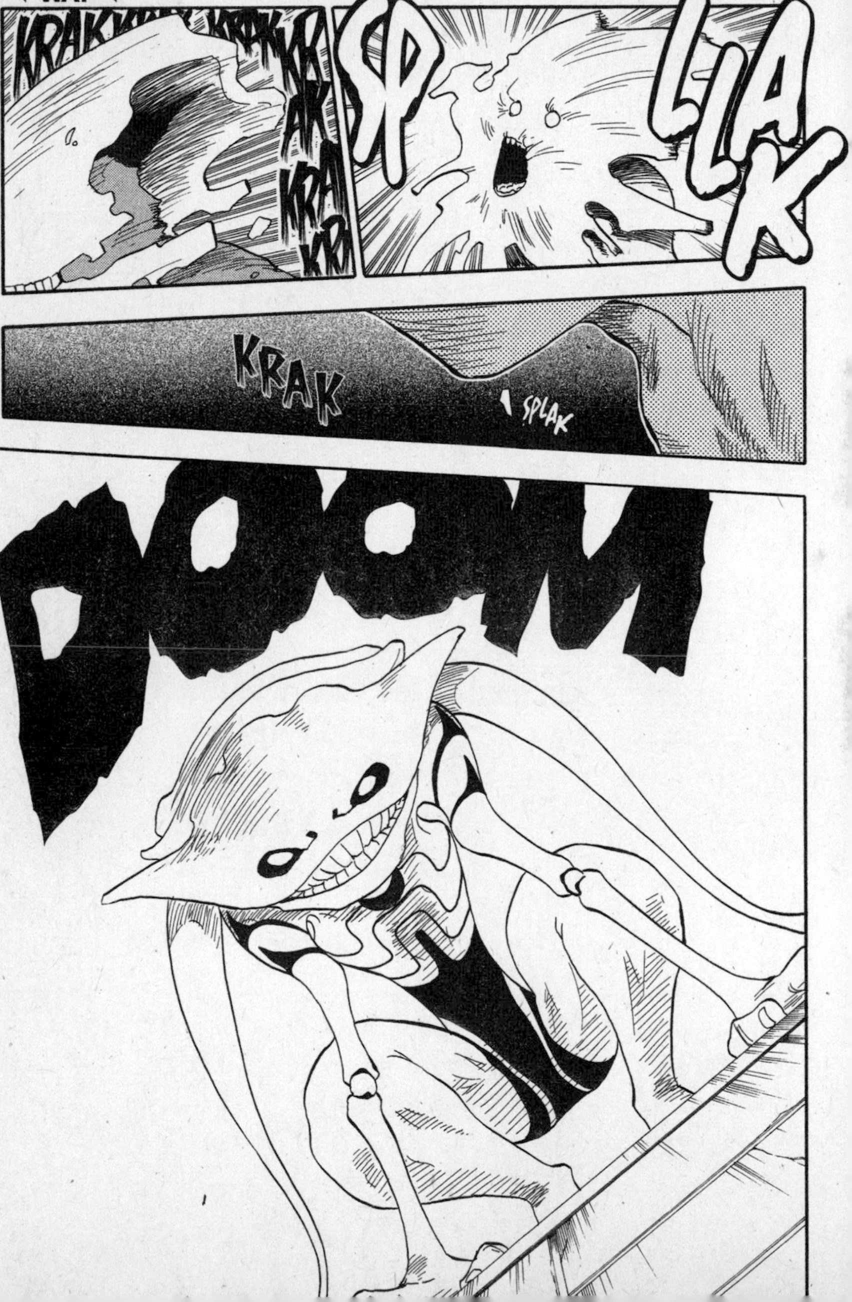
SPLLAK
KRAK KRAK KRAK KRAK KRAK
KRAK
SPLAK
DOOM

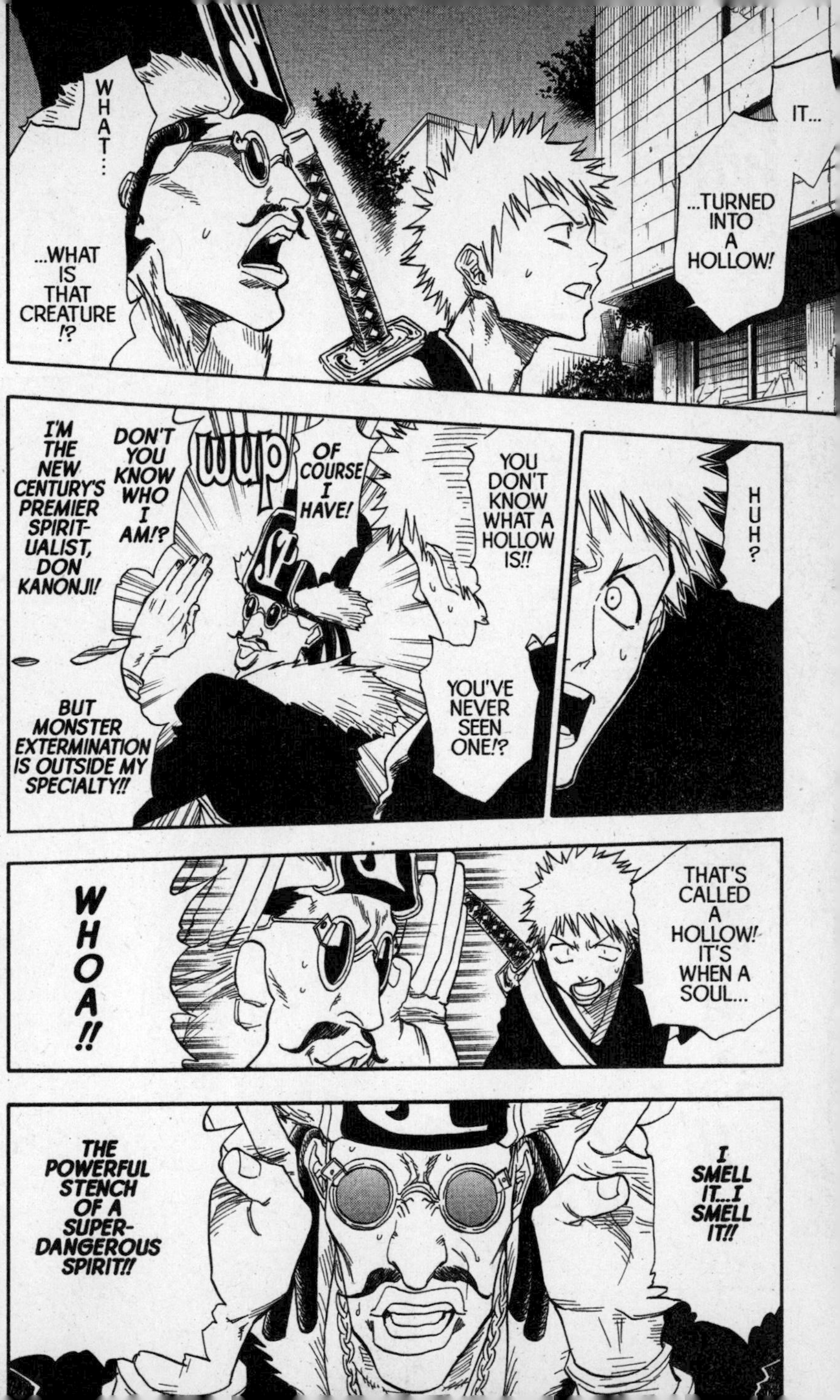
IT...
...TURNED INTO A HOLLOW!
WHAT...
...WHAT IS THAT CREATURE!?
HUH?
YOU DON'T KNOW WHAT A HOLLOW IS!!
YOU'VE NEVER SEEN ONE!?
OF COURSE I HAVE!
wup
DON'T YOU KNOW WHO I AM!?
I'M THE NEW CENTURY'S PREMIER SPIRITUALIST, DON KANONJI!
BUT MONSTER EXTERMINATION IS OUTSIDE MY SPECIALTY!!
THAT'S CALLED A HOLLOW! IT'S WHEN A SOUL...
WHOA!!
I SMELL IT...I SMELL IT!!
THE POWERFUL STENCH OF A SUPER-DANGEROUS SPIRIT!!

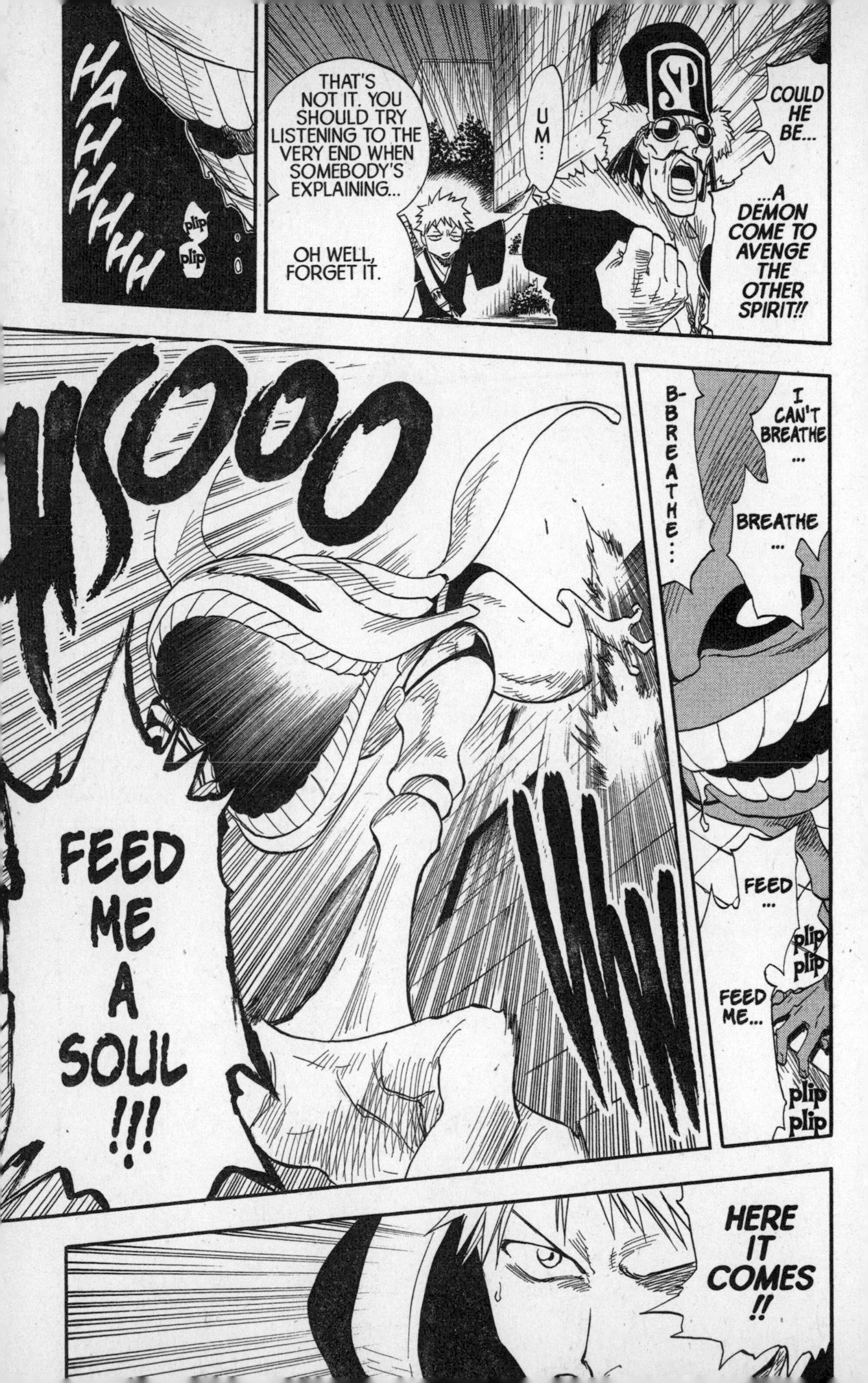
COULD HE BE...
...A DEMON COME TO AVENGE THE OTHER SPIRIT!!
UM...
THAT'S NOT IT. YOU SHOULD TRY LISTENING TO THE VERY END WHEN SOMEBODY'S EXPLAINING...
OH WELL, FORGET IT.
HAHHHHHH
plip plip
B-BREATHE...
I CAN'T BREATHE...
BREATHE...
FEED...
plip plip
FEED ME...
plip plip
HSOOO
FEED ME A SOUL!!!
HERE IT COMES!!

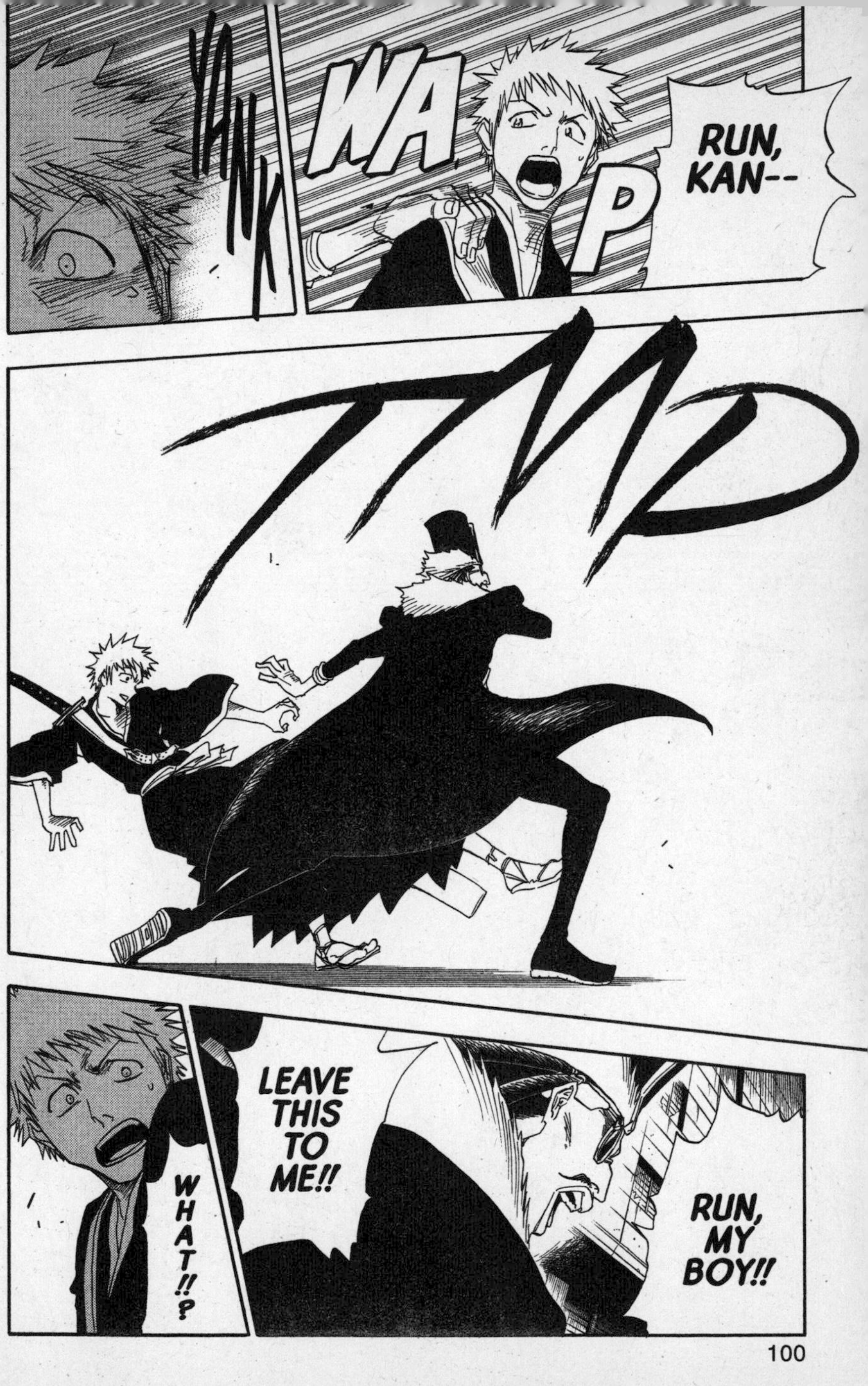

RUN, KAN--
WAP
YANK
TMP
RUN, MY BOY!!
LEAVE THIS TO ME!!
WHAT!!?

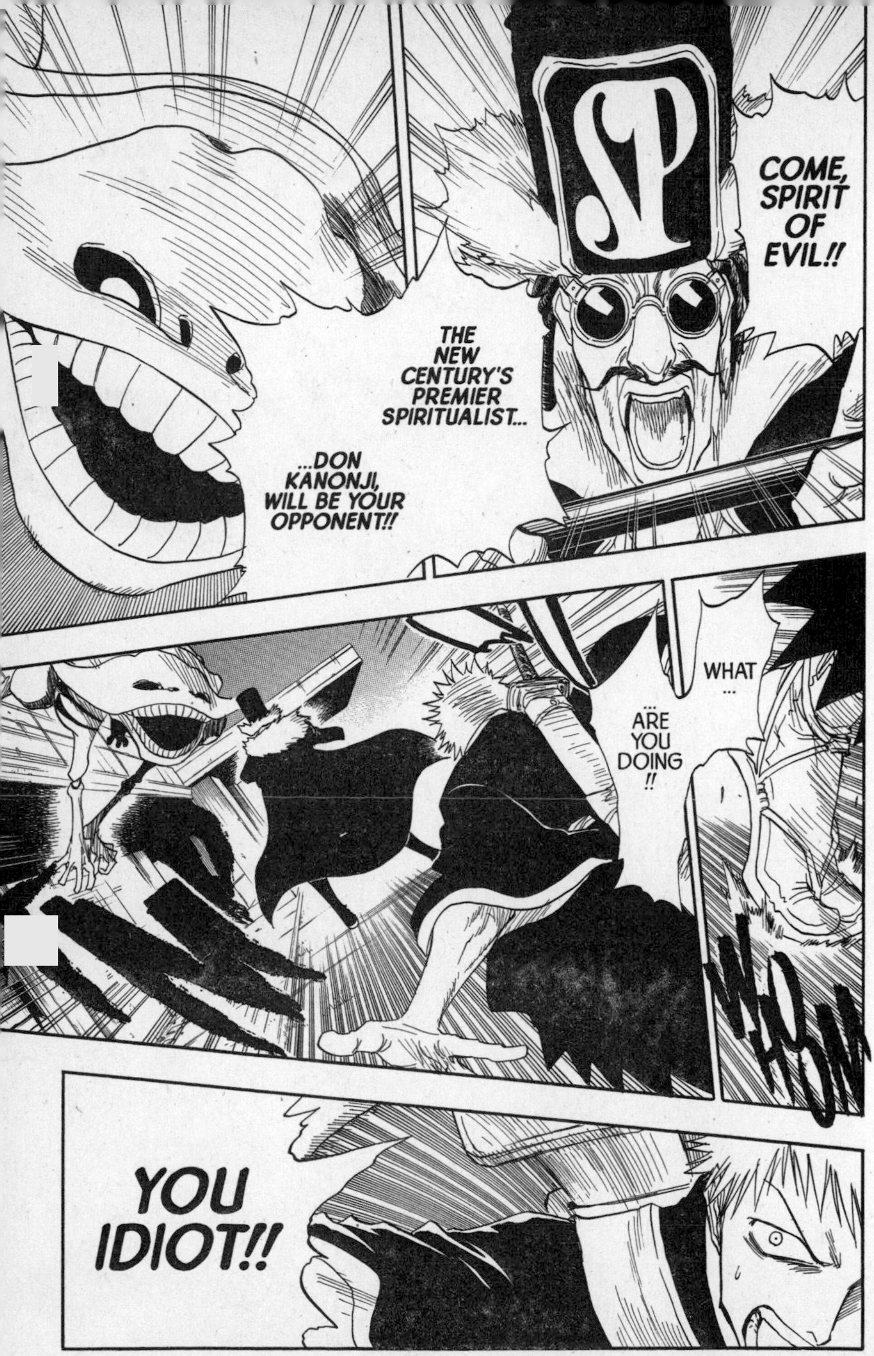
COME, SPIRIT OF EVIL!!
THE NEW CENTURY'S PREMIER SPIRITUALIST...
...DON KANONJI, WILL BE YOUR OPPONENT!!
WHAT ...
... ARE YOU DOING !!
WHOOM
YOU IDIOT!!

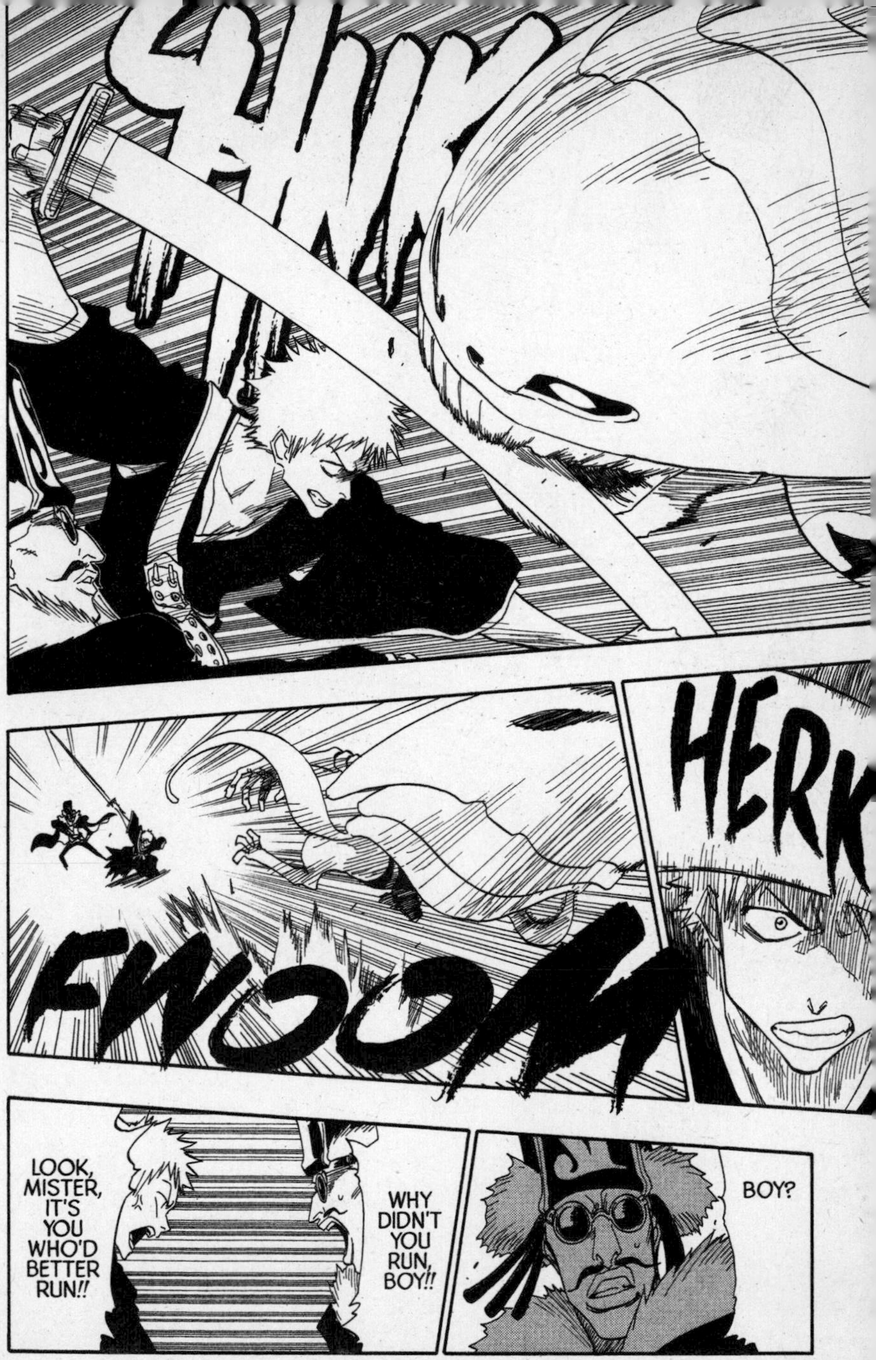
HERK
FWOOM
BOY?
WHY DIDN'T YOU RUN, BOY!!
LOOK, MISTER, IT'S YOU WHO'D BETTER RUN!!

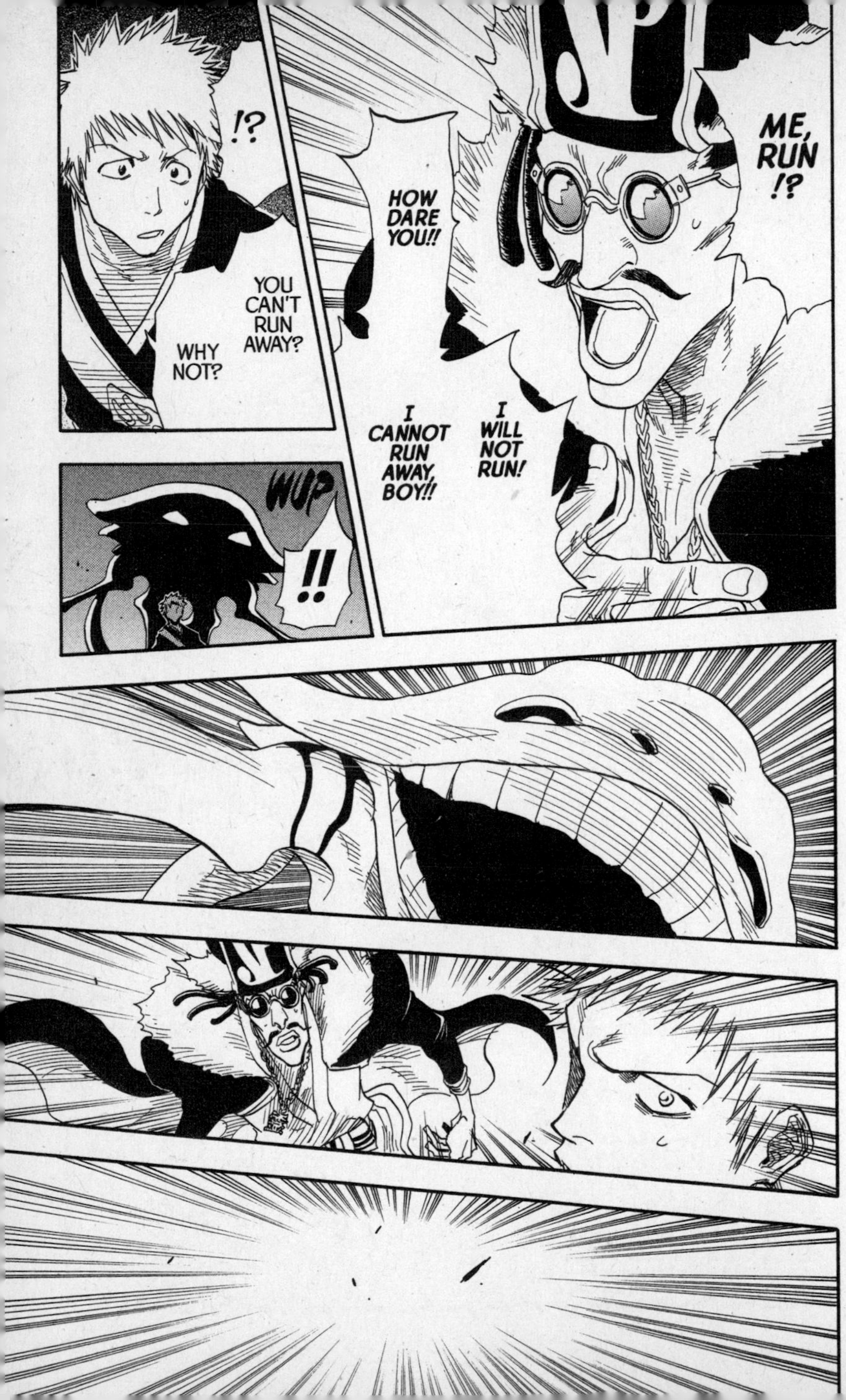
ME, RUN !?
HOW DARE YOU!!
I WILL NOT RUN!
I CANNOT RUN AWAY, BOY!!
!?
YOU CAN'T RUN AWAY?
WHY NOT?
WUP
!!

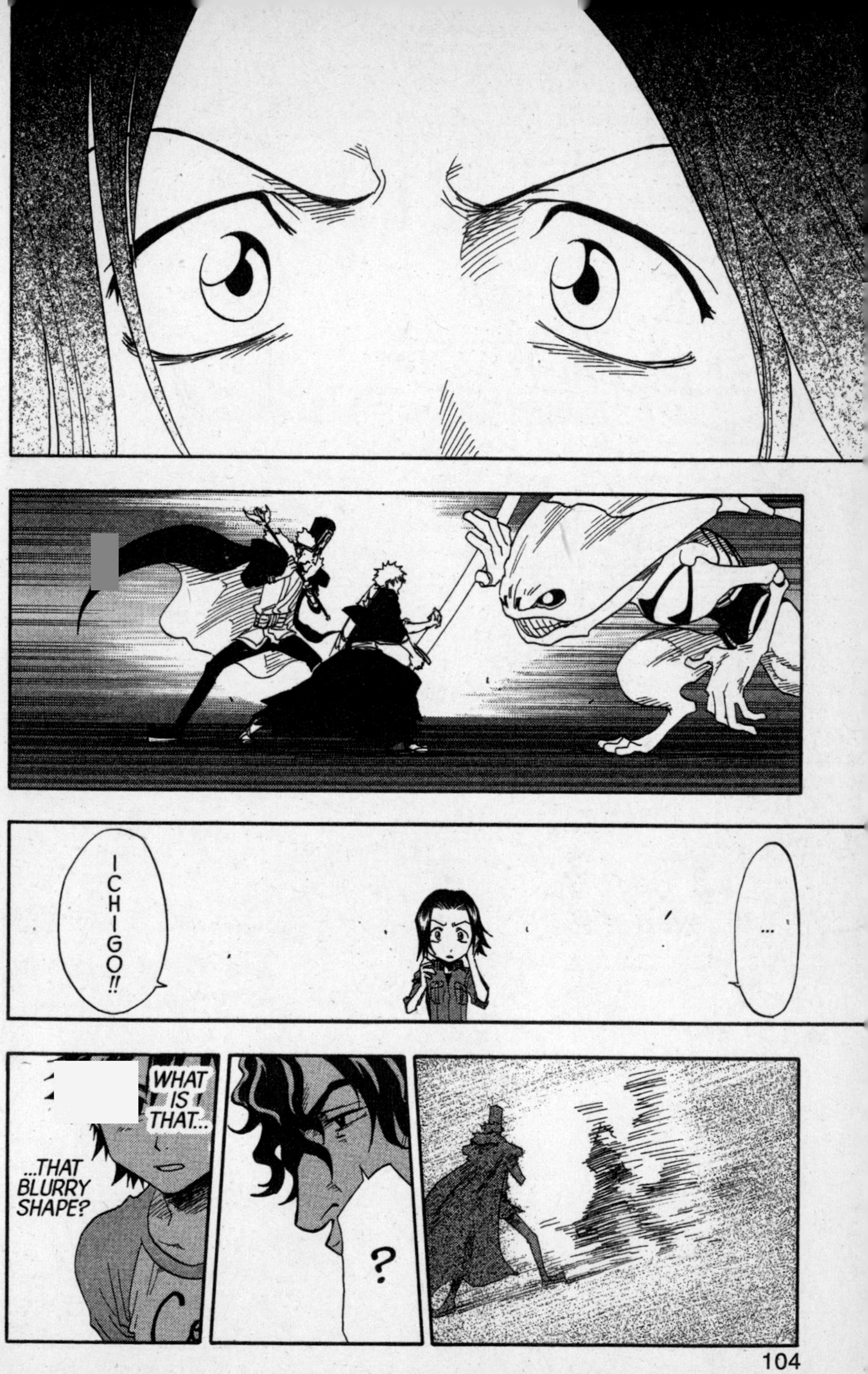
...
ICHIGO!!
?
WHAT IS THAT...
...THAT BLURRY SHAPE?

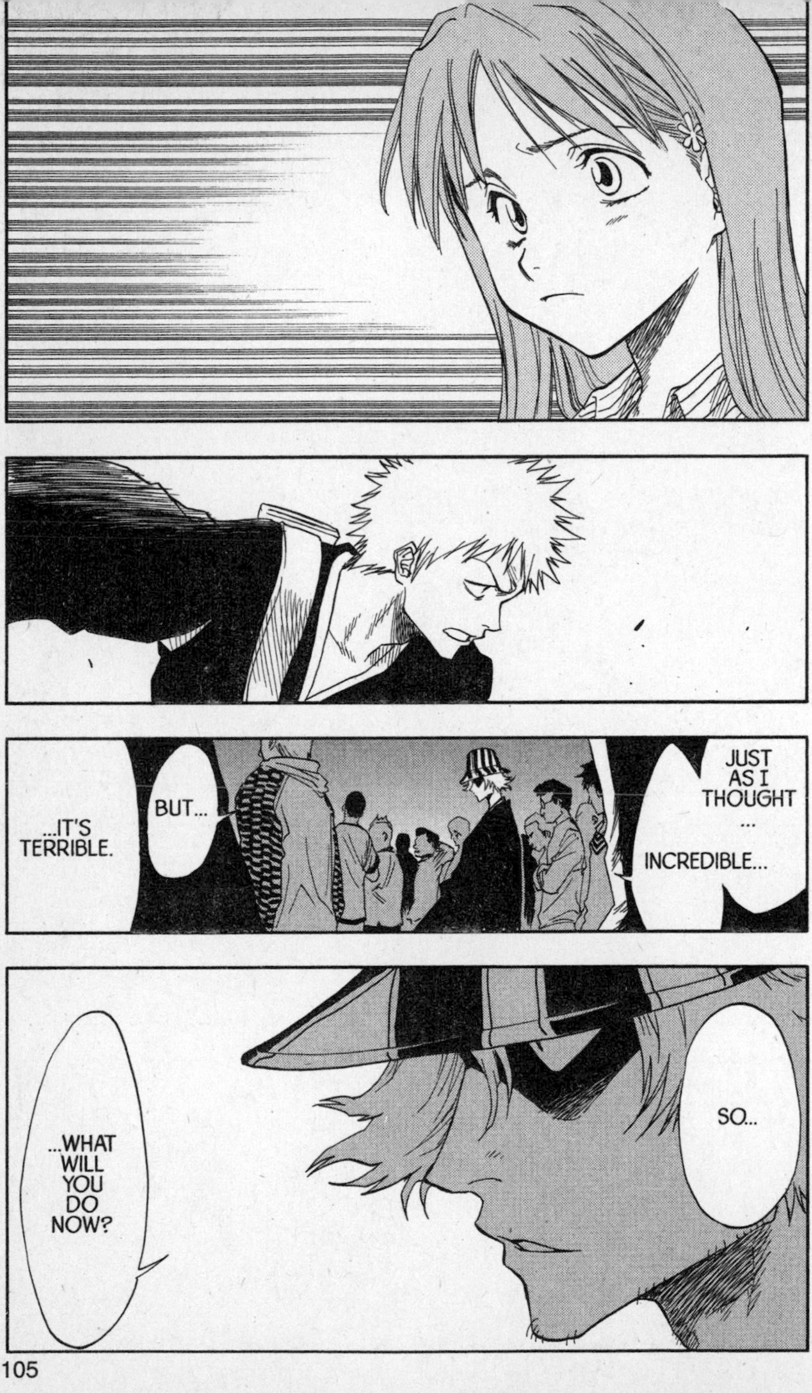
JUST AS I THOUGHT ...
INCREDIBLE...
BUT...
...IT'S TERRIBLE.
SO...
...WHAT WILL YOU DO NOW?

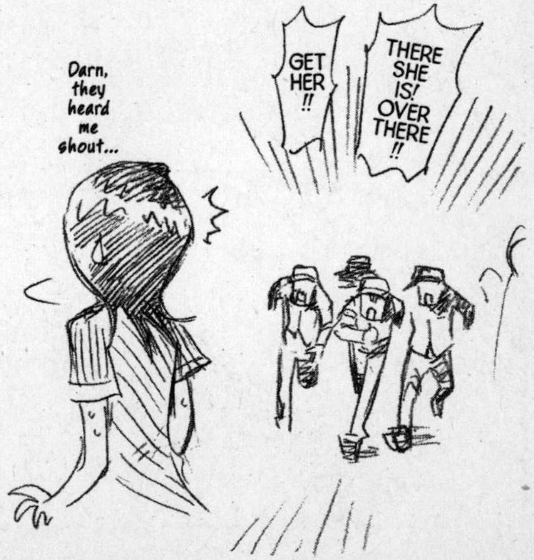
THERE SHE IS! OVER THERE!!
GET HER!!
Darn, they heard me shout...

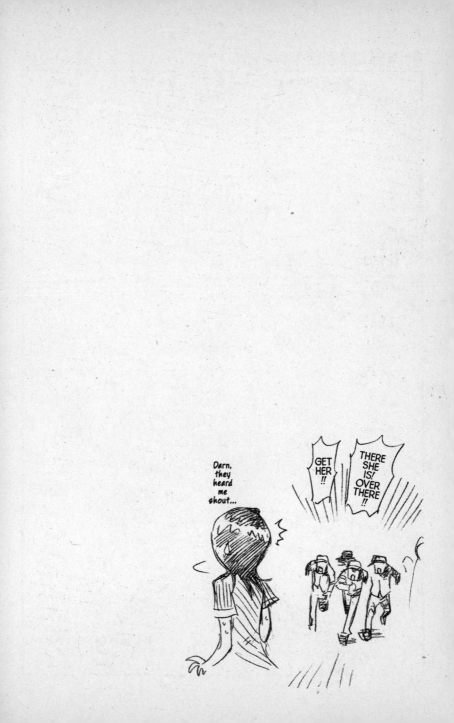

31. HEROES CAN SAVE YOU

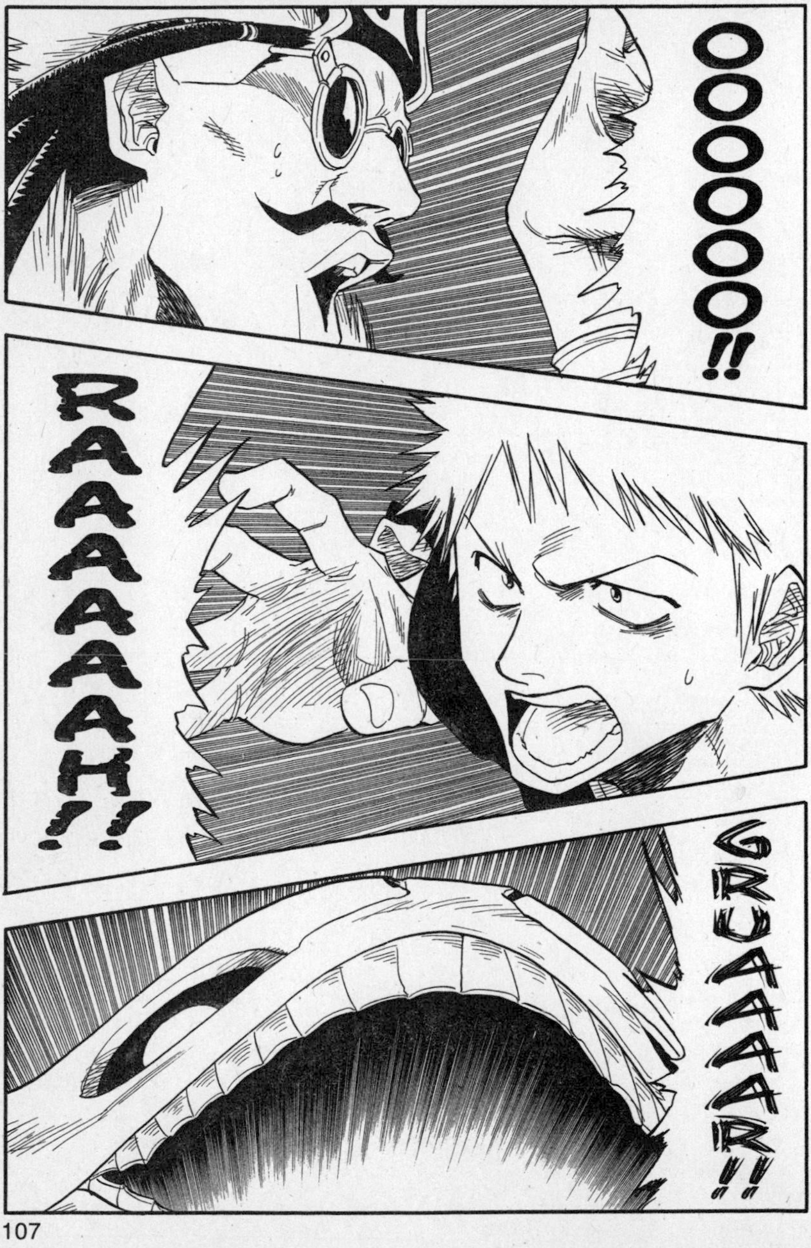
OOOOOO!!
RAAAAAAH!!
GRUAAAAR!!

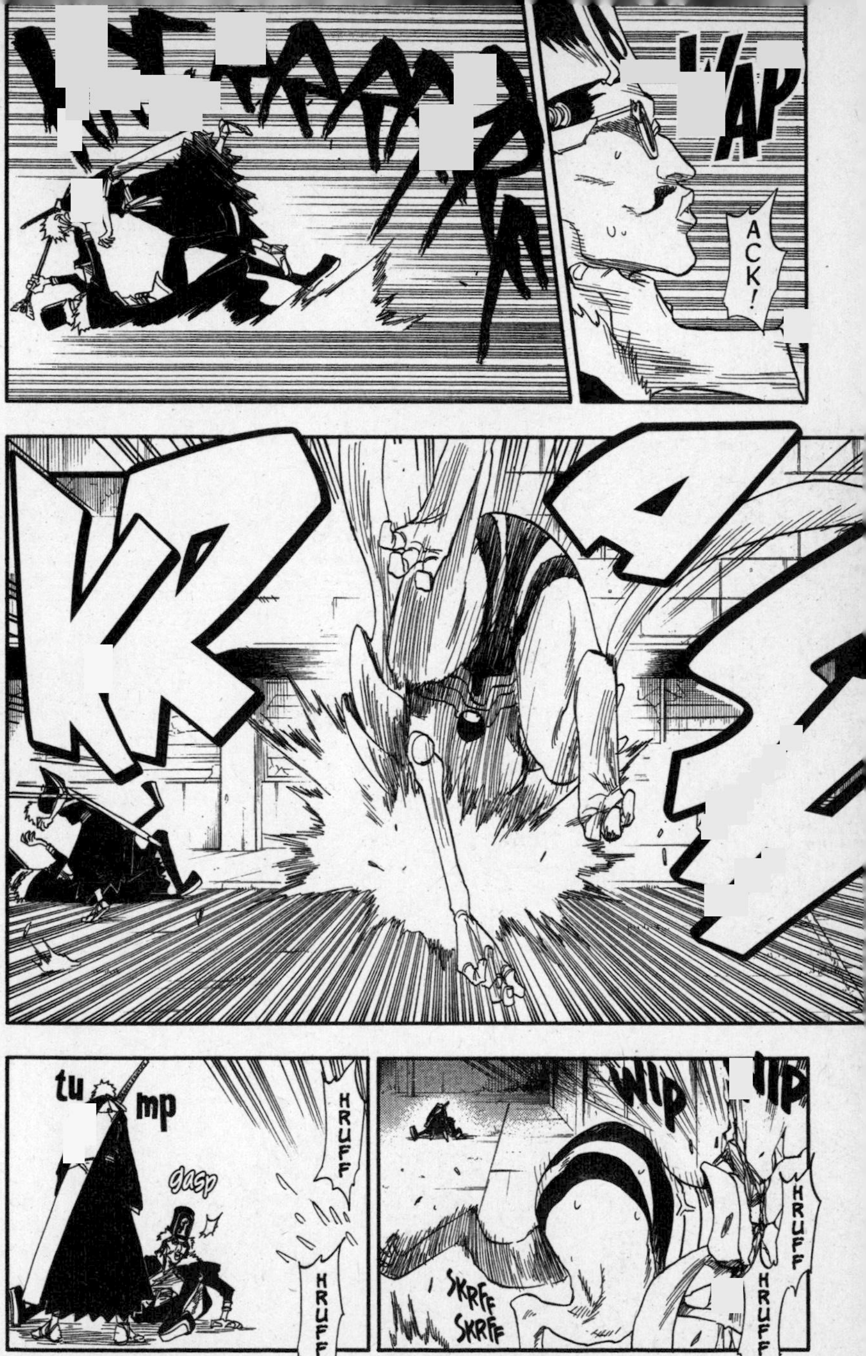
WAP
ACK!
WIP
HRUFF
HRUFF
SKRFF
SKRFF
HRUFF
HRUFF
gasp
tu mp

READ THIS WAY

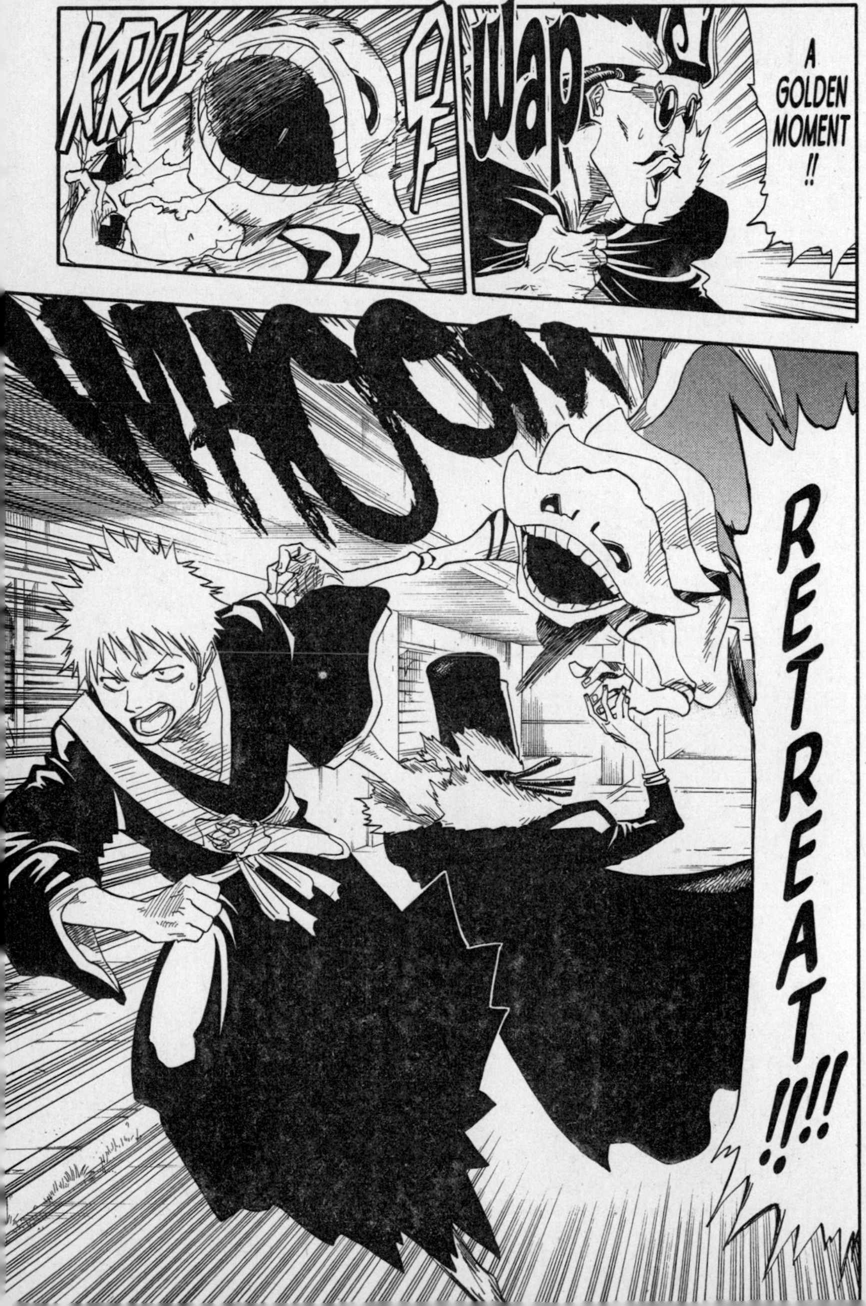
wap
A GOLDEN MOMENT !!
KROOF
RETREAT !!!!

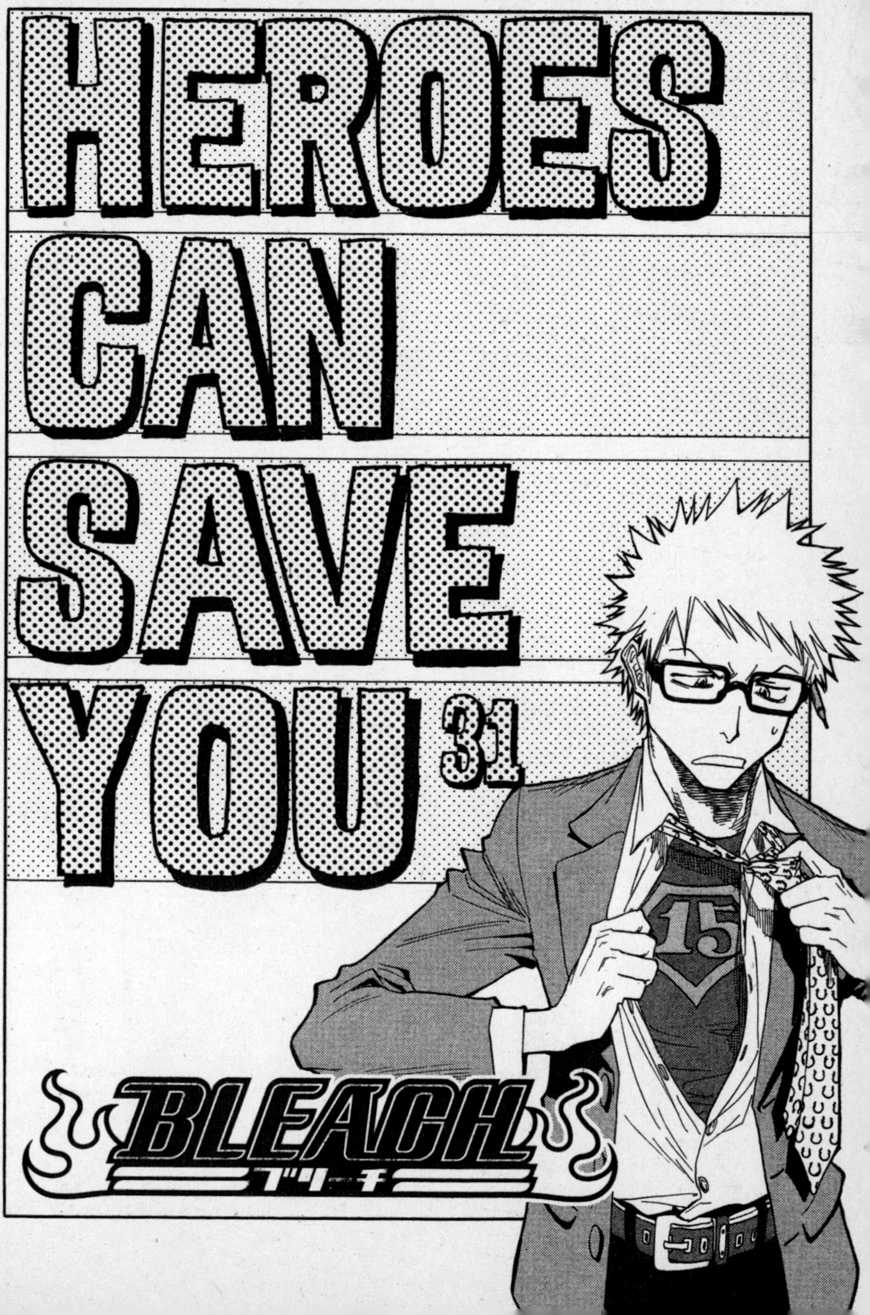
HEROES
CAN
SAVE
YOU
31
BLEACH
ブリーチ
15

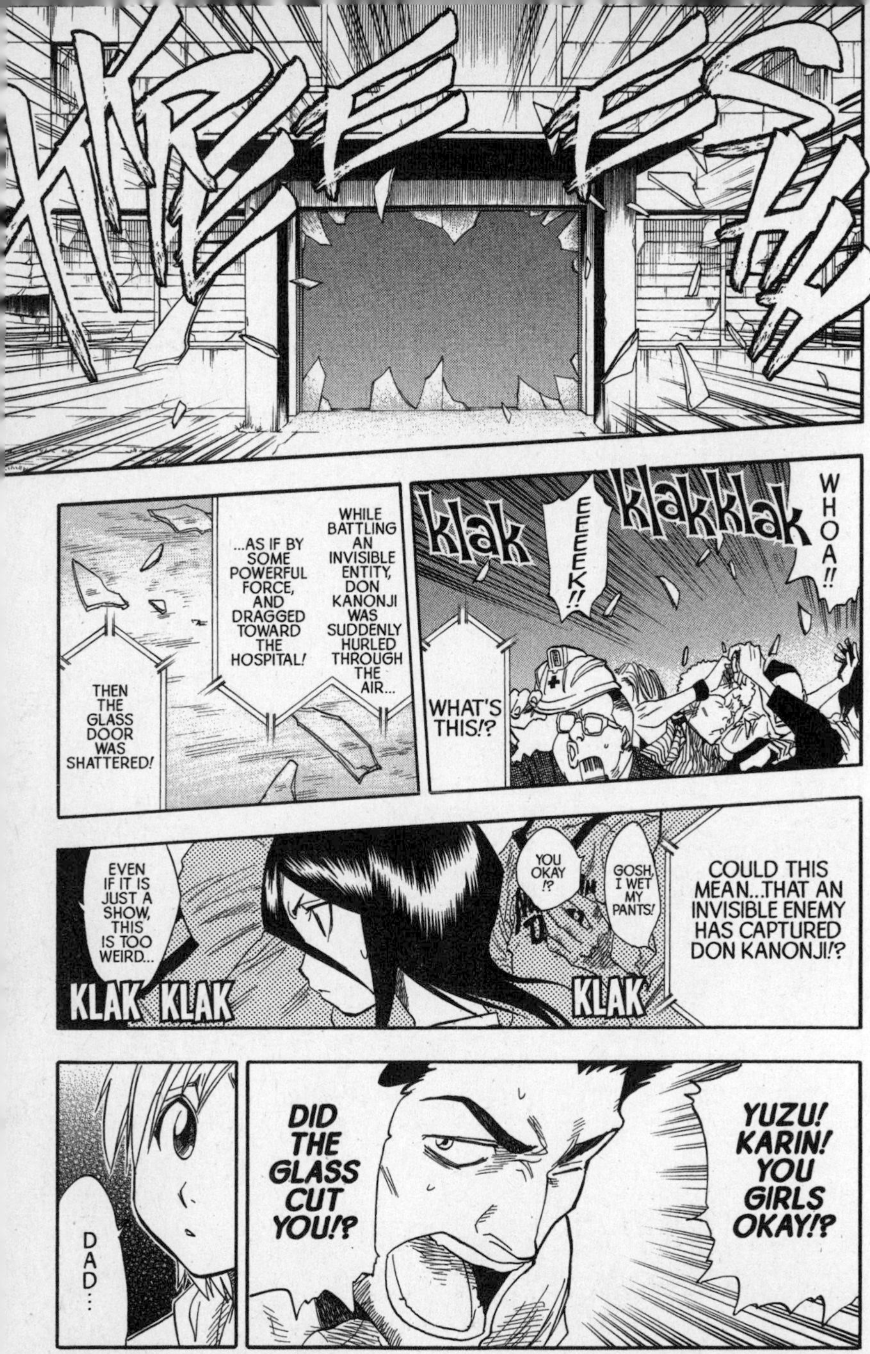
KREESH!!
WHOA!!
klakklak
EEEEK!!
klak
WHAT'S THIS!?
WHILE BATTLING AN INVISIBLE ENTITY, DON KANONJI WAS SUDDENLY HURLED THROUGH THE AIR...
...AS IF BY SOME POWERFUL FORCE, AND DRAGGED TOWARD THE HOSPITAL!
THEN THE GLASS DOOR WAS SHATTERED!
COULD THIS MEAN...THAT AN INVISIBLE ENEMY HAS CAPTURED DON KANONJI!?
GOSH, I WET MY PANTS!
YOU OKAY!?
KLAK
EVEN IF IT IS JUST A SHOW, THIS IS TOO WEIRD...
KLAK KLAK
YUZU! KARIN! YOU GIRLS OKAY!?
DID THE GLASS CUT YOU!?
DAD...

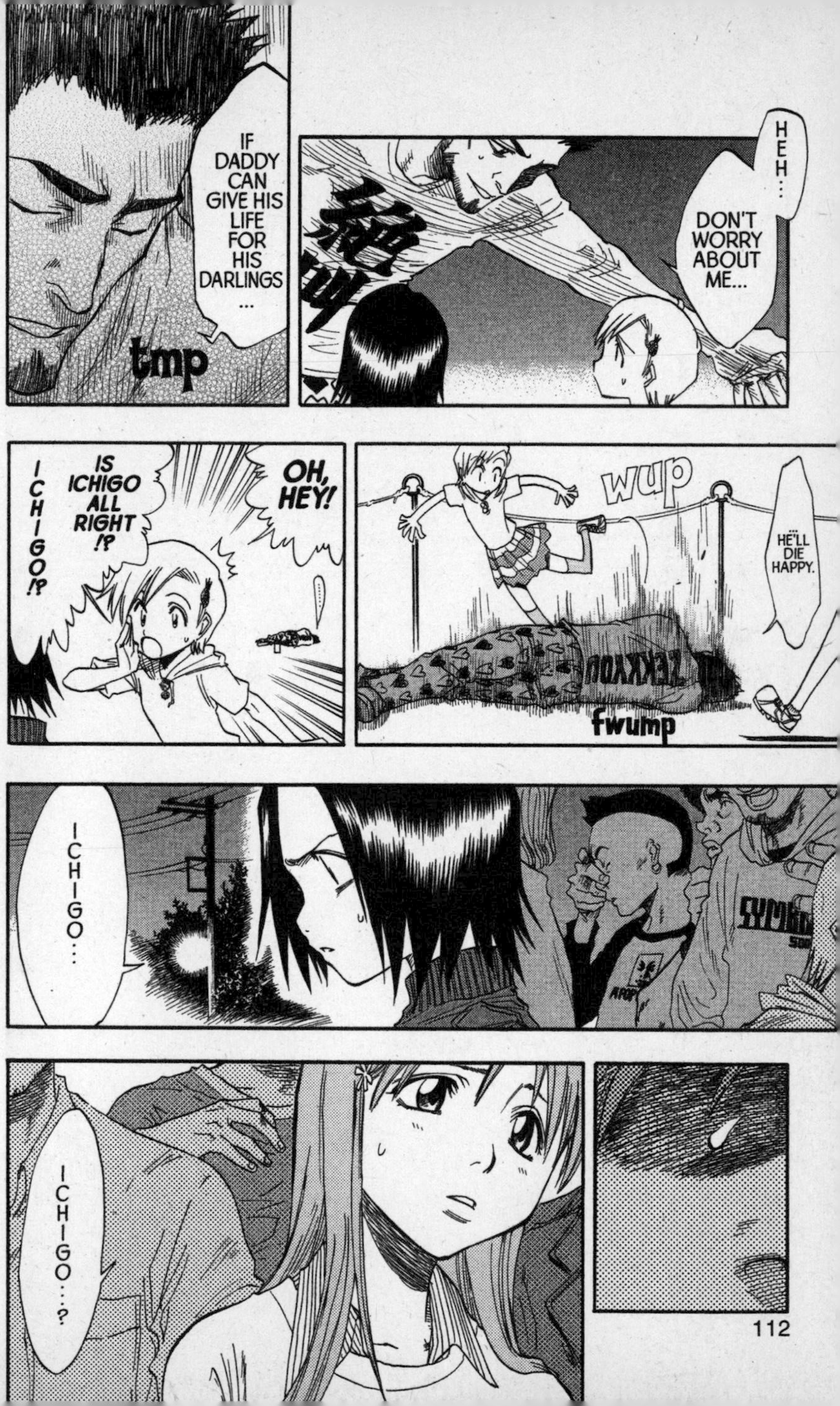
HEH... DON'T WORRY ABOUT ME...
IF DADDY CAN GIVE HIS LIFE FOR HIS DARLINGS...
tmp
wup
...HE'LL DIE HAPPY.
ZEKKYOU
fwump
OH, HEY!
IS ICHIGO ALL RIGHT!?
ICHIGO!?
ICHIGO...
ICHIGO...?

READ THIS WAY

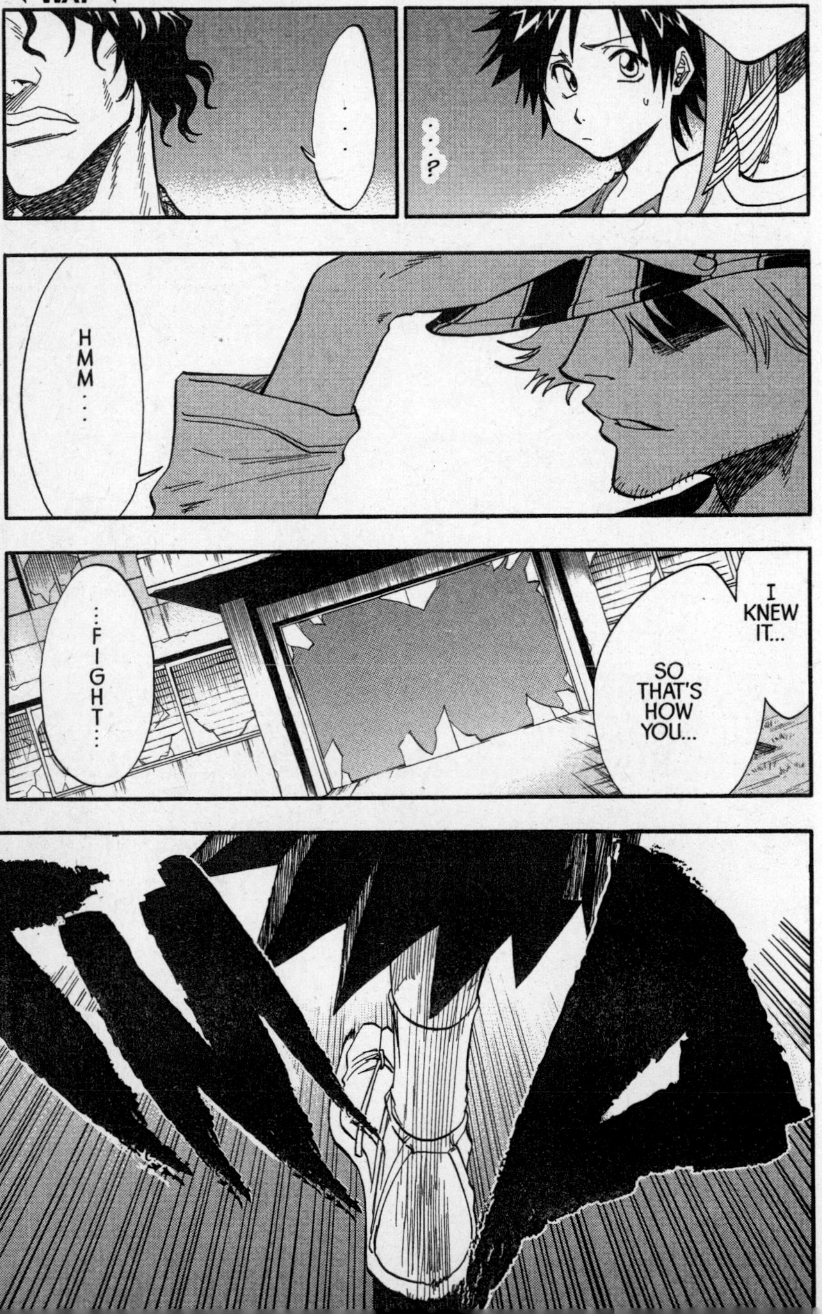
...?
...
HMM...
I KNEW IT...
SO THAT'S HOW YOU...
...FIGHT...

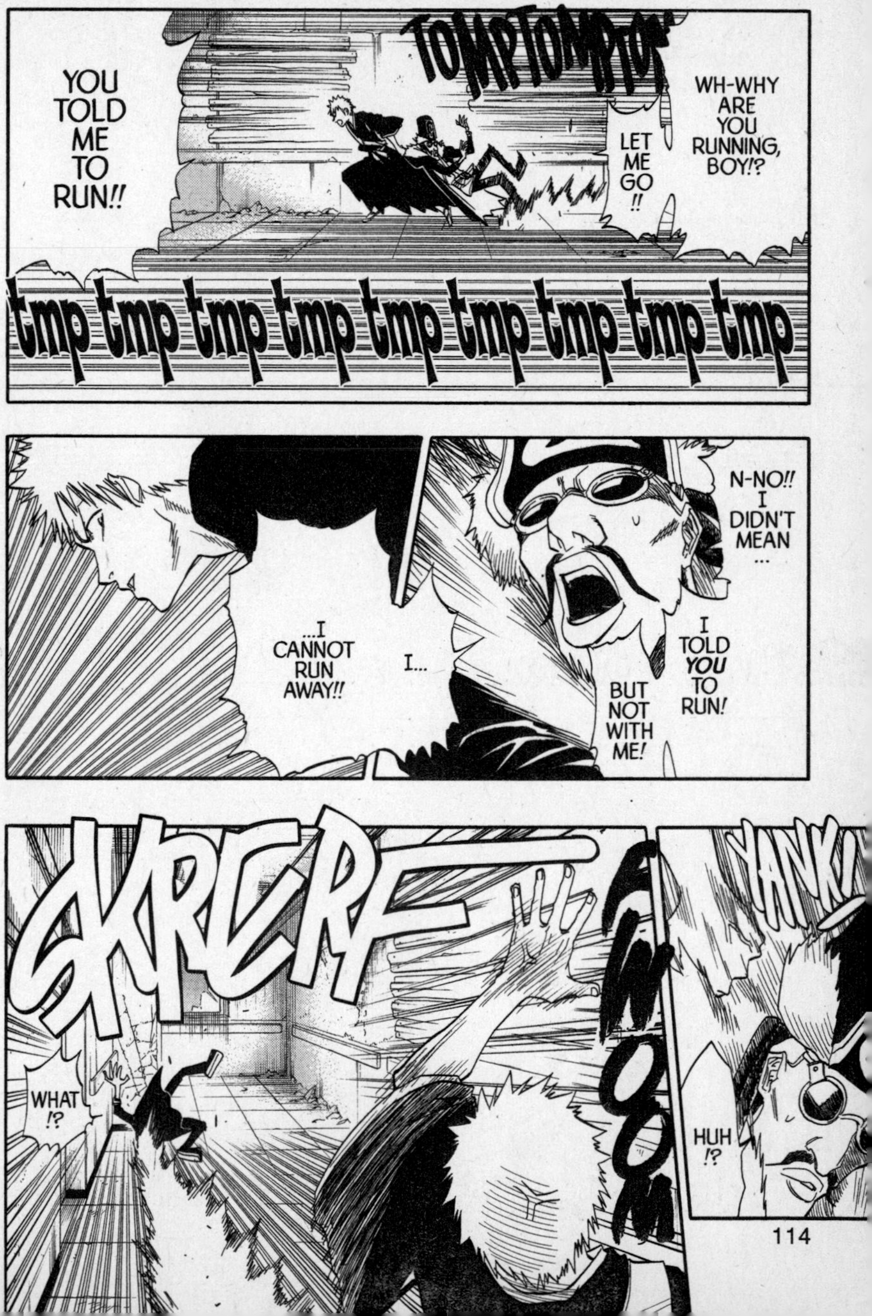
WH-WHY ARE YOU RUNNING, BOY!?
LET ME GO !!
YOU TOLD ME TO RUN!!
tmp tmp tmp tmp tmp tmp tmp tmp tmp
N-NO!! I DIDN'T MEAN ...
I TOLD *YOU* TO RUN!
BUT NOT WITH ME!
I...
...I CANNOT RUN AWAY!!
HUH !?
WHAT !?

READ THIS WAY

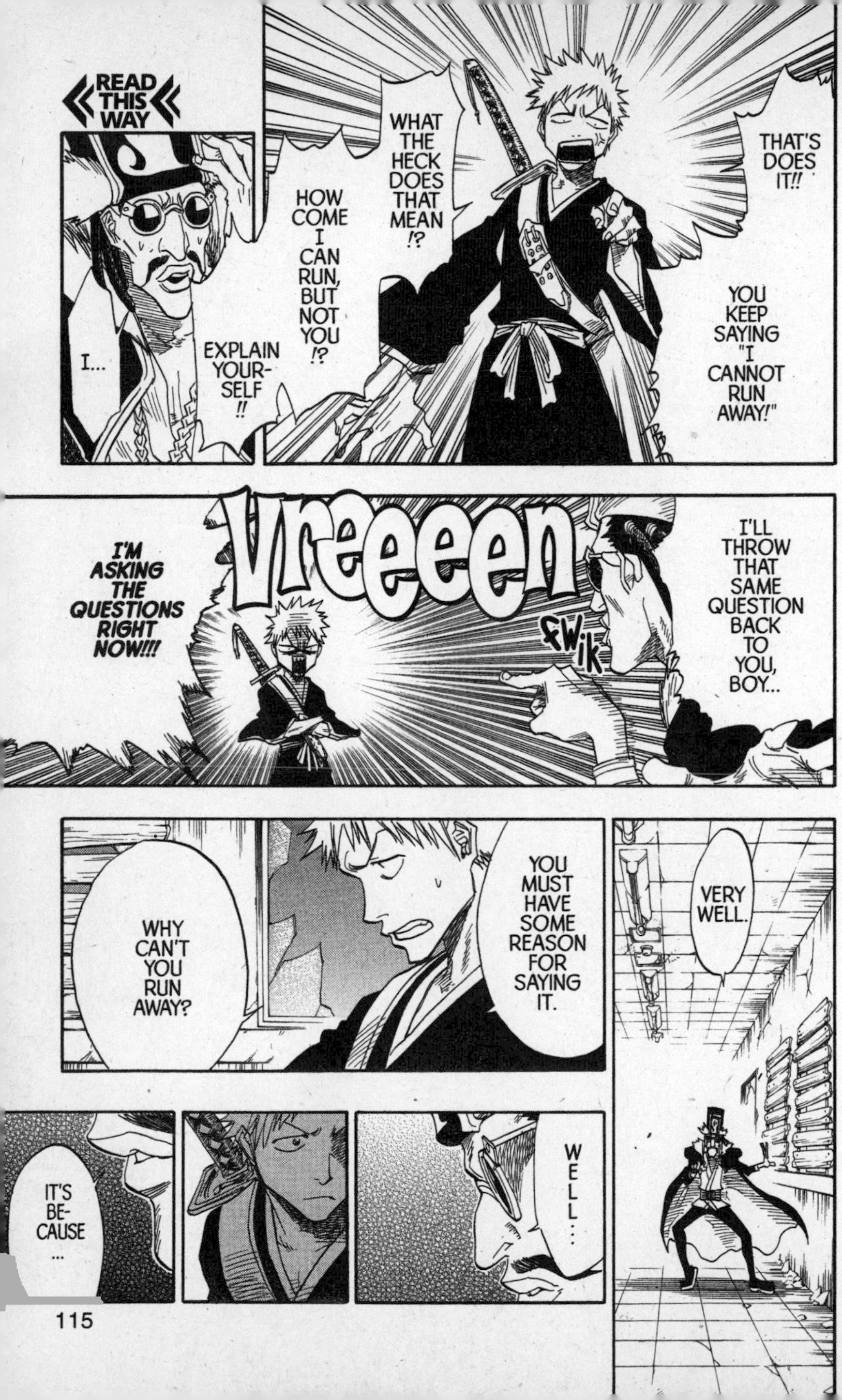
THAT'S DOES IT!!
YOU KEEP SAYING "I CANNOT RUN AWAY!"
WHAT THE HECK DOES THAT MEAN !?
HOW COME I CAN RUN, BUT NOT YOU !?
EXPLAIN YOUR-SELF !!
I...
I'LL THROW THAT SAME QUESTION BACK TO YOU, BOY...
fWik
Vreeeen
I'M ASKING THE QUESTIONS RIGHT NOW!!!
VERY WELL.
YOU MUST HAVE SOME REASON FOR SAYING IT.
WHY CAN'T YOU RUN AWAY?
WELL...
IT'S BE-CAUSE ...

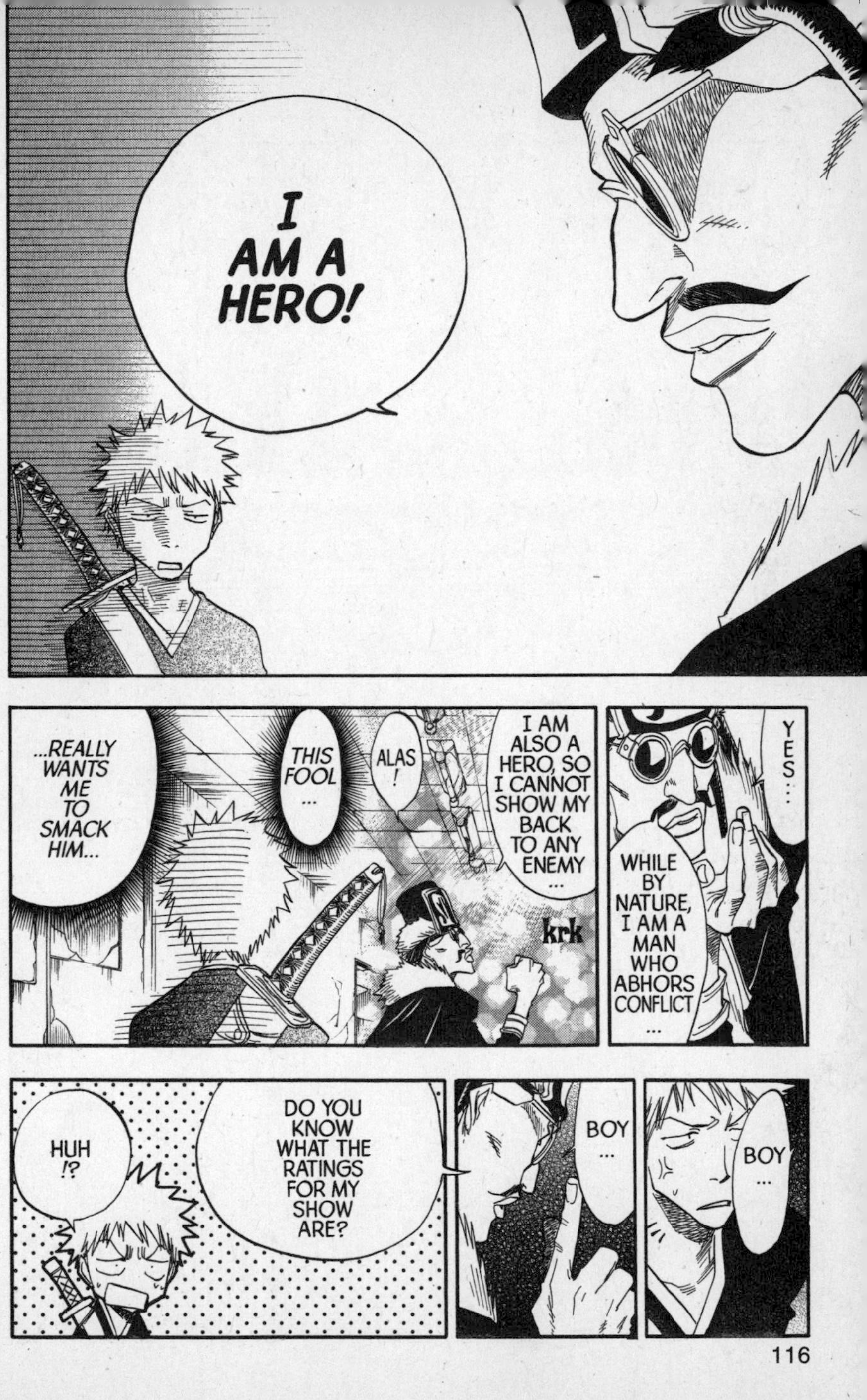
I AM A HERO!
YES...
WHILE BY NATURE, I AM A MAN WHO ABHORS CONFLICT...
I AM ALSO A HERO, SO I CANNOT SHOW MY BACK TO ANY ENEMY...
krk
ALAS!
THIS FOOL...
...REALLY WANTS ME TO SMACK HIM...
BOY...
BOY...
DO YOU KNOW WHAT THE RATINGS FOR MY SHOW ARE?
HUH!?

READ THIS WAY

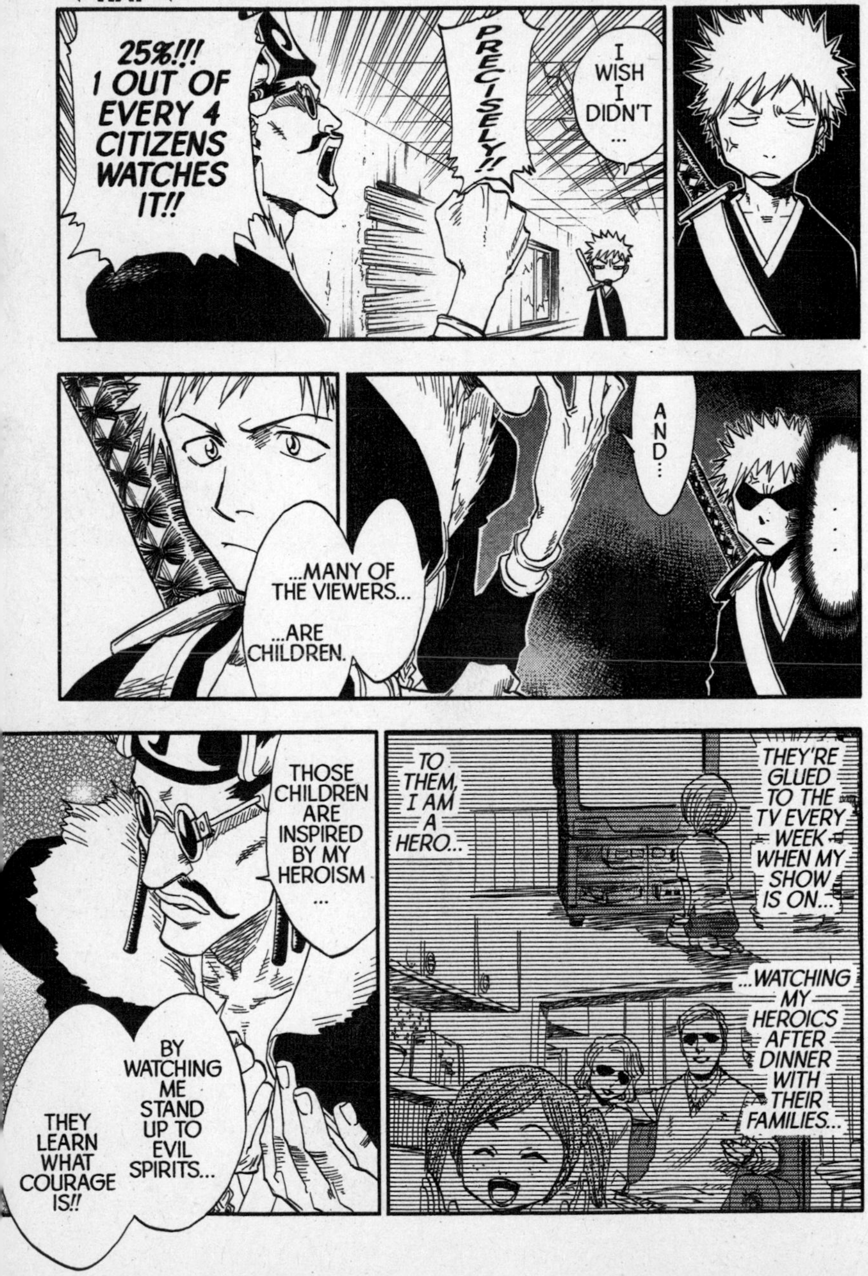

I WISH I DIDN'T ...
PRECISELY!!
25%!!! 1 OUT OF EVERY 4 CITIZENS WATCHES IT!!
AND...
...
...MANY OF THE VIEWERS... ...ARE CHILDREN.
THEY'RE GLUED TO THE TV EVERY WEEK WHEN MY SHOW IS ON...
TO THEM, I AM A HERO...
...WATCHING MY HEROICS AFTER DINNER WITH THEIR FAMILIES...
THOSE CHILDREN ARE INSPIRED BY MY HEROISM ...
BY WATCHING ME STAND UP TO EVIL SPIRITS...
THEY LEARN WHAT COURAGE IS!!

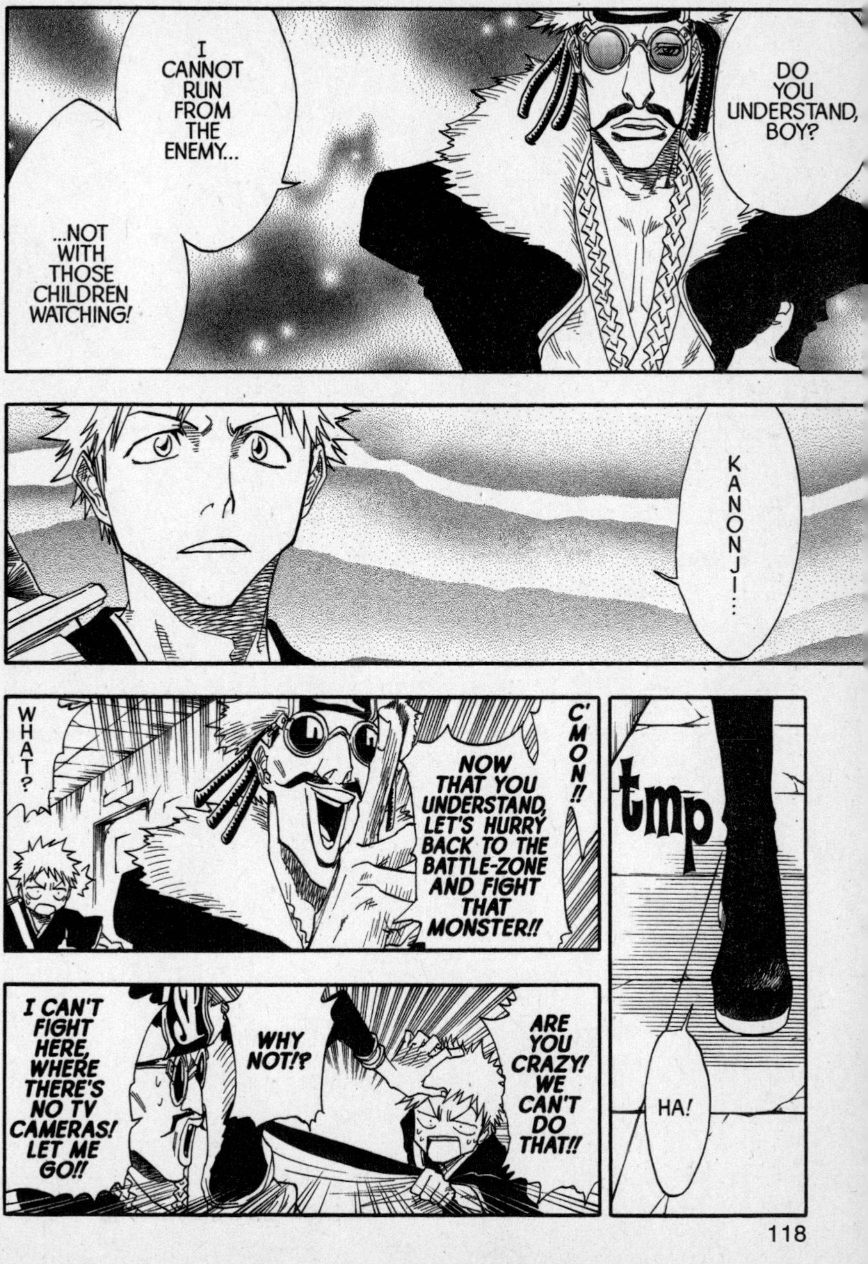
DO YOU UNDERSTAND, BOY?
I CANNOT RUN FROM THE ENEMY...
...NOT WITH THOSE CHILDREN WATCHING!
KANONJI...!
tmp
HA!
C'MON!!
NOW THAT YOU UNDERSTAND, LET'S HURRY BACK TO THE BATTLE-ZONE AND FIGHT THAT MONSTER!!
WHAT?
ARE YOU CRAZY! WE CAN'T DO THAT!!
WHY NOT!?
I CAN'T FIGHT HERE, WHERE THERE'S NO TV CAMERAS! LET ME GO!!

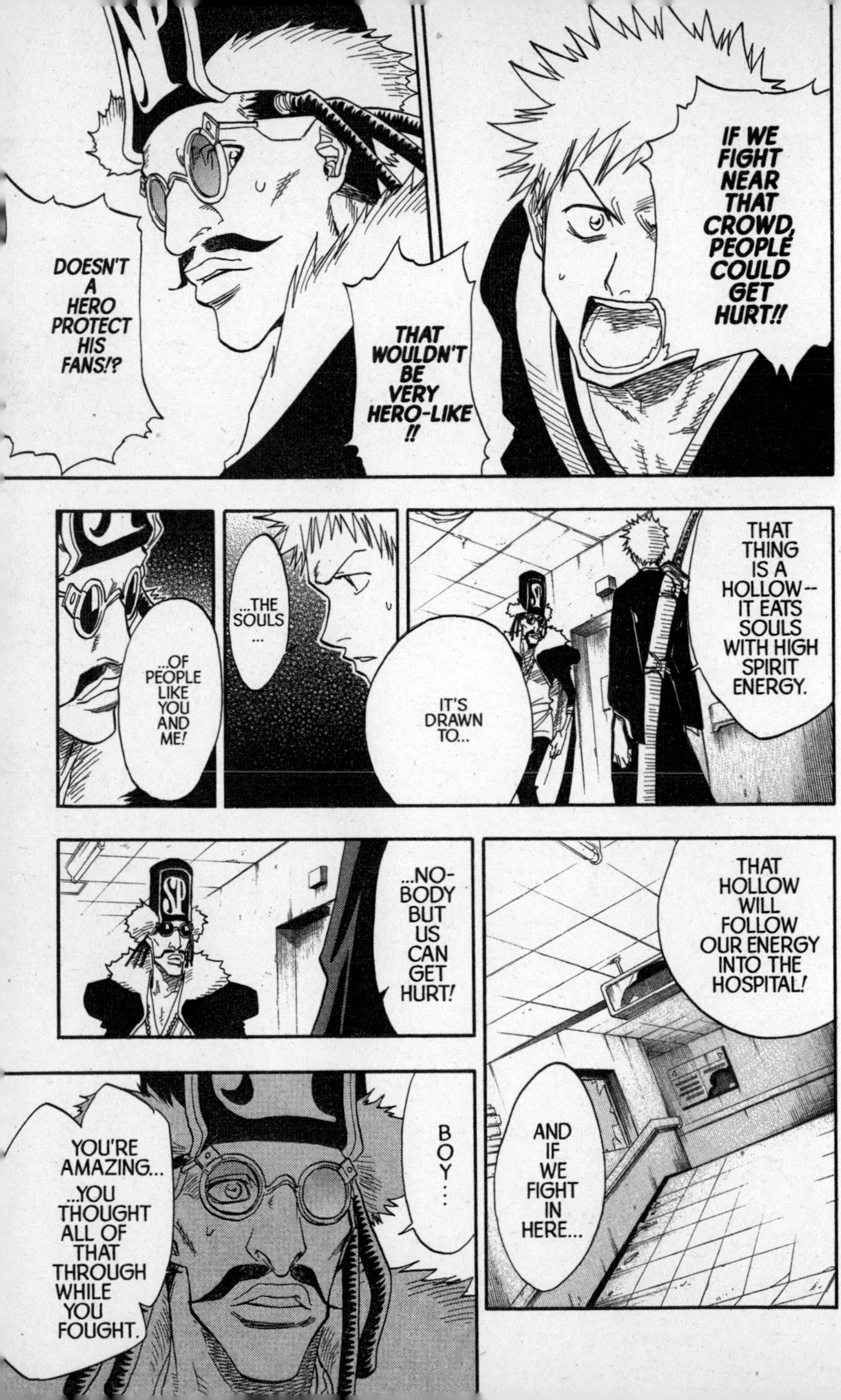
IF WE FIGHT NEAR THAT CROWD, PEOPLE COULD GET HURT!!
THAT WOULDN'T BE VERY HERO-LIKE!!
DOESN'T A HERO PROTECT HIS FANS!?
THAT THING IS A HOLLOW-- IT EATS SOULS WITH HIGH SPIRIT ENERGY.
IT'S DRAWN TO...
...THE SOULS...
...OF PEOPLE LIKE YOU AND ME!
THAT HOLLOW WILL FOLLOW OUR ENERGY INTO THE HOSPITAL!
AND IF WE FIGHT IN HERE...
...NOBODY BUT US CAN GET HURT!
BOY...
YOU'RE AMAZING...
...YOU THOUGHT ALL OF THAT THROUGH WHILE YOU FOUGHT.

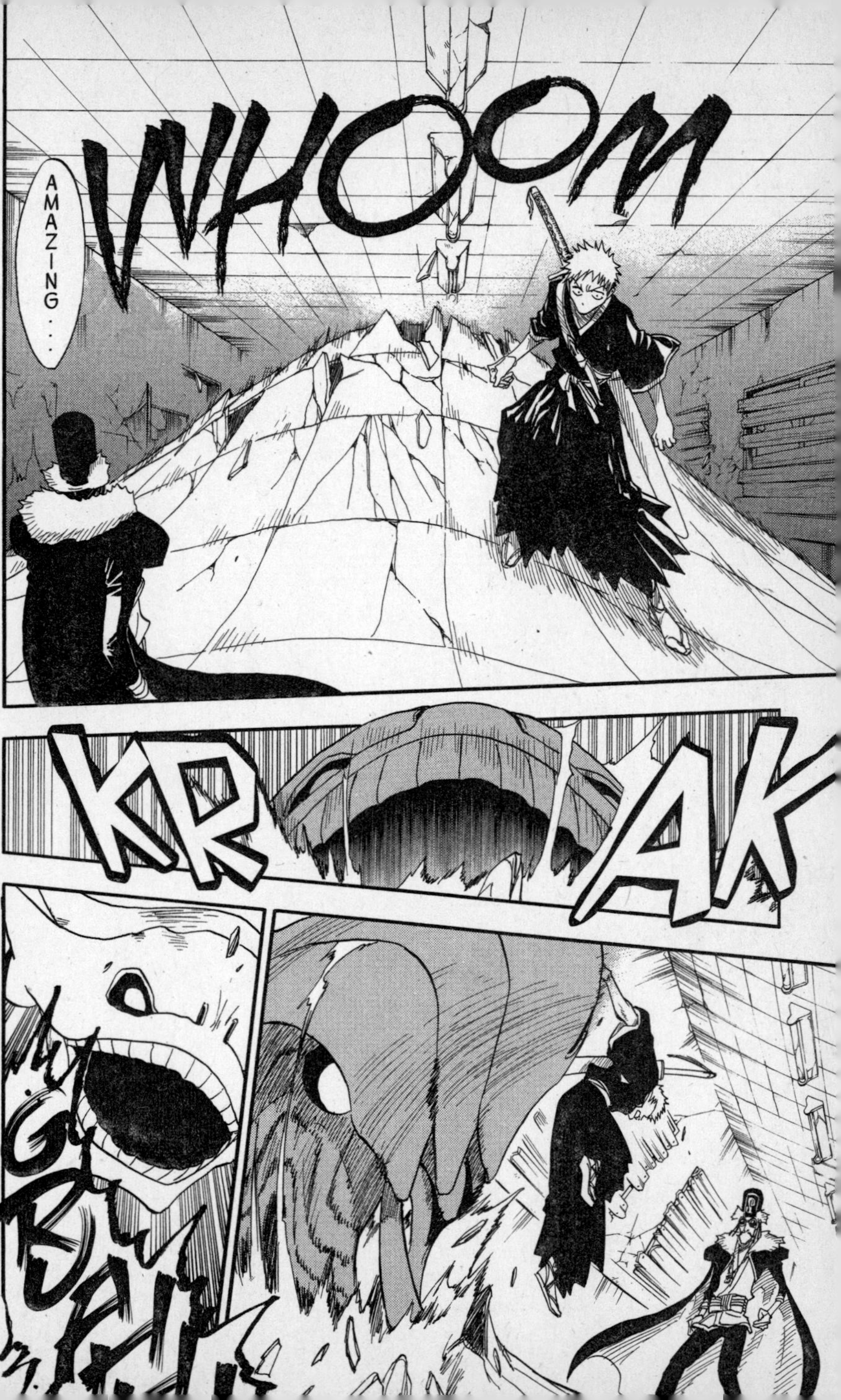
WHOOM
AMAZING...
KRAK

READ THIS WAY

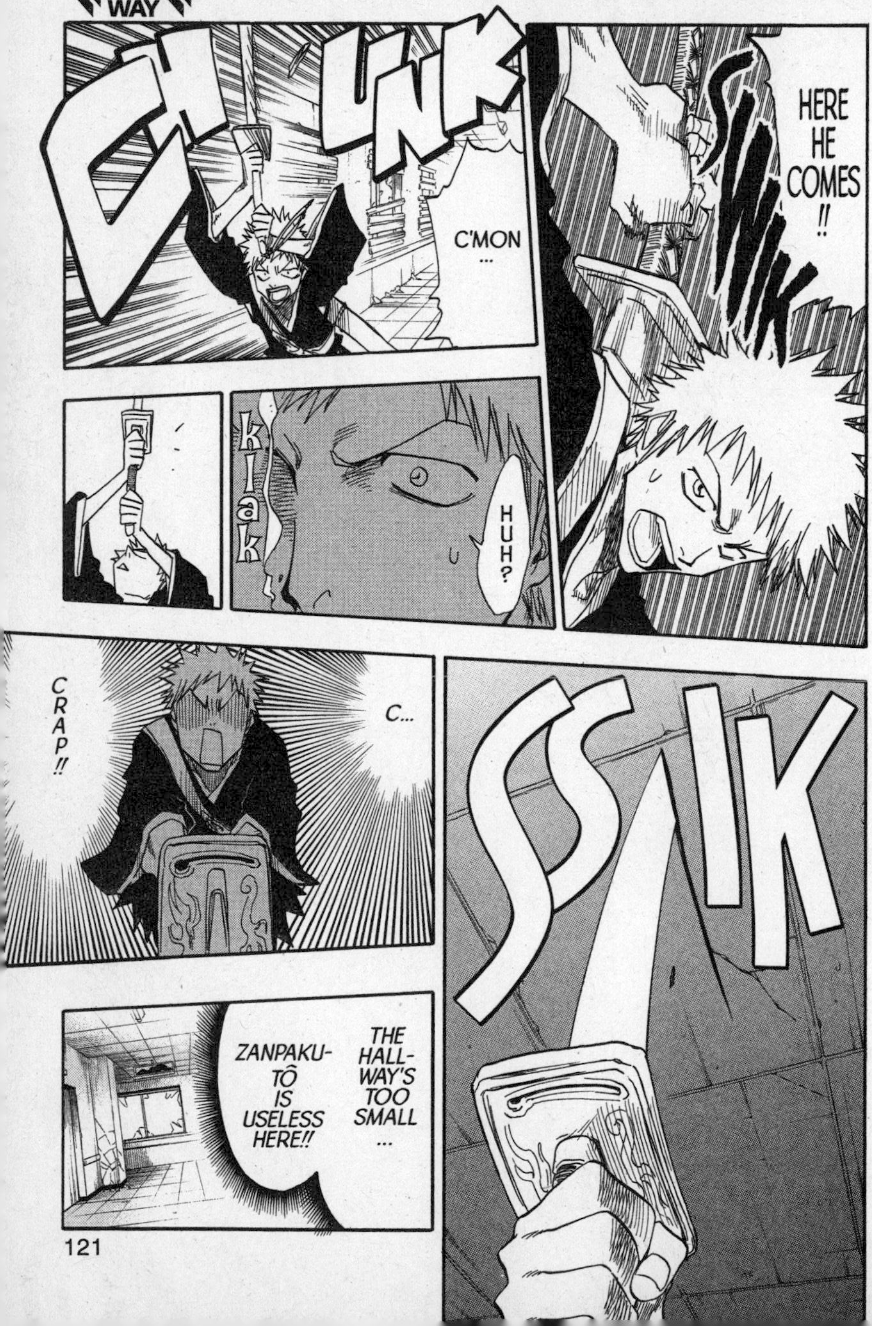
HERE HE COMES!!
SWIK
CHUNK
C'MON...
klak
HUH?
SSIK
C...
CRAP!!
THE HALLWAY'S TOO SMALL...
ZANPAKU-TÔ IS USELESS HERE!!

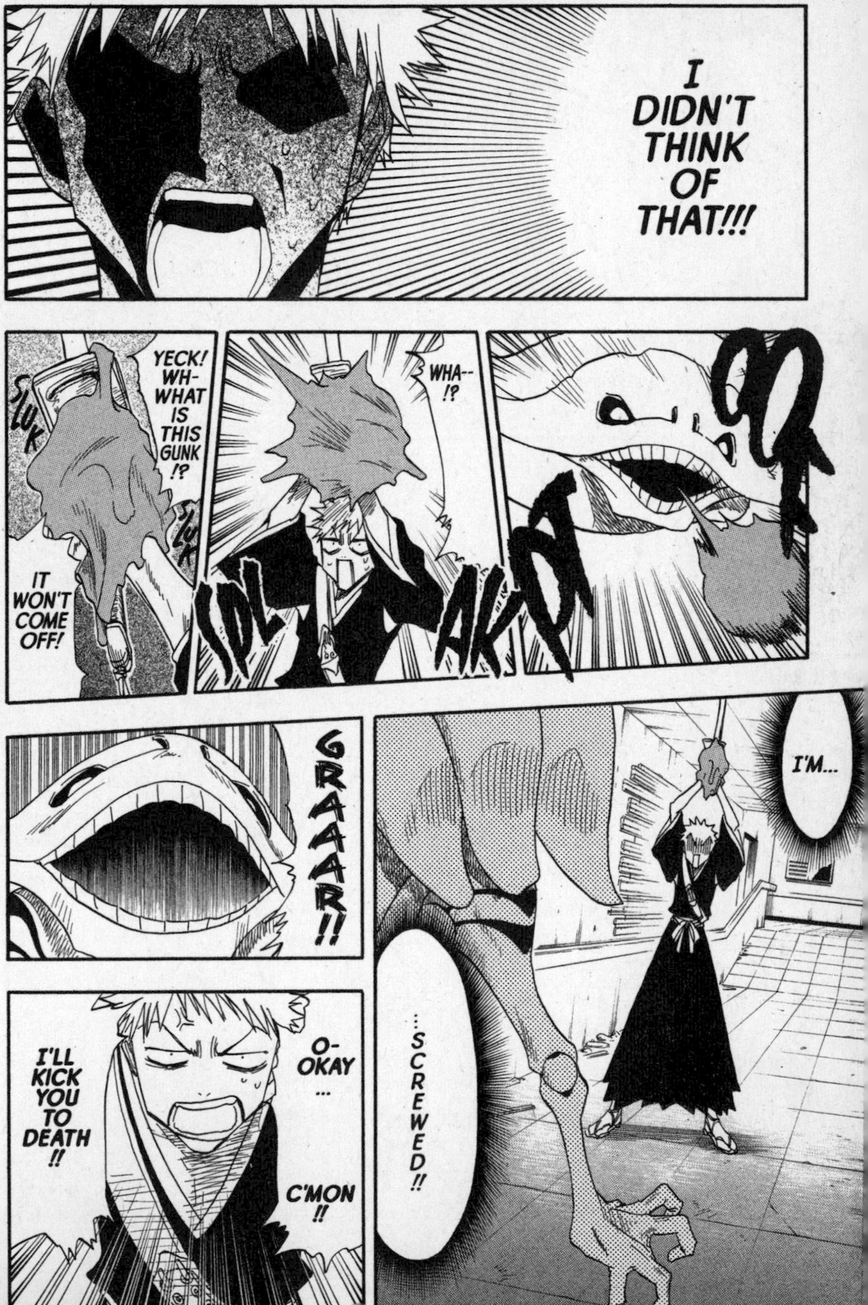
I DIDN'T THINK OF THAT!!!
WHA-- !?
YECK! WH-WHAT IS THIS GUNK!?
SLUK
SLUK
IT WON'T COME OFF!
I'M...
...SCREWED!!
GRAAAAR!!
O-OKAY ...
C'MON!!
I'LL KICK YOU TO DEATH!!

READ THIS WAY

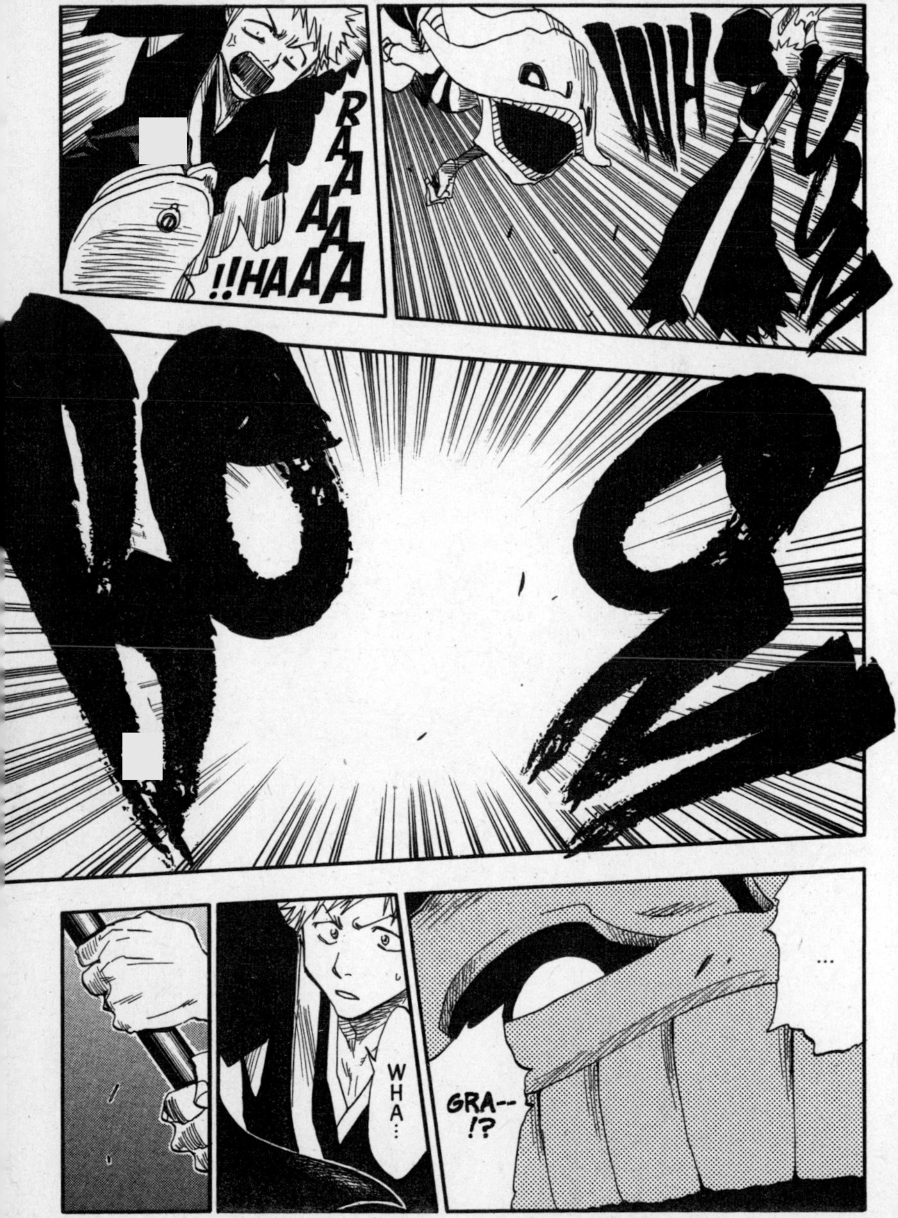

...
GRA--!?
WHA...

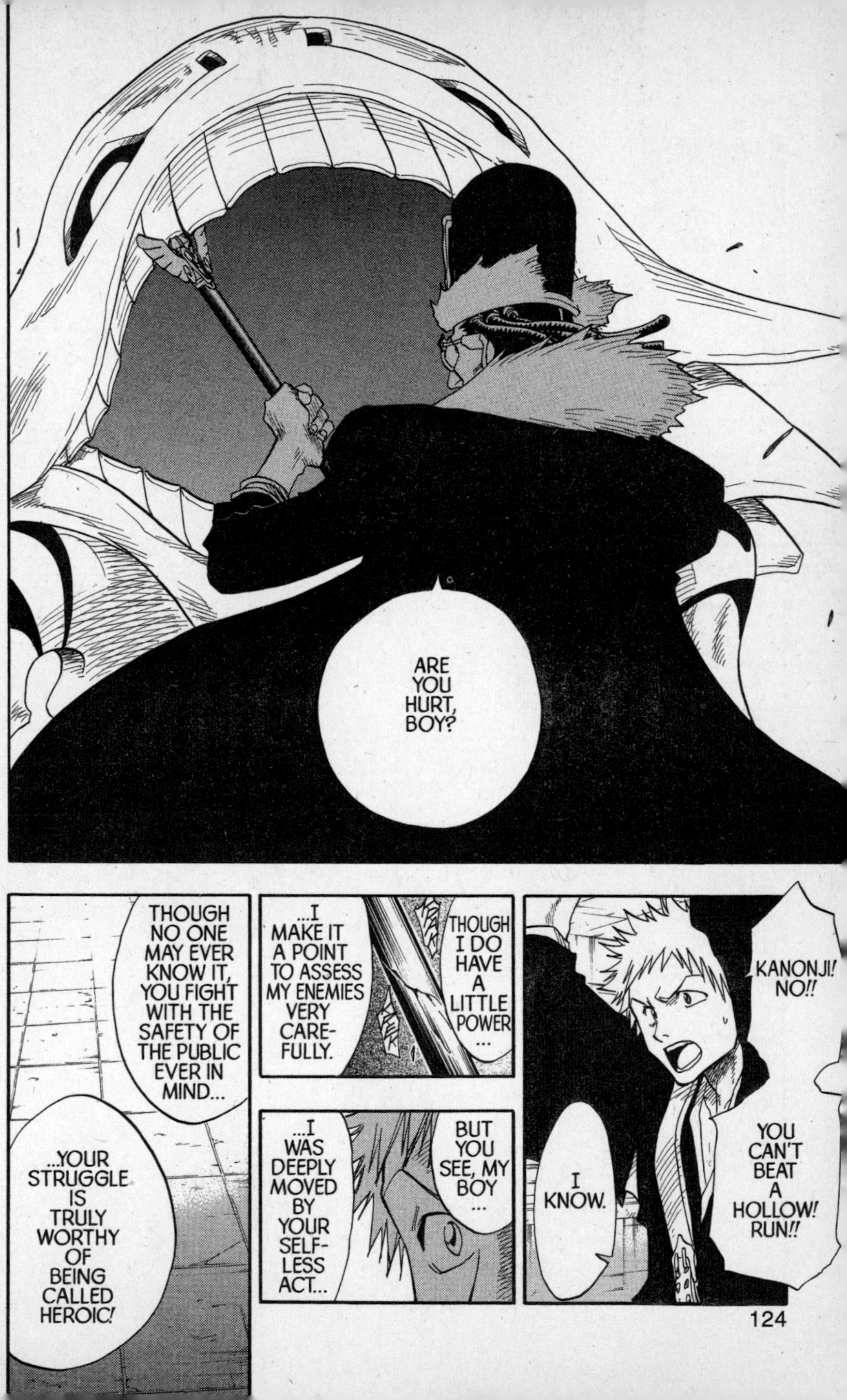
ARE YOU HURT, BOY?
KANONJI! NO!!
YOU CAN'T BEAT A HOLLOW! RUN!!
I KNOW.
THOUGH I DO HAVE A LITTLE POWER...
...I MAKE IT A POINT TO ASSESS MY ENEMIES VERY CAREFULLY.
BUT YOU SEE, MY BOY...
...I WAS DEEPLY MOVED BY YOUR SELFLESS ACT...
THOUGH NO ONE MAY EVER KNOW IT, YOU FIGHT WITH THE SAFETY OF THE PUBLIC EVER IN MIND...
...YOUR STRUGGLE IS TRULY WORTHY OF BEING CALLED HEROIC!

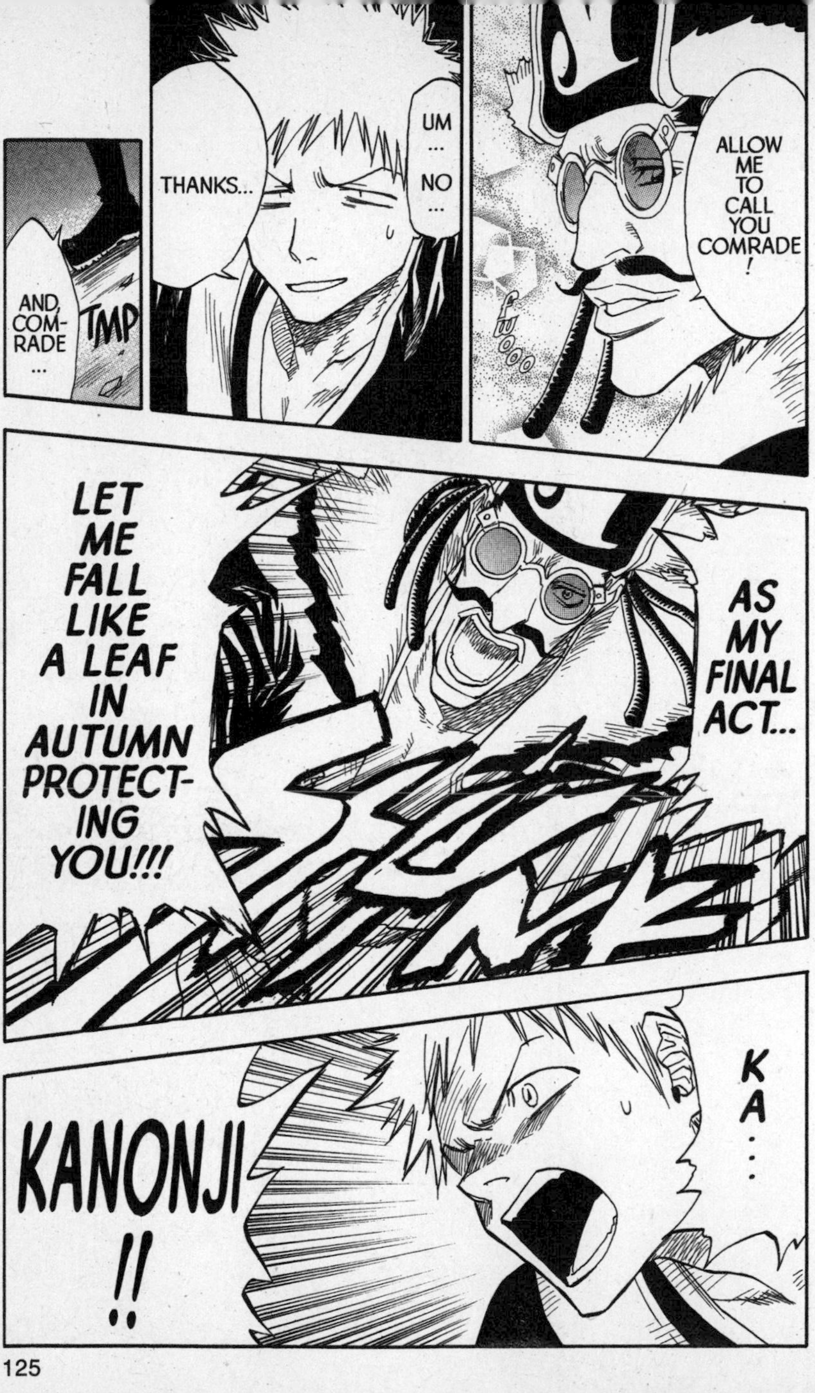
ALLOW ME TO CALL YOU COMRADE!
FWOOO
UM... NO...
THANKS...
TMP
AND, COMRADE...
AS MY FINAL ACT...
LET ME FALL LIKE A LEAF IN AUTUMN PROTECTING YOU!!!
KA...
KANONJI!!

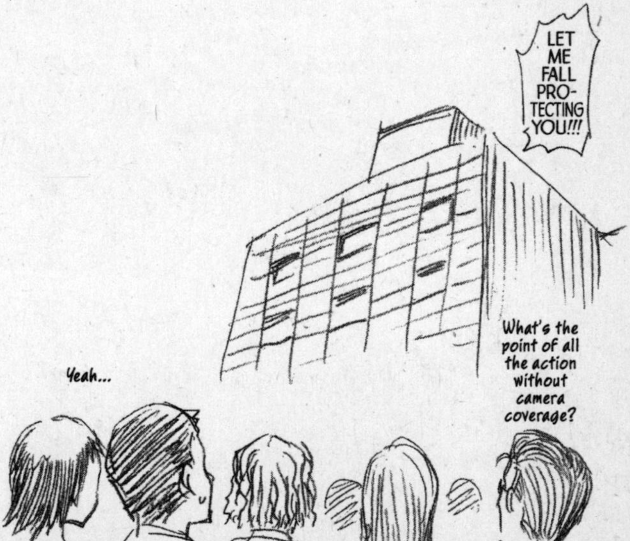
LET ME FALL PRO-TECTING YOU!!!
What's the point of all the action without camera coverage?
Yeah...

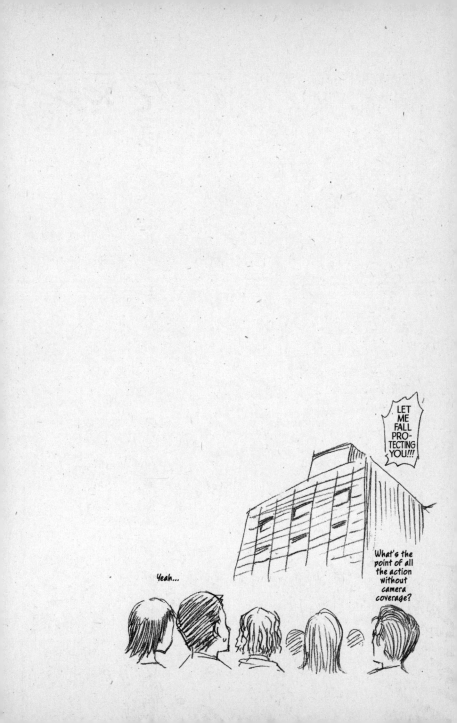

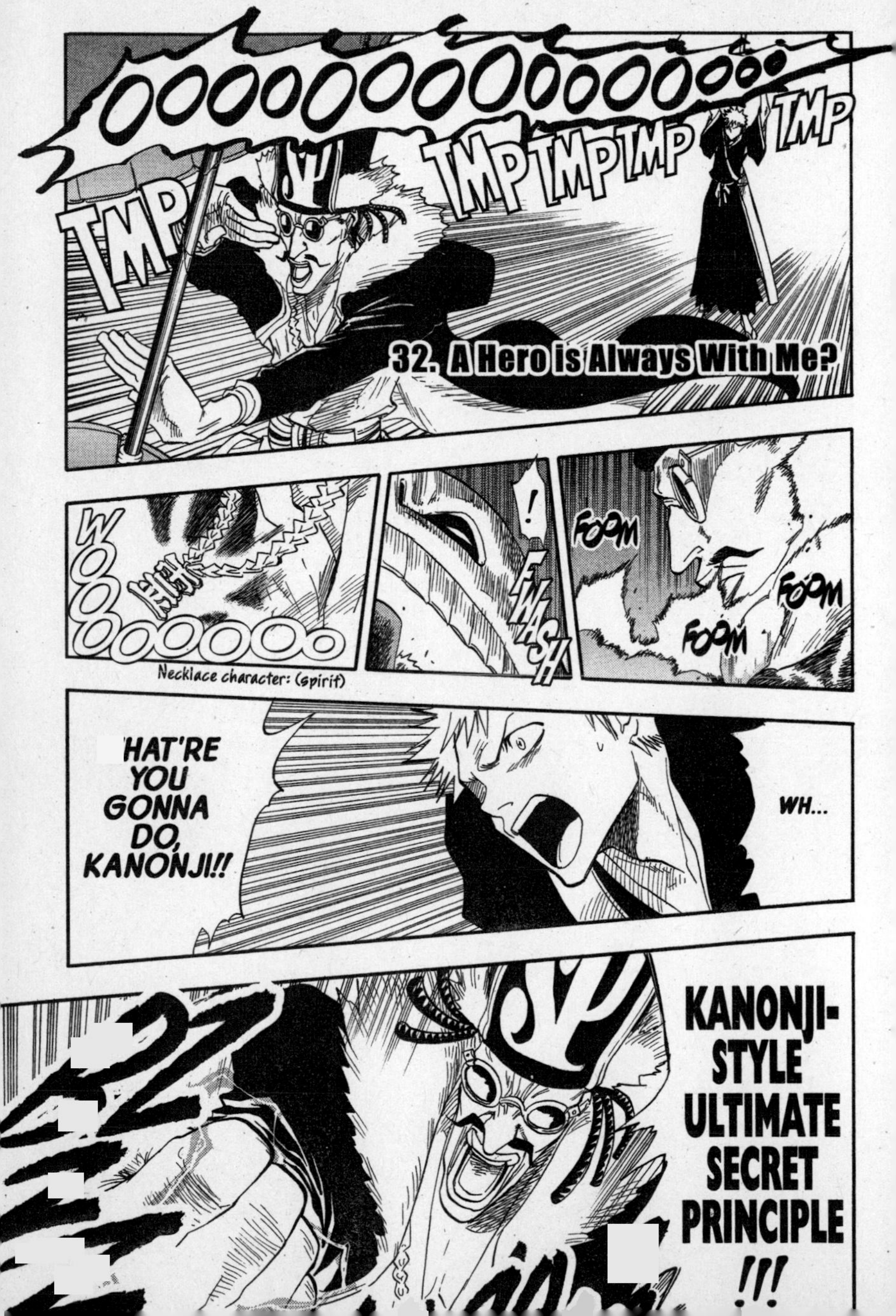
OOOOOOOOOOOOOOOO
TMP TMP TMP TMP TMP TMP
32. A Hero is Always With Me?
FOOM
FOOM
FOOM
!
FWASH
WOOOOOOOOOOO
Necklace character: (spirit)
WH...
HAT'RE YOU GONNA DO, KANONJI!!
KANONJI-STYLE ULTIMATE SECRET PRINCIPLE !!!

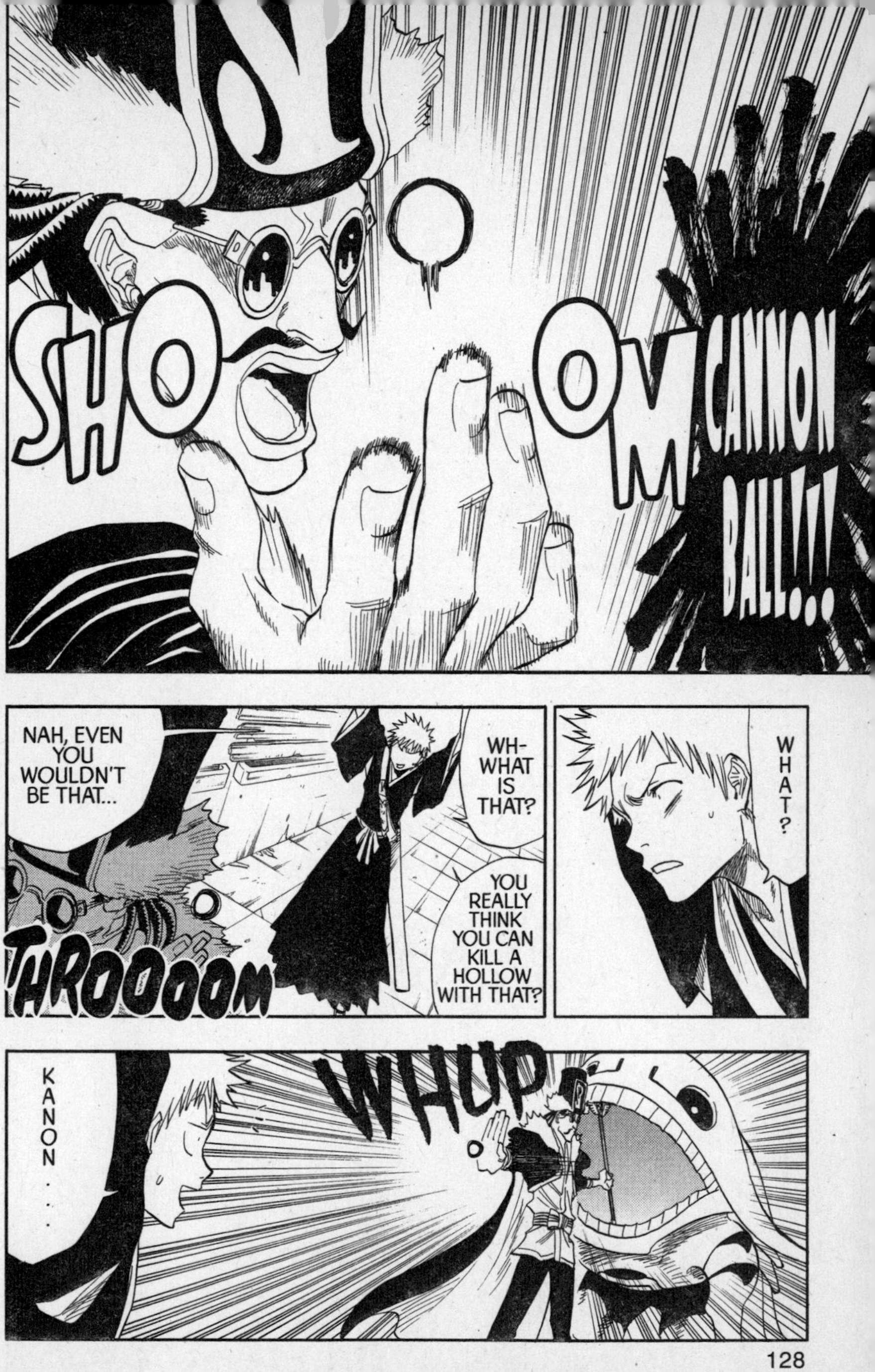
CANNON BALL!!!
SHOOM
WHAT?
WH- WHAT IS THAT?
YOU REALLY THINK YOU CAN KILL A HOLLOW WITH THAT?
NAH, EVEN YOU WOULDN'T BE THAT...
THROOOOM
WHUP
KANON . . .

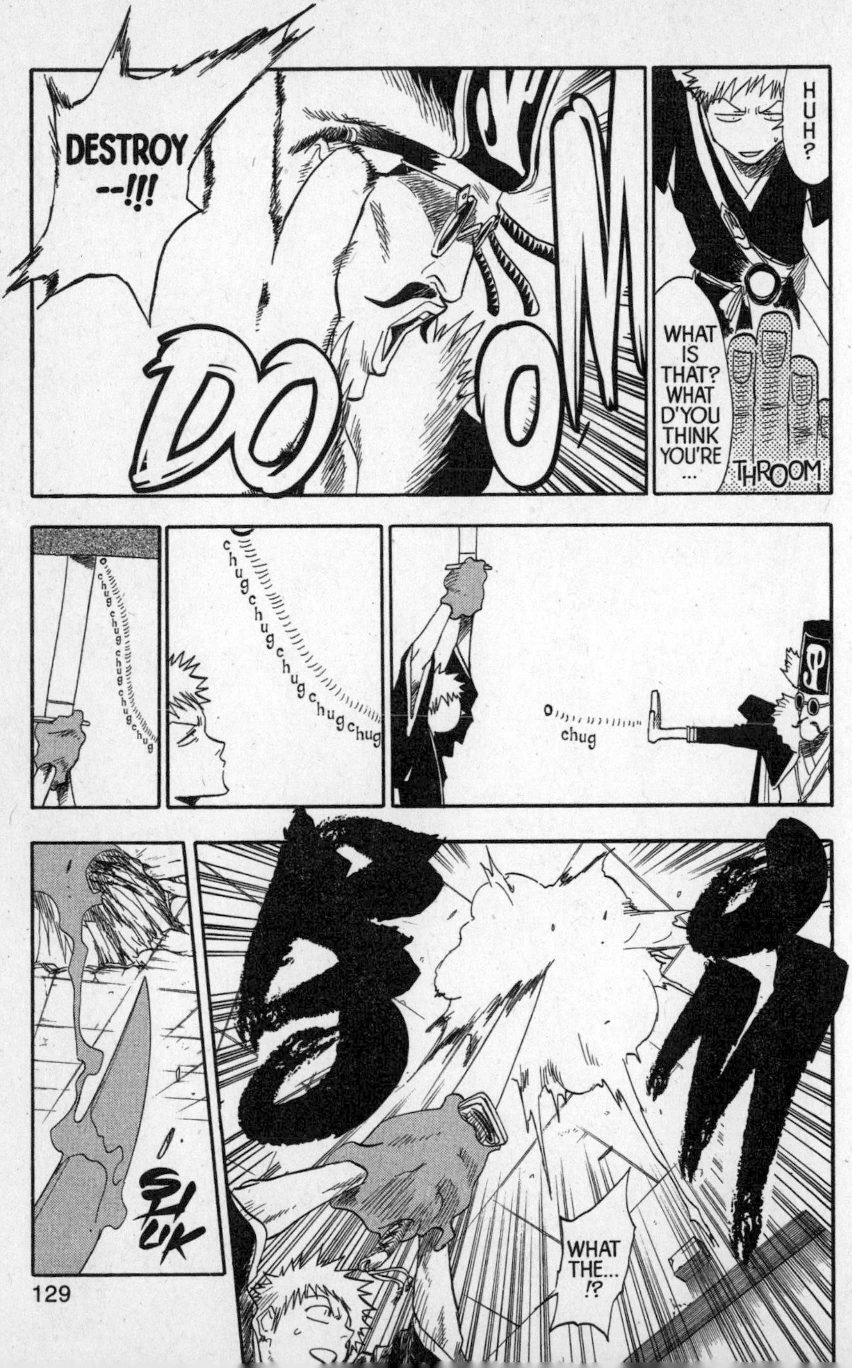
HUH?
WHAT IS THAT? WHAT D'YOU THINK YOU'RE ...
THROOM
DESTROY --!!!
DOOM
o chug
chug chug chug chug chug chug chug
o chug chug chug chug chug chug
BOOM
WHAT THE... !?
SHUK

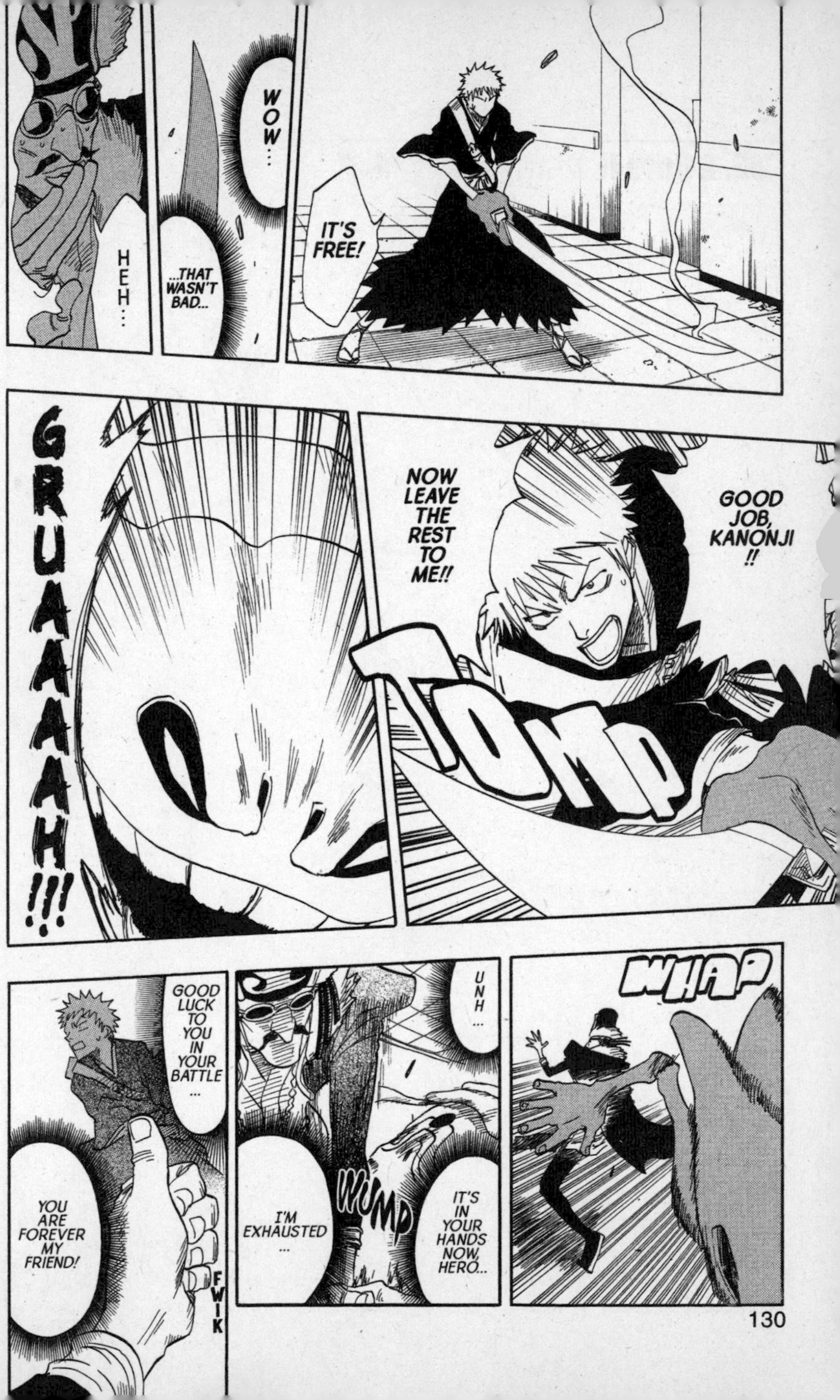

IT'S FREE!
WOW...
...THAT WASN'T BAD...
HEH...
GOOD JOB, KANONJI!!
NOW LEAVE THE REST TO ME!!
TOMP
GRUAAAAAAH!!!
WHAP
UNH...
IT'S IN YOUR HANDS NOW, HERO...
WUMP
I'M EXHAUSTED...
GOOD LUCK TO YOU IN YOUR BATTLE...
YOU ARE FOREVER MY FRIEND!
FWIK

32. A Hero is Always With Me?

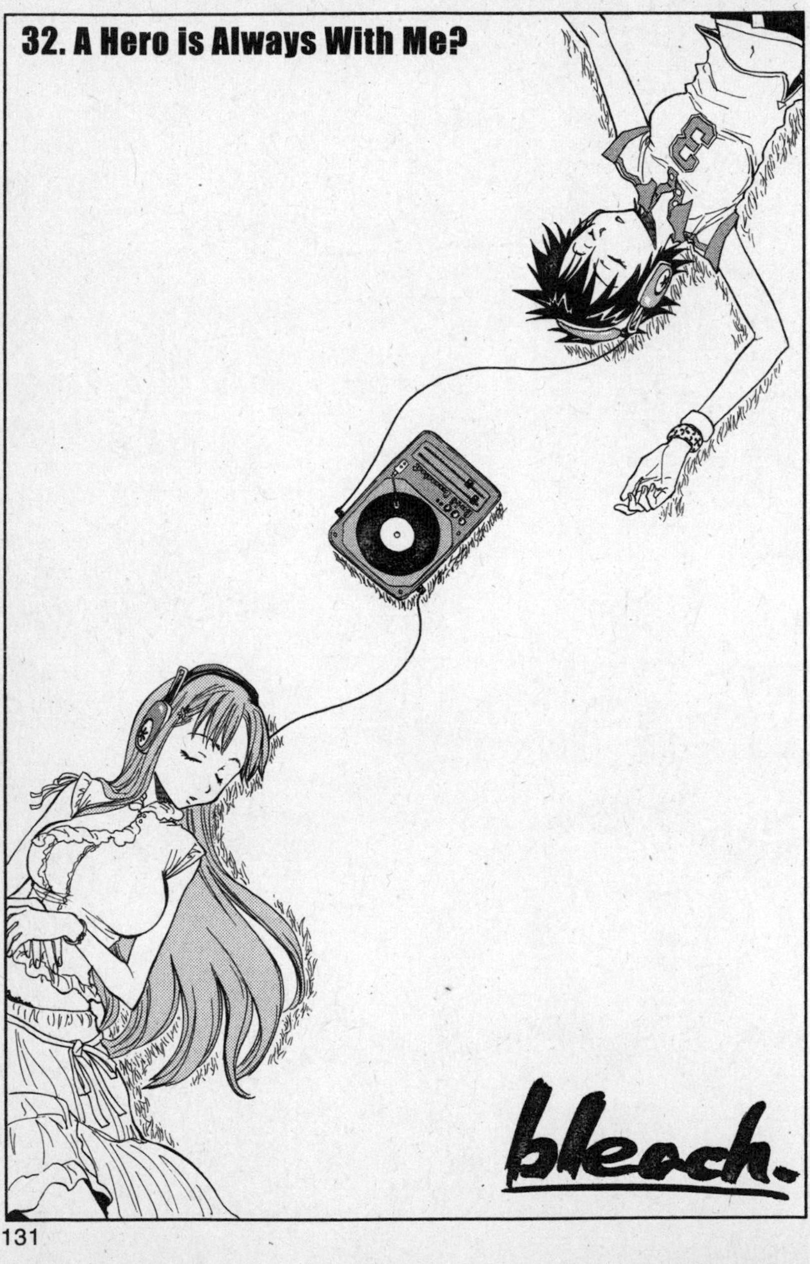
bleach.

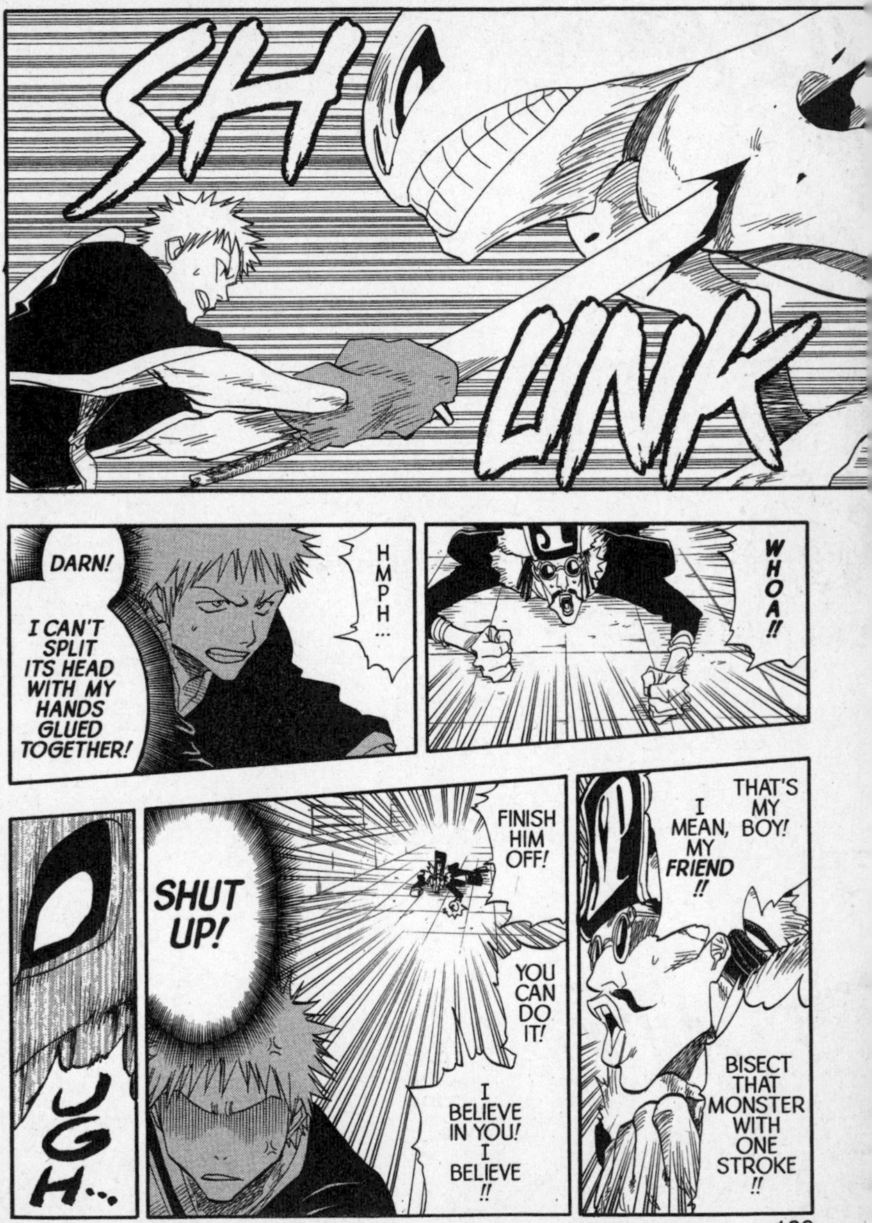
SH
LINK
WHOA!!
HMPH...
DARN!
I CAN'T SPLIT ITS HEAD WITH MY HANDS GLUED TOGETHER!
THAT'S MY BOY!
I MEAN, MY *FRIEND*!!
BISECT THAT MONSTER WITH ONE STROKE!!
FINISH HIM OFF!
YOU CAN DO IT!
I BELIEVE IN YOU! I BELIEVE!!
SHUT UP!
UGH...

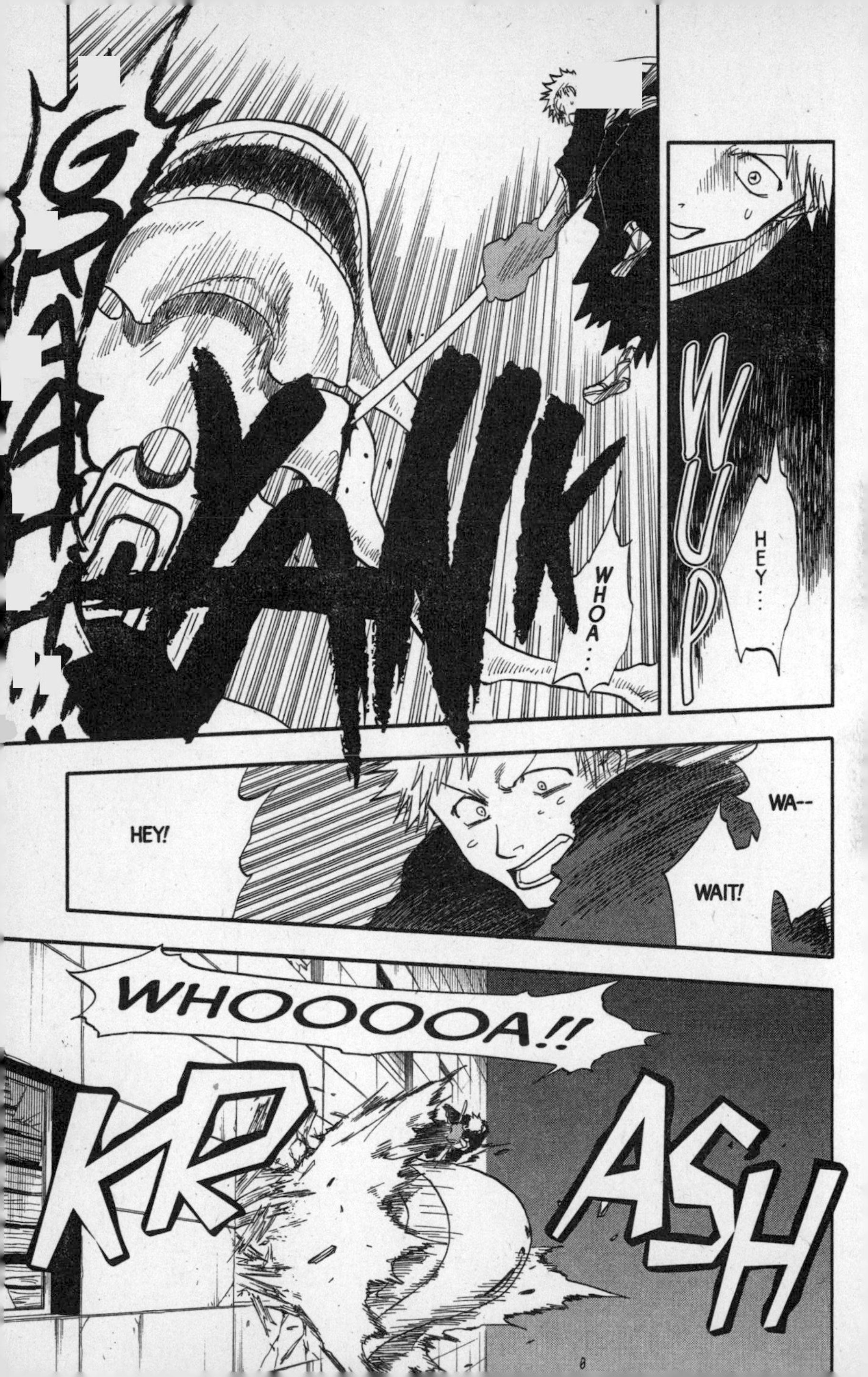
WUP
HEY...
YANK
WHOA...
WA--
WAIT!
HEY!
WHOOOOA!!
KRASH

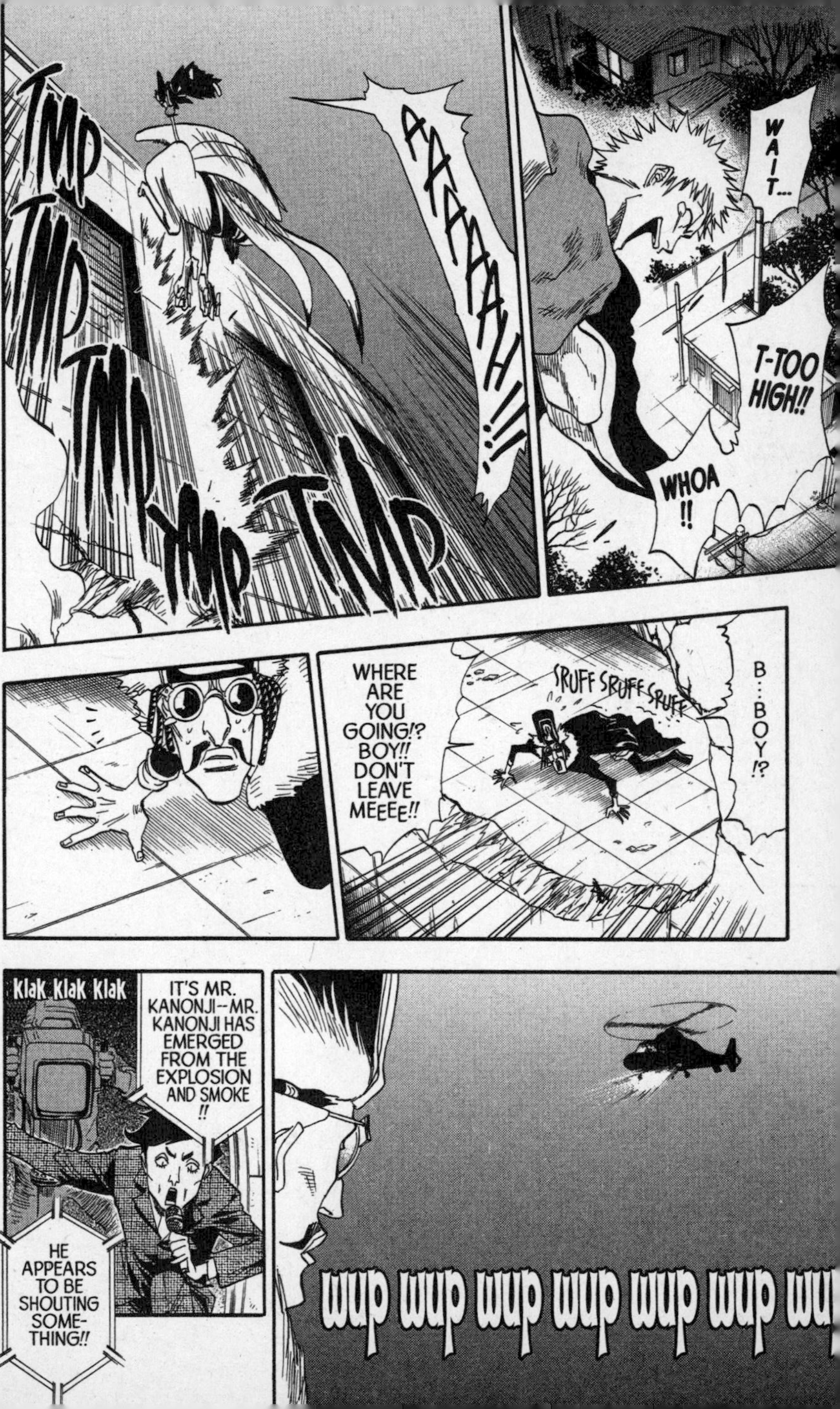
WAIT...
T-TOO HIGH!!
WHOA!!
AAAAAHH!!!
TMP TMP TMP TMP TMP TMP
B...BOY!?
SRUFF SRUFF SRUFF
WHERE ARE YOU GOING!? BOY!! DON'T LEAVE MEEEE!!
wup wup wup wup wup wup wup
Klak klak klak
IT'S MR. KANONJI--MR. KANONJI HAS EMERGED FROM THE EXPLOSION AND SMOKE!!
HE APPEARS TO BE SHOUTING SOME-THING!!

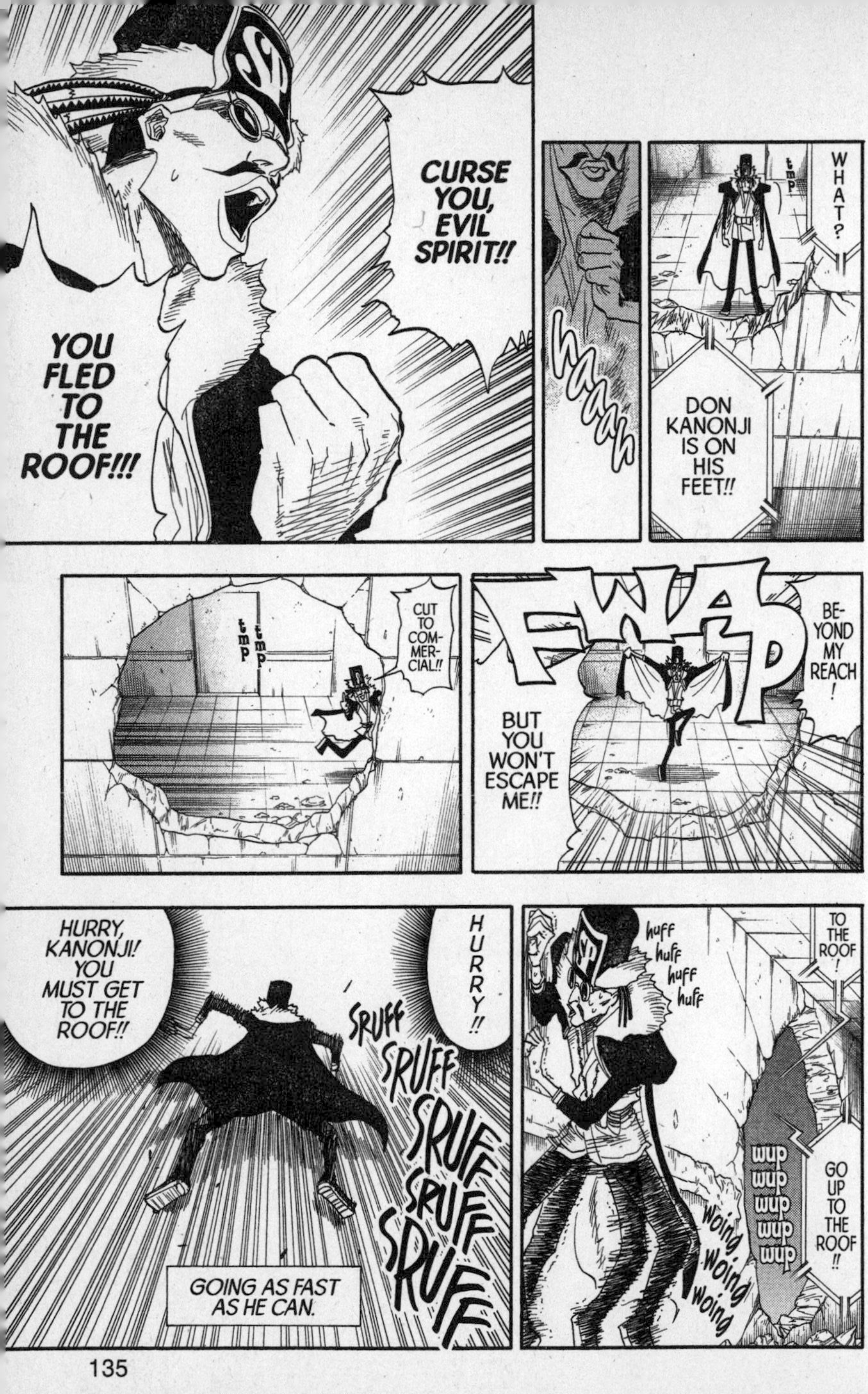
tmp
WHAT?
DON KANONJI IS ON HIS FEET!!
haaaah
CURSE YOU, EVIL SPIRIT!!
YOU FLED TO THE ROOF!!!
FWAP
BEYOND MY REACH!
BUT YOU WON'T ESCAPE ME!!
tmp tmp
CUT TO COMMERCIAL!!
TO THE ROOF!
huff huff huff huff
GO UP TO THE ROOF!!
wup wup wup wup wup
woing woing woing
HURRY!!
HURRY, KANONJI! YOU MUST GET TO THE ROOF!!
SRUFF SRUFF SRUFF SRUFF SRUFF
GOING AS FAST AS HE CAN.

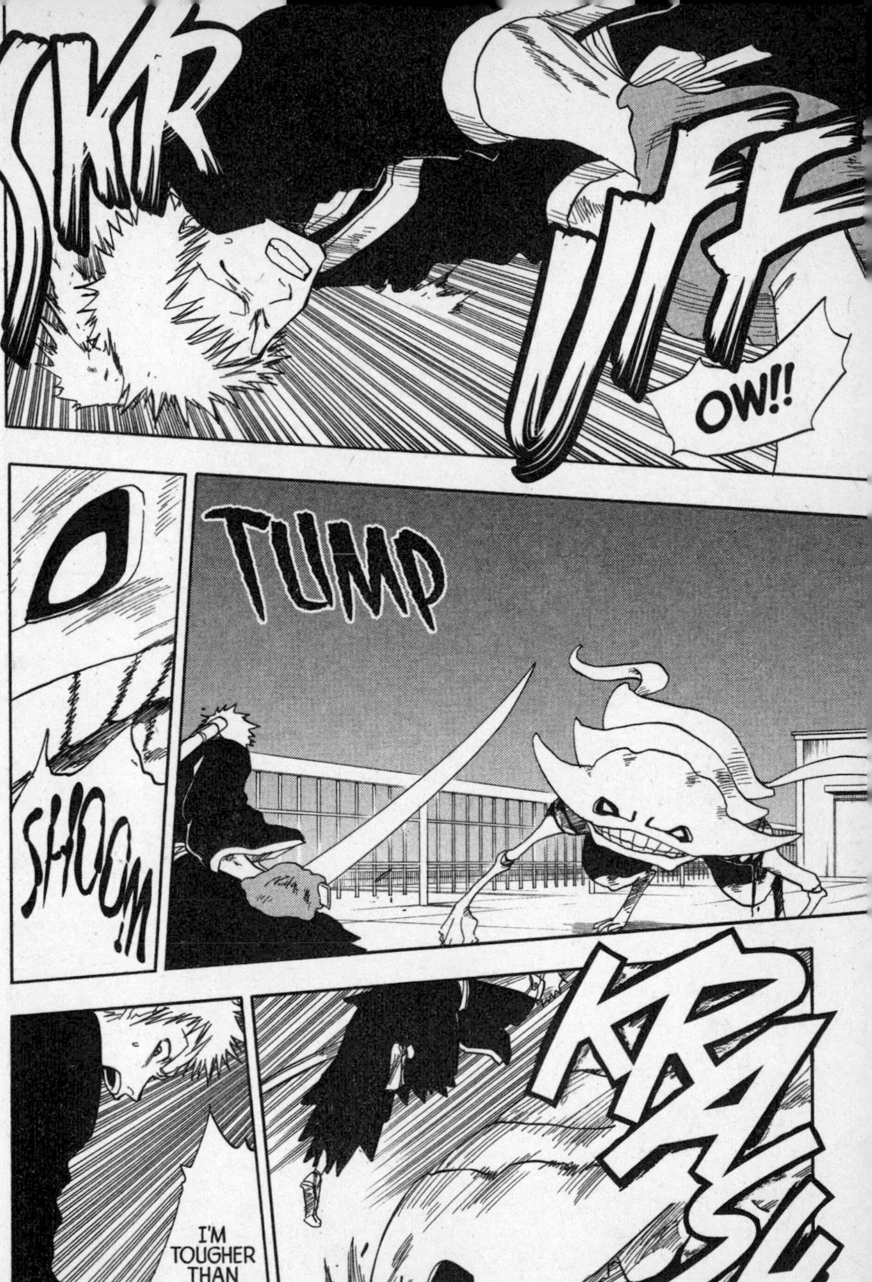
SKR
OW!!
TUMP
SHOOM!!
KRASH
I'M TOUGHER THAN YOU THINK!!

READ THIS WAY

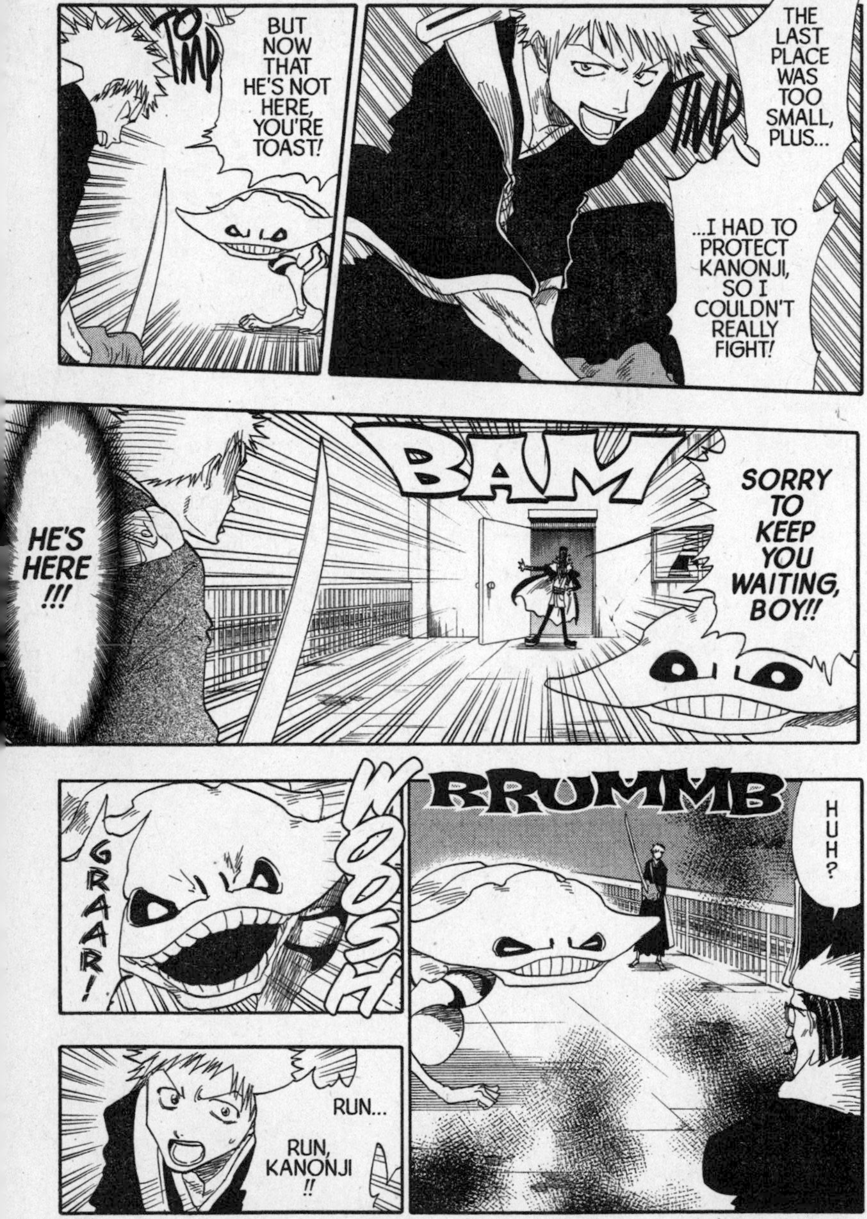
THE LAST PLACE WAS TOO SMALL, PLUS...
TMP
...I HAD TO PROTECT KANONJI, SO I COULDN'T REALLY FIGHT!
TMP
BUT NOW THAT HE'S NOT HERE, YOU'RE TOAST!
BAM
SORRY TO KEEP YOU WAITING, BOY!!
HE'S HERE!!!
RRUMMB
HUH?
WOOSH
GRAAR!
RUN...
RUN, KANONJI!!

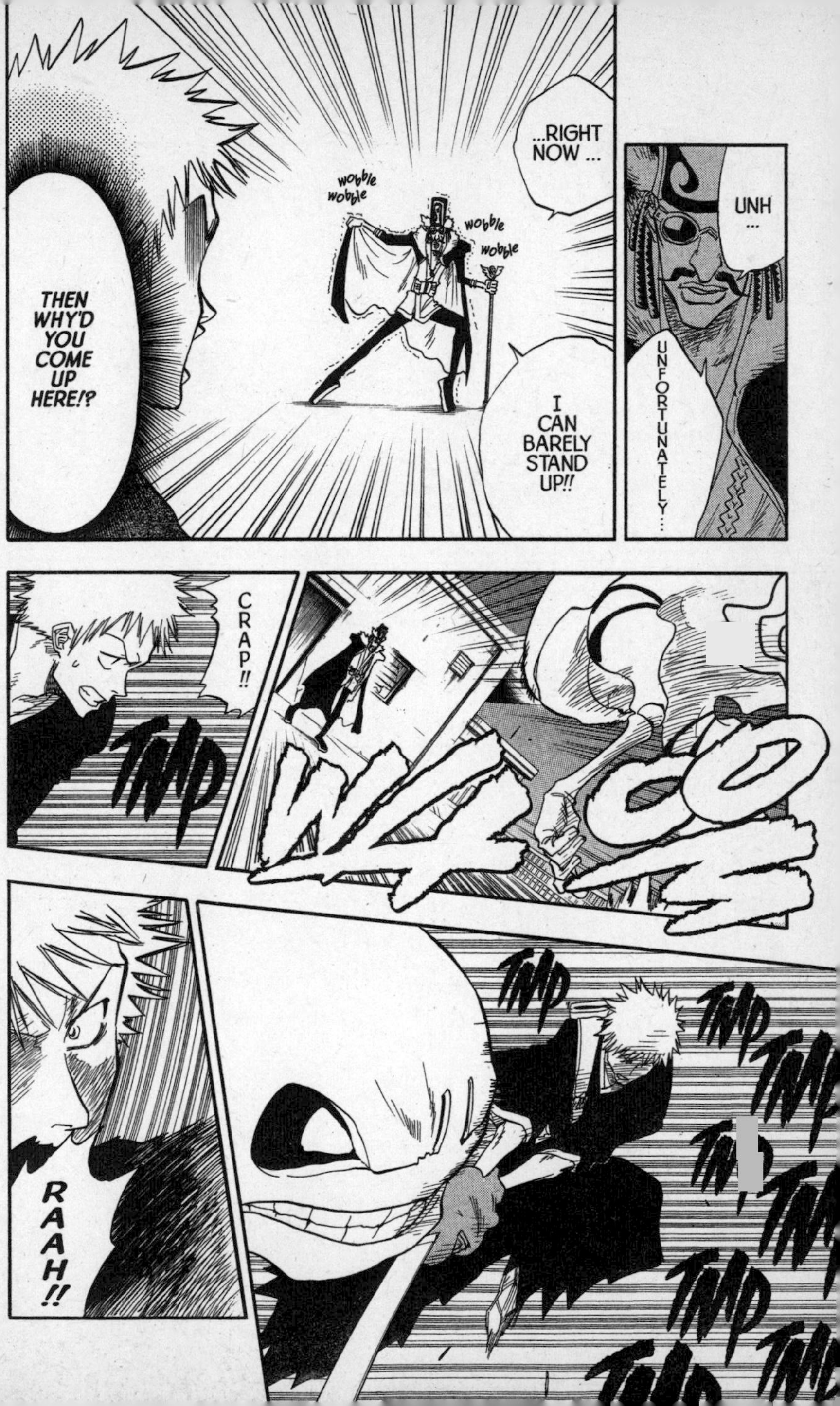
UNH ...
UNFORTUNATELY...
...RIGHT NOW ...
wobble wobble
wobble wobble
I CAN BARELY STAND UP!!
THEN WHY'D YOU COME UP HERE!?
CRAP!!
TMP
TMP
TMP
TMP
TMP
TMP
TMP
RAAAH!!

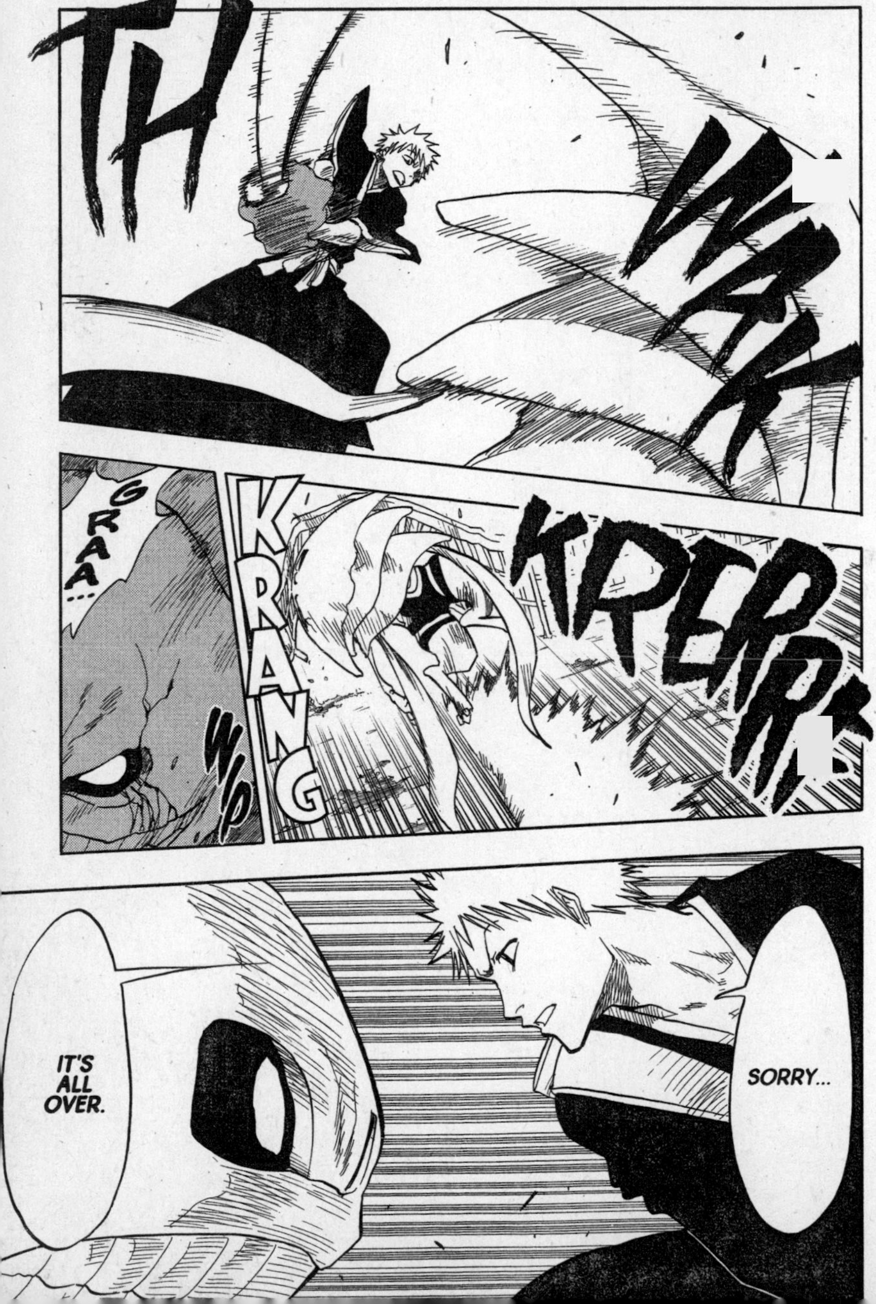
THWAK
KRERR
KRANG
WIP
GRAA...
SORRY...
IT'S ALL OVER.

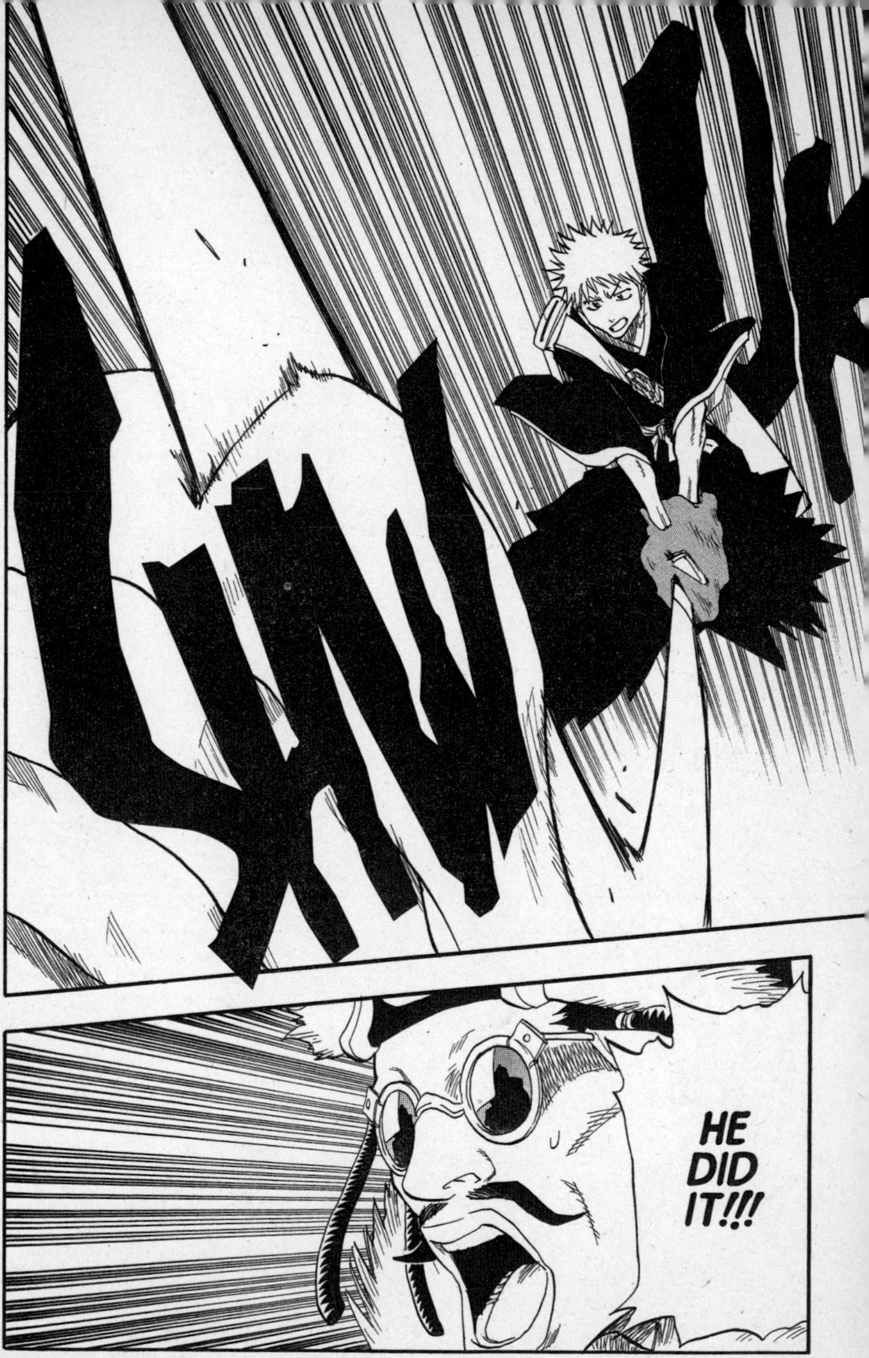
HE DID IT!!!

READ THIS WAY

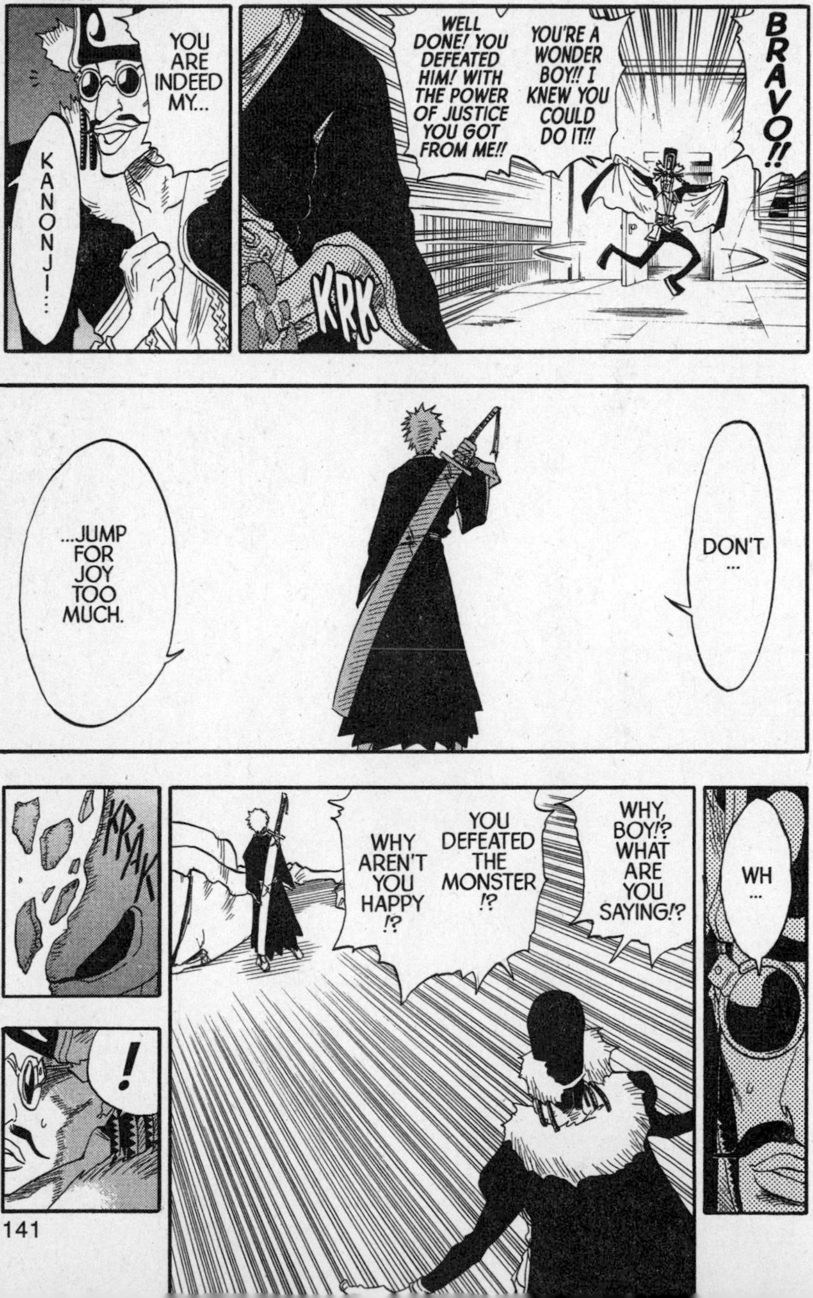

BRAVO!!
YOU'RE A WONDER BOY!! I KNEW YOU COULD DO IT!!
WELL DONE! YOU DEFEATED HIM! WITH THE POWER OF JUSTICE YOU GOT FROM ME!!
KRK
YOU ARE INDEED MY...
KANONJI...
DON'T...
...JUMP FOR JOY TOO MUCH.
WH...
WHY, BOY!? WHAT ARE YOU SAYING!?
YOU DEFEATED THE MONSTER!?
WHY AREN'T YOU HAPPY!?
KRAK
!

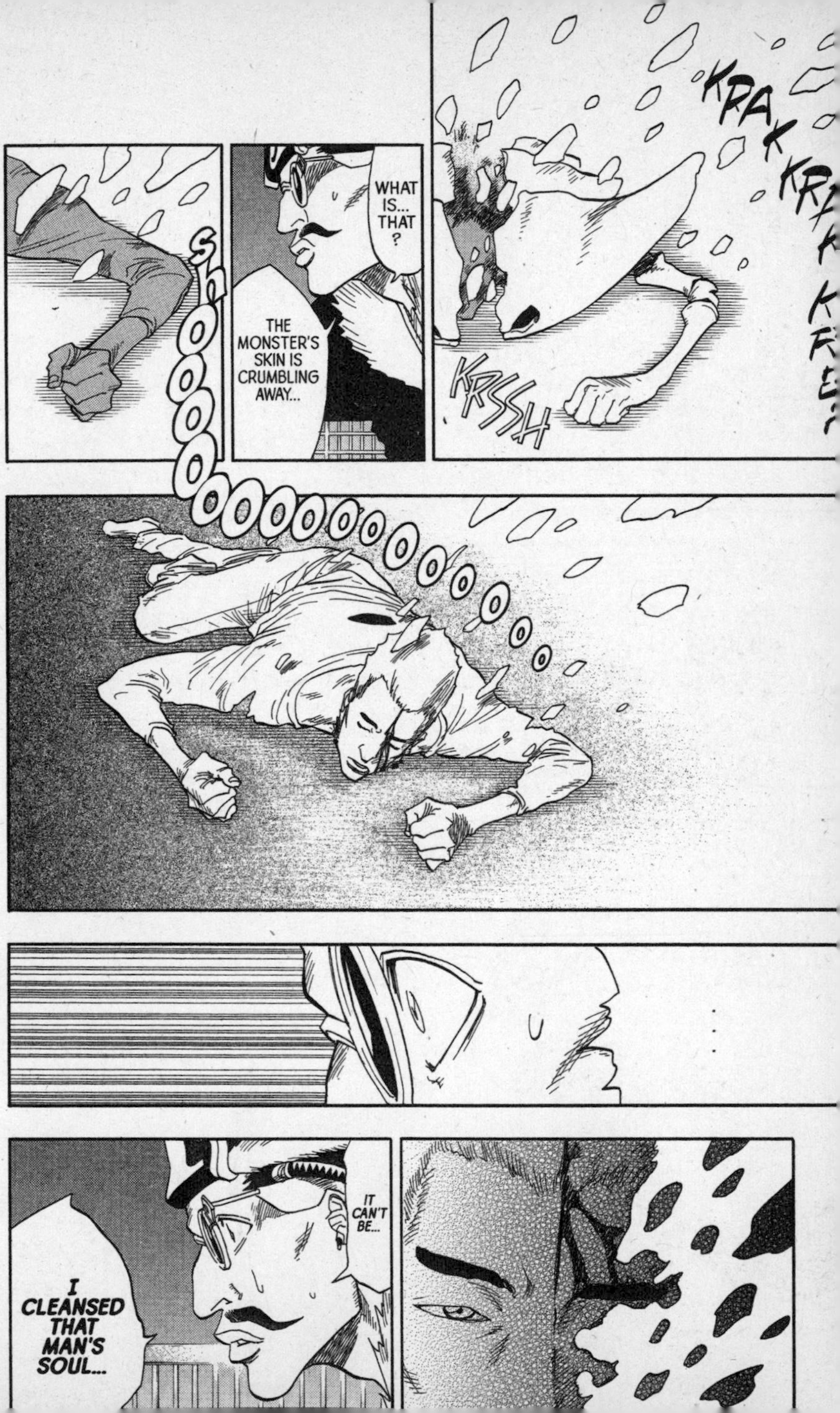
KRAK
KRSSH
WHAT IS... THAT?
THE MONSTER'S SKIN IS CRUMBLING AWAY...
SHOOOOOOOOOOOOOOOOOOOOO
IT CAN'T BE...
I CLEANSED THAT MAN'S SOUL...

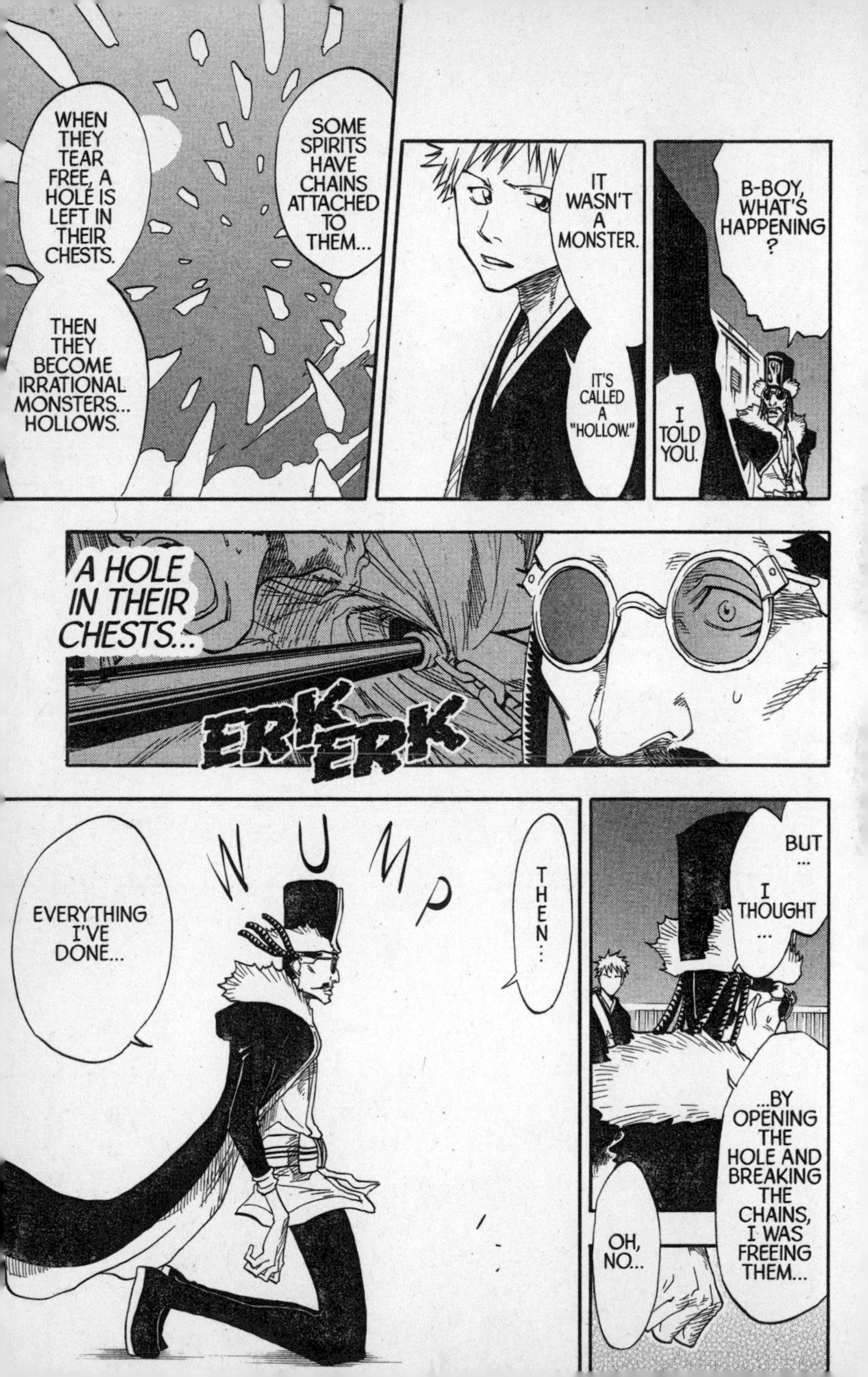
B-BOY, WHAT'S HAPPENING?
I TOLD YOU.
IT WASN'T A MONSTER.
IT'S CALLED A "HOLLOW."
SOME SPIRITS HAVE CHAINS ATTACHED TO THEM...
WHEN THEY TEAR FREE, A HOLE IS LEFT IN THEIR CHESTS.
THEN THEY BECOME IRRATIONAL MONSTERS... HOLLOWS.
A HOLE IN THEIR CHESTS...
ERK ERK
BUT... I THOUGHT...
...BY OPENING THE HOLE AND BREAKING THE CHAINS, I WAS FREEING THEM...
OH, NO...
THEN...
WUMP
EVERYTHING I'VE DONE...

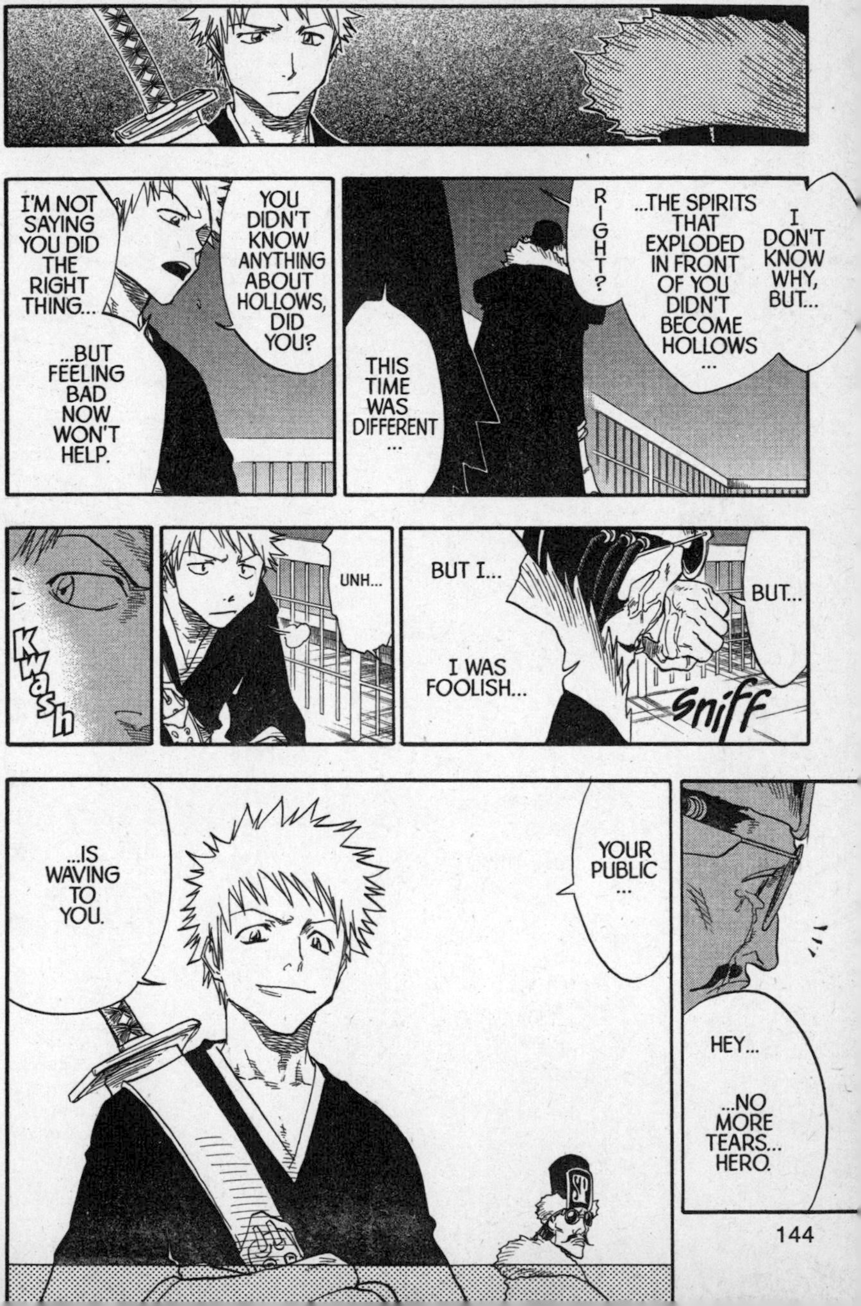
I DON'T KNOW WHY, BUT...
...THE SPIRITS THAT EXPLODED IN FRONT OF YOU DIDN'T BECOME HOLLOWS...
RIGHT?
THIS TIME WAS DIFFERENT...
YOU DIDN'T KNOW ANYTHING ABOUT HOLLOWS, DID YOU?
I'M NOT SAYING YOU DID THE RIGHT THING...
...BUT FEELING BAD NOW WON'T HELP.
BUT...
Sniff
BUT I...
I WAS FOOLISH...
UNH...
Kwash
HEY...
...NO MORE TEARS... HERO.
YOUR PUBLIC...
...IS WAVING TO YOU.

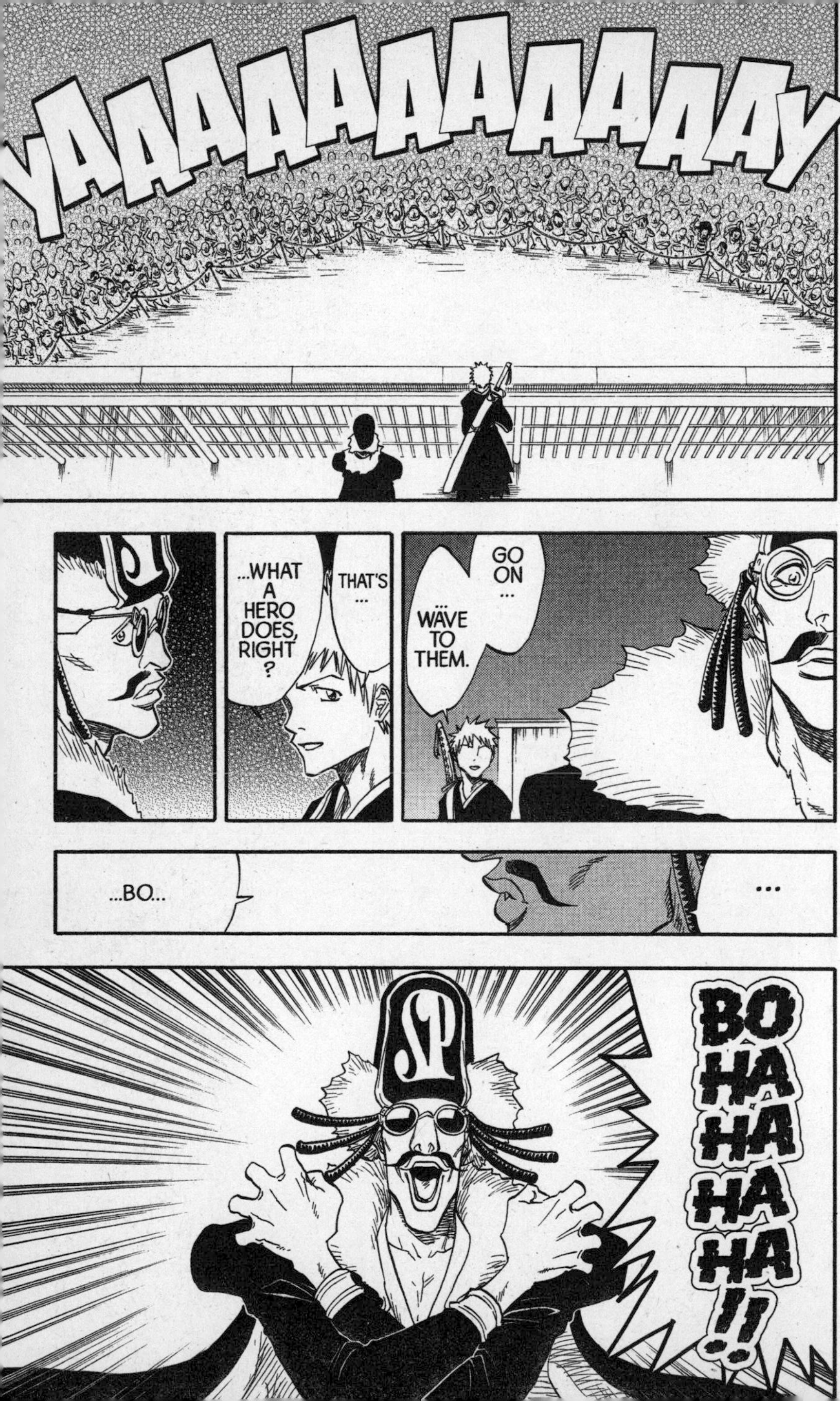
YAAAAAAAAAAAY
GO ON ...
... WAVE TO THEM.
THAT'S ...
...WHAT A HERO DOES, RIGHT?
...
...BO...
BOHAHAHAHAHA!!

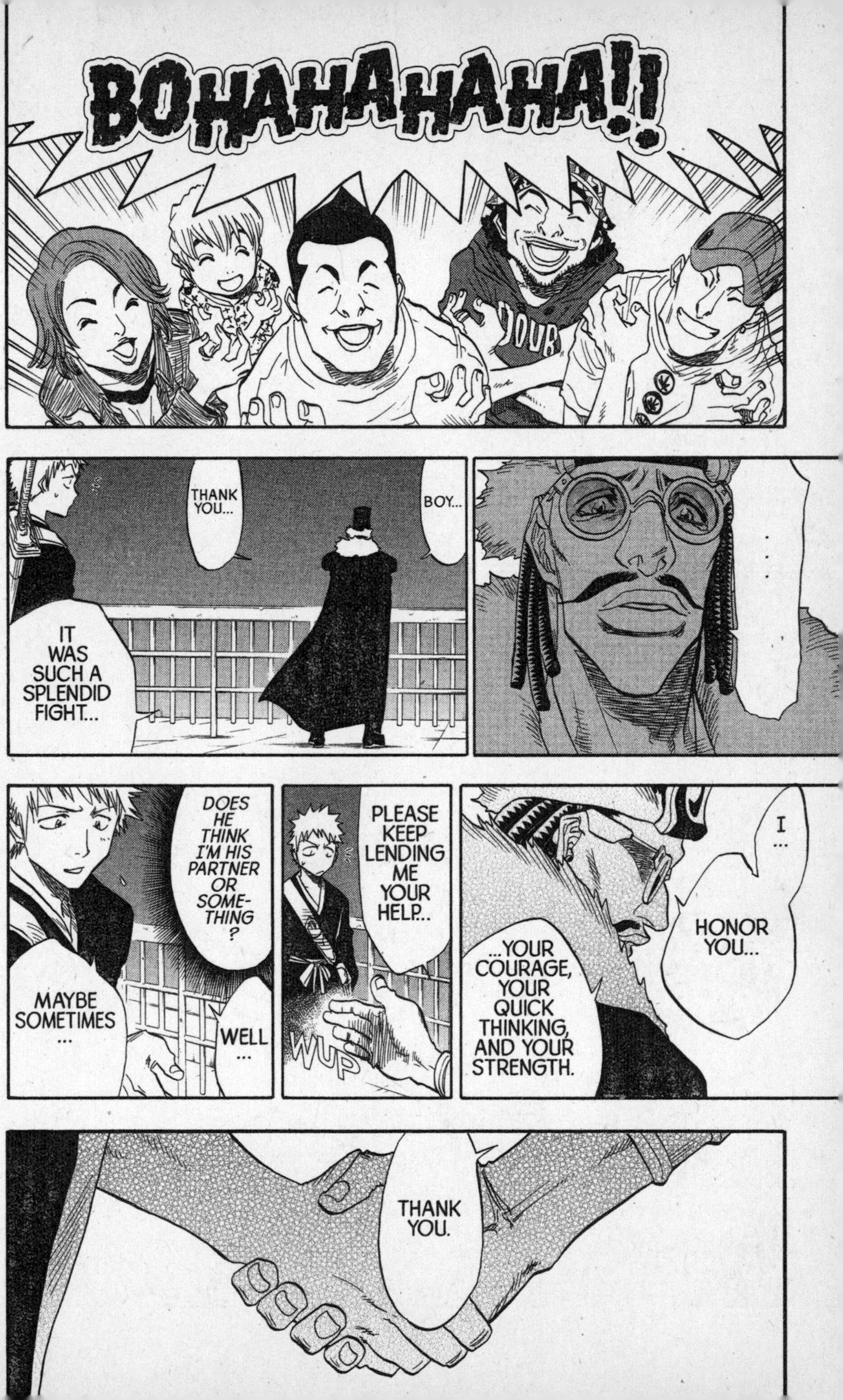
BOHAHAHAHA!!
BOY...
THANK YOU...
IT WAS SUCH A SPLENDID FIGHT...
I ...
HONOR YOU...
...YOUR COURAGE, YOUR QUICK THINKING, AND YOUR STRENGTH.
PLEASE KEEP LENDING ME YOUR HELP...
WUP
DOES HE THINK I'M HIS PARTNER OR SOME-THING?
WELL ...
MAYBE SOMETIMES ...
THANK YOU.

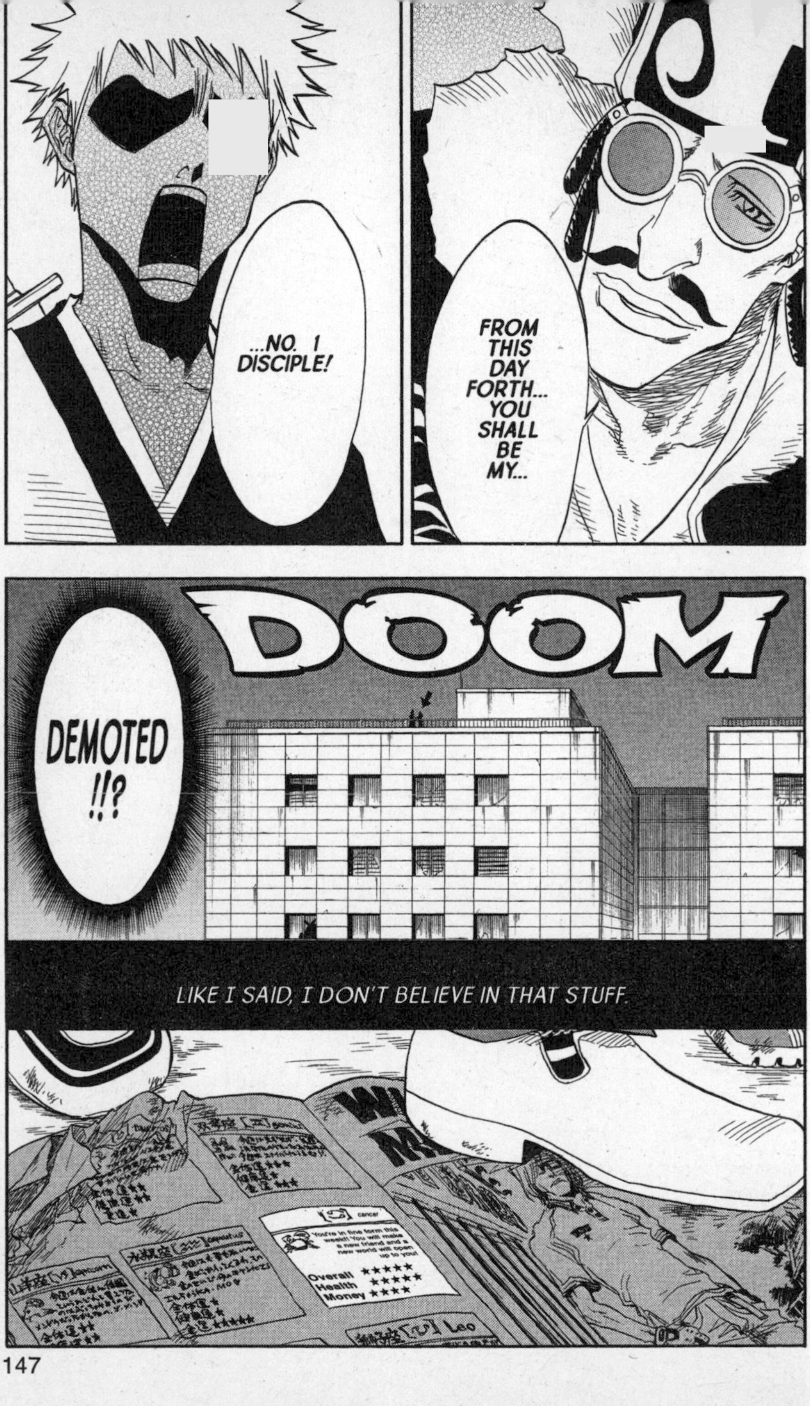
FROM THIS DAY FORTH... YOU SHALL BE MY...
...NO. 1 DISCIPLE!
DOOM
DEMOTED !!?
LIKE I SAID, I DON'T BELIEVE IN THAT STUFF.
cancer
You're in fine form this week!! You will make a new friend and a new world will open up to you!
Overall ★★★★★
Health ★★★★★
Money ★★★★
Leo

Trophy from this battle.

FAN CLUB

Don Kanonji
Fan Club

Special Membership Number: 0000000015

To. MY #1 DISCIPLE

Forced
upon
him as
he was
leaving.

Hmph

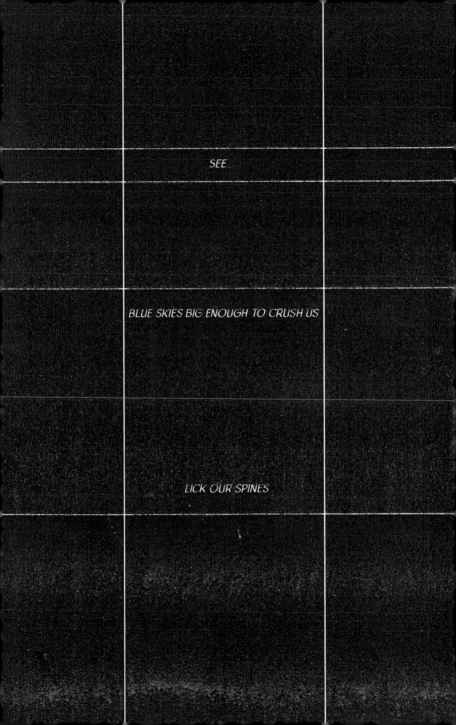

SEE

BLUE SKIES BIG ENOUGH TO CRUSH US

LICK OUR SPINES

33. ROCKIN' FUTURE 7

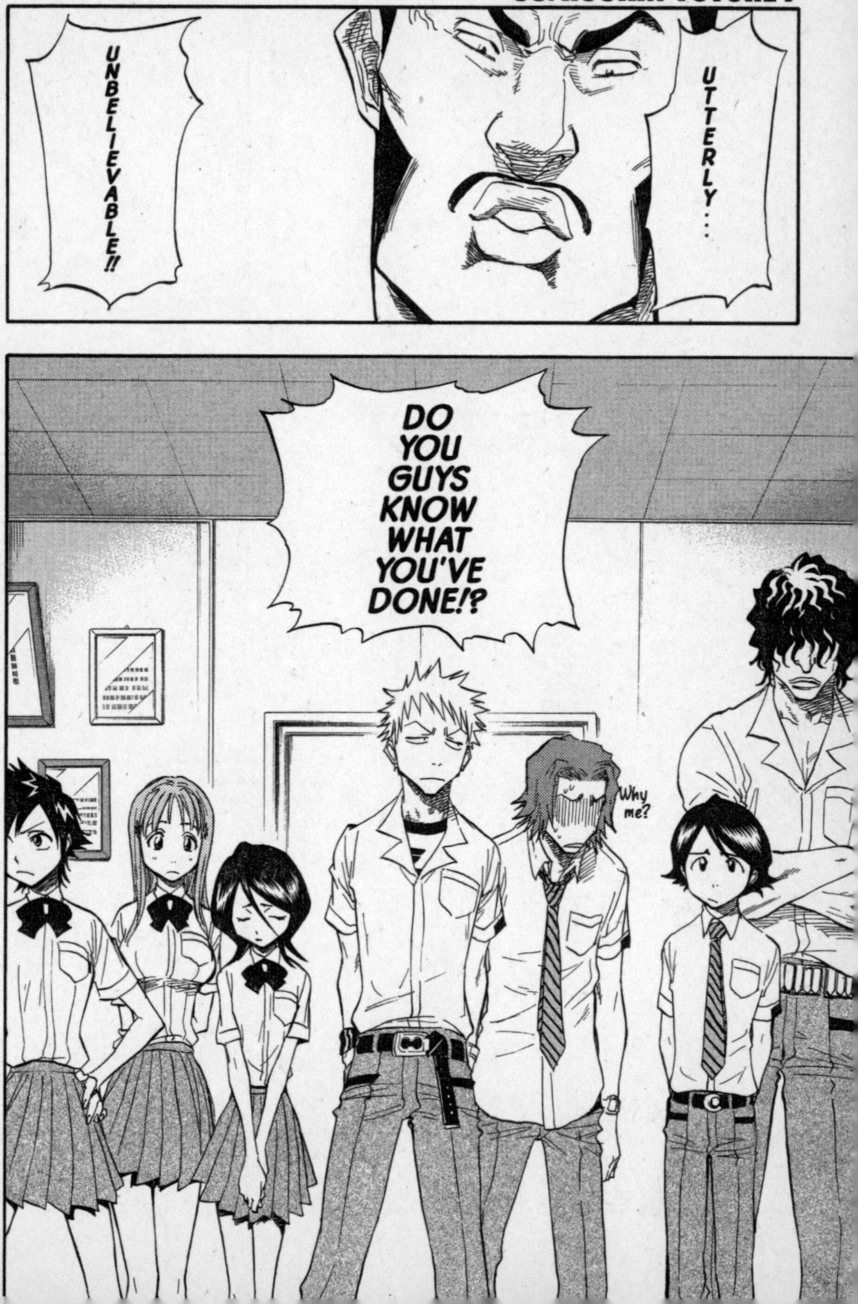
UTTERLY...
UNBELIEVABLE!!
DO YOU GUYS KNOW WHAT YOU'VE DONE!?
Why me?

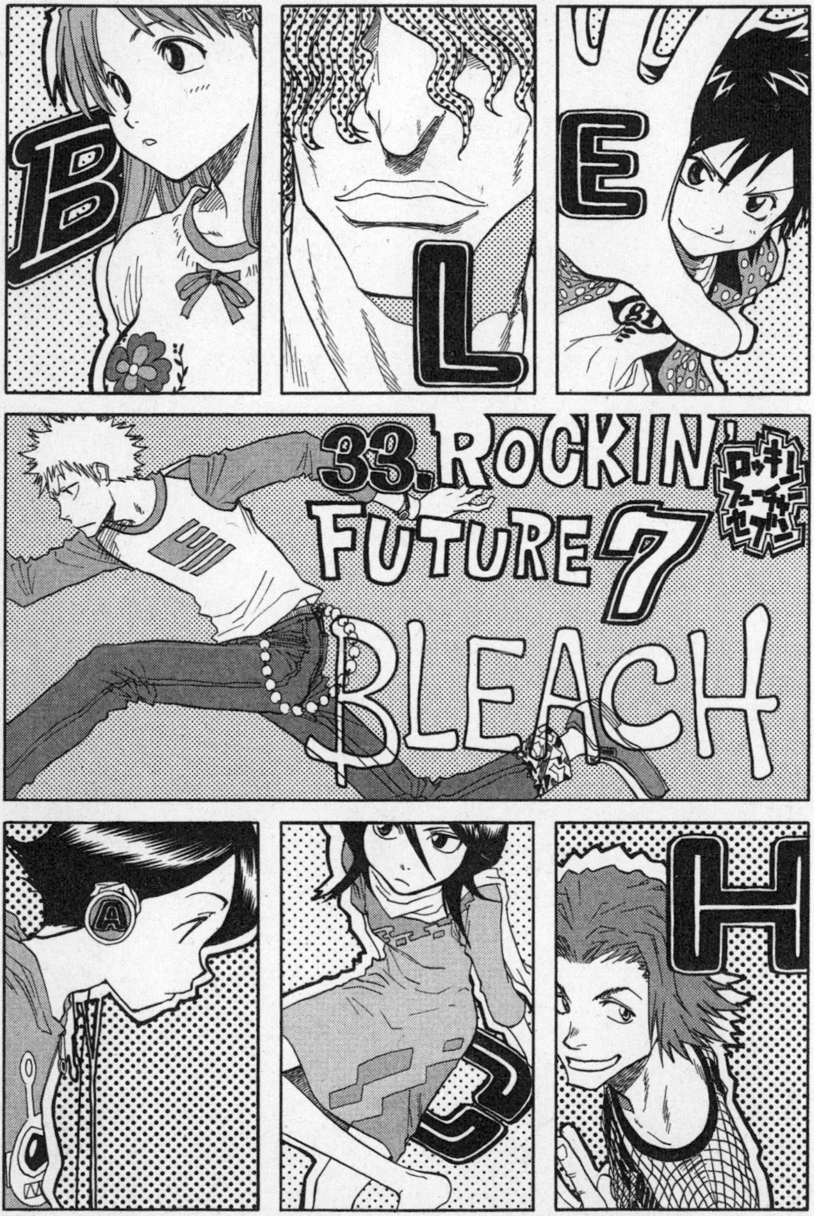

E
L
B
33. ROCKIN' FUTURE 7
BLEACH
H
C
A

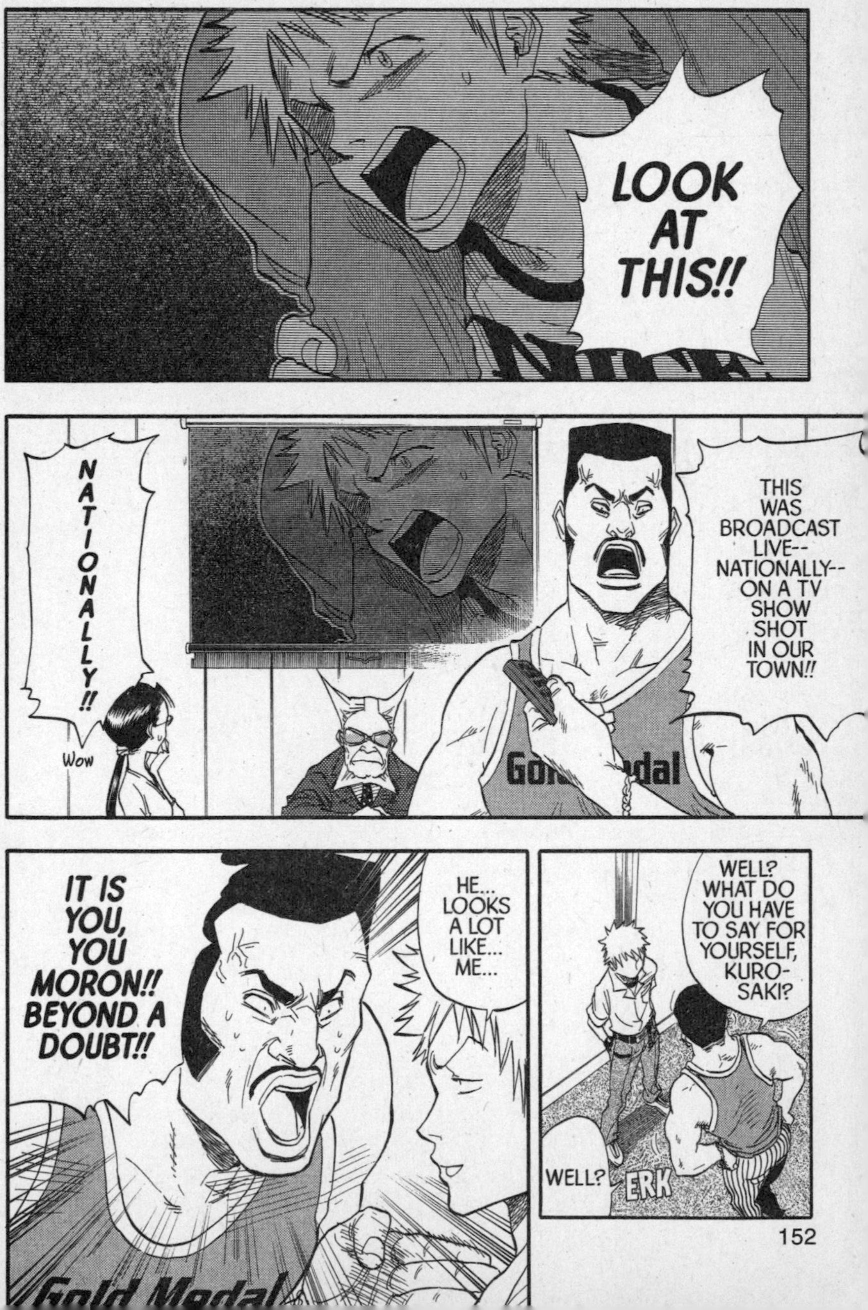
LOOK AT THIS!!
THIS WAS BROADCAST LIVE-- NATIONALLY-- ON A TV SHOW SHOT IN OUR TOWN!!
NATIONALLY!!
Wow
WELL? WHAT DO YOU HAVE TO SAY FOR YOURSELF, KURO-SAKI?
WELL?
ERK
HE... LOOKS A LOT LIKE... ME...
IT IS YOU, YOU MORON!! BEYOND A DOUBT!!

READ THIS WAY

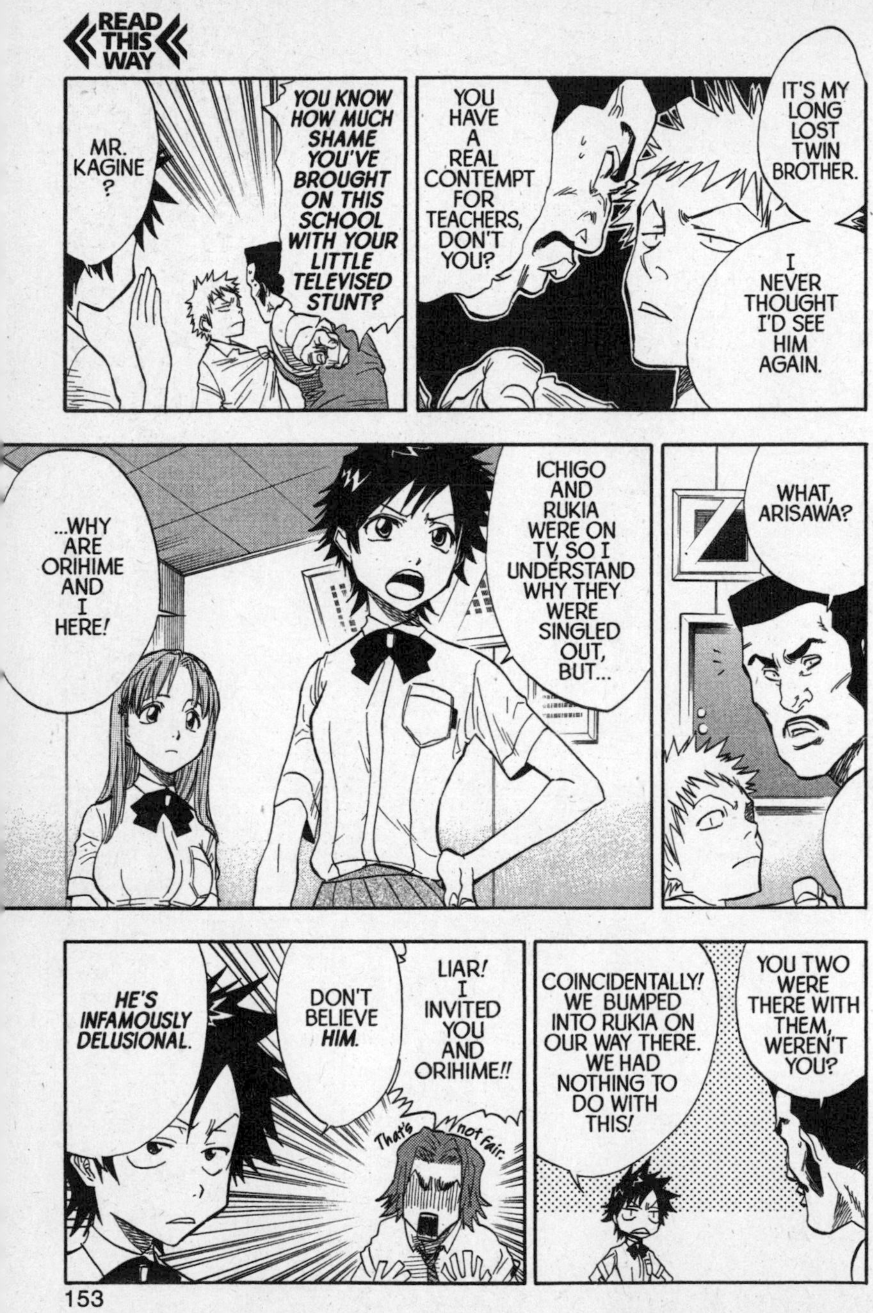
IT'S MY LONG LOST TWIN BROTHER.
I NEVER THOUGHT I'D SEE HIM AGAIN.
YOU HAVE A REAL CONTEMPT FOR TEACHERS, DON'T YOU?
YOU KNOW HOW MUCH SHAME YOU'VE BROUGHT ON THIS SCHOOL WITH YOUR LITTLE TELEVISED STUNT?
MR. KAGINE?
WHAT, ARISAWA?
ICHIGO AND RUKIA WERE ON TV, SO I UNDERSTAND WHY THEY WERE SINGLED OUT, BUT...
...WHY ARE ORIHIME AND I HERE!
YOU TWO WERE THERE WITH THEM, WEREN'T YOU?
COINCIDENTALLY! WE BUMPED INTO RUKIA ON OUR WAY THERE. WE HAD NOTHING TO DO WITH THIS!
LIAR! I INVITED YOU AND ORIHIME!!
That's not fair.
DON'T BELIEVE *HIM*.
HE'S INFAMOUSLY DELUSIONAL.

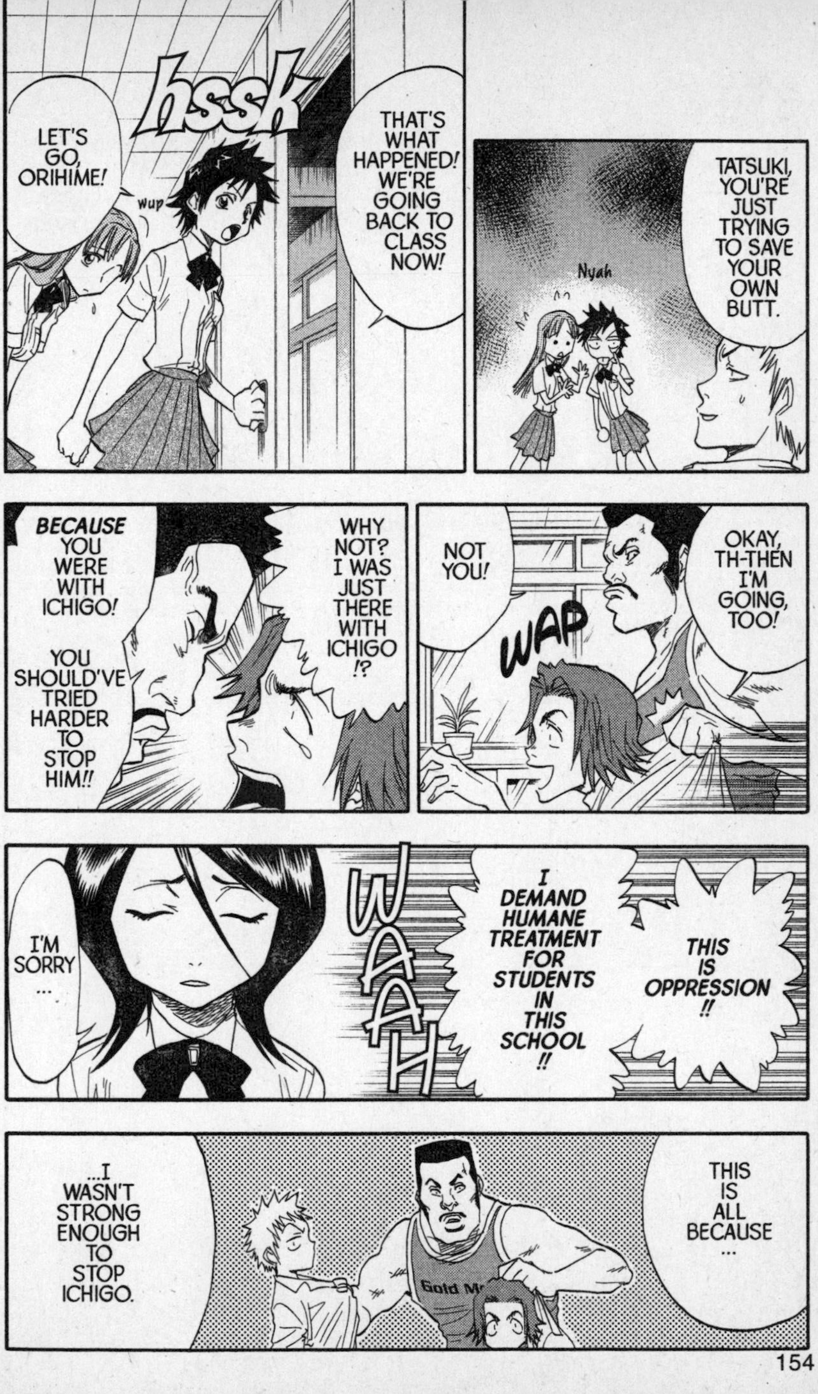
TATSUKI, YOU'RE JUST TRYING TO SAVE YOUR OWN BUTT.
Nyah
THAT'S WHAT HAPPENED! WE'RE GOING BACK TO CLASS NOW!
hssk
LET'S GO, ORIHIME!
wup
OKAY, TH-THEN I'M GOING, TOO!
NOT YOU!
WAP
WHY NOT? I WAS JUST THERE WITH ICHIGO!?
BECAUSE YOU WERE WITH ICHIGO!
YOU SHOULD'VE TRIED HARDER TO STOP HIM!!
THIS IS OPPRESSION!!
I DEMAND HUMANE TREATMENT FOR STUDENTS IN THIS SCHOOL!!
WAAH
I'M SORRY...
THIS IS ALL BECAUSE...
...I WASN'T STRONG ENOUGH TO STOP ICHIGO.

READ THIS WAY

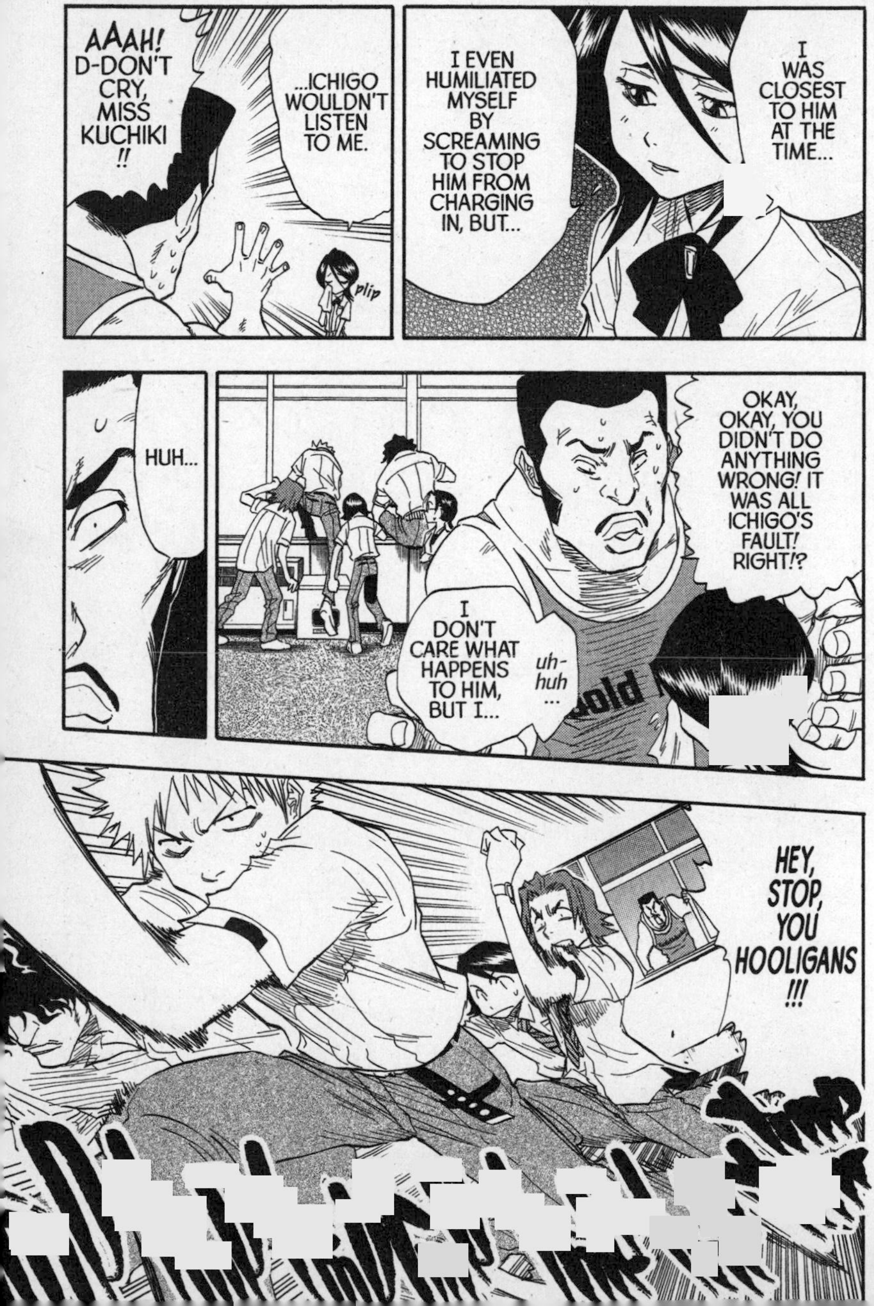
I WAS CLOSEST TO HIM AT THE TIME...
I EVEN HUMILIATED MYSELF BY SCREAMING TO STOP HIM FROM CHARGING IN, BUT...
...ICHIGO WOULDN'T LISTEN TO ME.
AAAH! D-DON'T CRY, MISS KUCHIKI!!
plip
OKAY, OKAY, YOU DIDN'T DO ANYTHING WRONG! IT WAS ALL ICHIGO'S FAULT! RIGHT!?
uh-huh...
I DON'T CARE WHAT HAPPENS TO HIM, BUT I...
HUH...
HEY, STOP, YOU HOOLIGANS!!!

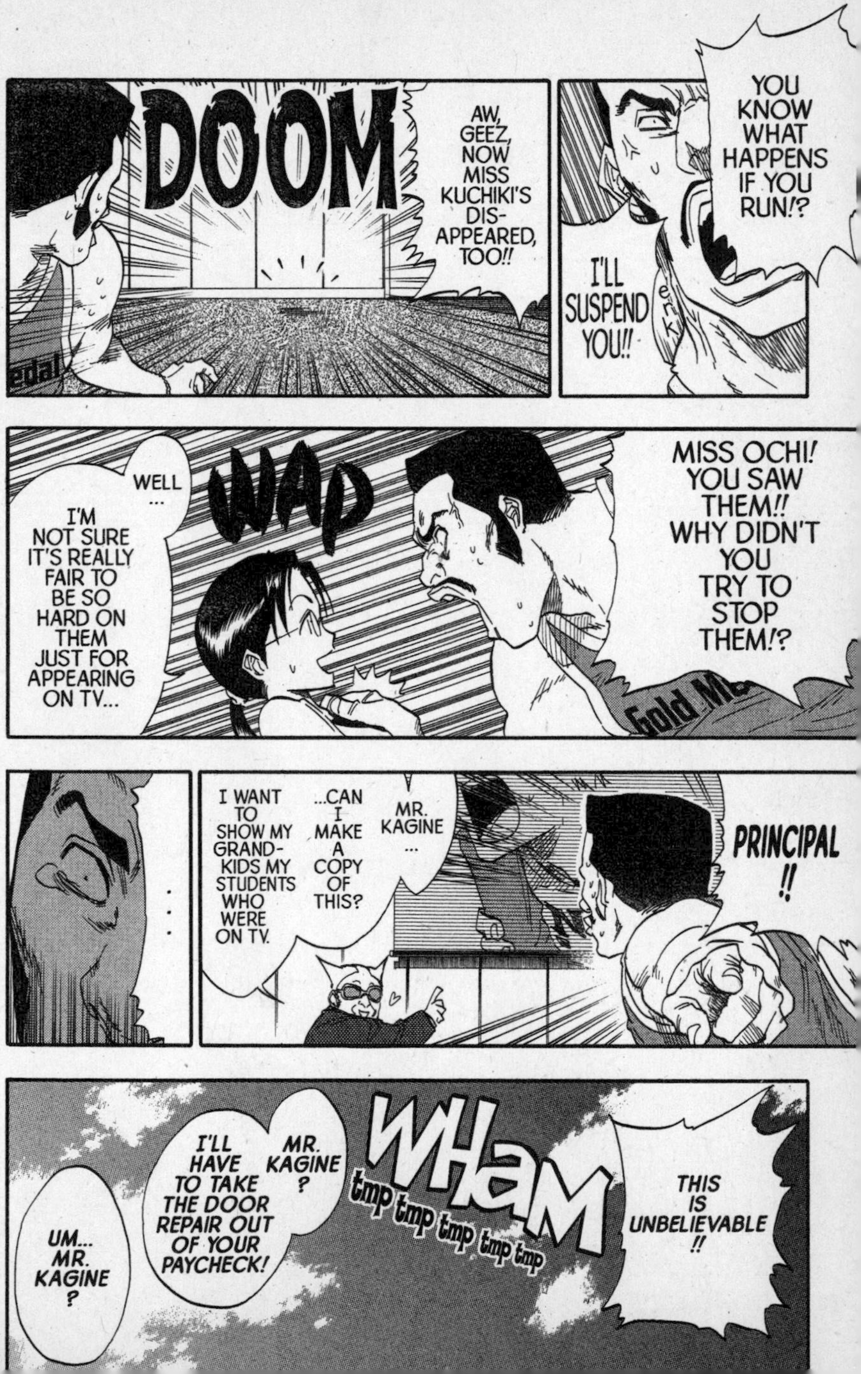
YOU KNOW WHAT HAPPENS IF YOU RUN!?
I'LL SUSPEND YOU!!
erk
DOOM
AW, GEEZ, NOW MISS KUCHIKI'S DIS-APPEARED, TOO!!
MISS OCHI! YOU SAW THEM!! WHY DIDN'T YOU TRY TO STOP THEM!?
WAP
WELL ...
I'M NOT SURE IT'S REALLY FAIR TO BE SO HARD ON THEM JUST FOR APPEARING ON TV...
PRINCIPAL !!
MR. KAGINE ...
...CAN I MAKE A COPY OF THIS?
I WANT TO SHOW MY GRAND-KIDS MY STUDENTS WHO WERE ON TV.
...
THIS IS UNBELIEVABLE !!
WHAM
tmp tmp tmp tmp tmp
MR. KAGINE ?
I'LL HAVE TO TAKE THE DOOR REPAIR OUT OF YOUR PAYCHECK!
UM... MR. KAGINE ?

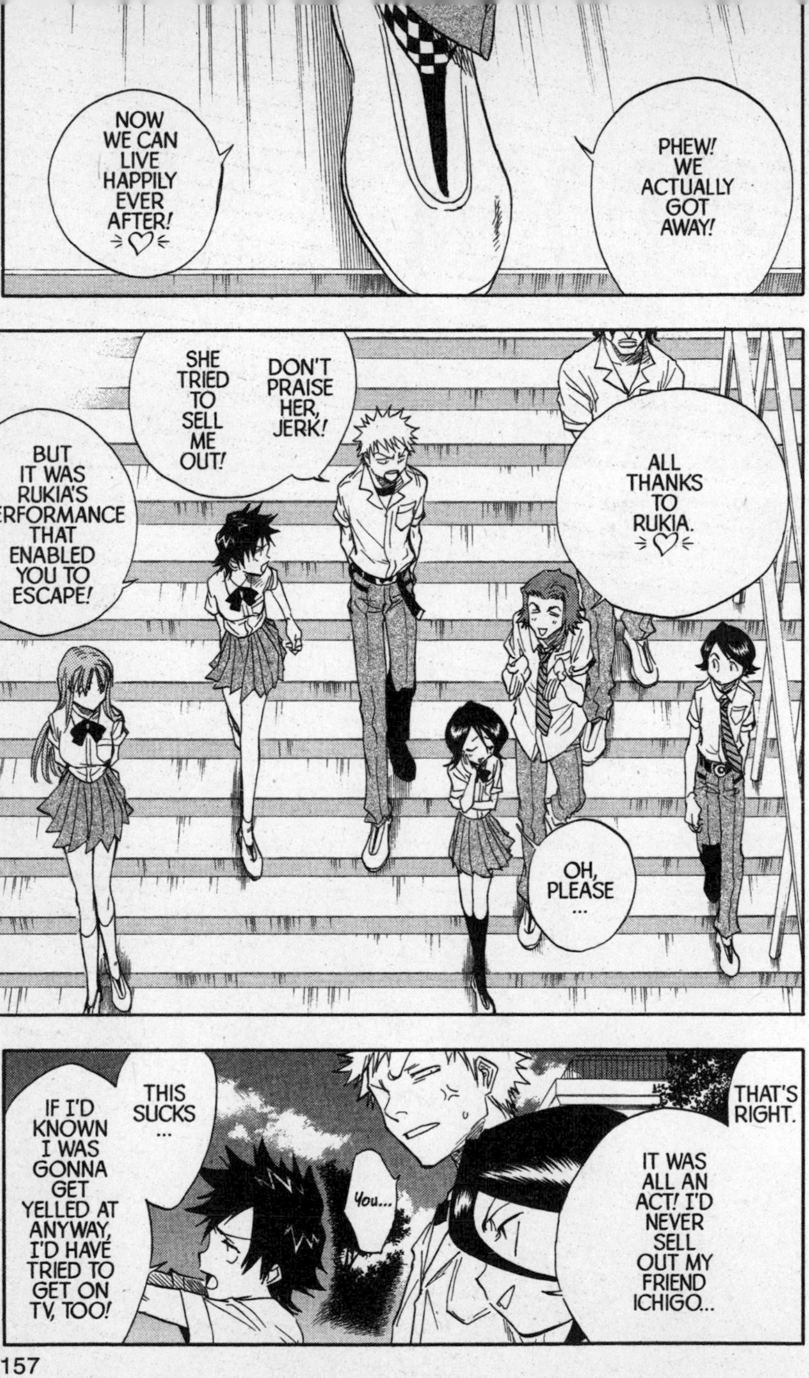
PHEW! WE ACTUALLY GOT AWAY!
NOW WE CAN LIVE HAPPILY EVER AFTER! ♡
ALL THANKS TO RUKIA. ♡
OH, PLEASE ...
DON'T PRAISE HER, JERK!
SHE TRIED TO SELL ME OUT!
BUT IT WAS RUKIA'S PERFORMANCE THAT ENABLED YOU TO ESCAPE!
THAT'S RIGHT.
IT WAS ALL AN ACT! I'D NEVER SELL OUT MY FRIEND ICHIGO...
You...
THIS SUCKS ...
IF I'D KNOWN I WAS GONNA GET YELLED AT ANYWAY, I'D HAVE TRIED TO GET ON TV, TOO!

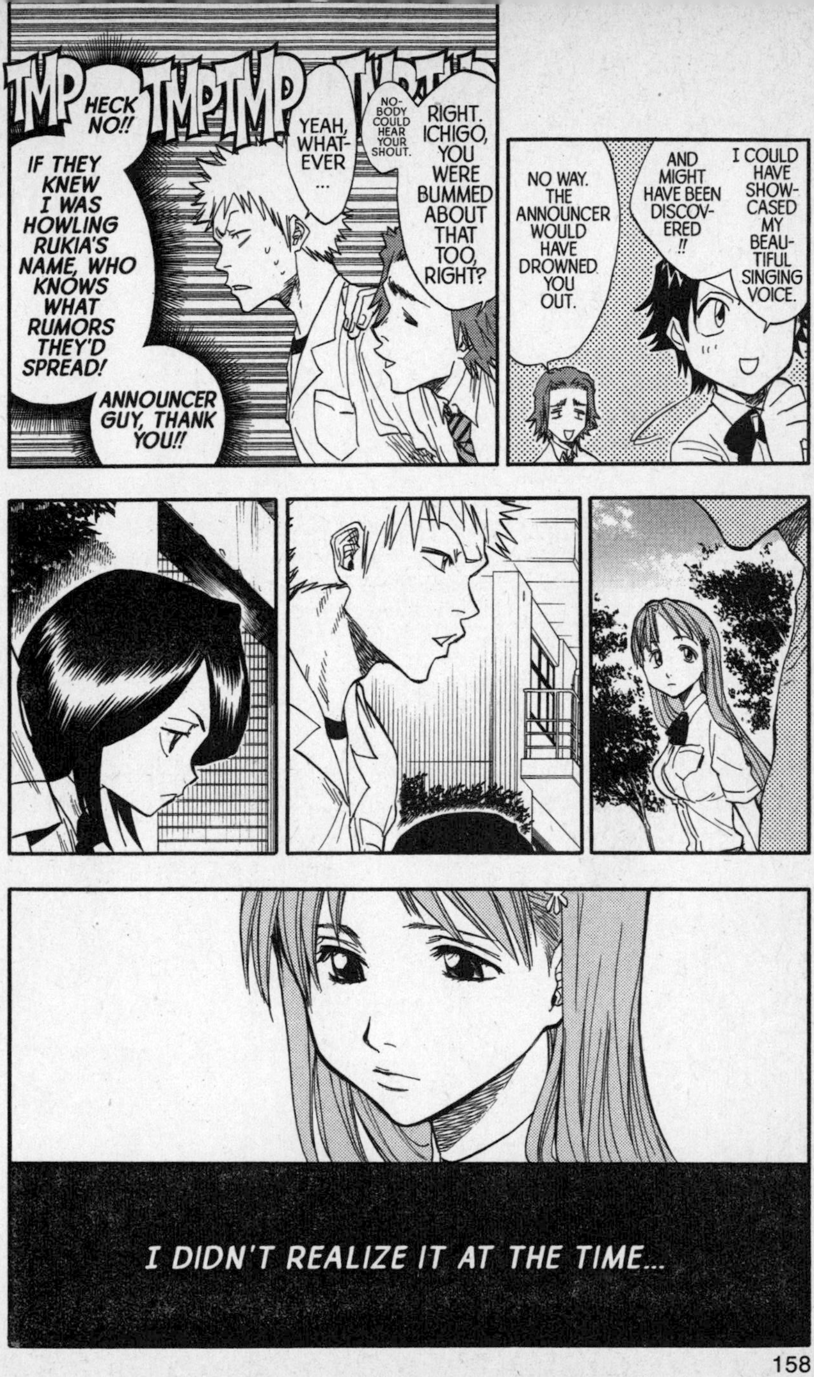
I COULD HAVE SHOWCASED MY BEAUTIFUL SINGING VOICE.
AND MIGHT HAVE BEEN DISCOVERED!!
NO WAY. THE ANNOUNCER WOULD HAVE DROWNED YOU OUT.
RIGHT. ICHIGO, YOU WERE BUMMED ABOUT THAT TOO, RIGHT?
NOBODY COULD HEAR YOUR SHOUT.
YEAH, WHATEVER...
TMP TMPTMP
HECK NO!!
TMP
IF THEY KNEW I WAS HOWLING RUKIA'S NAME, WHO KNOWS WHAT RUMORS THEY'D SPREAD!
ANNOUNCER GUY, THANK YOU!!
I DIDN'T REALIZE IT AT THE TIME...

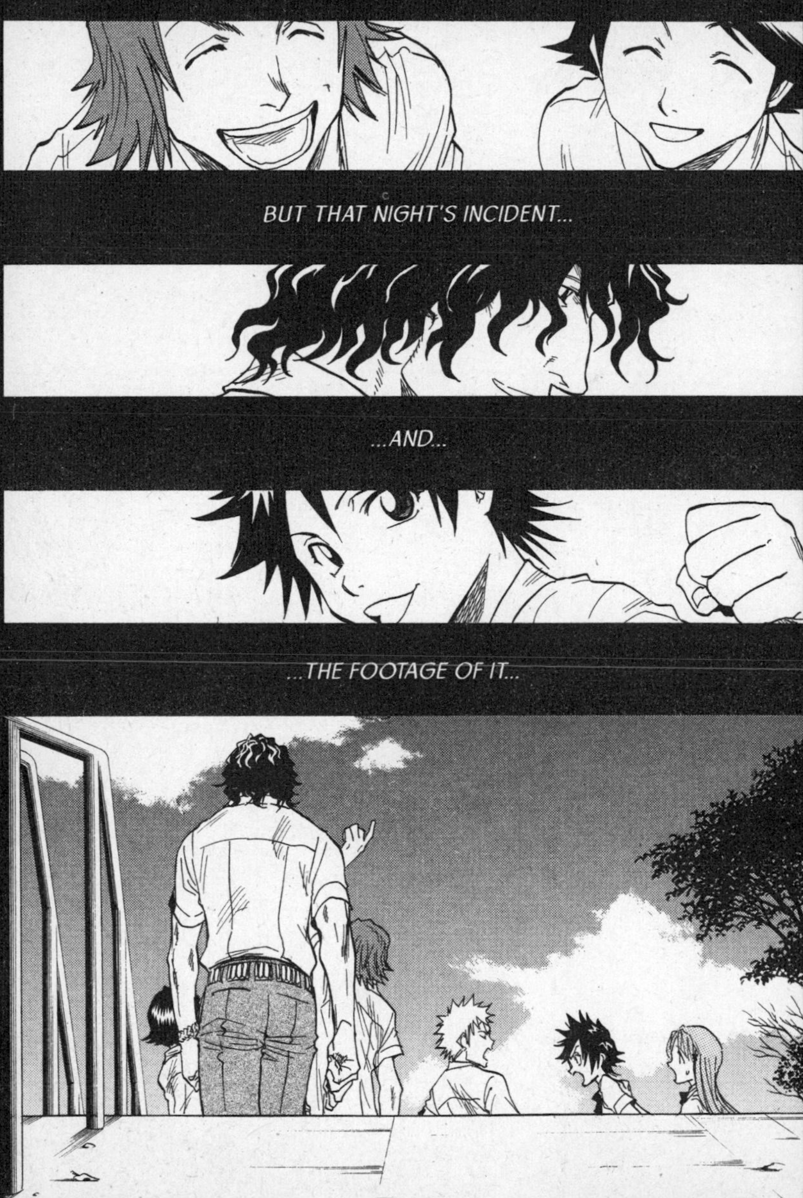
BUT THAT NIGHT'S INCIDENT...
...AND...
...THE FOOTAGE OF IT...

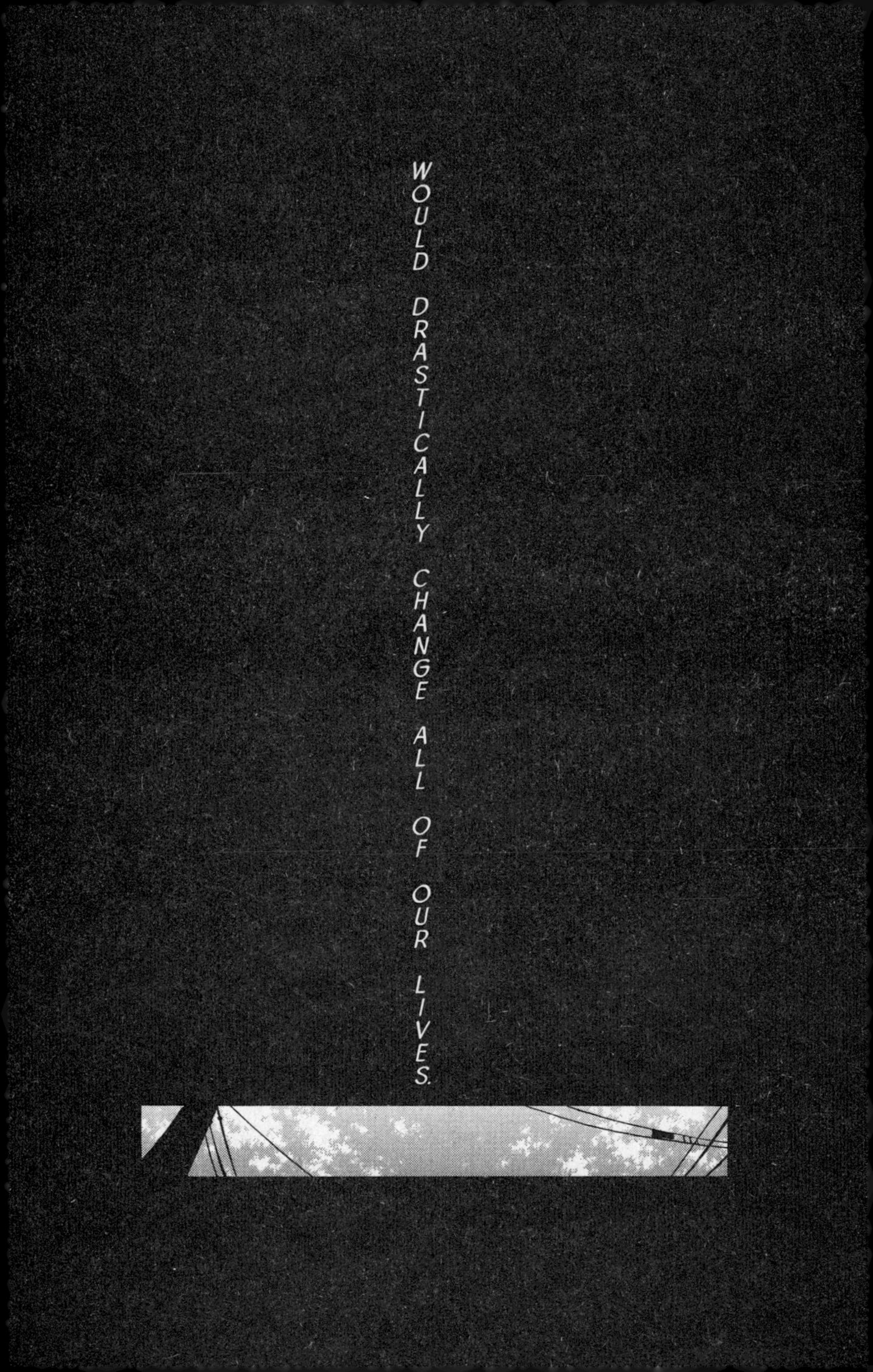
WOULD DRASTICALLY CHANGE ALL OF OUR LIVES.

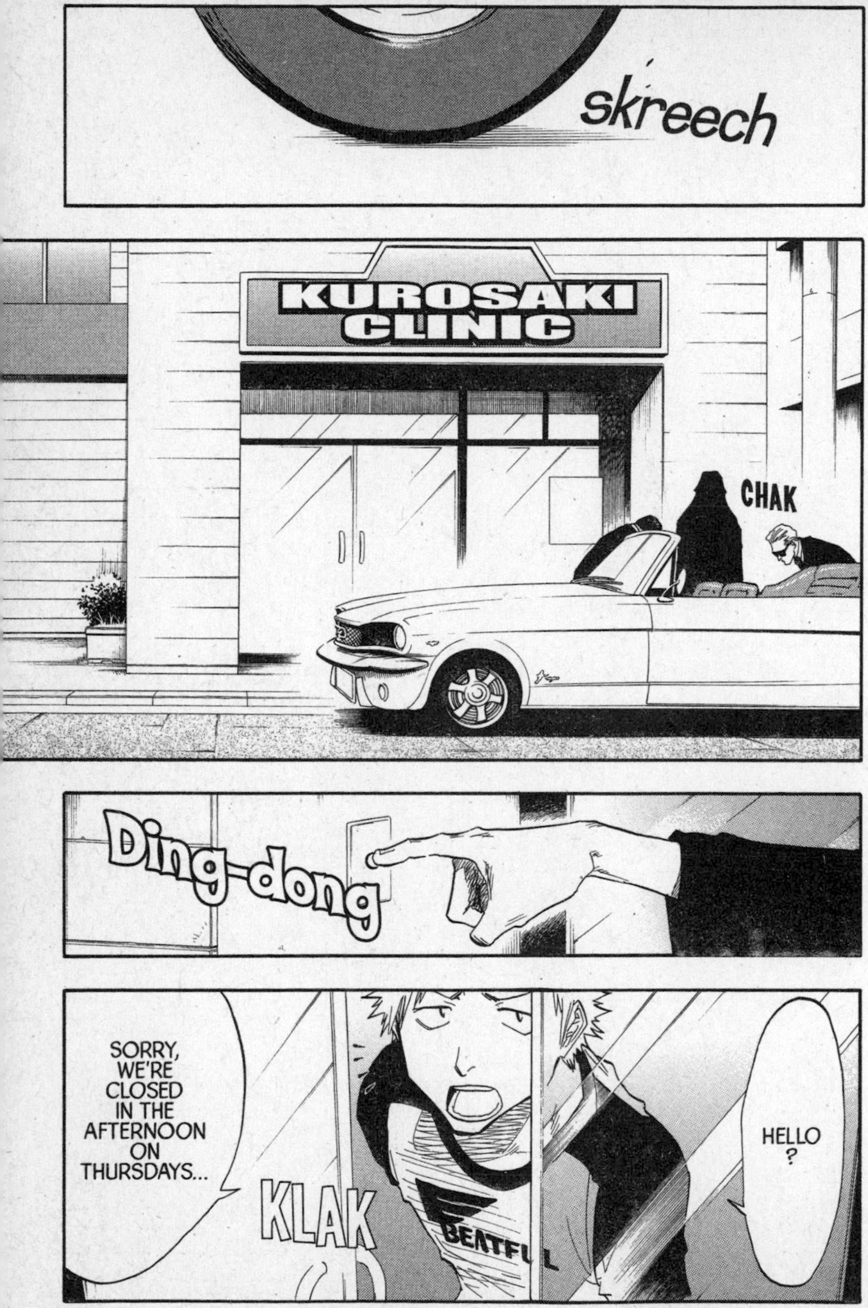
skreech
KUROSAKI CLINIC
CHAK
Ding-dong
HELLO?
SORRY, WE'RE CLOSED IN THE AFTERNOON ON THURSDAYS...
KLAK

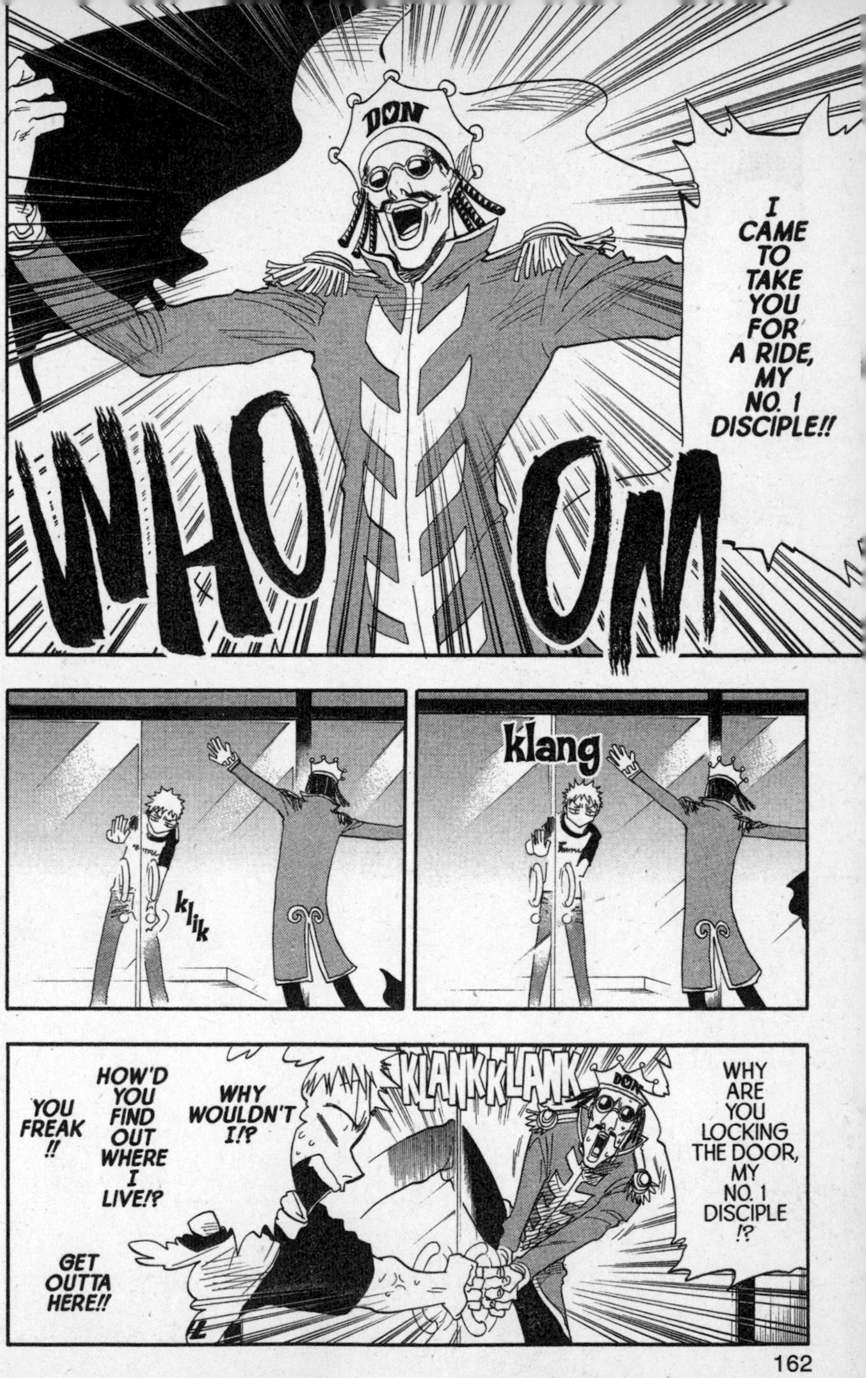
I CAME TO TAKE YOU FOR A RIDE, MY NO. 1 DISCIPLE!!
WHOOM
klang
klik
WHY ARE YOU LOCKING THE DOOR, MY NO. 1 DISCIPLE!?
KLANKKLANK
WHY WOULDN'T I!?
HOW'D YOU FIND OUT WHERE I LIVE!?
YOU FREAK!!
GET OUTTA HERE!!

READ THIS WAY

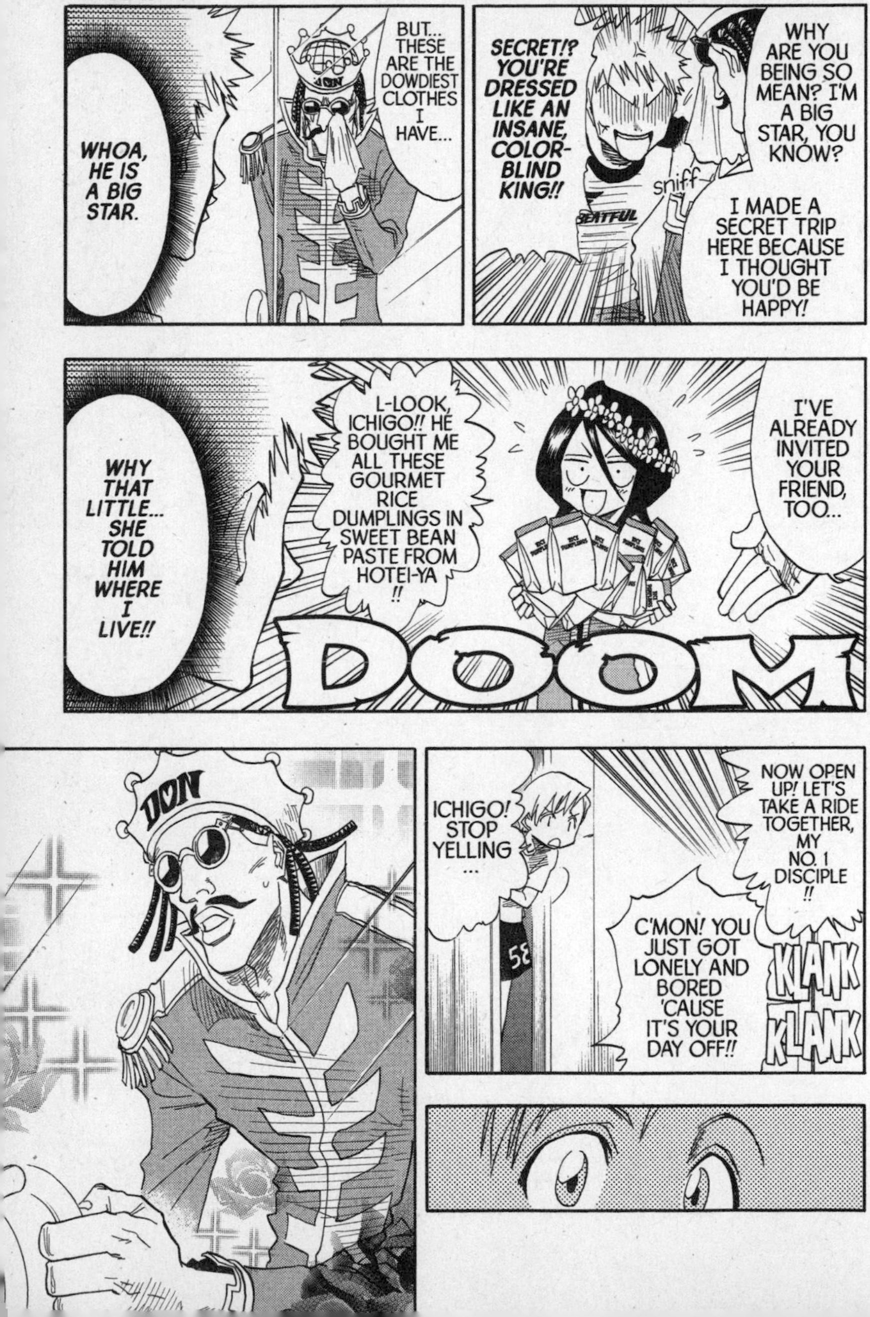
WHY ARE YOU BEING SO MEAN? I'M A BIG STAR, YOU KNOW?
sniff
I MADE A SECRET TRIP HERE BECAUSE I THOUGHT YOU'D BE HAPPY!
SECRET!? YOU'RE DRESSED LIKE AN INSANE, COLOR-BLIND KING!!
BUT... THESE ARE THE DOWDIEST CLOTHES I HAVE...
WHOA, HE IS A BIG STAR.
I'VE ALREADY INVITED YOUR FRIEND, TOO...
L-LOOK, ICHIGO!! HE BOUGHT ME ALL THESE GOURMET RICE DUMPLINGS IN SWEET BEAN PASTE FROM HOTEI-YA!!
DOOM
WHY THAT LITTLE... SHE TOLD HIM WHERE I LIVE!!
NOW OPEN UP! LET'S TAKE A RIDE TOGETHER, MY NO. 1 DISCIPLE!!
KLANK KLANK
C'MON! YOU JUST GOT LONELY AND BORED 'CAUSE IT'S YOUR DAY OFF!!
ICHIGO! STOP YELLING...
DON

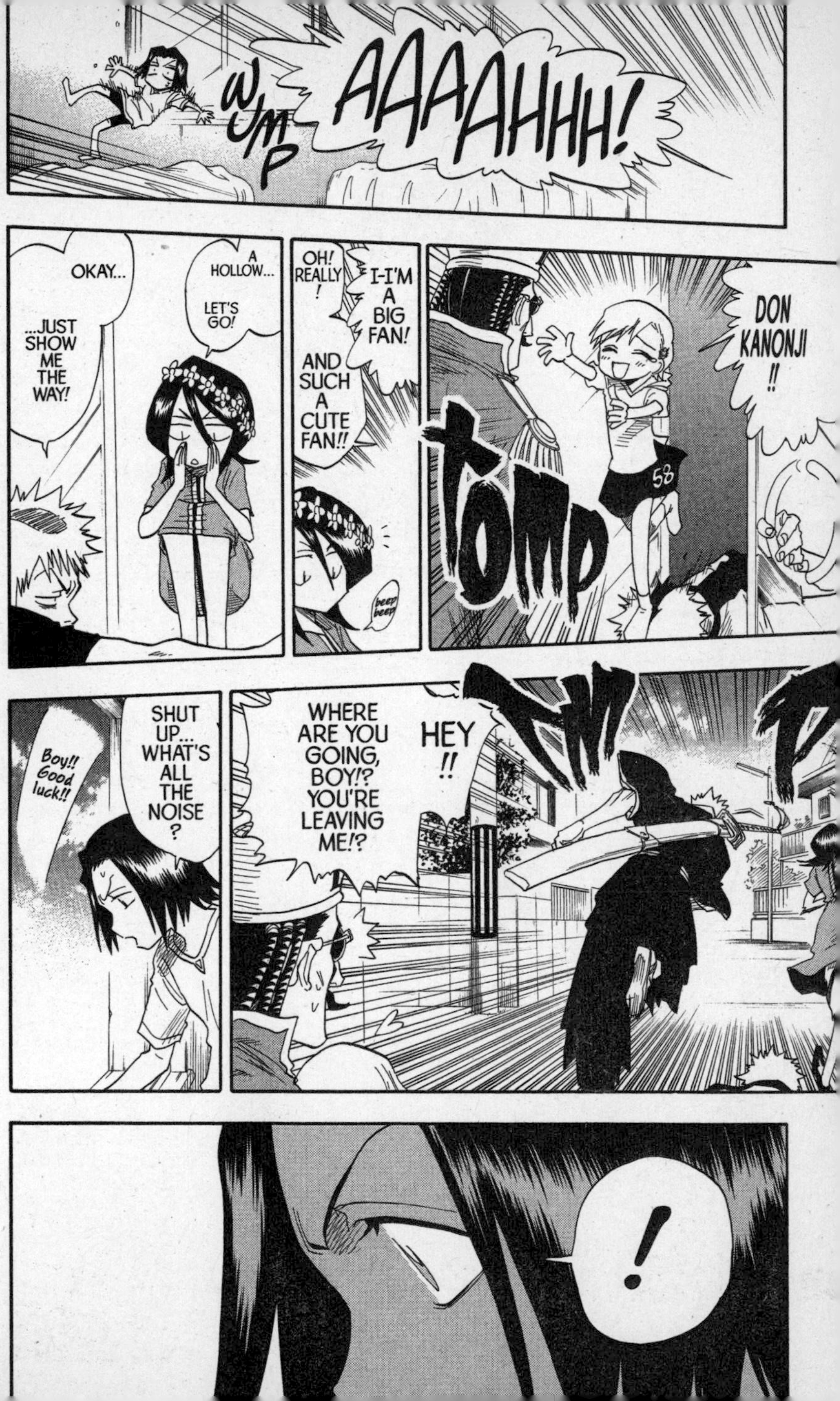
AAAAHHHH!
WUMP
DON KANONJI!!
TOMP
I-I'M A BIG FAN!
AND SUCH A CUTE FAN!!
OH! REALLY!
beep beep
A HOLLOW...
LET'S GO!
OKAY...
...JUST SHOW ME THE WAY!
HEY!!
WHERE ARE YOU GOING, BOY!? YOU'RE LEAVING ME!?
SHUT UP... WHAT'S ALL THE NOISE?
Boy!! Good luck!!
!

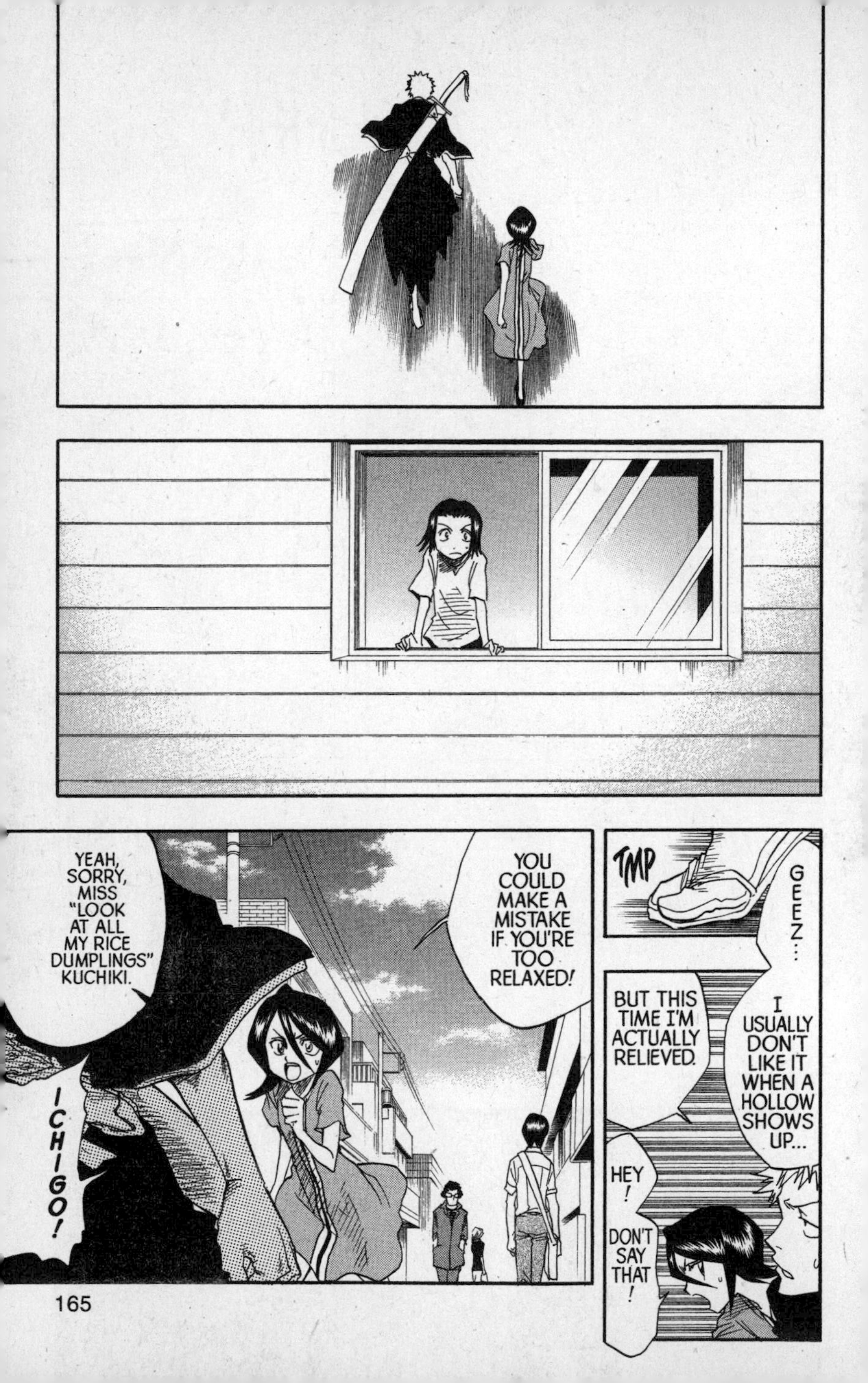
TMP
GEEZ...
I USUALLY DON'T LIKE IT WHEN A HOLLOW SHOWS UP...
BUT THIS TIME I'M ACTUALLY RELIEVED.
HEY! DON'T SAY THAT!
YOU COULD MAKE A MISTAKE IF YOU'RE TOO RELAXED!
YEAH, SORRY, MISS "LOOK AT ALL MY RICE DUMPLINGS" KUCHIKI.
ICHIGO!

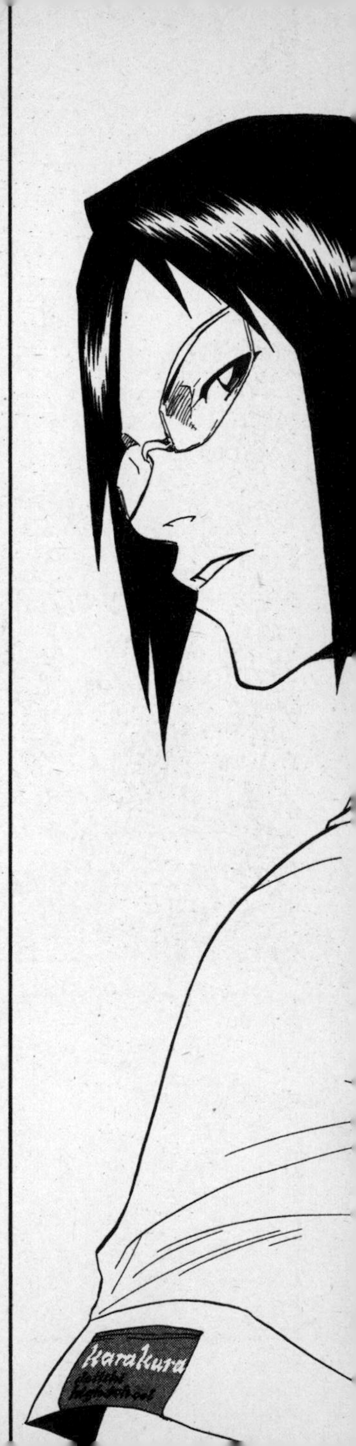
karakura
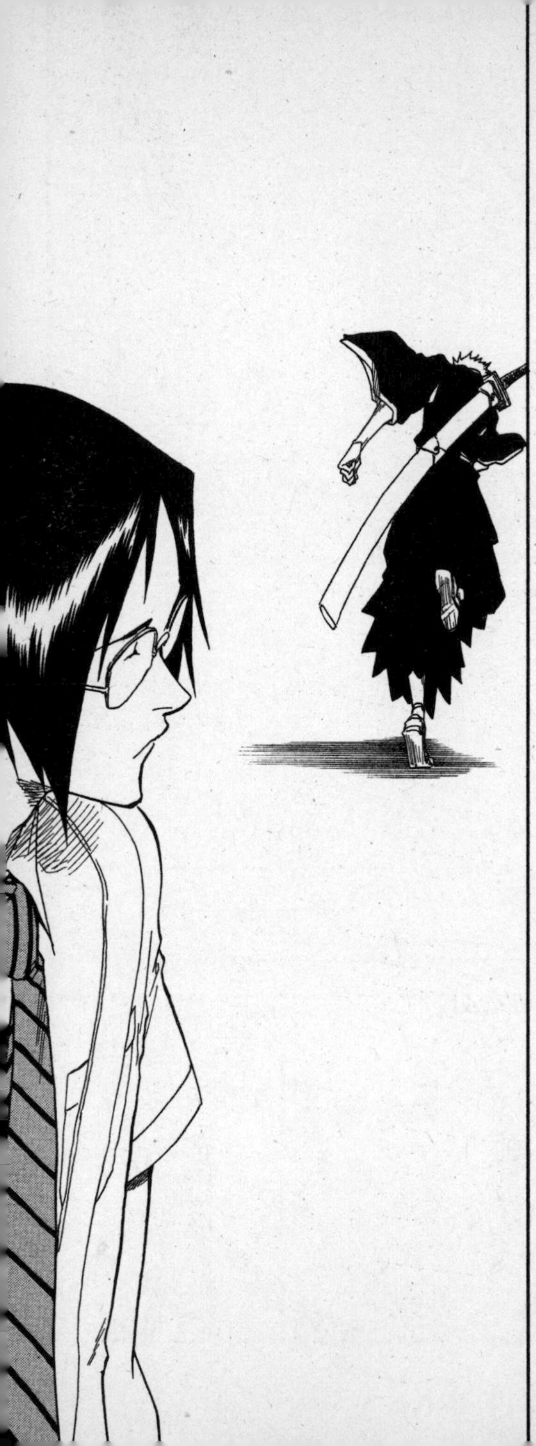

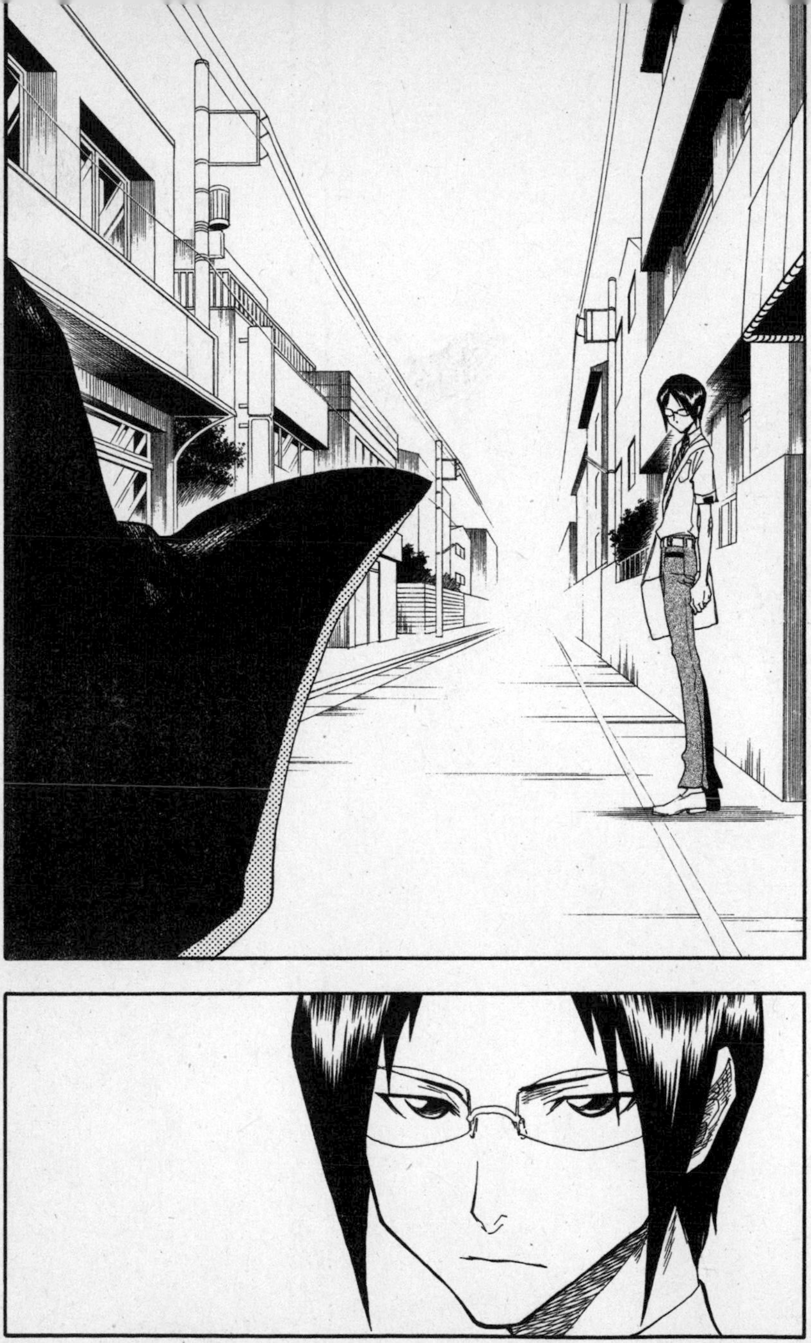

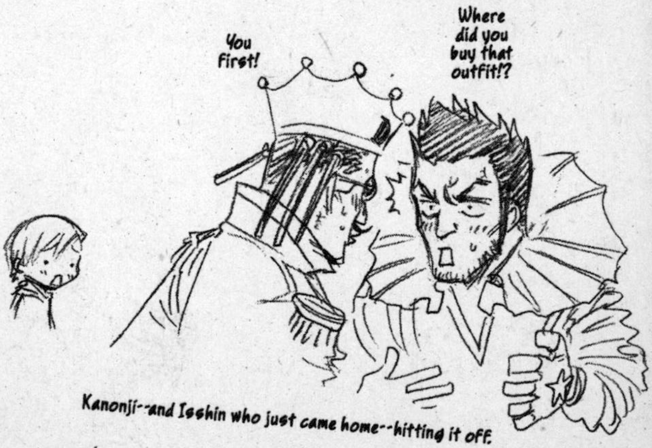
Where did you buy that outfit!?
You first!

Kanonji--and Isshin who just came home--hitting it off.

34. Quincy Archer Hates You

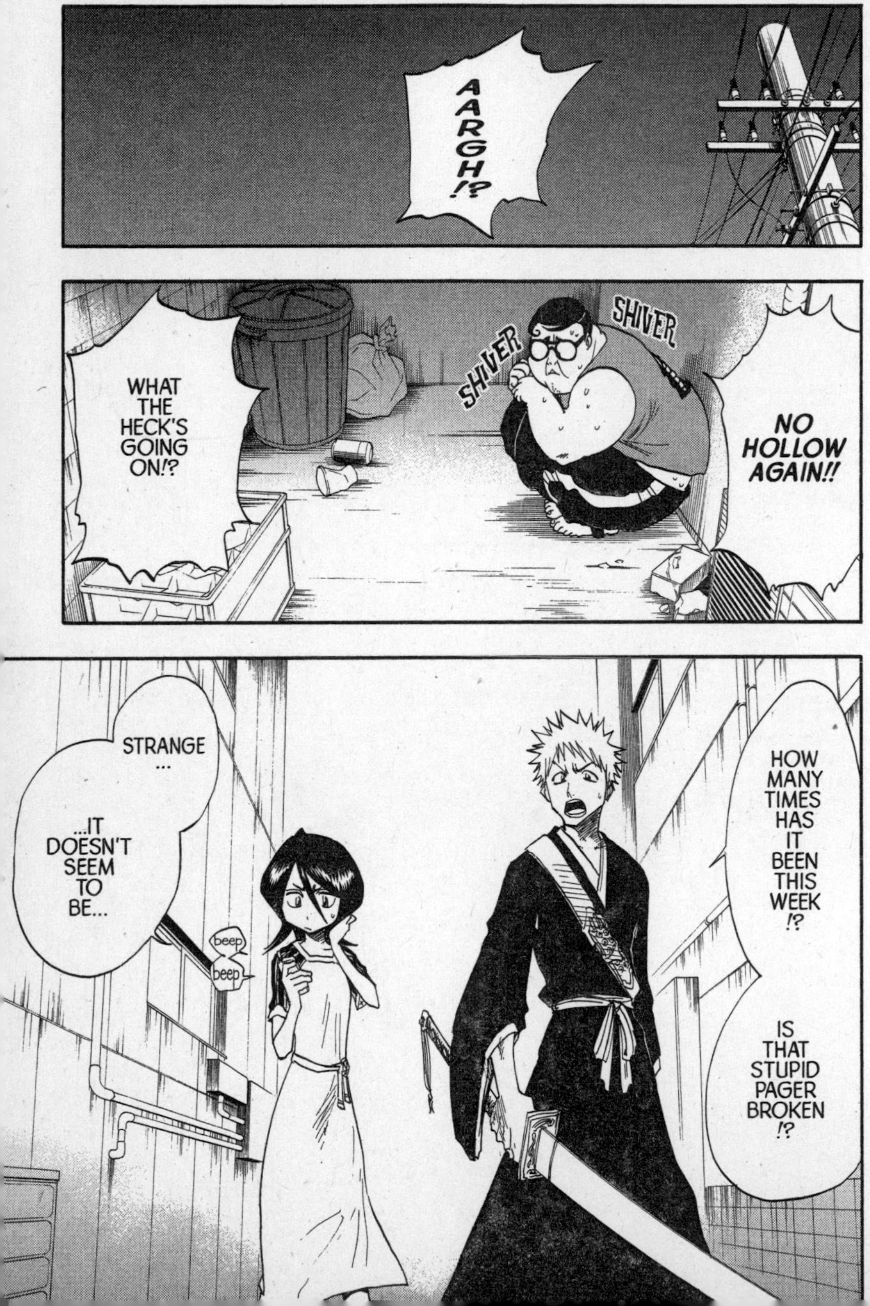
AARGH!?
NO HOLLOW AGAIN!!
SHIVER
SHIVER
WHAT THE HECK'S GOING ON!?
HOW MANY TIMES HAS IT BEEN THIS WEEK!?
IS THAT STUPID PAGER BROKEN!?
beep
beep
STRANGE...
...IT DOESN'T SEEM TO BE...

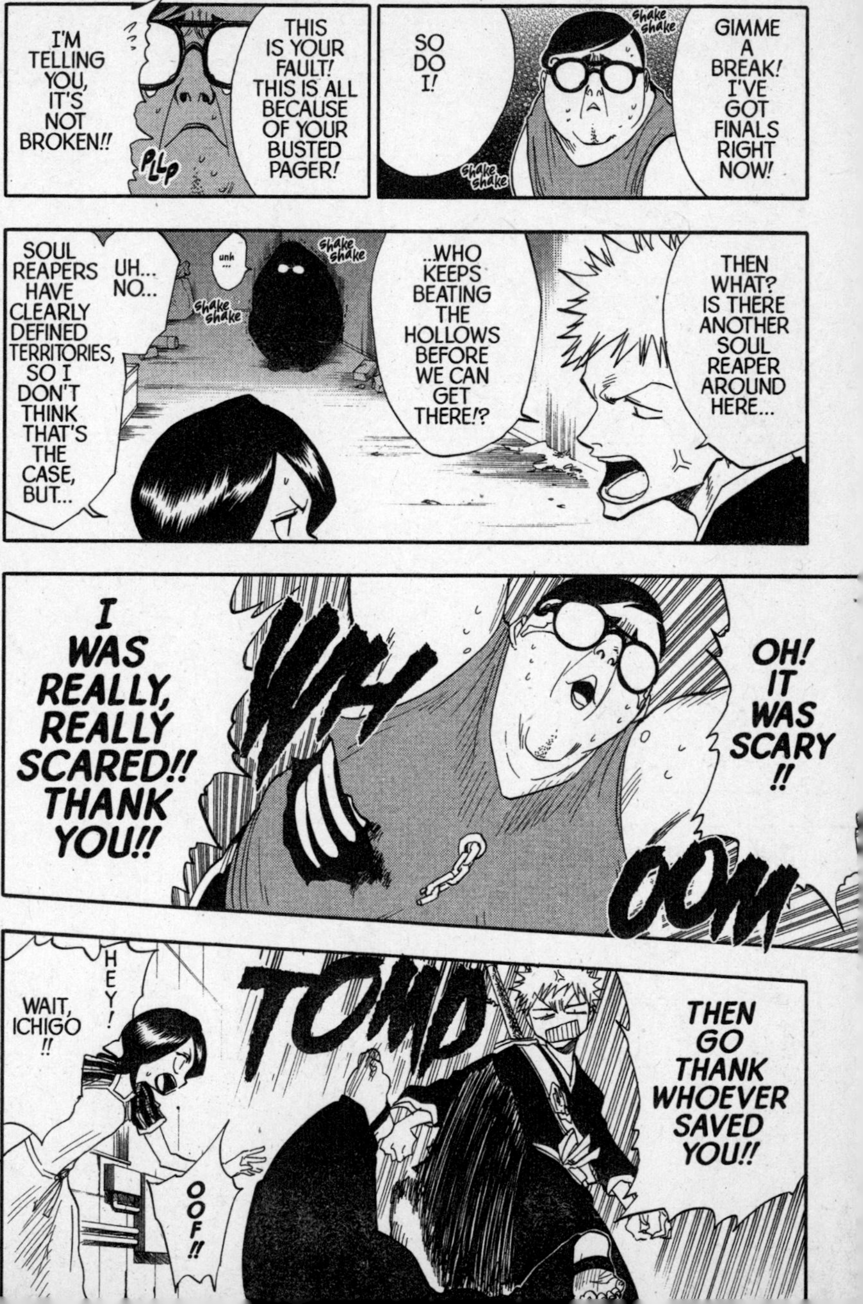
GIMME A BREAK! I'VE GOT FINALS RIGHT NOW!
shake shake
shake shake
SO DO I!
THIS IS YOUR FAULT! THIS IS ALL BECAUSE OF YOUR BUSTED PAGER!
I'M TELLING YOU, IT'S NOT BROKEN!!
PLLP
THEN WHAT? IS THERE ANOTHER SOUL REAPER AROUND HERE...
...WHO KEEPS BEATING THE HOLLOWS BEFORE WE CAN GET THERE!?
shake shake
unh ...
shake shake
UH... NO...
SOUL REAPERS HAVE CLEARLY DEFINED TERRITORIES, SO I DON'T THINK THAT'S THE CASE, BUT...
OH! IT WAS SCARY!!
I WAS REALLY, REALLY SCARED!! THANK YOU!!
WH
OOM
THEN GO THANK WHOEVER SAVED YOU!!
TOMD
HEY!
OOF!!
WAIT, ICHIGO!!

READ THIS WAY

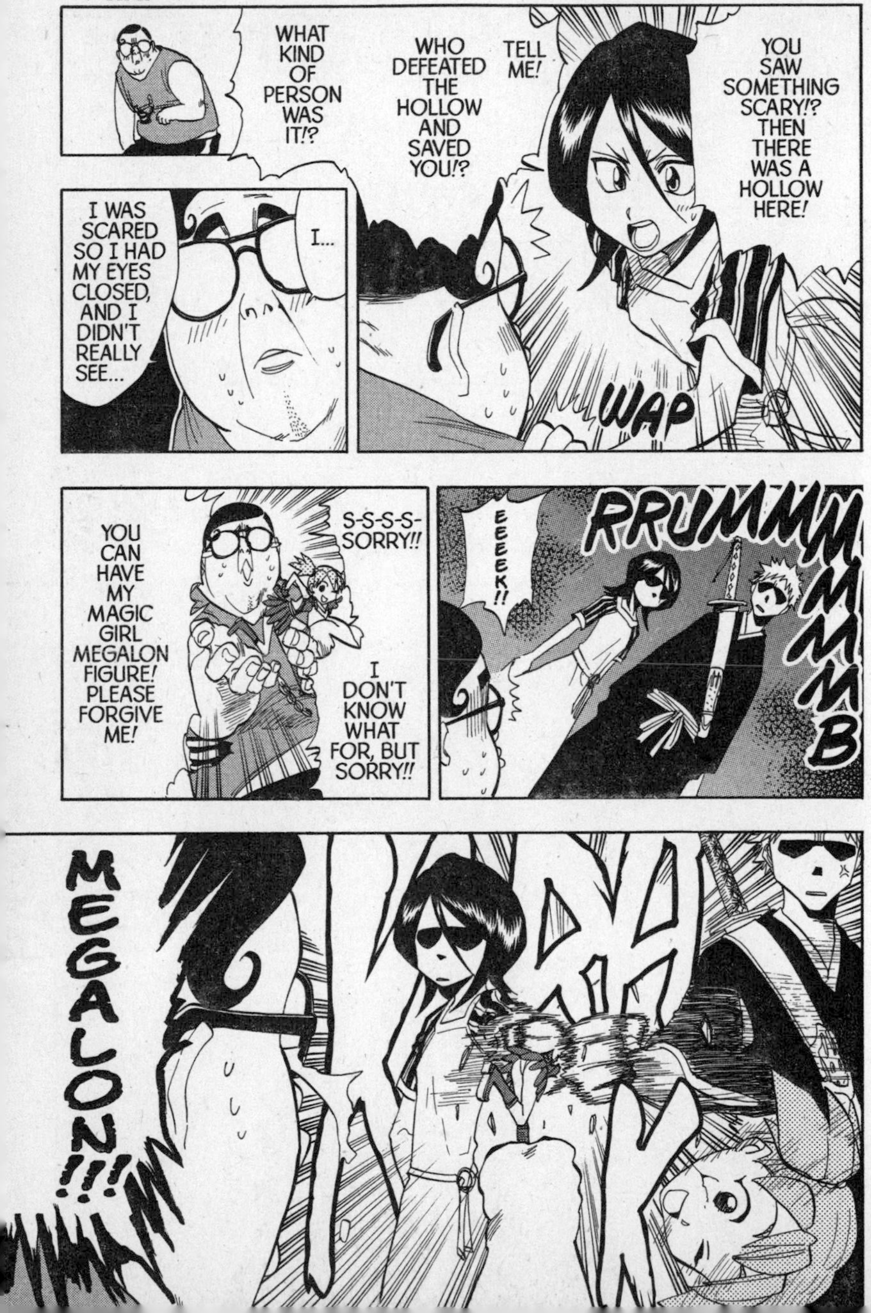

YOU SAW SOMETHING SCARY!? THEN THERE WAS A HOLLOW HERE!
TELL ME!
WHO DEFEATED THE HOLLOW AND SAVED YOU!?
WHAT KIND OF PERSON WAS IT!?
WAP
I...
I WAS SCARED SO I HAD MY EYES CLOSED, AND I DIDN'T REALLY SEE...
RRUMMMMMMMB
EEEEK!!
S-S-S-S-SORRY!!
I DON'T KNOW WHAT FOR, BUT SORRY!!
YOU CAN HAVE MY MAGIC GIRL MEGALON FIGURE! PLEASE FORGIVE ME!
MEGALON!!!

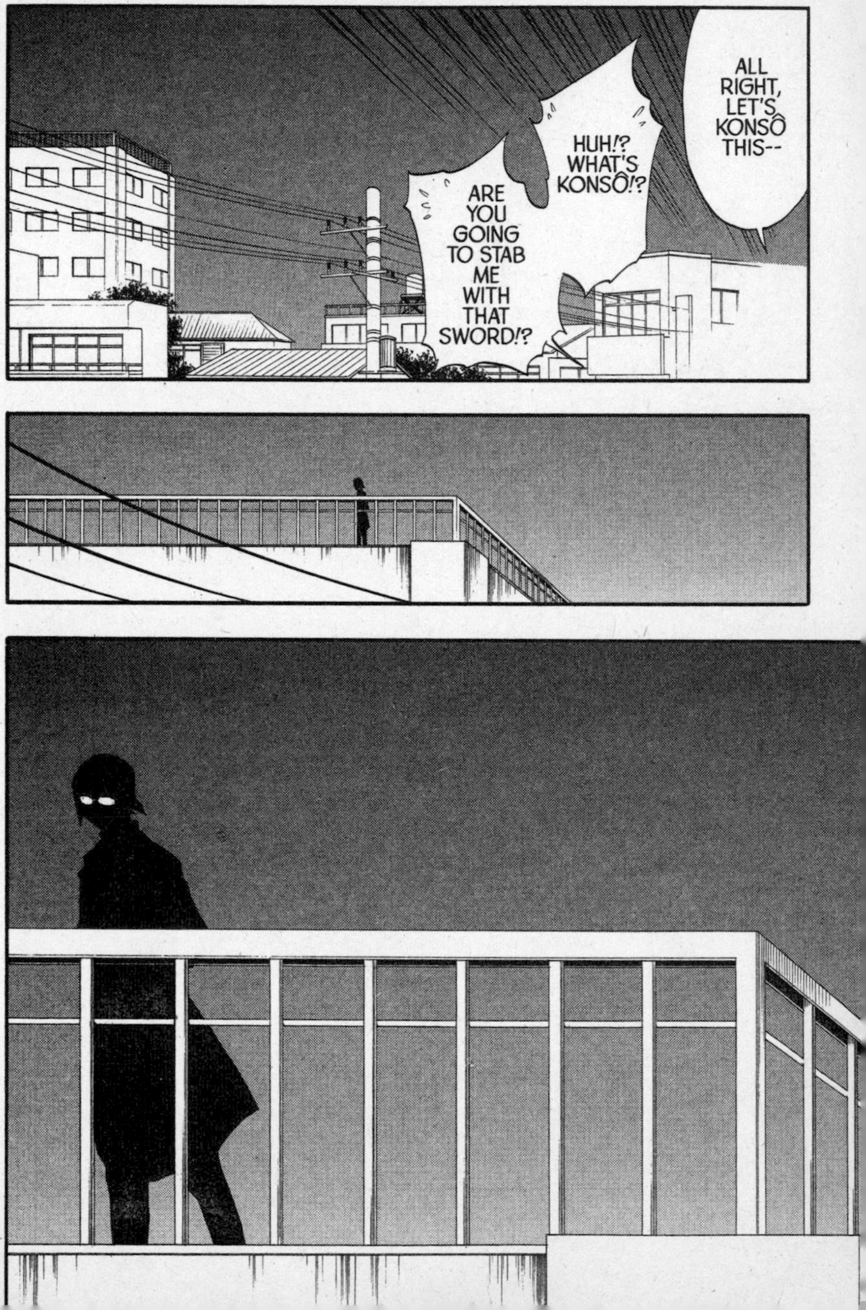
ALL RIGHT, LET'S KONSÔ THIS--
HUH!? WHAT'S KONSÔ!?
ARE YOU GOING TO STAB ME WITH THAT SWORD!?

34. Quincy Archer Hates You

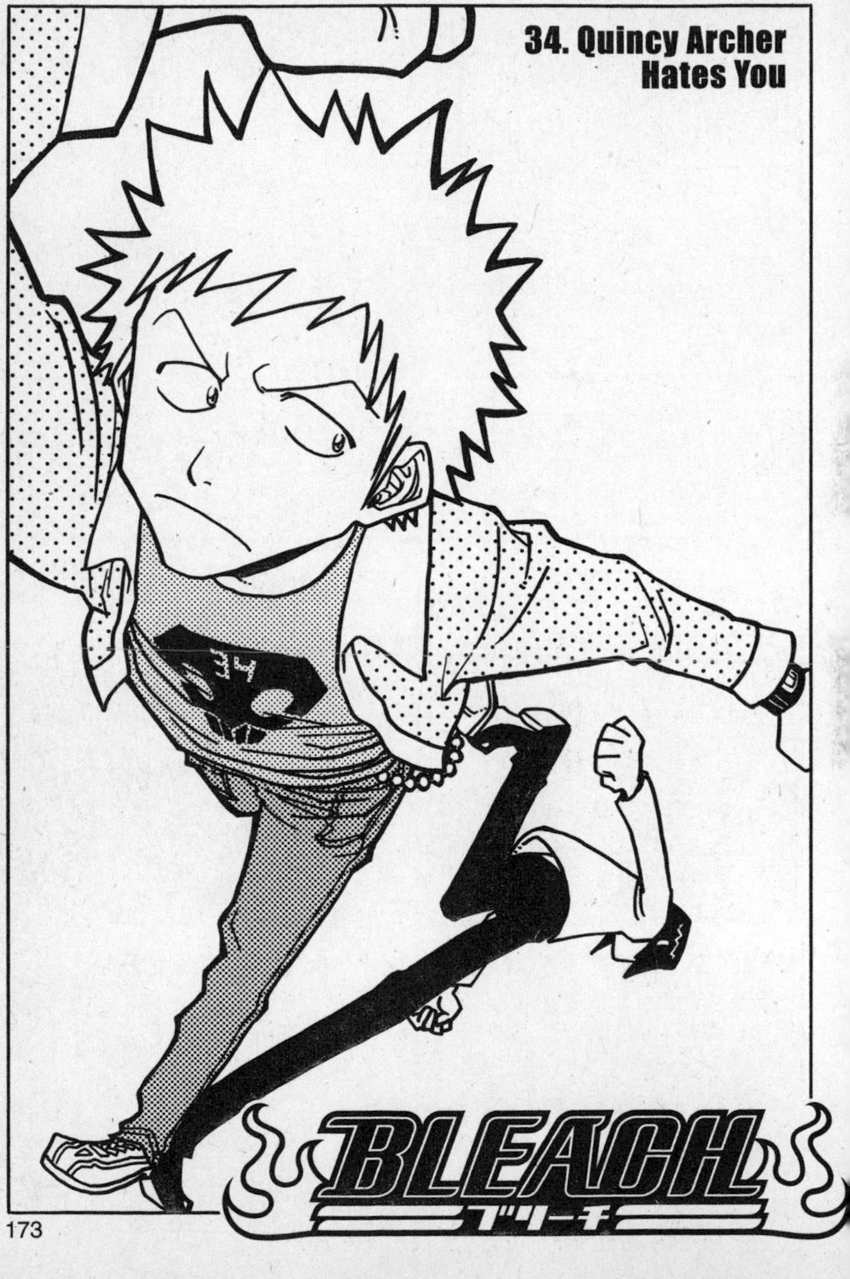
BLEACH
ブリーチ

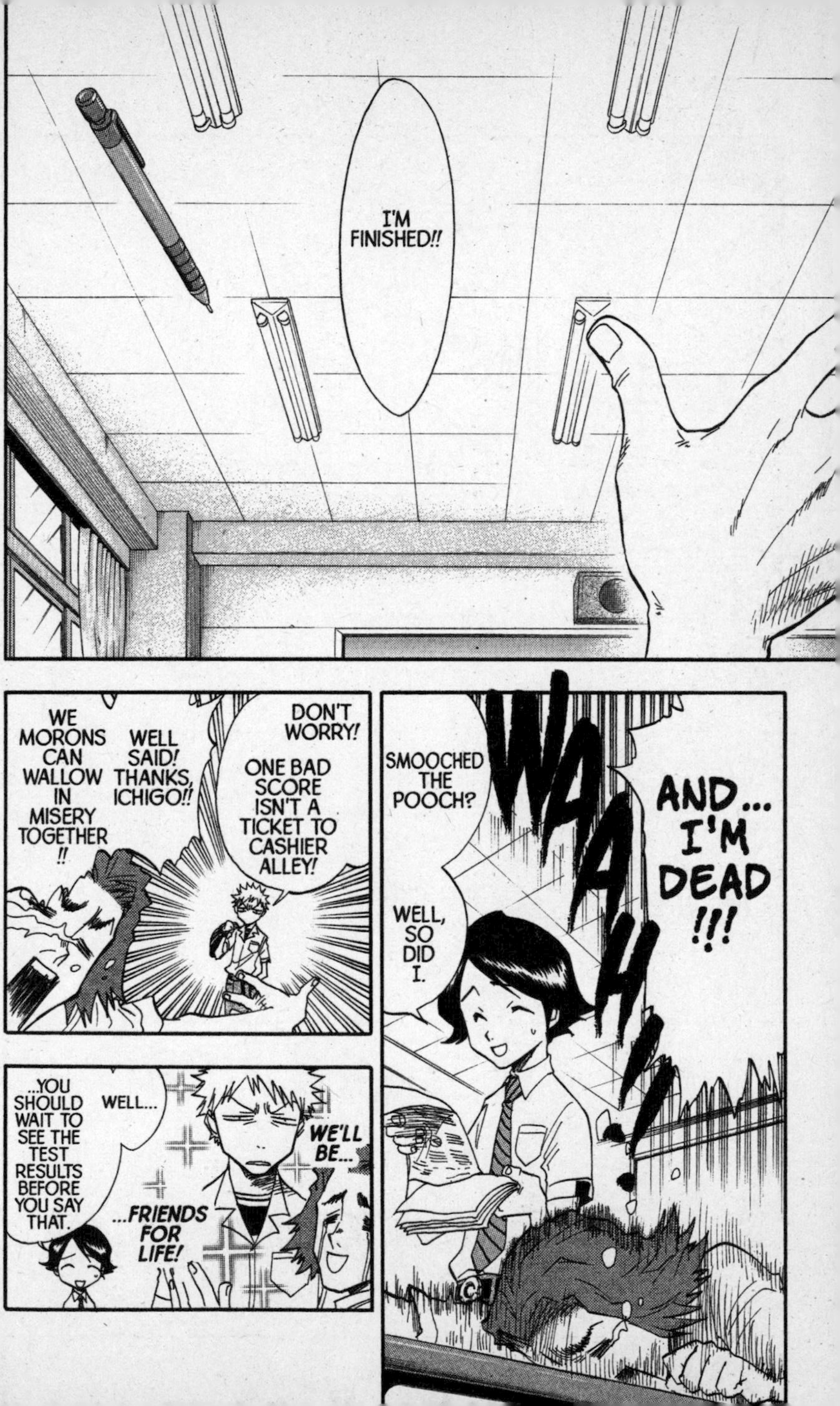
I'M FINISHED!!
AND... I'M DEAD!!!
WAAH!!!
SMOOCHED THE POOCH?
WELL, SO DID I.
DON'T WORRY!
ONE BAD SCORE ISN'T A TICKET TO CASHIER ALLEY!
WELL SAID! THANKS, ICHIGO!!
WE MORONS CAN WALLOW IN MISERY TOGETHER!!
WE'LL BE...
...FRIENDS FOR LIFE!
WELL...
...YOU SHOULD WAIT TO SEE THE TEST RESULTS BEFORE YOU SAY THAT.

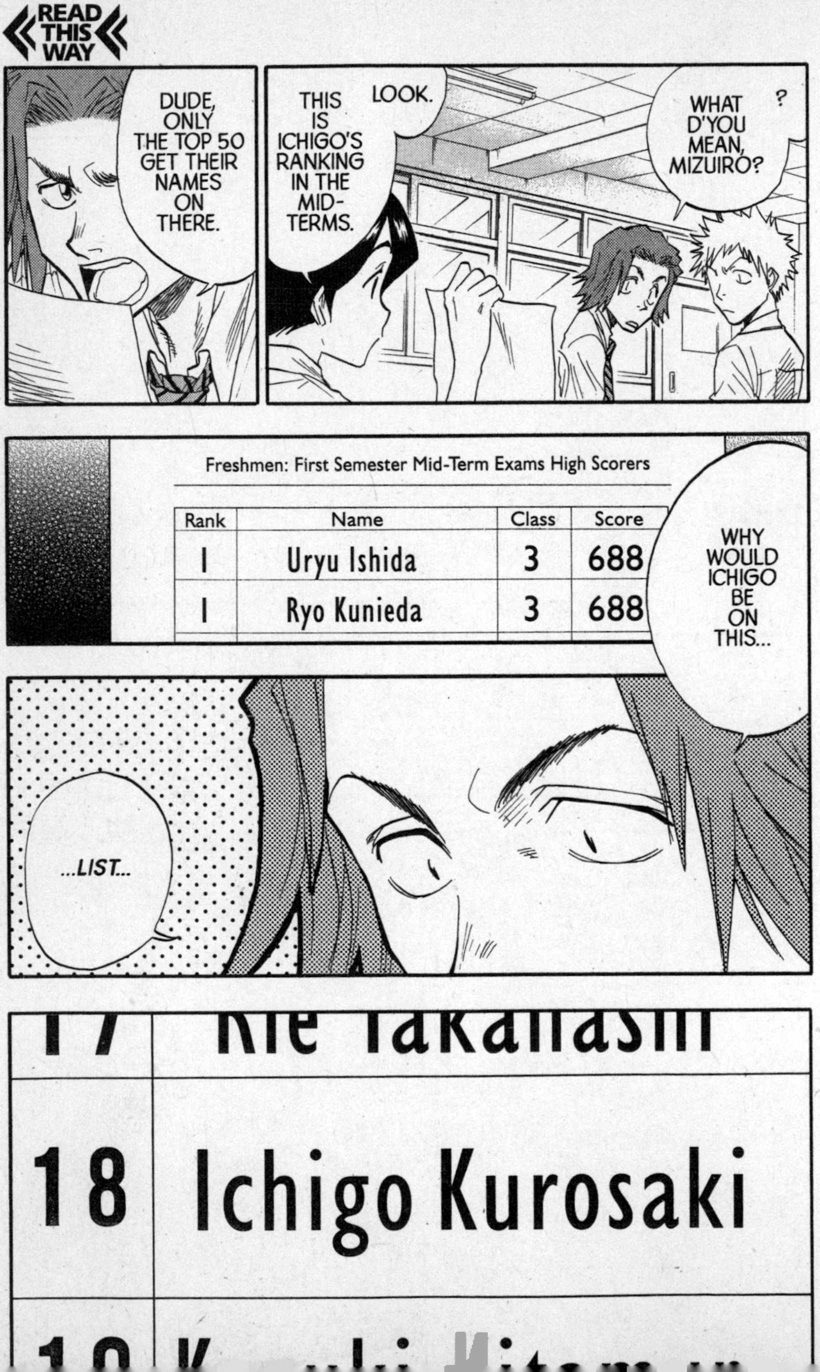
READ THIS WAY
WHAT D'YOU MEAN, MIZUIRO?
?
LOOK.
THIS IS ICHIGO'S RANKING IN THE MID-TERMS.
DUDE, ONLY THE TOP 50 GET THEIR NAMES ON THERE.
WHY WOULD ICHIGO BE ON THIS...
Freshmen: First Semester Mid-Term Exams High Scorers
Rank Name Class Score
1 Uryu Ishida 3 688
1 Ryo Kunieda 3 688
...LIST...
18 Ichigo Kurosaki

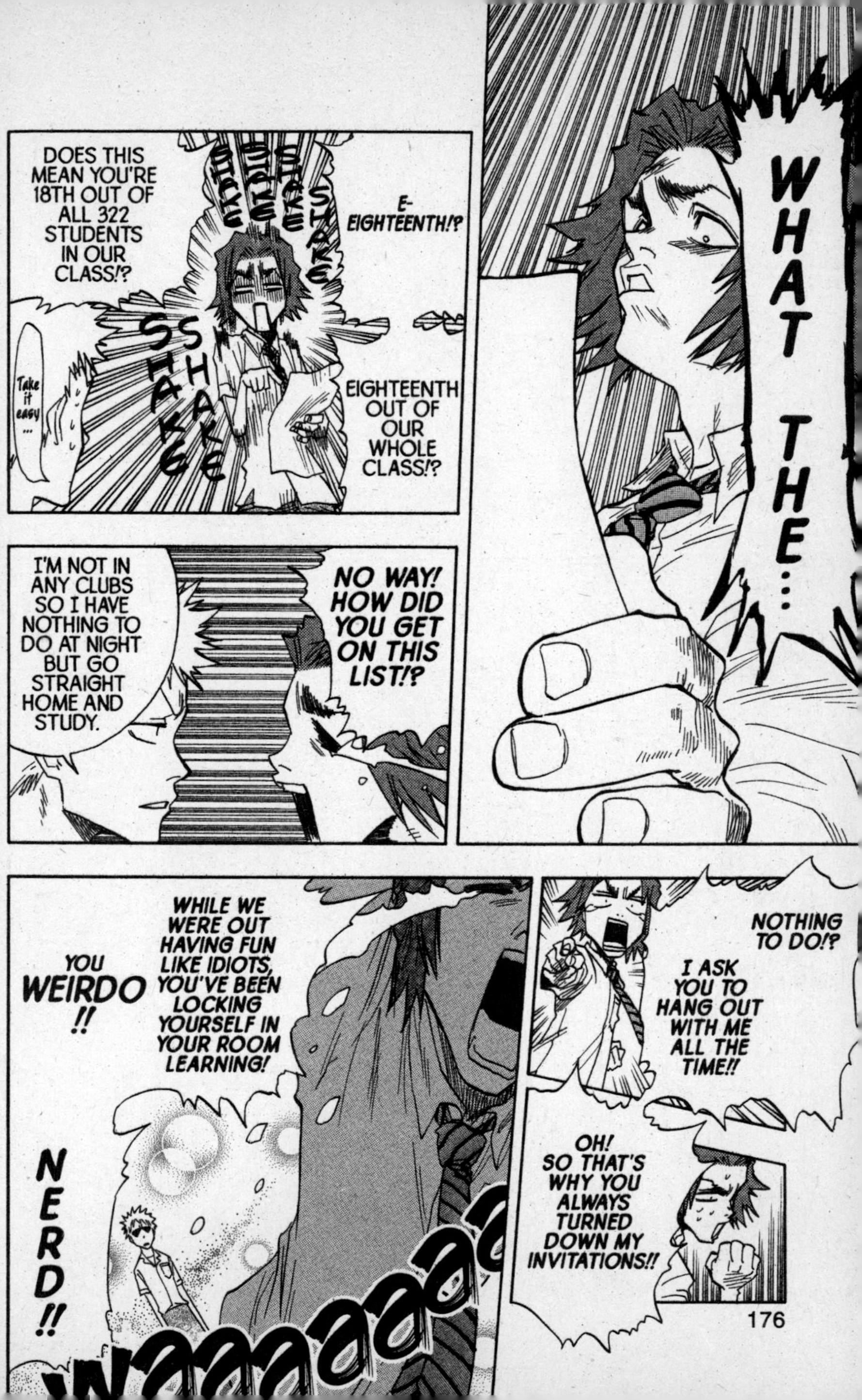
WHAT THE...
DOES THIS MEAN YOU'RE 18TH OUT OF ALL 322 STUDENTS IN OUR CLASS!?
SHAKE SHAKE SHAKE SHAKE
E-EIGHTEENTH!?
EIGHTEENTH OUT OF OUR WHOLE CLASS!?
SHAKE SHAKE
Take it easy...
NO WAY! HOW DID YOU GET ON THIS LIST!?
I'M NOT IN ANY CLUBS SO I HAVE NOTHING TO DO AT NIGHT BUT GO STRAIGHT HOME AND STUDY.
NOTHING TO DO!?
I ASK YOU TO HANG OUT WITH ME ALL THE TIME!!
OH! SO THAT'S WHY YOU ALWAYS TURNED DOWN MY INVITATIONS!!
WHILE WE WERE OUT HAVING FUN LIKE IDIOTS, YOU'VE BEEN LOCKING YOURSELF IN YOUR ROOM LEARNING!
YOU WEIRDO!!
NERD!!

READ THIS WAY

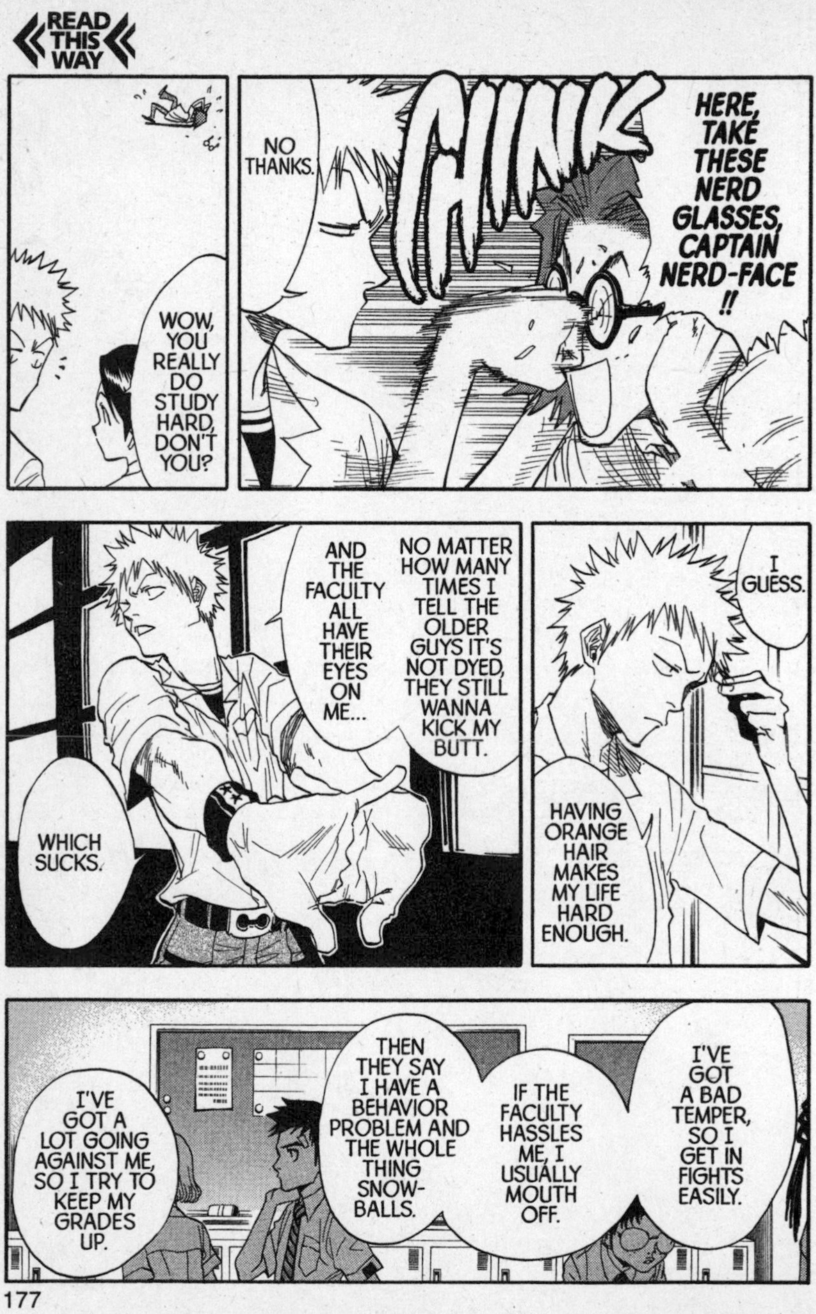

HERE, TAKE THESE NERD GLASSES, CAPTAIN NERD-FACE!!
CHINK
NO THANKS.
WOW, YOU REALLY DO STUDY HARD, DON'T YOU?
I GUESS.
HAVING ORANGE HAIR MAKES MY LIFE HARD ENOUGH.
NO MATTER HOW MANY TIMES I TELL THE OLDER GUYS IT'S NOT DYED, THEY STILL WANNA KICK MY BUTT.
AND THE FACULTY ALL HAVE THEIR EYES ON ME...
WHICH SUCKS.
I'VE GOT A BAD TEMPER, SO I GET IN FIGHTS EASILY.
IF THE FACULTY HASSLES ME, I USUALLY MOUTH OFF.
THEN THEY SAY I HAVE A BEHAVIOR PROBLEM AND THE WHOLE THING SNOW-BALLS.
I'VE GOT A LOT GOING AGAINST ME, SO I TRY TO KEEP MY GRADES UP.

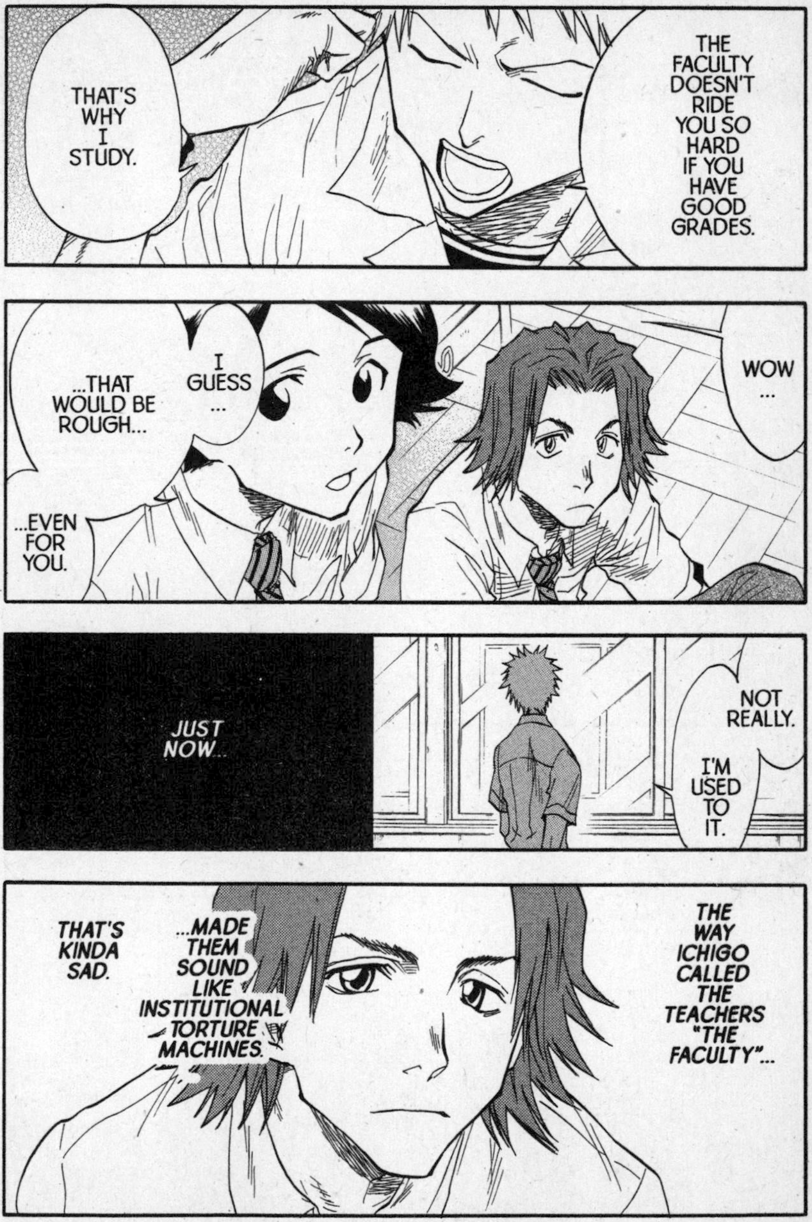
THE FACULTY DOESN'T RIDE YOU SO HARD IF YOU HAVE GOOD GRADES.
THAT'S WHY I STUDY.
WOW...
I GUESS...
...THAT WOULD BE ROUGH...
...EVEN FOR YOU.
NOT REALLY.
I'M USED TO IT.
JUST NOW...
THE WAY ICHIGO CALLED THE TEACHERS "THE FACULTY"...
...MADE THEM SOUND LIKE INSTITUTIONAL TORTURE MACHINES.
THAT'S KINDA SAD.

READ THIS WAY

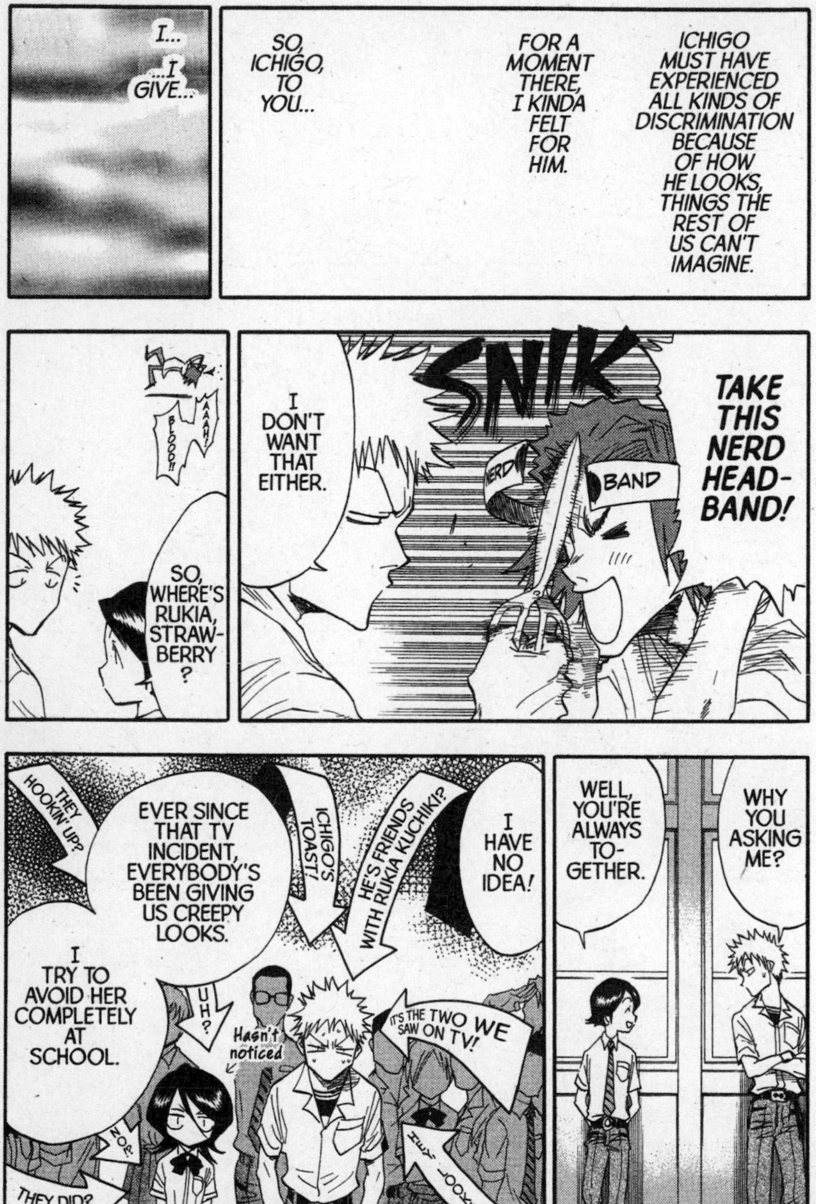

ICHIGO MUST HAVE EXPERIENCED ALL KINDS OF DISCRIMINATION BECAUSE OF HOW HE LOOKS, THINGS THE REST OF US CAN'T IMAGINE.
FOR A MOMENT THERE, I KINDA FELT FOR HIM.
SO, ICHIGO, TO YOU...
I...
...I GIVE...
TAKE THIS NERD HEAD-BAND!
SNIK
NERD
BAND
I DON'T WANT THAT EITHER.
AAAH!
BLOOD!!
SO, WHERE'S RUKIA, STRAWBERRY?
WHY YOU ASKING ME?
WELL, YOU'RE ALWAYS TO-GETHER.
I HAVE NO IDEA!
HE'S FRIENDS WITH RUKIA KUCHIKI?
ICHIGO'S TOAST!
EVER SINCE THAT TV INCIDENT, EVERYBODY'S BEEN GIVING US CREEPY LOOKS.
THEY HOOKIN' UP?
IT'S THE TWO WE SAW ON TV!
UH?
Hasn't noticed
I TRY TO AVOID HER COMPLETELY AT SCHOOL.
HEY, LOOK!
NO?!
THEY DID?

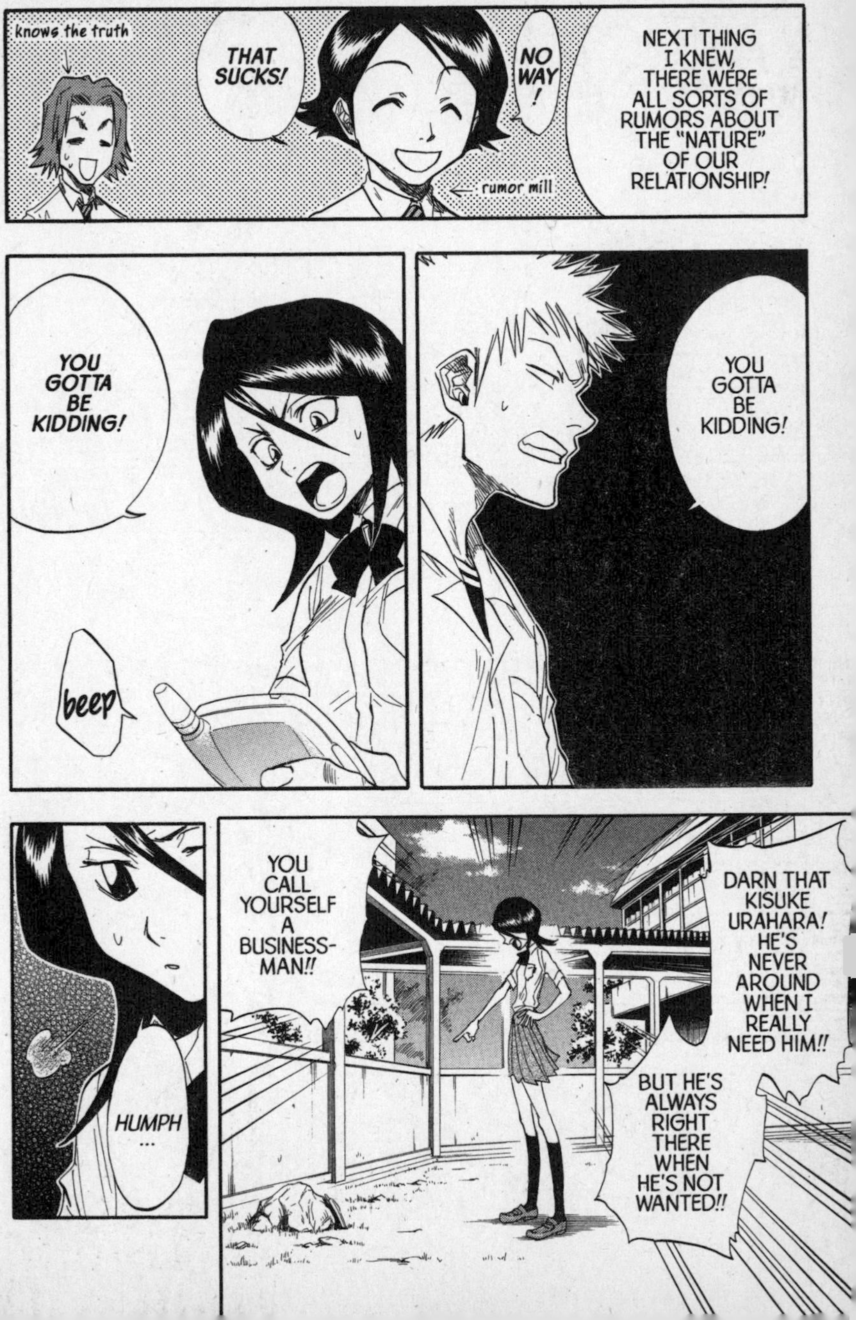
NEXT THING I KNEW, THERE WERE ALL SORTS OF RUMORS ABOUT THE "NATURE" OF OUR RELATIONSHIP!
NO WAY!
THAT SUCKS!
rumor mill
knows the truth
YOU GOTTA BE KIDDING!
YOU GOTTA BE KIDDING!
beep
DARN THAT KISUKE URAHARA! HE'S NEVER AROUND WHEN I REALLY NEED HIM!!
BUT HE'S ALWAYS RIGHT THERE WHEN HE'S NOT WANTED!!
YOU CALL YOURSELF A BUSINESS-MAN!!
HUMPH ...

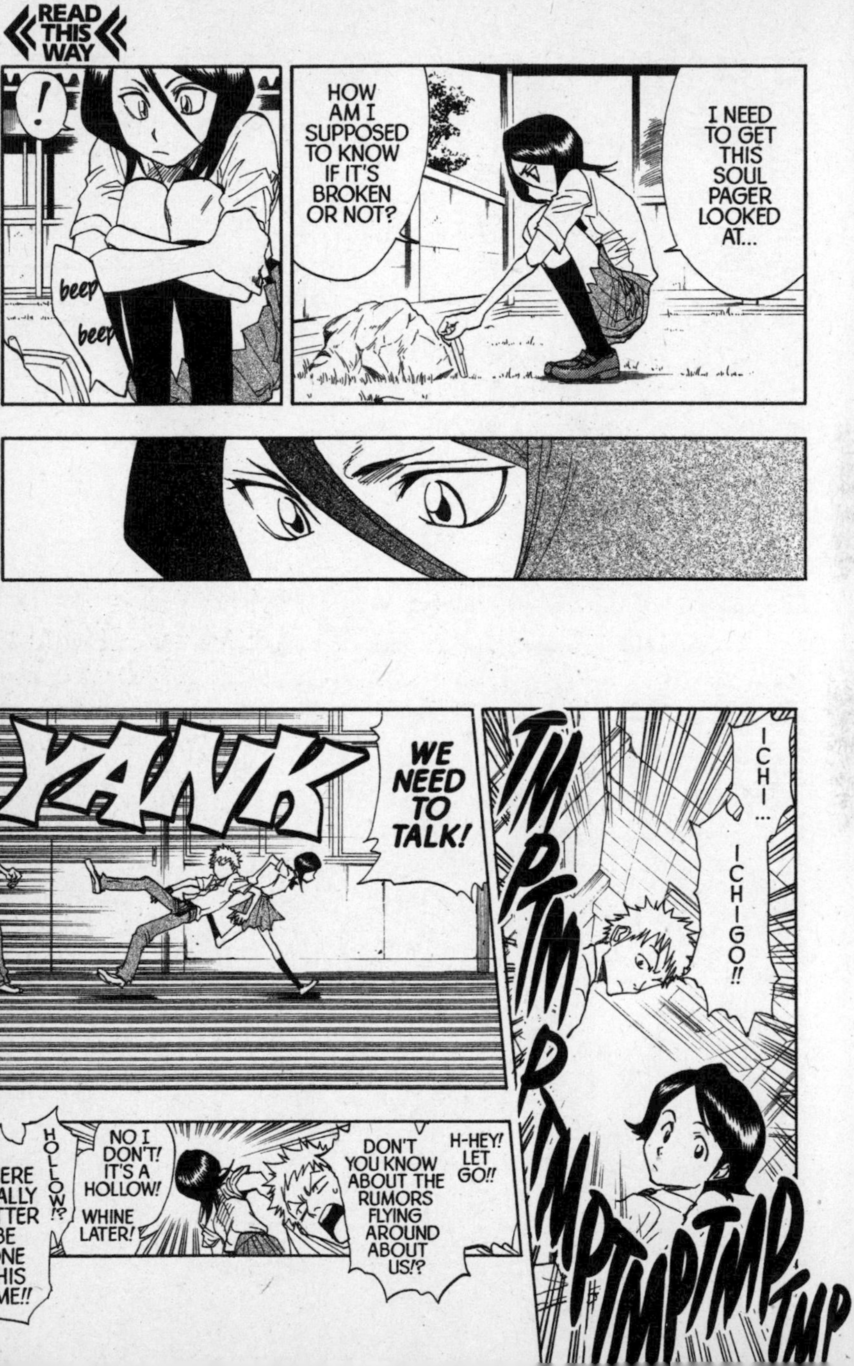
READ THIS WAY
I NEED TO GET THIS SOUL PAGER LOOKED AT...
HOW AM I SUPPOSED TO KNOW IF IT'S BROKEN OR NOT?
!
beep
beep
TMPTMPTMPTMPTMPTMP
TMP
ICHI...
ICHIGO!!
YANK
WE NEED TO TALK!
H-HEY! LET GO!!
DON'T YOU KNOW ABOUT THE RUMORS FLYING AROUND ABOUT US!?
NO I DON'T! IT'S A HOLLOW!
WHINE LATER!
HOLLOW!?
THERE REALLY BETTER BE ONE THIS TIME!!

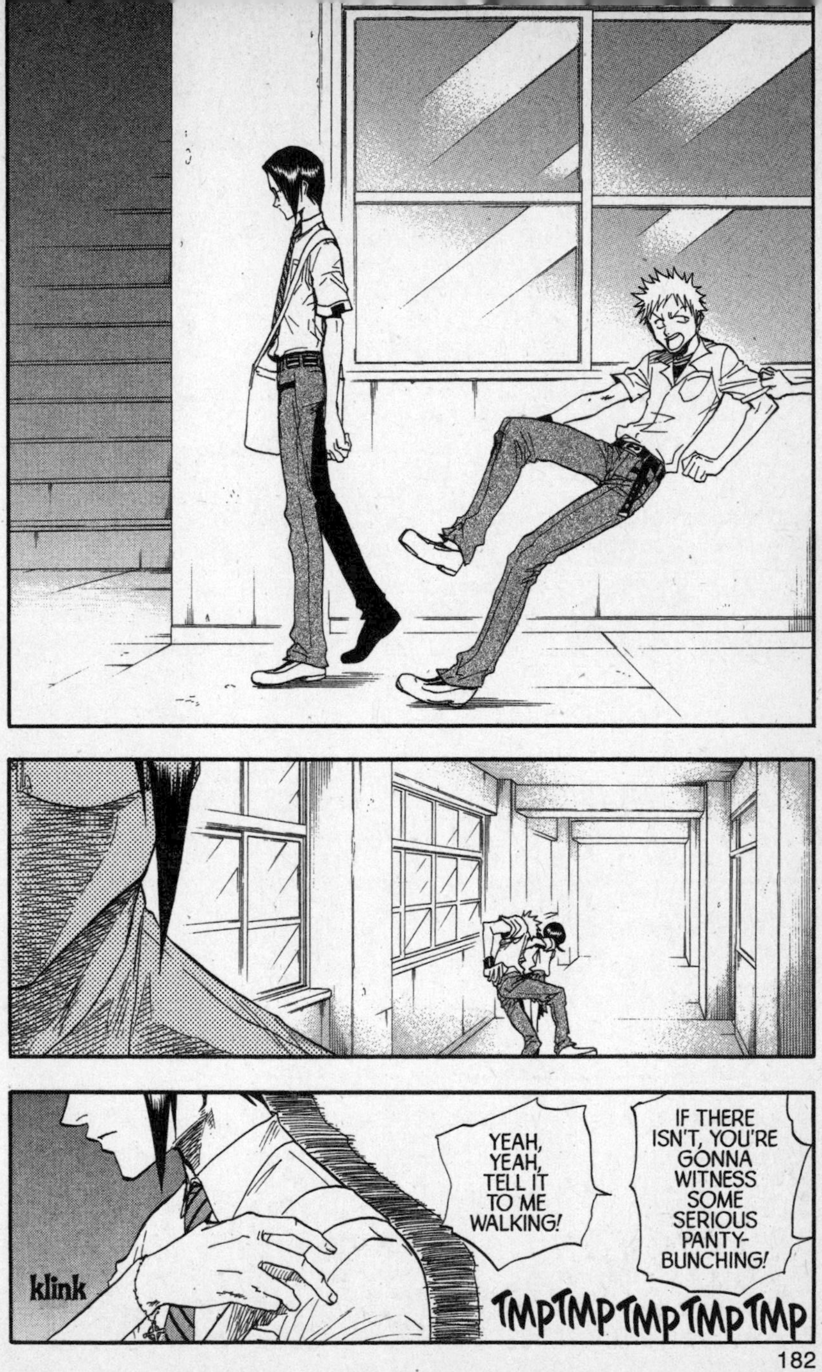
IF THERE ISN'T, YOU'RE GONNA WITNESS SOME SERIOUS PANTY-BUNCHING!
YEAH, YEAH, TELL IT TO ME WALKING!
TMPTMPTMPTMPTMP
klink

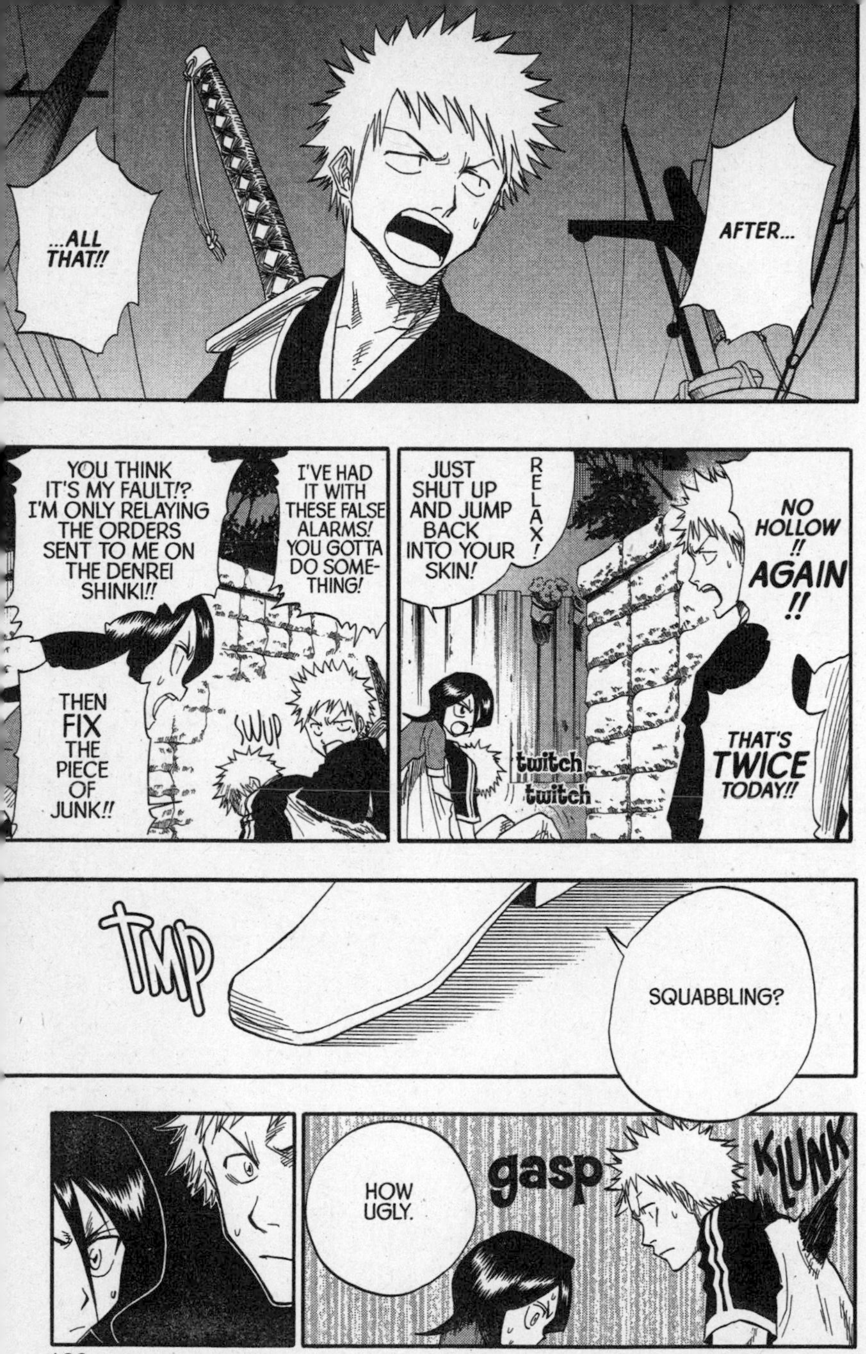
AFTER...
...ALL THAT!!
NO HOLLOW!! AGAIN!!
THAT'S TWICE TODAY!!
RELAX!
JUST SHUT UP AND JUMP BACK INTO YOUR SKIN!
twitch twitch
I'VE HAD IT WITH THESE FALSE ALARMS! YOU GOTTA DO SOME-THING!
YOU THINK IT'S MY FAULT!? I'M ONLY RELAYING THE ORDERS SENT TO ME ON THE DENREI SHINKI!!
SWUP
THEN FIX THE PIECE OF JUNK!!
SQUABBLING?
TMP
KLUNK
gasp
HOW UGLY.

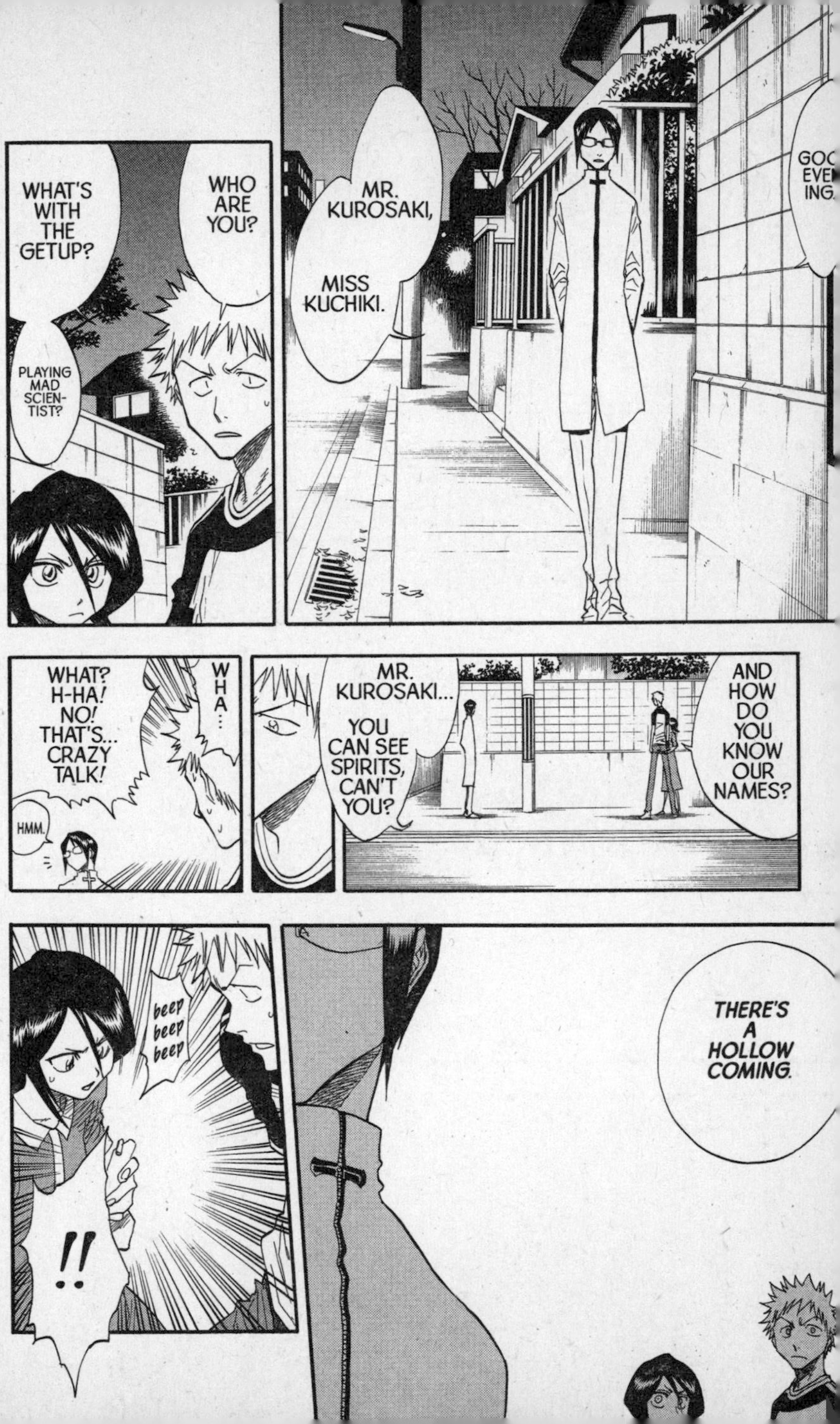
GOO EVEN ING.
MR. KUROSAKI, MISS KUCHIKI.
WHO ARE YOU?
WHAT'S WITH THE GETUP?
PLAYING MAD SCIEN- TIST?
AND HOW DO YOU KNOW OUR NAMES?
MR. KUROSAKI... YOU CAN SEE SPIRITS, CAN'T YOU?
WHA...
WHAT? H-HA! NO! THAT'S... CRAZY TALK!
HMM.
THERE'S A HOLLOW COMING.
beep beep beep
!!

READ THIS WAY

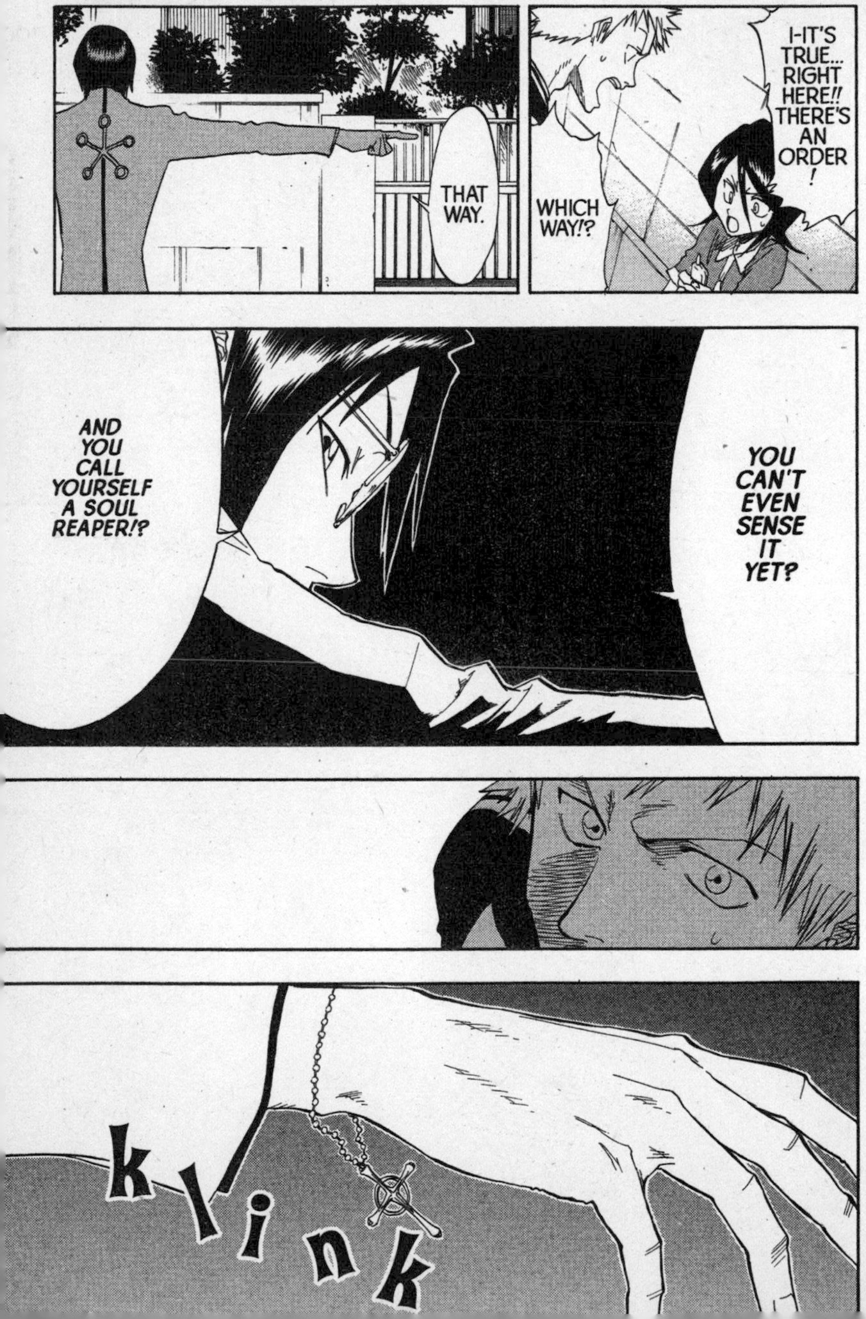
I-IT'S TRUE... RIGHT HERE!! THERE'S AN ORDER!
WHICH WAY!?
THAT WAY.
YOU CAN'T EVEN SENSE IT YET?
AND YOU CALL YOURSELF A SOUL REAPER!?
klink

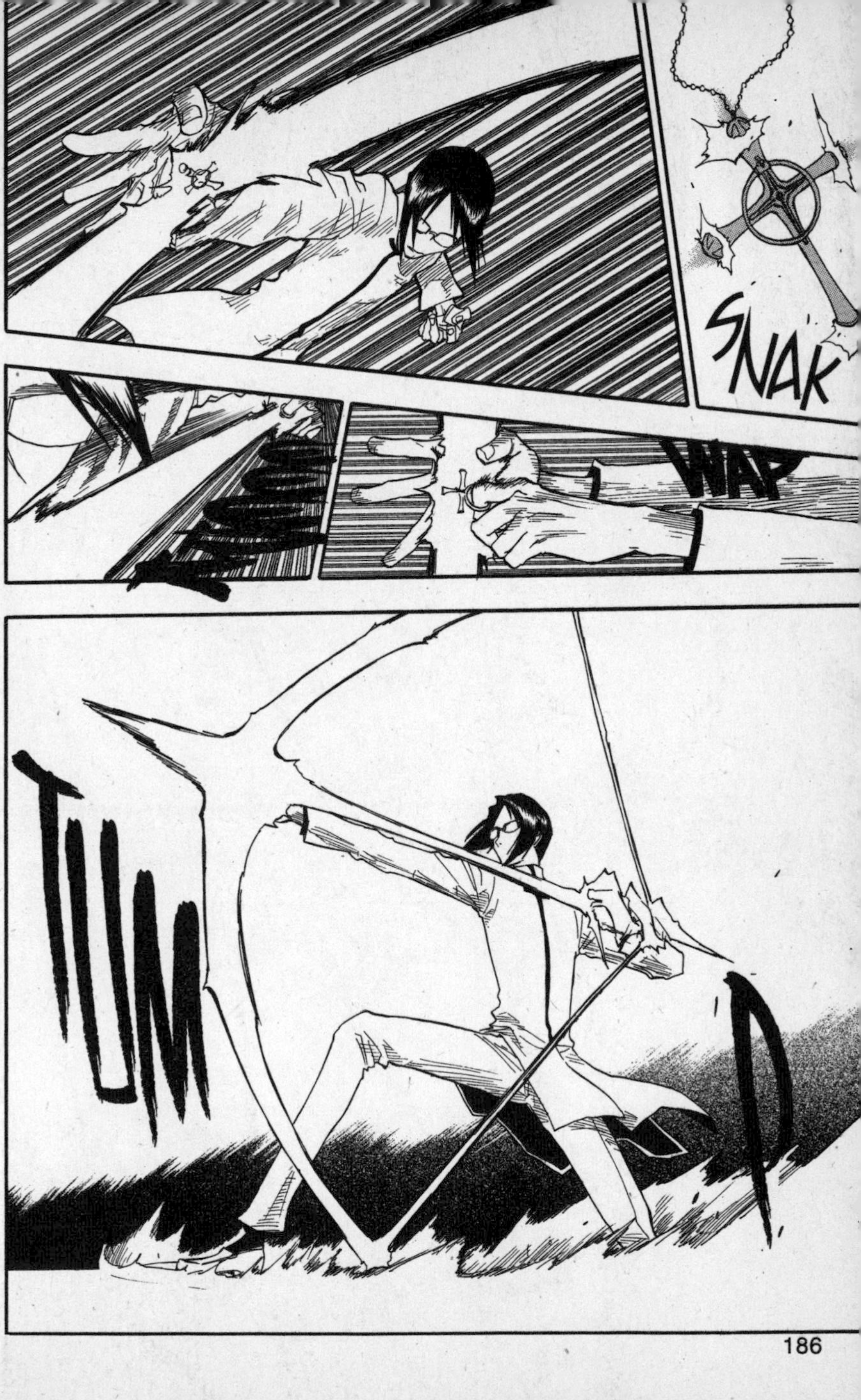
SNAK
WAP
TUMP

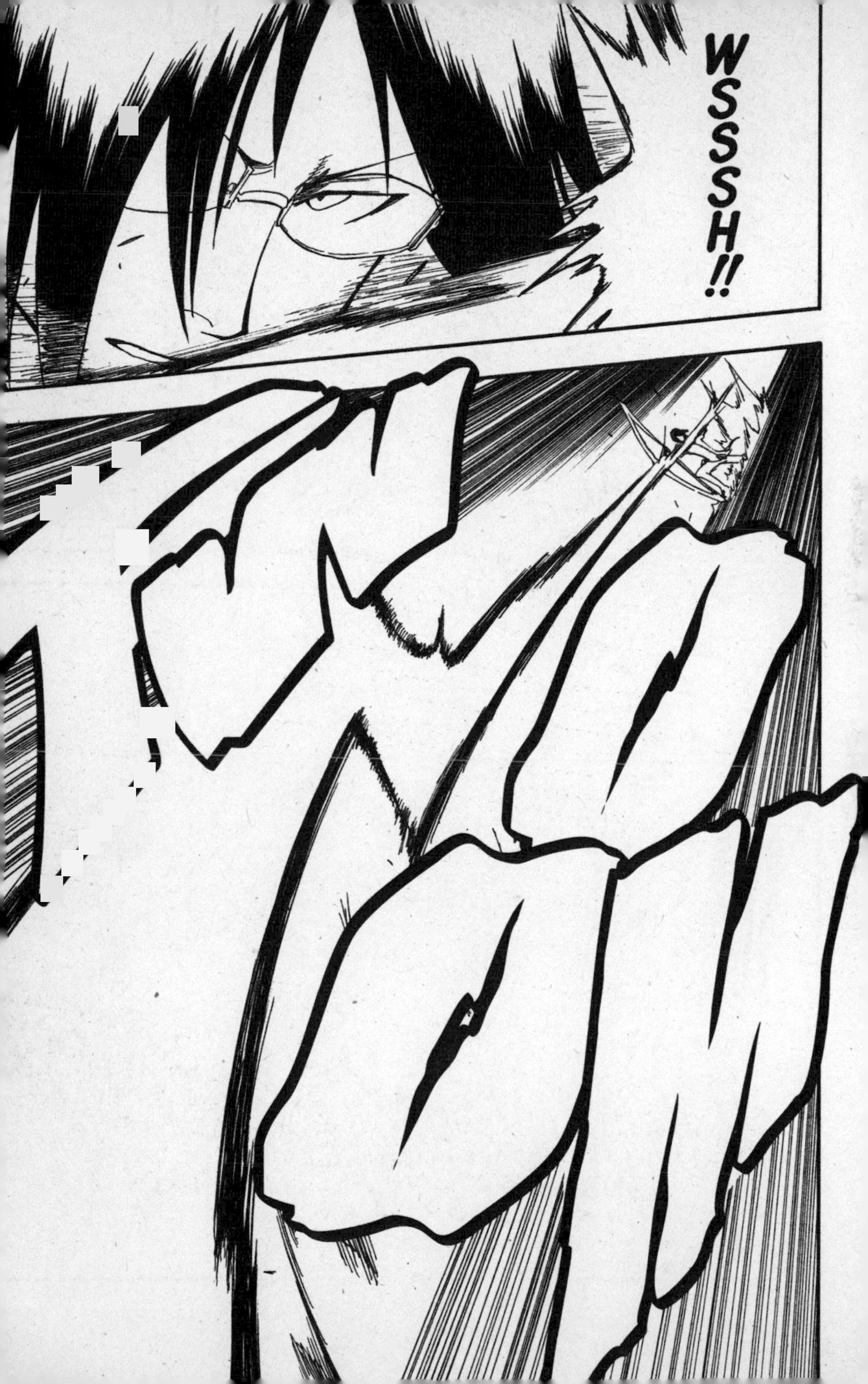
WSSSH!!

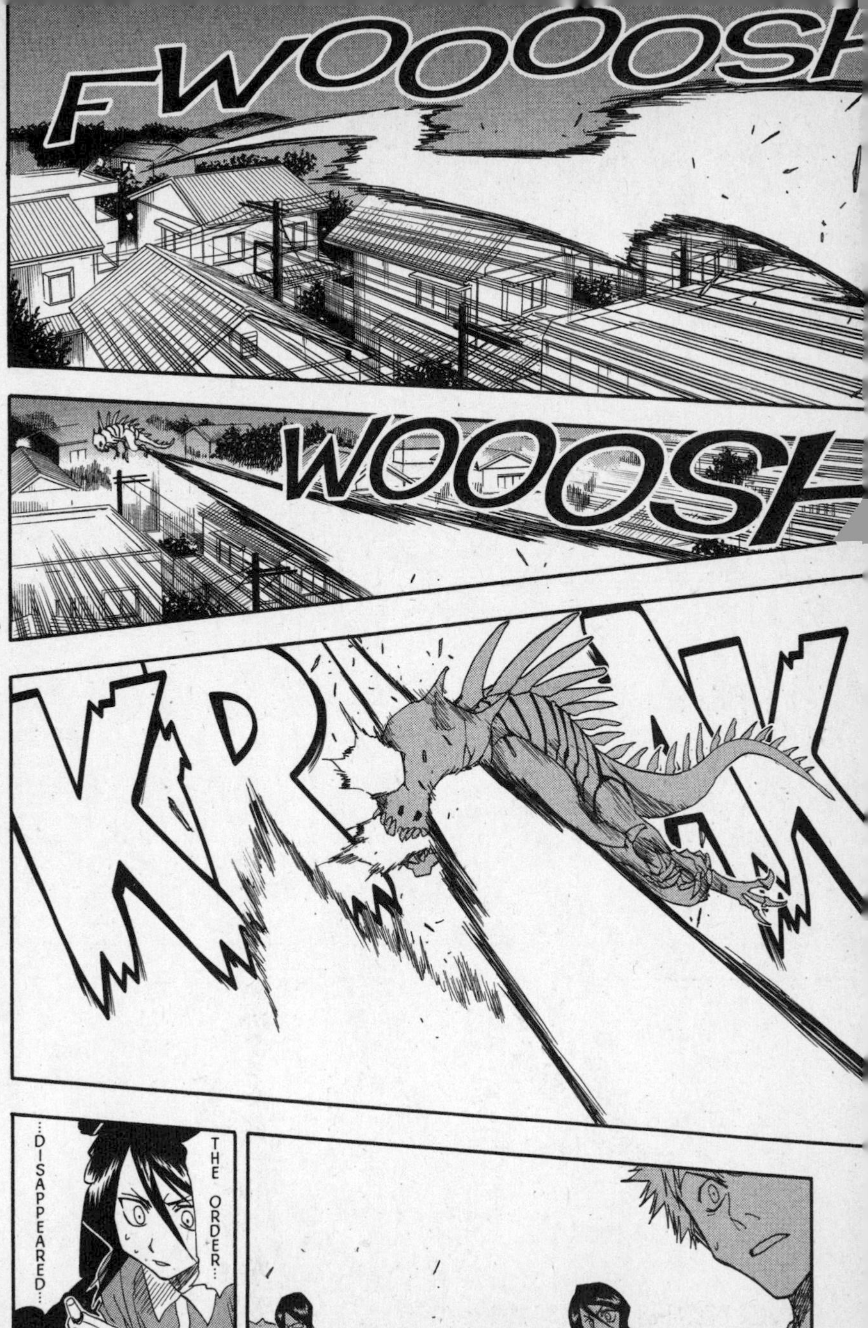
FWOOOOSH
WOOOSH
KRAK
THE ORDER...
...DISAPPEARED...

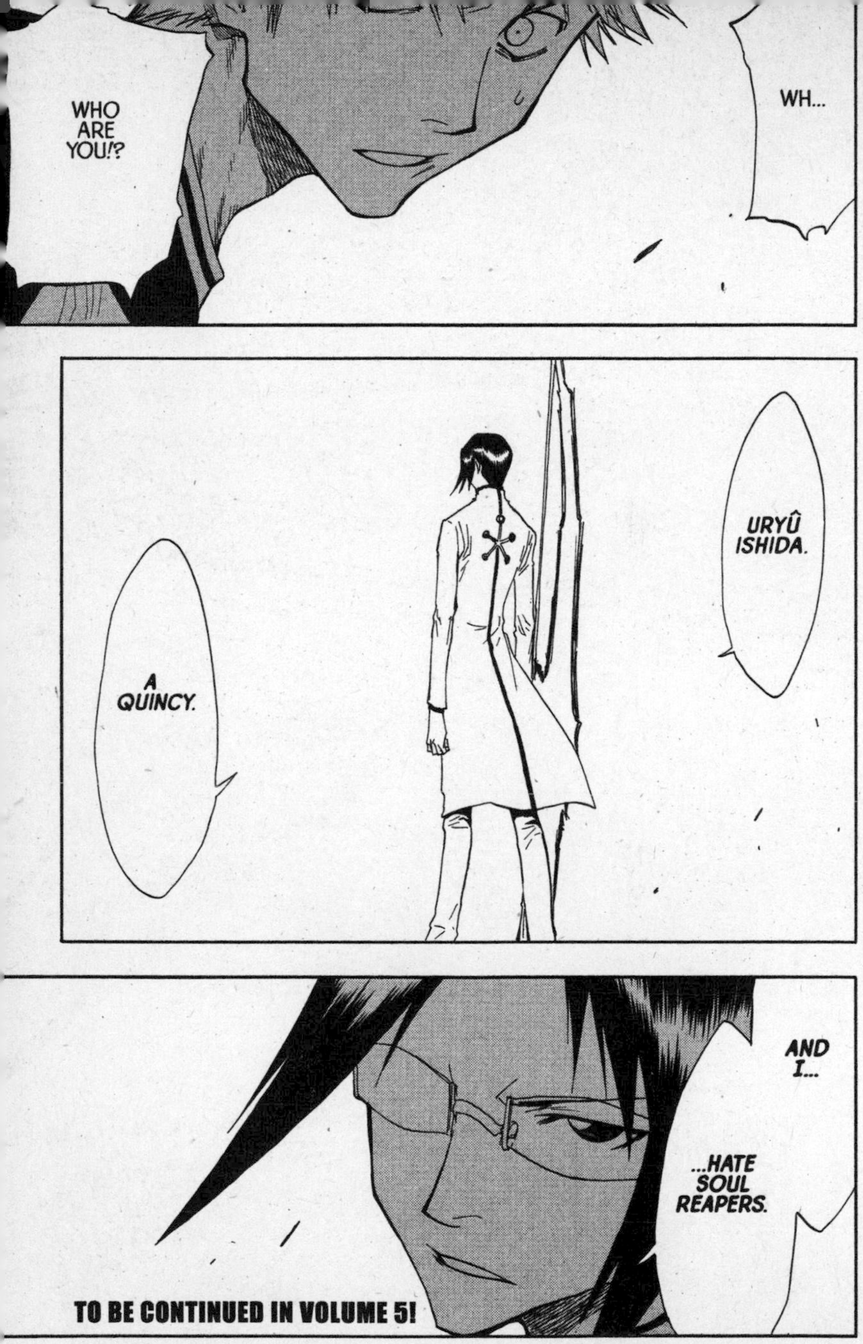
WH...
WHO ARE YOU!?
URYÛ ISHIDA.
A QUINCY.
AND I...
...HATE SOUL REAPERS.
TO BE CONTINUED IN VOLUME 5!

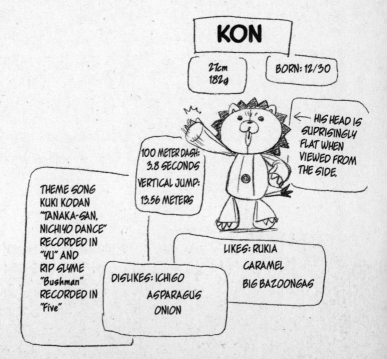

KON
27cm 182g
BORN: 12/30
HIS HEAD IS SUPRISINGLY FLAT WHEN VIEWED FROM THE SIDE.
100 METER DASH: 3.8 SECONDS VERTICAL JUMP: 13.56 METERS
THEME SONG KUKI KODAN "TANAKA-SAN, NICHIYO DANCE" RECORDED IN "YU" AND RIP SLYME "Bushman" RECORDED IN "Five"
LIKES: RUKIA CARAMEL BIG BAZOONGAS
DISLIKES: ICHIGO ASPARAGUS ONION

Next Volume Preview

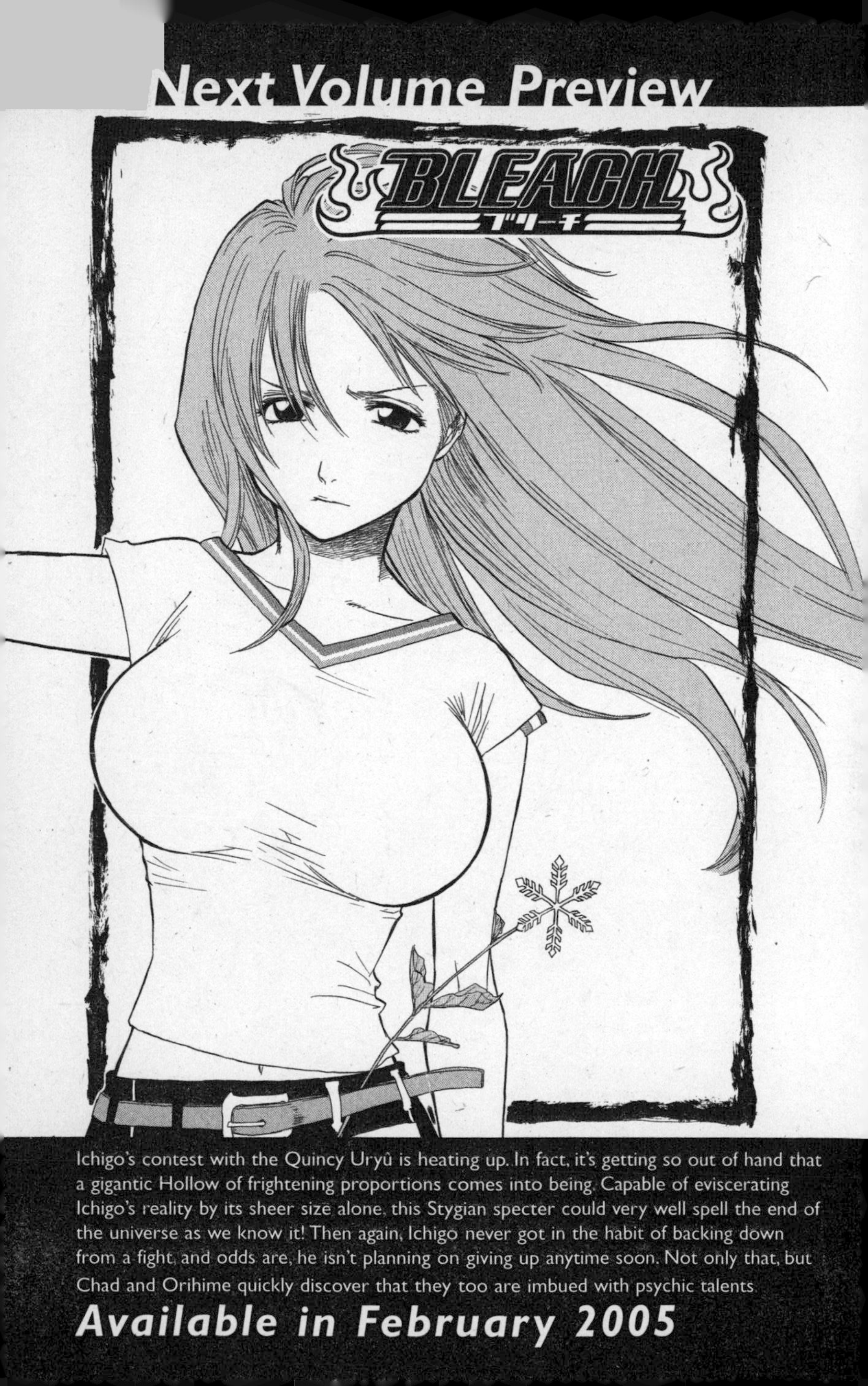
BLEACH
ブリーチ

Ichigo's contest with the Quincy Uryû is heating up. In fact, it's getting so out of hand that a gigantic Hollow of frightening proportions comes into being. Capable of eviscerating Ichigo's reality by its sheer size alone, this Stygian specter could very well spell the end of the universe as we know it! Then again, Ichigo never got in the habit of backing down from a fight, and odds are, he isn't planning on giving up anytime soon. Not only that, but Chad and Orihime quickly discover that they too are imbued with psychic talents.

Available in February 2005

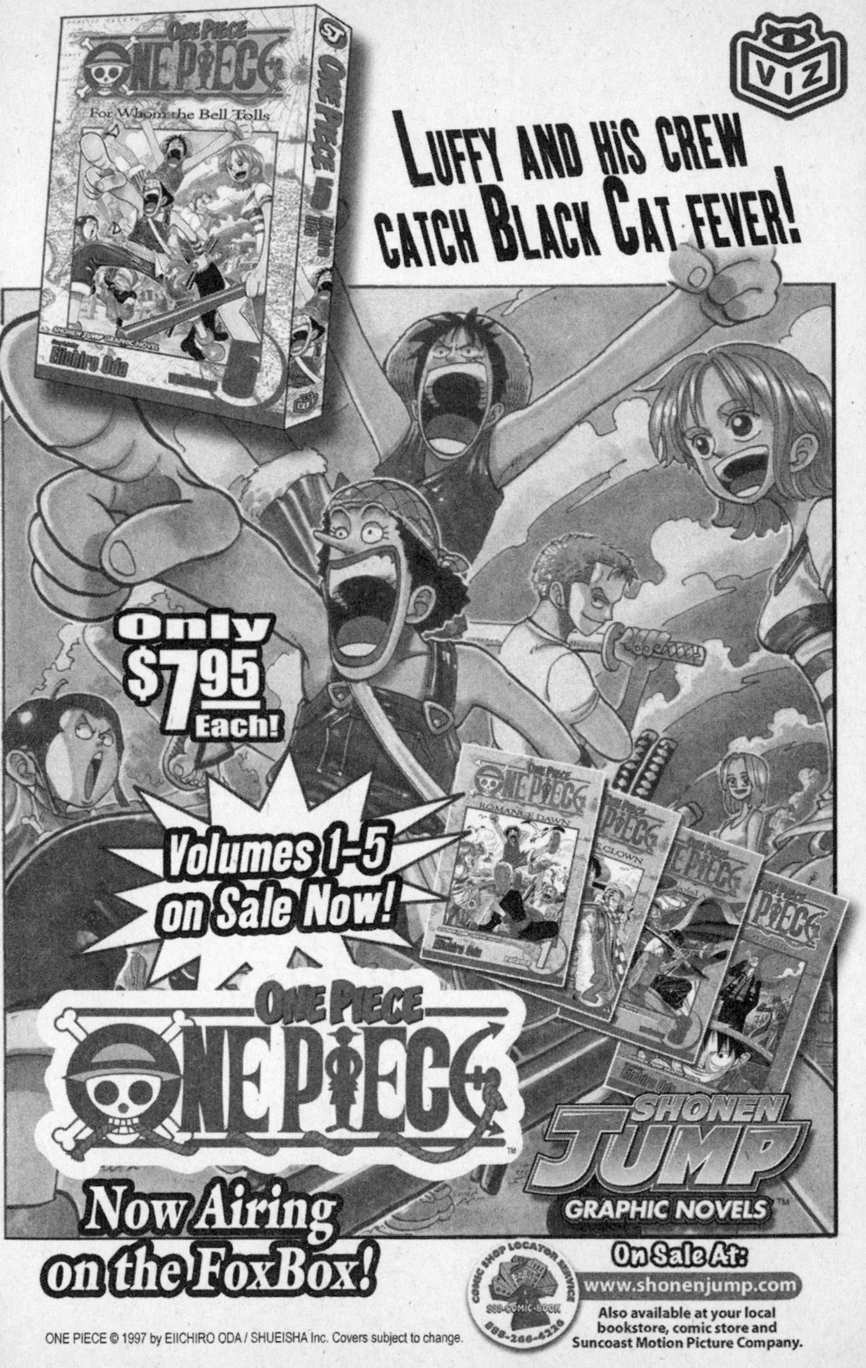
LUFFY AND HIS CREW CATCH BLACK CAT FEVER!
Only $7.95 Each!
Volumes 1-5 on Sale Now!
ONE PIECE
SHONEN JUMP GRAPHIC NOVELS
Now Airing on the FoxBox!
On Sale At:
www.shonenjump.com
Also available at your local bookstore, comic store and Suncoast Motion Picture Company.
COMIC SHOP LOCATOR SERVICE 888-COMIC-BOOK 888-266-4226
ONE PIECE © 1997 by EIICHIRO ODA / SHUEISHA Inc. Covers subject to change.

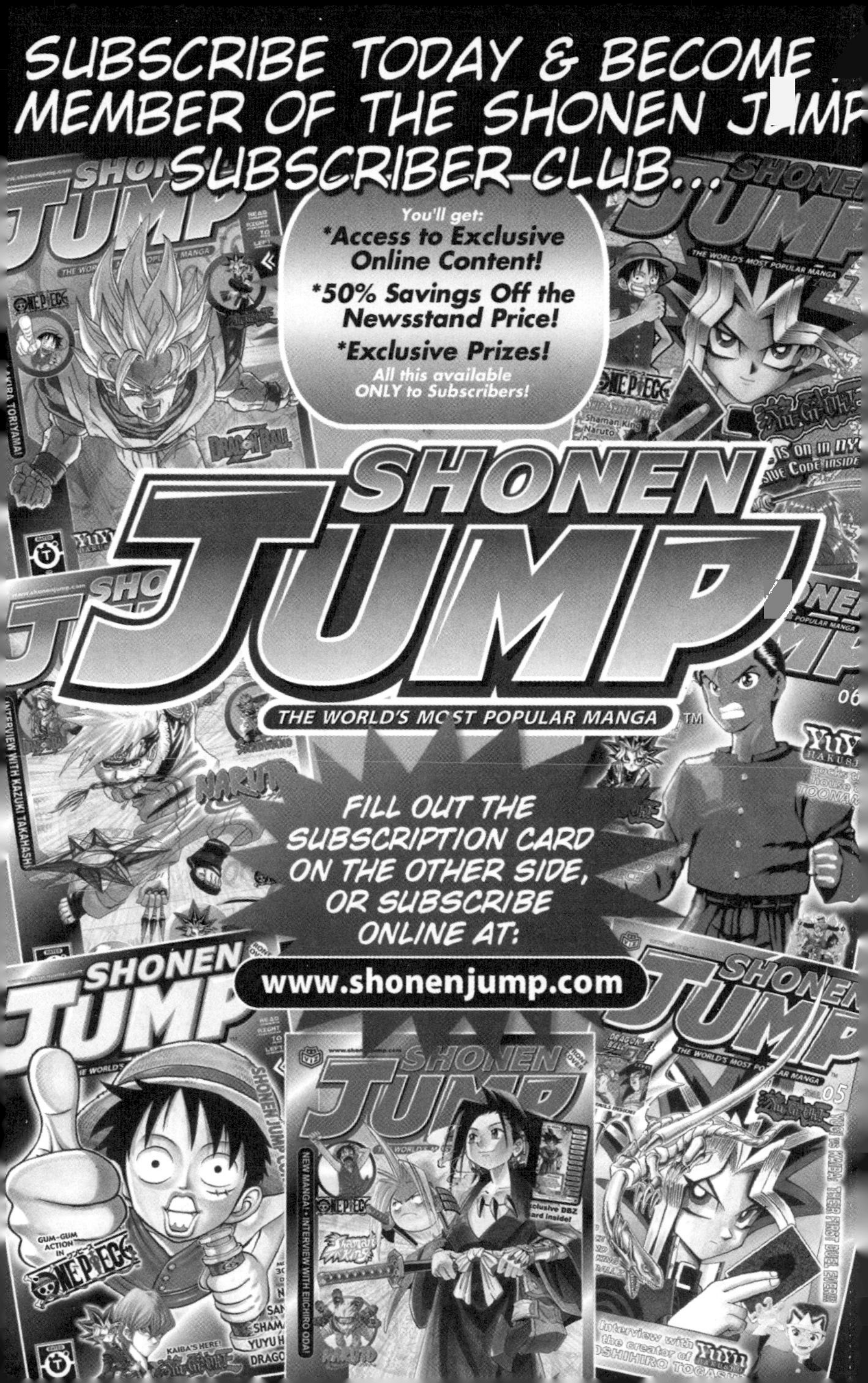

COMPLETE OUR SURVEY AND LET US KNOW WHAT YOU THINK!

☐ Please do NOT send me information about VIZ and SHONEN JUMP products, news and events, special offers, or other information.

☐ Please do NOT send me information from VIZ's trusted business partners.

Name: ______________________________

Address: ______________________________

City: ______________ **State:** ________ **Zip:** ____________

E-mail: ______________________________

☐ **Male** ☐ **Female** **Date of Birth** (mm/dd/yyyy): ___/___/______ (**Under 13? Parental consent required**)

What race/ethnicity do you consider yourself? (please check one)

☐ Asian/Pacific Islander ☐ Black/African American ☐ Hispanic/Latino

☐ Native American/Alaskan Native ☐ White/Caucasian ☐ Other: ____________

What SHONEN JUMP Graphic Novel did you purchase? (indicate title purchased)

____

What other SHONEN JUMP Graphic Novels, if any, do you own? (indicate title(s) owned)

____

____

Reason for purchase: (check all that apply)

☐ Special offer ☐ Favorite title ☐ Gift

☐ Recommendation ☐ Read in SHONEN JUMP Magazine

☐ Read excerpt in the SHONEN JUMP Compilation Edition

☐ Other ______________________________

Where did you make your purchase? (please check one)

☐ Comic store ☐ Bookstore ☐ Mass/Grocery Store

☐ Newsstand ☐ Video/Video Game Store ☐ Other: ____________

☐ Online (site: ______________________________)

Do you read SHONEN JUMP Magazine?

- [ ] Yes
- [x] No **(if no, skip the next two questions)**

Do you subscribe?

- [ ] Yes
- [ ] No

If you do not subscribe, how often do you purchase SHONEN JUMP Magazine?

- [ ] 1-3 issues a year
- [ ] 4-6 issues a year
- [ ] more than 7 issues a year

What genre of manga would you like to read as a SHONEN JUMP Graphic Novel?
(please check two)

- [x] Adventure
- [ ] Comic Strip
- [ ] Science Fiction
- [x] Fighting
- [ ] Horror
- [ ] Romance
- [ ] Fantasy
- [ ] Sports

Which do you prefer? (please check one)

- [ ] Reading right-to-left
- [x] Reading left-to-right

Which do you prefer? (please check one)

- [x] Sound effects in English
- [ ] Sound effects in Japanese with English captions
- [ ] Sound effects in Japanese only with a glossary at the back

THANK YOU! Please send the completed form to:

VIZ Survey
42 Catharine St.
Poughkeepsie, NY 12601

All information provided will be used for internal purposes only. We promise not to sell or otherwise divulge your information.